BRAZIL'S LONG REVOLUTION

ANTHONY PAHNKE

BRAZIL'S LONG REVOLUTION

*Radical Achievements of the
Landless Workers Movement*

THE UNIVERSITY OF
ARIZONA PRESS
TUCSON

The University of Arizona Press
www.uapress.arizona.edu

We respectfully acknowledge the University of Arizona is on the land and territories of Indigenous peoples. Today, Arizona is home to twenty-two federally recognized tribes, with Tucson being home to the O'odham and the Yaqui. Committed to diversity and inclusion, the University strives to build sustainable relationships with sovereign Native Nations and Indigenous communities through education offerings, partnerships, and community service.

© 2018 The Arizona Board of Regents
All rights reserved. Published 2018
First paperback edition published 2025

ISBN-13: 978-0-8165-3603-0 (cloth)
ISBN-13: 978-0-8165-5533-8 (paper)
ISBN-13: 978-0-8165-3883-6 (ebook)

Cover design by Carrie House, HOUSEdesign llc
Cover photo [*back*] by Anthony Pahnke

Unless otherwise noted, photos, illustrations, and tables are by the author.

Publication of this book is made possible in part by the proceeds of a permanent endowment created with the assistance of a Challenge Grant from the National Endowment for the Humanities, a federal agency.

Library of Congress Cataloging-in-Publication Data
Names: Pahnke, Anthony, author.
Title: Brazil's long revolution : radical achievements of the Landless Workers Movement / Anthony Pahnke.
Description: Tucson : The University of Arizona Press, 2018. | Includes bibliographical references and index.
Identifiers: LCCN 2017060968 | ISBN 9780816536030 (cloth : alk. paper)
Subjects: LCSH: Movimento dos Trabalhadores Rurais sem Terra (Brazil) | Social movements—Brazil—History. | Agricultural laborers—Brazil—History.
Classification: LCC HD1333.B6 P33 2018 | DDC 333.3/181—dc23 LC record available at https://lccn.loc.gov/2017060968

Printed in the United States of America
♾ This paper meets the requirements of ANSI/NISO Z39.48-1992 (Permanence of Paper).

For what is to come

CONTENTS

List of Illustrations	*ix*
Preface	*xi*
A Note on Names	*xiii*
List of Abbreviations	*xv*

	Introduction. From Horses to Health Care: Brazil's Landless Revolution	3
1.	Theory and Practice of Revolutionary Political Action	21
2.	The Revolution in Education, Economic Development, and Agrarian Reform	53
3.	Working with the Past: Incorporating Public Policy, Religion, and Prior Movement Tactics	87
4.	Mobilizing Through Neoliberalism: Revolutionary Persistence and Decline	124
5.	Dilemmas and Challenges When Confronting an "Allied" Government	157
	Conclusion. Lessons from the Landless Revolution? Post-Workers' Party Brazil and Revolutionary Political Action in the Global North	193

Notes	*217*
Bibliography	*243*
Index	*265*

ILLUSTRATIONS

FIGURES

1. Diagram of revolutionary resistance — 36
2. A mística at the tenth annual Jornada de Agroecologia, in Curitiba, Paraná — 60
3. Students at an MST elementary school beginning their day with the movement hymn and a little exercise — 61
4. Ascending and descending democracy in MST schools — 64
5. Agroecology training course and cooperative — 74
6. COOPTAR, collectively administered cooperative — 75
7. An encampment from the early stages of the movement — 91
8. Black tarp tents located in an encampment in Paraná state, 2011 — 92
9. Rural conflicts, southern Brazil: late 1970s to early 1980s — 97
10. Nucleo and assembly diagram of Nova Ronda Alta's organization — 114
11. Land conflicts, 1985–1990 — 135
12. People involved in conflicts, 1985–1990 — 136
13. Land conflicts, 1993–2000 — 142
14. People involved in conflicts, 1993–2000 — 143
15. Land occupations, 1990–2002 — 155
16. COOPERAL, regional cooperative — 161
17. COPTIL — 162
18. Evolution of INCRA's budget, 1995–2010 — 170

19. MST-led occupations, encampments, and protests, 2002–2015 — 174
20. Wall of Milton Santos School — 178
21. Grain production, fertilizer use, land use, 1990s–2000s — 189
22. Land conflicts, 2005–2014 — 190
23. People involved in land conflicts, 2005–2014 — 190

TABLES

1. Figures according to particular services (2000–2015) — 49
2. Agricultural production, 1970s–1980s — 98
3. Agricultural production, 1980s–1990s — 141
4. Agricultural production, 1990s–2000s — 189

PREFACE

I FINISHED THIS BOOK during uncertain times. The election of Donald Trump in the United States and the rise of the political right in Europe left many commentators to speculate on the nature of growing nationalist movements and parties. The persistence of violent conflict in Syria and concomitant refugee crisis, as well as the decades-long immigration disaster in the United States, daily reveal how millions live in extreme precarity. Meanwhile, the future of left-wing governments and movements in Latin America—Brazil included—is in doubt, whether due to corruption scandals or economic crisis. Standard social science has struggled to understand, as well as to predict, such developments. Still, social forces continue to operate. From what I read in the news and live daily, it looks like more and more people are choosing sides. If there was ever a time when one could be "apolitical," or "politically neutral," then those days are gone.

Gramsci wrote, "when the old world is dying and the new is born, then is the time of monsters." Perhaps that is true. Yet, especially during dark moments, we need to search for the light. And if there is none, then we make it. Nothing guarantees that the present historical moment is for the "monsters"—now very well could be the time when enemies, some of which we have tolerated for far too long, or thought had been defeated when really they lingered, are decisively confronted. Perhaps our time, which bears the trappings of transition, sees to the end of these monsters. Call me an optimist, or just plain dumb. I don't care. When one world is dying and another is being born, I choose my family, friends, and allies. Our community is strong. Woe to those that intend to harm it. There still is a world to win and spaces for new communities to proliferate.

Does this book help us understand the current historical moment? Maybe. I wrote it, sometimes consciously, but probably more than often unconsciously, thinking about myself and my origins. The last chapter applies what has taken place in Brazil over the last couple of decades to the United States. Latin American studies too often is conducted from the Global North with limited serious reflection on the part of academics. The standard approach to area studies research reifies non-Euro-American cultures and regions. Transnational connections, which are always there, are ignored, as politics is thought to take place "over there." I constantly struggle with this gap, with this book as the product of my many internal and external conflicts.

Thanks are in order for too many people. Everyone in the Landless Movement and its scores of allies, especially, deserve a thanks that any preface fails to deliver. I am especially thinking of the dozens of families with whom I stayed, conversed with, and shared experiences with during my time in Brazil. Some people I have managed to stay in contact with via Facebook; others I haven't. It's hard to express regret at losing contacts when one is writing a book, and some of the folks whom I interviewed are living in precarious conditions. I try to pay this unpayable debt and fail repeatedly. My parents, wife and daughter, sister, sister-in-law, brothers-in-law, nieces and nephews, aunts and uncles, and especially my grandparents, were also crucial in bringing this project to fruition. Each in their own way helped. My former colleagues at St. Olaf provided an exceptionally inviting work atmosphere. My colleagues at San Francisco State, likewise, have provided me numerous opportunities. Marlene, my wife, dealt often with my worries and anxieties. As political and life partners, we endlessly live political action, with me as her intern. She calls me her "voluntario estrella." It's a title that I accept with pride.

My parents and grandparents raised me to be politically aware *and* active. To divorce the two is all too easy, and in my early childhood, in rural and urban matters, it was ingrained into my being that the only ideas that mattered were the ones that became material.

How do I end this preface? I'm not sure. So, good luck. Fight the monsters.

San Francisco, Spring 2018

A NOTE ON NAMES

FOR THE SAKE OF THE INTERVIEWEES, I have refrained from using precise locations or specific names throughout this text. Instead, I reference general areas and positions of employment when applicable.

A NOTE ON NAMES

ABBREVIATIONS

AIM	American Indian Movement
ANDA	Associação Nacional para Difusão de Adubos (National Association for the Diffusion of Fertilizers)
ARENA	Aliança Renovadora Nacional (National Alliance for Renovation)
CDR	Comités de la Defensa de la Revolución (Revolutionary Defense Committees)
CEB	Comunidades Eclesiais de Base (Ecclesiastical Base Communities)
CEE	Conselho Estadual de Educação (State Educational Committee)
CLT	Consolidação das Leis do Trabalho (Consolidation of Labor Laws)
CNBB	Conferência Nacional do Bispos do Brasil (National Conference of Brazilian Bishops)
CNE	Conselho Nacional de Educação (National Council of Education)
CNI	Confederação Nacional da Indústria (National Confederation of Industry)

COANAL	Cooperativa Agrícola Novo Sarandi (New Sarandi Agricultural Cooperative)
CONAIE	La Confederación de Nacionalidades Indígenas del Ecuador (Confederation of Indigenous Nationalities of Ecuador)
CONATERRA	Cooperativa Nacional de Terra e Vida (National Cooperative of Land and Life)
CONCRAB	Confederação das Cooperativas de Reforma Agrária do Brasil (Brazilian Confederation of Agrarian Reform Cooperatives)
CONTAG	Confederação Nacional dos Trabalhadores na Agricultura (National Confederation of Workers in Agriculture)
COOPAN	Cooperativa de Produção Agropecuária Nova Santa Rita (Cooperative of Agricultural Production in New Santa Rita)
COOPERAL	Cooperativa Regional dos Agricultores Assentados (Regional Cooperative of Settled Farmers)
COOPTAT	Cooperativa de Produção Agropecuária dos Assentados de Tapes (Cooperative of Agricultural Production in Tapes)
COPAVI	Cooperativa de Produção Agropecuária Vitória (Victory Agricultural Production Cooperative)
COPTEC	Cooperativa de Serviços Técnicos (Cooperative of Technical Services)
COPTIL	Cooperativa de Produção e Trabalho Integração (Cooperative for Integrated Production and Work)
CPA	*cooperativa de produção agrícola* (agricultural production cooperative)
CPI	Comissões Parlamentares de Inquerito (Congressional Inquiries)
CPT	Comissão Pastoral da Terra (Pastoral Land Commission)

CUT	Central Única dos Trabalhadores (United Workers' Central)
CVSF	Comissão do Vale do São Francisco (Commission of São Francisco Valley)
DOPS	Departamento de Ordem Política e Social (Department of Political and Social Order)
EMBRAPA	Empresa Brasileria de Pesquisa Agropecuária (Brazilian Enterprise for Agricultural Research)
ETR	Estatuo do Trabalhador Rural (Rural Worker Statute)
EZLN	Ejército Zapatista de Liberación Nacional (Zapatista Army of National Liberation)
FSA	Farm Security Administration
FUNRURAL	Fundo de Apoio ao Trabalhador Rural (Rural Worker Support Fund)
GERA	Grupo Executivo da Reforma Agrária (Agrarian Reform Executive Group)
IBGE	Instituto Brasileiro de Geografia e Estatística (Brazilian Institute for Geography and Statistics)
IBOPE	Instituto Brasileiro de Opinião Pública e Estatística (Brazilian Institute of Public Opinion and Statistics)
IBRA	Instituto Brasileiro de Reforma Agrária (Brazilian Institute for Agrarian Reform)
IEJC	Instituto de Educação Josué de Castro (Institute of Education Josué de Castro)
IGRA	Instituto Gaucho de Reforma Agrária (Gaucho Institute for Agrarian Reform)
INCRA	Instituto Nacional de Reforma Agrária (Institute for Colonization and Agrarian Reform)
INDA	Instituto Nacional do Desenvolvimento Agrário (National Institute for Agrarian Development)
INEP	Instituto Nacional de Estudos e Pesquisas Educacionais (National Institute for Educational Study and Research)

INIC	Instituto Nacional de Imigração e Colonização (National Institute for Immigration and Settlement)
INRA	Instituto Nacional de Reforma Agrária (National Institute for Agrarian Reform)
ITERRA	Instituto Técnico de Capacitação e Pesquisa da Reforma Agrária (Technical Institute for Capacity-Building and Research for Agrarian Reform)
LDB	Lei de Diretrizes de Bases da Educação (Law of Educational Directives)
MAB	Movimento dos Atingidos por Barragens (Movement of People Affected by Dams)
MAPA	Ministério da Agricultura, Pecuaria e Abastecimento (Ministry of Agriculture, Livestock, Supply)
MDA	Ministério de Desenvolvimento Agrário (Ministry of Agrarian Development)
MDB	Movimento Democrático Brasileiro (Brazilian Democratic Movement)
MEC	Ministério da Educação e Cultura (Ministry of Education and Culture)
MLST	Movimento de Libertação dos Sem Terra (Movement for the Liberation of the Landless)
MP	Ministério Público (Public Prosecutor's Office)
MPA	Movimento dos Pequenos Agricultores (Movement of Small Farmers)
MST	Movimento de los Sin Tierra (Landless Movement)
MST	Movimento dos Trabalhadores Rurais Sem Terra (Landless Workers Movement)
MTD	Movimento dos Trabalhadores Desempregados (Movement of Unemployed Workers)
PA	Brazilian state of Pará
PAA	Programa de Acquisão dos Alimentos (Program for Acquiring Food)
PCB	Partido Comunista Brasileiro (Brazilian Communist Party)

PC do B	Partido Comunista do Brasil (Communist Party of Brazil)
PE	Brazilian state of Pernambuco
PIN	Plano de Integração Nacional (National Integration Plan)
PL	Partido Liberal (Liberal Party)
PLANALSUCAR	Programa Nacional de Melhoramento de Cana-de-Açúcar (National Plan to Improve Sugarcane)
PMDB	Partido do Movimento Democrático Brasileiro (Brazilian Democratic Movement Party)
PNAE	Programa Nacional Alimentar Escolar (National School Food Program)
PNRA	Plano Nacional de Reforma Agrária (National Plan for Agrarian Reform)
POLAMAZONIA	Programa de Pólos Agropecuários e Agrominerais da Amazônia (Programs for Agricultural and Agromineral Exploration in the Amazon)
POLONORDESTE	Programa de Desenvolvimento de Áreas Integradas do Nordeste (Program for the Integrated Development of the Northeast)
PR	Brazilian state of Paraná
PROCERA	Programa de Crédito Especial para a Reforma Agrária (Special Program for Agrarian Reform Credit)
PRONAF	Programa Nacional de Fortalecimento da Agricultura Familiar (National Program for Strengthening Family Farming)
PRORURAL	Programa de Assistência ao Trabalhador Rural (Program for Rural Worker Assistance)
PROTERRA	Programa de Redistribuição de Terras e de Estímulo à Agro-indústria do Norte e do Nordeste (Land Redistribution and Agroindustry Stimulation Program for the North and Northeast)
PROVALE	Programa Especial para o Vale do São Francisco (Special Program for the São Francisco Valley)

PSD	Partido Social Democratica (Social Democratic Party)
PSP	Partido Socialista Popular (Socialist Popular Party)
PT	Partido dos Trabalhadores (Workers' Party)
PTB	Partido Trabalhista Brasileiro (Brazilian Labor Party)
RS	Brazilian state of Rio Grande do Sul
SAF	Secretário de Agricultura Familiar (Secretary of Family Farming)
SEIU	Service Employees International Union
SP	Brazilian state of São Paulo
SPVEA	Superintendência do Plano de Valorização Econômica da Amazônia (Superintendent of Economic Valorization Plans in the Amazon)
STFU	Southern Tenant Farmers' Union
SUDENE	Superintendência do Desenvolvimento Econômico do Nordeste (Superintendent of Economic Development in the Northeast)
SUDOESTE	Superintendência do Plano de Valorização Econômica da Região da Fronteira Sudoeste do País (Superintendent of Economic Valorization Plans for the Southeast Border Region)
SUPRA	Superintendência de Política Agrária (Superintendent for Agrarian Politics)
TCU	Tribunal das Contas da União (National Audit Court)
UDN	União Democrática Nacional (National Democratic Union)
ULTRAB	União dos Lavradores e Trabalhadores Agrícola do Brasil (Union of Farmers and Agricultural Workers in Brazil)

BRAZIL'S LONG REVOLUTION

INTRODUCTION

FROM HORSES TO HEALTH CARE

Brazil's Landless Revolution

FIRST SCARED, THEN RELIEVED (AND SURPRISED)

MY LEG WAS CUT OPEN while I was horseback riding in a remote, rural area in the Brazilian state of Pernambuco. Two members of the Movimento dos Trabalhadores Rurais Sem Terra (Landless Workers Movement, or MST) were showing me the entirety of the ranch a few dozen families recently had occupied, when all of a sudden on my not-so-trusty-steed I scraped against a brush-covered barbed-wire fence. Fear set in after I pulled the horse away from the fence to see blood running down my leg. One of my MST escorts jokingly said, "Oxi, agora você tem uma lembrança!" (Oh man, looks like you got a souvenir!) I nervously laughed along with them, trying to show that I was not scared out of my wits. I was miles away from any city. Where were the doctors, hospitals, and medicine? What would I do if my leg were infected?

After the ride, we went to one movement member's tent in the *acampamento* (encampment). This encampment was like the various others I had visited and lived in during my twenty months of fieldwork in Brazil. The smell of cooking beans and meat floated between the hundred or so black tarp tents that were lumped together in an area no larger than a football field. A few mangy horses and run-down cars moved women, children, and men to school, work, movement meetings, and church. A red MST flag—not the Brazilian—flew above everything. In addition to its color, the flag's image of a man and woman holding tools served as a reminder of the movement's socialist identity. Below the flag, people moved with determination, in spite of the mud that made everything difficult. Some were on their way to harvest, while others were planning land occupations at different sites. One *núcleo* (nucleo)—a term used by the MST to denote a small group—was leaving to repair buildings at a movement-run school. Still others were attending classes on the movement's history. At night people told stories, played music, and drank. The hustle and bustle made me think of Tocqueville's description of township life in *Democracy in America*, with the MST version in Portuguese.

The movement's land occupations and encampments exist in a juridical gray area. According to the Brazilian Constitution of 1988 and the Estatuo da Terra (Rural Land Statute)—this latter piece of legislation inaugurating official agrarian reform policy in 1964—land not serving its *função social* (social function) can be expropriated by the government for redistribution. The social function clause sanctions expropriation in the event that an owner violates environmental and/or labor law, or fails to productively use 80 percent of the area.[1] While de jure expropriation is conducted only after assessment by the Instituto Nacional de Reforma Agrária (INCRA; Institute for Colonization and Agrarian Reform) and a subsequent executive decree issued by the president, there are few legal guidelines for who, or what, may allege that a certain parcel is in violation of its social function. As such, land occupations and the ensuing encampments have an ambivalent status within the Brazilian legal order. Brazil's highest legal authority—the Supremo Tribunal Federal (Federal Supreme Court)—in case ADIN-MC n. 2.213 in 2002 equated occupations with labor strikes. Despite this vague recognition, the similarity between the two kinds of tactics is minimal. Brazil's Consolidação das Leis do Trabalho (CLT; Consolidation of Labor Laws) and supplementary legislation (Law 7789/1989) detail when, where, and how strikes are to take place. No supplementary legislation exists to detail the conduct of occupations.

Even with the steady increase in research on the MST and the various other social movements, religious organizations, and labor unions that together compose what is known as the Landless Movement,[2] scholars have struggled to understand the precise legal nature of the land occupation tactic. Miguel Carter describes the MST as having a "complex" relationship to the Brazilian legal order without explaining in detail what this means.[3] Wendy Wolford, who has written extensively on the movement, in one article notes that "land occupations are technically illegal," while in her co-authored book with Angus Wright, she comments in passing that the movement's tactics create "legal confusion."[4] Another longtime scholar of the movement, Jack Hammond, in a relatively early treatment, simply calls land occupations "illegal."[5] George Mészáros provides the most comprehensive account of the movement's relationship to Brazil's legal system, describing the movement practices as exemplary of "offensive legal action."[6] While I partially agree with Mészáros's description of the movement's tactics as offensive, as well as with comments by other scholars, a central argument in this book is that we need to place the tactical repertoire that has been developed by MST and its allies in a greater political, economic, and legal context to gain a better understanding of the movement's mode of resistance.

The legal ambiguity of the movement's actions, while essential for analyzing tactics, should not distract us from acknowledging the Landless Movement's radical and innovative mode of organization. I first became aware of the movement's organizational dynamics when I was sitting in a tent after my horseback riding mishap. After I waited a short time, a woman entered and brought me some ointment and bandages. She told me that she was a member of the *setor de saúde* (health sector) who, along with a small team, provides similar attention to others when necessary. A week later while visiting a movement-run training school for early childhood educators, I met someone else who was also a member of the movement's health care sector, not on any particular encampment, but nationally. She explained that in every encampment there is either a single person or a group in charge of treating people who have accidents. I also learned that the movement works in partnership with Brazilian and Cuban universities to train members to become doctors. These courses, which are funded by the Brazilian government, but managed by the MST and the other members of the Landless Movement, teach people how to use traditional herbs and medicines in opposition to corporate, for-profit health care. Health care was explicitly politicized: on the one hand it was about basic survival and well-being, while on the other hand, the movement's collective management approach explicitly incorporated anti-capitalist elements into the service's delivery. The health care that I received explicitly opposed the current neoliberal orthodoxy that privileges individualism and deregulated, privatized modes of service provision.

I was surprised—what at first seemed like accidental, ad hoc care for my wound was actually part of regularized activity. My care was not only standard, but also characteristic of well-established movement practices locally, nationally, and even internationally. The movement, for lack of a better description, was governing a service that is also provided by the Brazilian government. Yet, in their mode of governance, movement members delivered the service while simultaneously altering its content and method of provision. As I later found, how the MST and its allies provide health care is similar to the organization of land occupations and encampments, as well as to the movement's work in education, economic development, and other areas. In effect, the movement claims a particular service, such as agrarian reform or health care, from the Brazilian government. It demands not only that the government make modifications, but also that the movement itself ought to implement the changes. Over the course of its three decades of existence, the Landless Movement has developed an intriguing set of tactics: one side of the movement's practices features controversial actions that challenge easy definitions of what constitutes legal action, and that often generate intensive, protracted conflicts with public and private authorities. Obversely, efforts to request and access public policies recognize and work fully according to Brazilian laws. Through these actions, the movement challenges status quo modes of service design and implementation through the development of a transformative, revolutionary mode of political action.

THE CONTRADICTIONS OF REVOLUTIONARY POLITICAL ACTION

Reflecting on the Landless Movement's practices reveals various provocative contradictions. Consider the content found in certain documents that have been produced by the movement for training purposes. Concerning its efforts in education, some manuals detail how to organize every aspect of school life, from daily building maintenance to creating lesson plans. This apparent autonomy contrasts with the movement's dependence on the federal government and many subnational administrations to provide resources to pay teachers, build schools, and certify courses. Additionally, initiatives central to creating the movement's collectivized production cooperatives, where land is held in common and profit is divided equally among members, have in part been achieved by members demanding special lines of subsidized credit and production policies for small farmers from Brazilian institutions like the Ministério de Desenvolvimento Agrário (MDA; Ministry of Agrarian Development) and the Ministério da Agricultura, Pecuaria e Abastecimento (MAPA; Ministry of Agriculture, Livestock, Supply). These institutions emphasize private property and individual entrepreneurship. Revolutionaries like Che Guevara and Carlos

Marighella, who promoted guerrilla warfare, are regularly referenced in the Landless Movement's documents, songs, and chants. Yet the movement's frequent demands to increase the amount of resources for Brazilian institutions in charge of education, agriculture, and health care seems precisely the antithesis of revolutionary conduct. At times, the MST and its allies give the impression that their project exists parallel to state power, while at others the movement appears dependent on it, or even its accessory.

The argument I advance in this book makes two contributions concerning the growing scholarship on Brazilian social movements, revolutionary politics, and contentious politics in general. First, I contend that we ought to consider the movement's contradictory relationship with state authority as resulting from a combination of legal and extralegal tactics. Scholars who have written on tactics and the Landless Movement, as referenced above, acknowledge some peculiarities of the movement's practices. Still, they have struggled to document the nature of the movement's tactical repertoire. The Landless Movement's tactics, which include the MST's and its allies' use of land occupations, their ensuing encampments, and ways of appropriating resources from the Brazilian government, are best understood as indicative of what I call extralegal political action. I define extralegal political action as neither legal nor illegal practices, but a form of collective action that appears similar to illegal conduct, but that lacks clear statutory guidelines for punishment and/or approval. In the first chapter I further document the meaning of extralegality, especially in my expansion and adaptation of the concept from the Marxist tradition's analysis of tactics.

Second, I argue that the Landless Movement's form of resistance is best considered as revolutionary, particularly in the creation and development of a dual power form of organization vis-à-vis the Brazilian state. In making this argument, I explicitly challenge Jeff Goodwin and Theda Skocpol's claim that "the ballot box has proven to be the coffin of revolutionary movements."[7] Or in other words, the emergence and even consolidation of liberal democratic institutions—free and fair elections that feature competitive political parties, transparent public policy-making mechanisms, the protection and promotion of private property—does not spell the end for the development of revolutionary modes of political conduct. Dual power, as I explain, does not entail a strict separation between state and social actors, and can develop within a liberal democratic context. Upon analysis, we find the Landless Movement working simultaneously within, through, and outside the Brazilian state to produce an alternative mode of organizing political, economic, and cultural relationships in particular spaces. The movement's tactics, organization of certain production cooperatives and schools, and overall style of governance constitute what I call revolutionary political action—transformative undertakings that challenge state power and already-existing, dominant cultural, political, and economic relations. Such a form of political action runs through every moment of the MST's and its allies' practices, from occupations and encampments to more recent attempts to develop agroecological production and access public programs for education, health care, and other services.

Previous studies of the MST and the other groups that compose the Landless Movement document the ebbs and flows of contentious politics, as well as the movement's history. In English, Gabriel Ondetti's *Land, Protest, and Politics: The Landless Movement and the Struggle for Agrarian Reform in Brazil* is the first application of social science theory and concepts to the movement, followed by Wendy Wolford's *This Land Is Ours Now: Social Mobilization and the Meanings of Land in Brazil*.[8] Miguel Carter's edited volume *Challenging Social Inequality* offers a comprehensive collection of essays on the movement's origin and growth through Luiz Inácio Lula da Silva's first term (2002–6).[9] Bernardo Mançano Fernandes's work in Portuguese, *A formação do MST no Brasil* (The Formation of the MST in Brazil), is likewise a necessary scholarly resource for anyone interested in the movement, as is Sue Branford and Jan Rocha's *Cutting the Wire: The Story of the Landless Movement in Brazil* and Angus Wright and Wendy Wolford's *To Inherit the Earth: The Landless Movement and the Struggle for a New Brazil*.[10] Central to these works is a focus on the MST's territorial expansion throughout Brazil in the 1980s and 1990s. Multiple other studies in Portuguese document movement practices in particular settlements and encampments, as well as efforts in education, cooperative administration, and health care.[11] While acknowledging insights from these studies, I feature in this book a novel theoretical framework concerning the movement's form of resistance and fieldwork and textual analysis of developments from the 2000s and 2010s.

Leandro Vergara-Camus's *Land and Freedom: The MST, the Zapatistas, and Peasant Alternatives to Neoliberalism* comes closest to understanding the movement's tactics and mode of resistance that I propose, specifically in his understanding of how MST is creating "autonomous rural communities."[12] Yet, in overemphasizing autonomy, this study misses the productive contradictions at the root of the MST's relationship to state power. Elsewhere, Vergara-Camus describes the MST as a new form of peasant rebellion.[13] Despite recognizing a certain transformative quality in the movement's resistance, something that potentially indicates that the Landless Movement is not simply seeking reform, he does not differentiate between rebellion and revolution. As a result, the use of rebellion is question-begging. Wolford, in *This Land Is Ours*, highlights the diversity of ideas and beliefs within the movement and their potential in creating "new revolutionary subjectivities."[14] Despite this recognition of revolutionary subjects, we are left without a clear understanding of whether the MST is in rebellion, constitutes a bona fide case of revolution, or simply demands that the Brazilian government make policy changes on its behalf. Fernandes conceives of the MST as a "social-territorial movement."[15] This is similar to how I analyze the movement's resistance in light of theorists of revolutionary movement organization and governance. The conceptual apparatus that I construct over the course of this book builds from Fernandes's work on the territorial quality of the movement, while supplementing it by highlighting what I call the movement's sovereign claim to space.

THE THEORETICAL AND EMPIRICAL RELEVANCE OF RESEARCHING REVOLUTION

Theoretically, this book addresses a gap in the literature on the meaning and practice of collective action. As has been addressed by various scholars, Marxist, Post-Marxist, and Critical theoretical approaches have been largely kept separate from studies of social movements and revolution. In reflecting on social movement theory in general, Jeff Goodwin and James Jasper note that scholarship has largely "ignored the Marxist tradition."[16] Elsewhere, in critically evaluating the current state of social movement studies, Jasper notes that the dominance of the rational choice approach has led theorists of collective action to postulate "the wrong micro-foundations."[17] Steven Buechler, in *Understanding Social Movements*, similarly recognizes that "work on social movements and theories of revolution progressed on almost parallel paths that rarely intersected."[18] The point is that even while theorists such as Charles Tilly began their careers with a focus on revolutionary contention in the 1970s, the vast majority of subsequent scholarship in the field tended to sideline empirical and theoretical studies of radical social transformation.

Some Marxist and Post-Marxist theories, especially in the 1980s, appeared in research on Latin American contention. For instance, insights from Ernesto

Laclau and Chantal Mouffe's *Hegemony and Socialist Strategy* impacted the theoretical frameworks of various studies found within Arturo Escobar and Sonia Alvarez's edited volume *The Making of Social Movements in Latin America*, as well as Daniel Slater's and Ilse Sherer-Warren's research.[19] A few of the current studies of the Landless Movement, notably the scholarship by Rebecca Tarlau and Leandro Vergara-Camus, incorporate a neo-Gramscian framework to analyze contention in the Brazilian countryside.[20] Fernandes, James Petra and Henry Veltmeyer, Henry Bernstein, and Tom Brass also explicitly adopt a Marxist approach to rural movements.[21] There exists a somewhat scattered group of scholars who have worked with the Marxist theoretical tradition, as well as a growing recognition for how this tradition can inform social movement research. This book works with, and complements, this growing body of research theoretically and empirically.

In addressing Goodwin and Jasper's concern, as well as in building off of the literature on social movement studies inspired by the Marxist tradition, this book squarely focuses on the meaning and practice of revolutionary contention. Concerning the Brazilian Landless Movement especially, Wendy Wolford and Leandro Vergara-Camus have passingly alluded to the movement's revolutionary elements. Central to my theoretical orientation, which I detail at length in the first chapter, is how charting the growth and development of the Brazilian Landless Movement helps us reexamine the conditions for and the nature of revolutionary political action. The Landless Movement is especially suited for this endeavor. First, the movement has explicitly embraced a Marxist posturing with respect to its goals, symbols, and demands. Still, it is possible that the movement could claim such an identity without actually displaying radical, revolutionary forms of resistance. My response to this critique is primarily found in chapter 2. In that chapter, I take the theoretical framework I develop in the first chapter to show that the actual practices initiated and organized by the MST and its allies do display a revolutionary form of social transformation. Additionally, the movement helps us think through the dynamics of revolutionary transformation and resistance given its longevity and territorial presence. With over a million and a half people mobilized, for over three decades, the Landless Movement provides a case for documenting the ebbs and flows of contention that intends to transform social relations.

Moreover, my study of the Landless Movement is timely because of the growing interest in food politics and the continuing debates surrounding neoliberal policy reforms: for example, privatizing social services, eliminating public policies, and/or cutting government spending. Even in the United States with the Trump administration's embrace of seemingly protectionist policy positions, slashing the budgets of various government agencies and promoting "trickle-down" tax cut plans remain at the center of the president's political and economic vision. Furthermore, the most recent global recession has spurred government and corporate elites to express the notion that such neoliberal policy prescriptions can address persistent social problems. Such policy proposals are far from new. In the 1980s, Ronald Reagan in the United States and Margaret Thatcher in Great Britain heralded the neoliberal era with a "rollout" of tax cuts, privatizations, and deregulations. Not only in Brazil but around Latin America, neoliberal restructuring—in both its more macro- and microlevel varieties—characterized political, economic, and cultural life for decades. Drastic cuts to social programs and privatizations of public firms, from Venezuela to Argentina, were initiated in the 1980s and throughout the 1990s. Later experiments in micro-finance, and other targeted social programs launched under the banner of "entrepreneurship," have been a staple of agricultural policy in Brazil and elsewhere. Revisiting how the Landless Movement engaged such changes as they took place, which is the focus of chapter 4, should be of interest to readers in the Global North.

One danger brought with neoliberalism is the depoliticization of social relations. This may seem like a strange claim, especially when privatizing education and social security, as well as expanding free-trade agreements that feature clauses that enable corporations to sue governments,[22] appear more of a cause for concern. Furthermore, politics is often considered a "dirty word," usually considered tantamount to corruption. Nobel Prize–winning economist Milton Friedman contributed to this general denigration of political action by equating nearly every government action with politics, inefficiency, and anti-capitalism. Friedman's free markets, with the atomistic individuals that compose them, are best if left alone and "free." In many Latin American states, international institutions made financial assistance contingent on privatizing state-owned enterprises, allowing foreign capital to invest by eliminating tariff protections and privatizing social services. Accompanying and promoted by such macroeconomic changes was a culture where people first and foremost believe that they are separate and isolated, instead of constituting collectives or existing within a variety of relationships. This seemingly innocent notion of freedom conceals an extensive political project. Politics-as-anti-politics was, and remains, rooted in delegating state power to those with so-called economic expertise who promote the pursuit of profit without limits and equate public policies with tyranny.

Organizing and sustaining political action, or rather, attempting to politicize social affairs, in Latin America and elsewhere is difficult. Most students, burdened by debt, are ever increasingly trying to graduate in three instead of four years to save money. This contrasts with the 1960s and 1970s, when student organizations in Europe, the United States, and in various Latin American countries were organizing protests that challenged wars, imperialism, and the growing consumerist culture. Now, "politics" for students is found in carefully planned internships for credit that are required to satisfy a general education requirement. Unions, where they still exist, struggle to prove their relevance and retain the few remaining protections for members. Labor organizations in both the Global North and South, from the Service Employees International Union (SEIU) to the Brazilian Central Única dos Trabalhadores (CUT; United Workers' Central), have been engaging in new organizing campaigns. Yet, it is hard to tell if their practices show new, innovative actions or are mainly defensive in nature. Meanwhile, a never-ending discussion in the United States concerns the national debt and the government's budget. Debates usually degenerate into petty arguments about the size of cuts to public spending. In these discussions, politics is reduced to balancing a checkbook.

The worry about depoliticization is that the desire and commitment to search for and experiment with alternatives is being foreclosed. If movements, organizations, and individuals mainly devote their attention to managing expenses, then the potential for conflict and antagonism is repressed. When one's calculus begins with a cost-benefit analysis, without trying to conceive of larger collectives, an instrumental logic dominates practice. Such practices most often betray a desire for immediate gratification, as well as the tendency for individuals to accept status quo political, economic, and cultural relations.

In spite of this climate of depoliticization, the Landless Movement and transnational social movements such as La Via Campesina (LVC) display some of the most radical, transformational political demands and projects in both the Global North and South. The LVC's concept of food sovereignty—developed and practiced in opposition to the United Nation's notion of food security—postulates the need to radically change food and natural resource economies in ways that promote alternative modes of production, distribution, and circulation.[23] Primary among such demands is agrarian reform, in Africa, Europe, and throughout the Americas. In Brazil, the MST is one among a variety of social movements that proclaim and practice the principles of food sovereignty, inspiring dozens of LVC chapters and affiliated movements throughout North, Central, and South America. In the United States, the Rural Coalition and National Family Farm Coalition (NFFC) are umbrella organizations that feature dozens of LVC groups with thousands of members that are working with the concept of food sovereignty. From the United States to Tanzania, movements protest in favor of legislation to address climate change, create collectively administered cooperatives, and demand greater gender equality. As of 2017, over seventy countries host LVC movements, with approximately 200 million farmworkers, farmers, Indigenous people, and peasant producers affiliated. Food politics, which may be more conventionally associated with consumer advocates and local food cooperatives, is an area where movements are increasingly becoming politicized. I explore the history and potential for such actors' projects more in the conclusion of this book.

One lesson from the Brazilian Landless Movement when thinking about the possibilities for present-day revolutionary politics is found in how many of the movement's leaders studied and appropriated the past. It is likely that demands raised by current movements, in the United States or elsewhere, are not new. Many of the principal problems that the MST and its allies draw attention to—monocultural production, political and economic inequality, land rights—were also acknowledged by movements that predated the Landless Movement. Demanding rural settlements, for instance, has a long history in Brazil. What the MST and its allies show is the intergenerationality of collective action. Leaders do not discover a particular social grievance and create, ex nihilo, the ways to address it. Movements that study the past learn from past successes and failures, which inform efforts to create projects suitable to their current historical moment.

An additional lesson is the movement's claim to space. Of late, the multiple "Occupy" movements in the United States and Europe squatted in public places in their demand for economic justice. While such acts are, in a sense, occupations, they do not demand the transfer of ownership of the particular site where people encamped. Neither do they attempt to sustain a transformation of political, economic, or cultural relations in an area. Multiple movements in Brazil make such direct claims to space. The nature of the claim is mutually exclusive—something must be given to the occupiers and taken from someone, or something else.

Revolutionary transformative projects are protracted movements. Castro's 26th of July Movement in Cuba took years to construct its alternative, beginning in 1956 after Che Guevara and a small group of insurgents landed near the Sierra Maestra mountain range.[24] After deposing the Batista regime in 1959, the Cuban Revolution did not end, but continued as the enemy changed from Batista's government to economic inequality, large landowners, and illiteracy. Or in other words, in this classic, often-referenced case of revolutionary resistance, the end of a period of armed insurrection did not mean the conclusion of revolutionary political action. Briefly reflecting on the Cuban case, and as this book's in-depth study of the Landless Movement will also make clear, taking state power and engaging in revolutionary political action does not necessarily mean deposing and replacing governments. Revolutions are not marked by specific dates when one government replaces another, but by extended periods of time when transformation is planned and carried out.

Revolutionary resistance unfolds simultaneously inside and outside of state structures of authority. A movement's "insider" nature is seen in negotiations with officials, the use of public policies, and/or alliance-building efforts. "Outside" state authority means mobilizing in ways that construct new, or alternative forms of community by deploying extralegal tactics. Again, to draw a parallel with Cuba, Castro frequently referenced the 1940 Constitution in the early stages of the Cuban Revolution, in particular the document's declaration of social rights, as a way for his 26th of July Movement to claim legitimacy, organize their encampments, claim space, and seek allies. In Brazil, the MST and its allies similarly appeal to laws and the constitution in their efforts. Dual power unfolds at once in, against, and through state power to produce alternative modes of collective organization.

In addition this book addresses the current status of the Landless Movement. Especially during President Luiz Inácio Lula da Silva's second term (2006–10), and then during President Dilma's time in office (2011–16), the movement experienced what some would consider a period of decline. According to the Commissão Pastoral da Terra (CPT; Pastoral Land Commission)—a longtime ally and religious organization that collects figures on rural issues—there was a 60 percent decrease in occupations from 2004 to 2016.[25] As I argue more in chapter 5, this change represents a shift on behalf of the movement and does not simply indicate that the MST and its allies have seen better days. Especially with respect to how the movement has reoriented its actions in economic development and education, the Landless Movement's revolutionary mode of contention has continued, but through attempting to consolidate its gains and strengthen itself internally. In short, revolutionary resistance continues to characterize the movement's actions, yet more so in a way that shows consolidation instead of expansion.

The Landless Movement revolutionary project forces us to rethink property relations in light of dominant conceptions of productivity. Neoliberal restructuring and its accompanying policies usurp how to think about economic production. The fall of the Soviet Union was accompanied by a general disapproval of state-led development. In the 1980s and 1990s, various scholars disputed the praise of a minimalist state in their reading of East Asian industrial development in light of intricate connections between bureaucratic expertise, nationalism, private actors, and government regulation.[26] Besides this literature and the periodic critiques of corporate welfare and subsidies, the sanctity of free market capitalism has seemingly been accepted. In stark contrast, the MST and its allies draw our attention to the notion that property, instead of being primarily an input or factor in economic production, has a social function. The social function clause found within the Brazilian Constitution is part of many other constitutions that were written in the twentieth century.[27] The rationale for the social function clause can be traced to the English philosopher John Locke's theory of property from his *Treatise on Government*. In Locke, we find the ideas that property has value only when labor is invested in it and that wasting land, that is, allowing spaces to sit idle, is a social wrong. The Landless Movement's mobilization of social function shows that property does not necessarily have roots in individual ownership, but can also be conceived of as having greater, more collective uses intended to develop alternative social relations.

The Landless Movement challenges our thinking about property and production in still other ways. The movement's cooperatives and subsequent promotion of agroecology counter Brazil's history of monocultural production and export agriculture. It also contests agribusiness corporations, such as Monsanto and Syngenta, which attempt to disseminate a mode of appropriating agricultural space that is dependent on privatized seed technologies, chemical inputs, and heavy machinery. The movement's economic project directly contests such goals of agribusiness. It also offers a socially grounded view of production, encompassing culture, politics, and economics. MST cooperatives, especially, are interesting for their communal orchards, lack of private property, and ability to free families for political work during certain times of the year. Thus, the movement's actions cannot be reduced to subsistence or meeting so-called basic needs.

Throughout this book I document the Landless Movement's practices, neither denouncing nor cheerleading its projects. At various points in my study, I discuss challenges facing the movement owing to overcentralization, a lack of planning, the misuse of resources, and internal divisions. It is too easy to find revolution in moments prior to engaging with state power when movements and organizations are "in the streets" or "at the barricades." This naïve celebration of spontaneous outbursts of autonomy in some studies of Latin American movements emphasizes the purely disruptive, "outsider" nature of resistance. I see similar qualities in the MST, its allies, and other movements at particular times, but also understand that conceiving of political action as solely oppositional, or at isolated moments, is an oversimplification of dynamics and a partial depiction of events.

Comments on the Landless Movement's project abound. Some call it socialist, others totalitarian. Some say it educates; others allege that the movement indoctrinates. Critiques espoused by opponents of the MST and its allies call encampments with their crowd of black tents "rural favelas." To the contrary, visitors from around the world, especially from the United States and Europe, look to the movement as a model. While I do not believe that the Landless Movement contains a perfect model for reproduction outside of Brazil, its form of political action indicates the potential to think and act contrary to the dominant political and economic depoliticizing orthodoxy.

MY TIME IN BRAZIL AND OVERVIEW OF THE BOOK

The research for this book took place from 2009 to 2016, featuring information collected from semistructured interviews and participatory observation when I lived in Brazil from 2009 and 2011. Afterword, I engaged in textual analysis of primary source materials published from 2012 to 2016, as well as from the 1980s and 1990s, which included newspapers, movement newsletters and training manuals, and Brazilian legislation. At first, I was intrigued by the MST's organization. I became aware of the movement's sophisticated constitution in meetings with leaders that presented me with somewhat stressful, yet productive obstacles. Some initial discussions I had with leaders, from my perspective, seemed like interviews—of me—to verify my identity and ultimate intentions. Once "on site" with the movement, once in a while a leader ensured that I was performing my stated objective. Such surveillance did not entail control over my research, as various members spoke frankly with me about movement weaknesses and problems. From central offices in São Paulo to remote areas in the Amazonian state of Pará, networks of movement activists and leaders helped me find the people I needed to interview and locate settlements, encampments, schools, and cooperatives. On the one hand, it felt at times like I was under constant watch. On the other hand, without this organization, I would not have been able to locate the places and people necessary to understand the movement's actions. Eventually, I gained the trust of various members and leaders. At one point, I was called upon by the movement to escort a Palestinian movement leader throughout MST settlements and schools. I also assisted in an international LVC event, hosted by the MST in São Paulo, by offering my translation abilities for a week.

Something I learned from my regular interactions with leaders was the high degree of movement organization. The initial interviews of me showed a necessary sense of caution, especially given that while I was in Brazil a Wikileaks cable was released that detailed how the U.S. consulate had repeatedly spoken with academics about the MST to understand its weaknesses and if the movement posed a threat to agribusiness transnationals.[28] The long history of CIA involvement in dismantling governments and supporting right-wing military regimes throughout Latin America was well known by Landless Movement leaders who took initial precautions with me. The movement's practices revealed an internal structure with well-established rules, procedures, and practices. As I found out, this organization also characterizes the MST's and its allies' form of revolutionary resistance.

The research for this book mainly took place in the states of Rio Grande do Sul, Paraná, and São Paulo. I also spent weeks in the states of Pará and Pernambuco. My interviews with INCRA representatives and some Landless Movement allies, as well as opponents, were held in Brasília. I interviewed leaders of the movement, young and old, while also living with member families in settlements and encampments. I had the privilege to attend movement schools, becoming part of núcleos that cleaned, cooked, and worked on pedagogical goals. Many times I rode on the back of motorbikes on unpaved roads to get from one place to another. I helped slaughter a cow on a settlement and chopped wood to keep a black tarp tent warm during one of Paraná's colder winter months. Like many visitors to movement areas, I took extremely valuable time away from members who could have been with their families, growing food, or participating in meetings. The ethical dilemma of whether or not to research a social movement, as well as how to treat its practices critically without being a cheerleader or a disparager, was—and remains—my concern.

To assuage these worries, I drew extensively on secondary sources, in Portuguese and English. In addition to academic articles, I read countless dissertations written in Portuguese. I began researching the MST by studying their occupations and production cooperatives because many members of my family were involved in rural movement mobilization in the United States in the 1960s and 1970s. I wanted to know how and why this agrarian movement in Brazil persisted, with apparent success, while efforts in the United States seemed to flounder.

While in Brazil, I also interviewed movement opponents. One official in the state of Rio Grande do Sul, who was an outspoken critic of the Landless Movement, told me that the movement was "terrorist," employing tactics "similar to those used by guerrillas in the Vietnam War," with children in movement schools "never learning to read or write anything but the name Karl Marx."[29] In an official state document that I obtained, the Public Ministry "declared the MST illegal," in the name of "protecting children" from the movement's alleged "disruption of public order," and "use of public resources for criminal behavior."[30] Right before I arrived in Rio Grande do Sul, the PSDB governor Yeda Crusius (2006–10) left power after earning a reputation for repressive actions against social movements and unions, which drew mass protests and federal investigations. Trying to strike a balance between movement allies and opponents often drew me into local political conflicts, as well as Manichean depictions of the Landless Movement.

I have removed actors' names from citations to protect their identity. I took other ethical actions while I conducted my fieldwork. For instance, instead of only extracting information from members and leaders, I tried to return a little by regularly giving short lectures about agricultural practices and social movement activity in the United States to interested movement members, allies, and leaders. I got the idea for this kind of activity from one movement leader who told me that foreigners come to study the MST, yet leave movement members with little to no understanding of the politics and movements outside of Brazil. Fortunately, I was from a farm. I grew up with stories of how my great-grandfather organized penny auctions during the Great Depression. My grandfather discussed the 1980s farm crisis with me often, as well as taught me about his days organizing farmers in dairy cooperatives in the 1960s with the National Farmers Organization (NFO). My father and mother involved me in local farming organizations such as 4-H, taught me how to grow and sell produce locally, and warned me never to go into the pasture when the bull was out. In my presentations to movement members, I complemented my own stories of agrarian and social movement history with academic research. This developed into presentations on the farm bill, 4-H, milking parlors, bankruptcies, and the Dust Bowl for Landless Movement high school students, middle-aged movement leaders, and, on one occasion, a group of engineers who ally with the MST to design settlements. Whenever possible, I tried to dialogue, creating a friendly environment and allowing people whom I was interviewing to interview me.

This book is organized into five chapters and a conclusion. In the first, I provide a general theoretical approach to revolutionary political action. In the second, I make this more abstract discussion concrete in analyzing the Landless Movement's revolutionary resistance in education, economics, and agrarian reform. My objective in this chapter is to show the result of the movement's resistance. Chapters 3, 4, and 5 track how the Landless Movement has developed over time. Throughout, I discuss movement tactics and their intersection with certain external conditions to produce opportunities. Chapter 3 deals with the movement's emergence. This chapter takes my conceptual apparatus and applies it to past struggles to show its application. While this moment is well researched, my theoretical and conceptual framework offers a novel take on the movement's origins, as well as the emergence of its tactical repertoire. Chapter 4 documents the movement's revolutionary expansion and how it maneuvered neoliberal restructuring. Chapter 5 brings readers up to date with the Landless Movement's current actions and challenges.

In the conclusion I summarize the book's key arguments and apply my study to the United States. The second half of that chapter attempts to search out specific parallels in U.S. history. Essentially, I am condensing what I did over five chapters on the Landless Movement into one section. Despite the conclusion's brevity, the chapter is a valuable contribution to thinking about revolutionary political action in the Global North. Many people, from the United States and Europe, visit the MST and its allies and think about the potential application of what they learn to their home countries. Most books written by scholars in the Global North, despite their intentions, represent objects of study in the Global South as "out there" and removed from the realities of their own societies. This, too often, assumes a certain kind of presumed, unstated stability in home countries while suggesting that disruption and resistance take place somewhere else. Such a manner of representation also leaves readers in the Global North idealistically dreaming about possibilities. I have no interest in continuing this kind of exercise. My conclusion is meant to explicitly engage and provoke reader-dreamers.

1

THEORY AND PRACTICE OF REVOLUTIONARY POLITICAL ACTION

MOBILIZING THE CONTRADICTIONS OF REVOLUTIONARY RESISTANCE

"LISTEN, PUBLIC POLICIES FROM THE STATE, they are always compensatory policies [*políticas compensatórias*]. I mean, they are good, but what are the priorities? They never are based on our class interests."[1] This comment, from an MST activist who had worked for years in the movement's educational initiatives, contains some provocative contradictions. To parse the statement's meaning, it is necessary to figure out the meaning of the word "compensatory." As I learned, one sense is literal—public policies are intended to compensate people for a social injustice, whether owing to a history of racial discrimination or economic exploitation. Miguel Arroyo argues that this sense of compensation is behind the government's rural education policy, which attempts to confront "the debt" that Brazilian society owes to historically marginalized rural populations.[2] Another, less literal meaning of "compensatory" that I discerned when interviewing other Landless activists carried a more dismissive tone. As the activist quoted above remarked, many movement leaders believe that there are really two kinds of policies—compensatory ones that are partial and incomplete, and others that could lead to substantive change based on "class interests." In this other conception of "compensatory," even though public policies are "good," they are half-hearted attempts to confront social problems when compared to the social transformation envisioned by the MST and its allies.

The contradictory meanings of "compensatory"—on the one hand, the movement dismisses government initiatives as inadequate, while on the other, it embraces and accepts public policies—reveal dynamics that are central to the Landless Movement's mode of revolutionary resistance. Demanding and accepting public policies, no matter how incomplete they seem with respect to overall objectives, offers the movement a way to gain resources, continue mobilization, and pressure for more transformative alternatives. Yet, such actions are not the only mode of interaction practiced by the movement. Land occupations, encampments, as well as large marches are also routine practices found within the movement's repertoire of contention. Or, as summarized by another longtime MST leader, "it's how we do things, you know, with force and words [*com pau e prosa*]."[3] *Pau*, the Portuguese word for stick, connotes direct action tactics that are disruptive and unconventional. Occupations count as the *pau*. Leaders and members often negotiate and discuss problems with government elites—acts of *prosa*—in order to make demands and seek concessions. Revolutionary resistance is neither solely one form of action nor the other, never fully outside or inside state power. Rather, as is theorized in this chapter, revolutionary contention works simultaneously inside, outside of, and through state power to build an alternative that transforms existing political, economic, and cultural relations.

In this chapter, I present the main theoretical components of revolutionary political action that will orient the subsequent analysis of the Landless Movement. I develop a way of conceiving of revolutionary resistance that emphasizes the use of collective, extralegal tactics, sometimes in combination with legal tactics, in the claim to transform political, economic, and cultural relations within a particular space. Building off other scholars and theorists of revolutionary contention and social movements, from Lenin and Skocpol, to Gamson, Piven and Cloward, and McAdam, this chapter provides an alternative way to conceive of structures, tactics, and political action. Combining the scholarship on revolutionary resistance with social movement studies makes explicit two theoretical points: first, that the concept of structure as analyzed by social movement theorists needs refining, and second, that insights from Marxist and Critical Theory approaches complement other traditional accounts of tactics and political action. With respect to the first point, the use of the concept of structure in research on collective action—as I elaborate in this chapter—needs to distinguish between state, political, and economic conditions. Revolutionary movements provoke this recognition, especially given their claim to control space and create what Lenin termed the "dual power." How revolutionary movements engage authorities, or rather, their tactics, is likewise clarified when we combine theories from the Marxist tradition with those of scholars who specialize in social movements. The synthesis I conduct in this chapter addresses the gap in the literature between studies from the Marxist tradition and social movement studies.

I begin this chapter by highlighting the shortcomings in the study of contentious politics, namely, the relative failure to combine theoretical insights from Marxist studies with social movement research. One notable exception I discuss includes the research on rural social movements, which highlights capitalist development and the persistence of the peasantry. After also acknowledging the research on the meaning and practice of food sovereignty, I detail how my conceptual and theoretical framework builds from and complements existing scholarship on sovereignty and revolutionary political action. The next section features a prolonged discussion of sovereignty and revolution, drawing upon Lenin, Schmitt, Dussel, and Negri, while at the same time synthesizing their works with social movement studies. I then present how I conceive of conditions, showcasing the distinction between state, political, and economic structures. I describe each condition with a brief historical discussion of how each exists within the Brazilian context. The last section of the chapter notes how many people have participated in the Landless Movement. This section, which is less abstract than the others, is intended to show that the movement's achievements are quite extensive. For readers skeptical that the Landless Movement qualifies as a revolutionary actor, this section should persuade by documenting the scale of the movement's practices.

SYNTHESIZING THE MARXIST TRADITION WITH SOCIAL MOVEMENT STUDIES

Studies of revolutionary political action within the Marxist tradition and scholarship on social movements share a common concern with theory and practice. Marx himself, as well as Vladimir Lenin, Rosa Luxemburg, and Mao Zedong, are well known for their political activities and the subsequent theorization of their conduct.[4] Antonio Negri's work on revolution, in part, arose not from reflecting on events as a bystander, but from his participation in Italian revolutionary movements in the 1960s and 1970s.[5] Scholar-activists more associated with social movement studies, Saul Alinsky, for instance, in *Rules for Radicals*, as well as others such as Marshall Ganz, who was active in the creation of the United Farmworkers Movement in the U.S. Southwest, used their real-world experiences to inform their academic works on collective action.[6] Resource mobilization theory, as John McCarthy and Mayer Zald remind us, was intended to speak to "social movement leaders and practical theorists."[7] The concern with bridging academic scholarship with political practice motivated Douglas Bevington and Chris Dixon to bemoan the tendency in social movement research to become detached from real practitioners.[8]

Despite this common acknowledgement of the importance of incorporating theory with practice, the Marxist tradition has only tangentially found its way into social movement research. Sidney Tarrow, in *Power in Movement*, begins with recognizing the importance of Marxism for analyzing collective action, principally the works of Marx, Lenin, and Gramsci, yet quickly concludes that their contributions are more succinctly found in rationalist approaches of social movement theory.[9] Doug McAdam notes that his political-process model follows from Marxist theories of society, due to the way he conceives of power inequalities and disparities. Still, despite this nod, Marxist theorists and scholars do not reappear in his seminal work on the U.S. civil rights movement.[10] One exception in the literature is Charles Tilly's *From Mobilization to Revolution*. In this work, Tilly works with ideas developed by Lenin and Trotsky on the nature of dual power, multiple sovereignties, and revolution.[11] Yet, most other studies of social movements, as seen in various edited volumes, pay nearly no attention to Marxist, Post-Marxist, and/or Critical Theory perspectives.[12]

Notable exceptions exist, mainly in agrarian studies. Multiple scholars who explicitly focus on the resurgence of peasant movements in the Global South foreground certain insights gained from Marxist theories by emphasizing the role of capitalist development and class consciousness in rural mobilization. This scholarship features comparative and single case studies on African, Southeast Asian, and Latin American rural movements.[13] In embracing the Marxist tradition, and through rehabilitating the concept of the peasantry, these scholars draw attention to rural agency, the concepts of de/re-peasantization, and the effects of peripheral capitalist development on mobilization. Such studies, moreover, underscore the materiality of social conflict, whether over food, land, or natural resources.

What the current incorporation of Marxism into social movement studies lacks is an explicit theorization of revolutionary political action, and concomitantly, the concept of sovereignty. One of the more recent studies of the Brazilian MST, Wilder Robles and Henry Veltmeyer's "The Politics of Agrarian Reform in Brazil," fits squarely in this burgeoning area of scholarship, situating the movement in the context of capitalist growth and development in the Global South. Oddly, while asserting that the MST is a central actor in the struggle for food sovereignty, the authors refrain from exploring the meaning of a social movement that includes sovereignty among its demands.[14] If the practice of sovereignty within the MST's and its allies' actions is to have any real meaning, then a more theoretically and empirically informed analysis of food sovereignty is required. Even though the MST emerged prior to the official emergence of the LVC in the 1990s, applying the concept of sovereignty to the Landless Movement's mode of resistance does not pose a problem. The attempt to transform social relations in a particular space characterizes the movement's practice of food sovereignty, as well as its tactics and mode of organization before and after joining LVC.

Others have concretely explored movements that embrace the notion of food sovereignty. Such research features studies that theorize the meaning of the term, analyze its history, and document the practices of certain movements that have adopted it.[15] One standard theme has been democratization, usually depicted as involving historically marginalized people in participatory practices of food production.[16] Democratic practice, in most of these studies, extends beyond formal political rights to claiming control of material resources such as land, seeds, and crops. Peter Rosset's extensive research on movements and cases of food sovereignty has highlighted many different qualities, including the need for greater involvement of national governments to oppose free markets in agriculture, as well as grassroots initiatives to use territory in less capital-intensive ways.[17]

Still, even with this rich body of research, the meaning and practice of sovereignty remains underexplored. Scholar-activist Raj Patel inadvertently shows the need for further empirical and conceptual work by stating that "integral to the functioning of Via Campesina is the absence of a sovereign authority" while also mentioning that "no organisation can be a part of Via Campesina without subscribing to the organisation's principles [of food sovereignty]."[18] Patel's analysis, and the growing literature on rural social movements that explicitly adopt food sovereignty, provokes many questions. For instance, is it possible for a set of ideas, or principles, to be sovereign? Does there need to be a single actor that is recognized as "*the* sovereign" to adequately conceive of sovereignty? Furthermore, is democratic practice commensurable with sovereignty, or are the two concepts irreconcilable? Also, is democratizing the food system mainly a demand, or is it a series of practices that contain more radical, transformative potential?

Some theorists that are particularly useful in connecting sovereignty, revolution, and democracy come to us from the traditions of Marxism and Critical Theory. Principally, I draw upon Lenin, Carl Schmitt, Enrique Dussel, and Antonio Negri. To draw on Lenin and Schmitt may, at first glance, seem odd, for a variety of reasons. First, Lenin and Schmitt were engaged in theoretical debates and political action during the first half of twentieth century, which some might think makes their contributions outdated. Others might question bringing together two thinkers with radically different political perspectives. Superficially, it would appear that Lenin, the Marxist theoretician and first leader of the Soviet Union, has nothing in common with Carl Schmitt, the right-wing authoritarian thinker who during Nazi rule in Germany played a central role in designing National Socialist jurisprudence.[19]

Each apprehension can be easily addressed. As to whether Lenin and Schmitt are outdated, there has been a relatively recent flurry in revisiting their political-theoretical works. Among such endeavors is the work of Antonio Negri and Enrique Dussel. Additionally, Lenin's writings on revolution have drawn the attention of Slavoj Žižek and Fredric Jameson, while his analysis of tactics was recently the focus of a book by August Nimtz.[20] Schmitt has been incorporated by various other scholars, especially for his analysis of the meaning of political action. From Chantal Mouffe to Giorgio Agamben, Schmitt has been reappropriated for conceptual debates concerning sovereignty, pluralism, and democracy.[21] Some of Schmitt's work has received relatively little attention. Specifically, his *Theory of the Partisan*, which first appeared in the 1960s, and then was reissued in 2007, has been used by only a few scholars when compared to his other works. Lenin and Schmitt's political differences should not lead us to forgo combining their insights. Contributions from each can be extracted and further developed, principally related to the concepts of revolution and sovereignty. At the time of their writing, Lenin and Schmitt were at the forefront of revolutionary thought and radical political action. Multiple other anarchist, Marxist, and right-wing theorists explicitly acknowledged their contributions, either in adhering to certain precepts, or in critique.[22] Besides their relative intellectual weight, each thinker draws our attention to the connection between sovereignty and revolution, which has been relatively neglected in social movement studies. Returning to these early twentieth-century thinkers, therefore, is a reasonable point of departure for providing a framework to understand the connection.

DUAL POWER AND THE PARTISAN: CONCEIVING OF EXTRALEGALITY IN TACTICS AND ORGANIZATION

Constitutive of their understandings of revolution and sovereignty are Lenin's and Schmitt's contributions concerning tactics and political action. In arguing against his European contemporaries who claimed that revolutionaries should not participate within government, Lenin emphasized the importance of legal *and* illegal tactics.[23] Legal tactics are straightforward: they include negotiating with government elites and forming political parties. In this sense, Lenin agreed with other Marxist theorists of the time such as Georg Lukács and Rosa Luxemburg, who believed that legal tactics were useful to secure resources, illustrate how liberal democracy is not fully democratic, and/or recruit new members.[24] Illegal tactics include practices that are strictly proscribed by a country's legal order, for example, robberies and treason. Various other acts that Lenin promoted, such as mass marches, forming trade unions, and leading general strikes were at times illegal, yet during other periods no legislation sanctioned or prohibited their practice. In repressive, more authoritarian contexts, engaging in any kind of oppositional activity requires disregard for laws and institutions. Still, while the goals for using legal tactics are clear, the reasons why revolutionary contention requires illegal acts is left somewhat vague.

Carl Schmitt's conceptual differentiation between illegality and extralegality offers a way to link revolutionary contention to certain kinds of tactics, as well as to a collective sense of political action. In the *Concept of the Political*, Schmitt emphasizes that political action is not about technical, problem-solving practices such as negotiations over the level of deficit spending or discussions of the amount of resources to be spent on social programs, but instead is concerned with establishing the "friend/enemy" division. Schmitt tells us that "the distinction between friend and enemy denotes the utmost degree of intensity of a union and separation, of an association or dissociation. . . . Each participant is in a position to judge whether the adversary intends to negate his opponent's way of life and therefore must be repulsed or fought in order to preserve one's own form of existence."[25] For Schmitt, political action is first and foremost existential—it is about defending and potentially entering into conflicts over ways of life. This is not strictly about biological life, but involves cultural, economic, moral, and/or religious self-understandings used to represent a human collectivity. Furthermore, setting up the friend/enemy distinction creates opportunities for subsequent antagonism and potential conflict.[26] Or in other words, political action is an ongoing process. Political action is ultimately about processes that create new openings, or opportunities for collective action where groups become self-aware of difference by establishing clear distinctions between ways of life.

Schmitt provokes us to reflect on political action in a way that is simultaneously material, ideational, and all-encompassing. This makes establishing the friend/enemy distinction similar to but different from how social movement theorists have noted the centrality of frames in collective action. As discussed in the literature, frames are practices of meaning construction and interpretation.[27] Frames simplify, condense, label, and identify pertinent aspects of reality for the purposes of social movements, which may include practices of coalition-building and identity formation.[28] Such practices allow movements to draw distinctions between challengers and allies. Political action, for Schmitt, includes but also moves beyond the framing literature's focus on signs and language. Or rather, there is a tendency in social movement studies to conceive of discourse as primarily linguistic in nature. David Snow betrays such an understanding of frames in claiming that movements are best conceived of as "signifying agents engaged in the production and maintenance of meaning for protagonists, antagonists, and bystanders."[29] Signs denote the friend/enemy distinction, yet political action, for Schmitt, is much more than this—in addition to language, politics is about the representation as well as the actual material organization of conflicting ways of life.

Schmitt's later work that foregrounds political action by nonstate actors offers additional and more specific ways to bridge revolutionary politics with extralegal forms of conduct. Specifically, Schmitt defines what he calls "the partisan" with reference to political commitment, irregular conduct, and the defense of space. Irregularity is found in the partisan's agility, speed, ability to surprise, and more precisely, in *not* being a regular, formal army that represents a particular government. The partisan's irregularity places its practices outside the legal order, but not in a criminal sphere. Collective, not individual, action is where we take from Schmitt the conceptual difference between illegality and extralegality. The former, exemplified by actors like pirates, knowingly break laws for "private enrichment," while partisans are groups with "intense political commitments."[30] Partisans also defend their way of life in a certain delimited area. For Schmitt, the partisan has a strict relationship "to the soil," which includes an intimate knowledge of people, terrains, and customs within a certain space.[31] The partisan can represent anything as a threat to its collective way of life—examples that Schmitt alludes to include colonialism, capitalism, and foreign invasion.

Schmitt's understanding of irregularity is what I call extralegal tactics. Such tactics are not sanctioned by the legal order and may even resemble illegal acts. A bank robber steals other people's money from banks. Hundreds of protestors riot and take food from supermarkets while denouncing their government's efforts to privatize education, lower the minimum wage, and raise the age when people can access social security. The former act is individualistic, without collective ideals. The latter, which may appear similar to the robbery in so far as objects are taken, takes on an extralegal quality because of its collective, political quality. Further discerning whether a certain tactic is extralegal, legal, or illegal entails knowledge of a country's legal code, which may or may not contain specifics for acts such as robbery. Yet another aspect of extralegal, irregular action is its production of opportunities for the friend/enemy distinction to become manifest and for the partisan, or in our case a social movement, to perpetuate and reproduce itself while recreating the divisions that it establishes in opposition to another actor. Exploiting legal ambiguities causes confusion and discord among authorities, and thus when deploying such tactics movements buy time to develop. Furthermore, in extending Schmitt's theorization of the partisan, extralegal political action combines offensive and defensive practices. Offensive, irregular tactics allow agents to surprise and catch opponents off guard. The same tactics also contain defensive elements in so far as movements attack in order to protect their own way of life.

Research on tactics is not a new area of study. According to Charles Tilly's concept of repertoires of contention,[32] tactics are contentious if they are deployed by movements that collectively make claims that potentially conflict with the plans of another actor. Many scholars define social movements in terms of their ability to engage in such disruptive, collective forms of protest.[33] Concerning kinds of tactics and their effects, for Frances Piven and Richard Cloward, demobilization resulted once U.S. movements in the 1960s and 1970s traded public disruption for involvement in public policy administration.[34]

Others similarly find that coordinated collective action diminished when leaders began dedicating time and energy to work within government institutions.[35] William Gamson's classic study, likewise, noted that "unruly" groups, or rather, actors that challenged authorities through adopting violent or direct-action tactics were more successful than movements that opted for nondisruptive forms of action.[36] Janice Hellman complicates these findings in noting that movements demobilize after demands are met; they become part of a political party or are co-opted by a populist leader.[37] Alvarez noticed that neoliberal reforms increased the professionalization of economically privileged organizations, contributing to fragmentation and the marginalization of more disruptive elements within the Latin American feminist movement.[38]

Some research on Latin American movements problematizes establishing a simple connection between certain kinds of tactics and outcomes. On Brazilian movements, Gabriel Ondetti—in contradicting those who emphasized the effectiveness of unruly action—noticed how the MST's use of more confrontational acts in the 1990s led to a loss in popular support.[39] Rebecca Tarlau's study of movement success in educational initiatives notes the centrality of combining disruptive action *with* negotiation.[40] Jeffrey Webber's work on Bolivia and collective action is also informative. He describes the protest actions in Bolivia that contributed to the rise of Evo Morales and electoral success of MAS (Movimiento al Socialismo) as "extra-parliamentary."[41] In a similar fashion, Pablo Ramirez describes the tactics of setting up roadblocks and destroying property as "quasi" or "semi-legal" forms of resistance that helped galvanize popular support for the election of Morales in 2005.[42]

Here we find the need for conceptual interventions from Lenin and Schmitt, namely the differentiation between extralegal and illegal practices, as well as how the combination of defensive and offensive tactics potentially leads to an extended process of movement-building. Some have noticed the use of novel tactics that blur conventional senses of legality. What is missing is how to conceive of such acts per se. Moreover, what has not been shown in the literature overall is whether disruptive tactics tend toward movement success or failure. If anything, what the literature on tactics and outcomes reveals is that we need more conceptual, country-specific research. Furthermore, most social movement scholarship conceptualizes tactics in isolation from a country's particular legal order. My exploration of extralegal action requires paying attention to a specific country's laws and norms. Or in other words, what may be considered extralegal in one country may not have the same quality elsewhere. Social movement theory, which emphasizes noting how tactics relate to outcomes, tends to lack country-specific analyses that trace how movement development is related to a given country's legal order.

Extralegal, or irregular, tactics allow a movement to confuse and surprise opponents. Who or what is opposed may not have the ability to respond swiftly or adequately, which grants movements time to develop. Meanwhile, legal tactics potentially allow a movement to gain legitimacy and material resources. Operating solely in the legal realm, however, can place a movement at a disadvantage, especially if organizers lack experience or the means to persistently engage with status quo actors. While illegal tactics offer the ability to surprise opponents, they are limited by the legal order. Illegal acts are present within laws due to their exclusion; for example, acts that constitute robbery are explicitly prohibited in the law. People who break the law find clear and direct punishments. The Landless Movement's extralegal land occupations and encampments, combined with the legal use of public policies, are the main factors internal to the movement that contribute to the development of its revolutionary contention. Even as land occupations have dropped in numbers since 2004, the movement continues to combine extralegal and legal action in consolidating educational and economic development political projects.

Schmitt's conception of political action is also central to questions of how social movements can claim sovereignty. In *Political Theology*, Schmitt defines sovereignty as "he who decides on the exception," which does not mean the use of arbitrary discretionary power, but instead the ability to define and demarcate one political order from another.[43] Later incorporations of Schmitt into radical democratic theory have claimed that his notion of sovereignty as exception is about preserving and establishing order in the face of an enemy, or antagonist, and thus not necessarily state-centric.[44] Mouffe, notably, attempts to read into Schmitt's friend/enemy distinction the potential to create a unified sense of a "people" that includes a coalition of diverse groups to the exclusion of others.[45] Ernesto Laclau's understanding of populism in like manner seeks to introduce pluralism into a Schmittian-inspired conception of radical democracy. Here we find Laclau's concept of "the logic of equivalence," which relies on the construction of a subject from multiple, diverse agents who together are unified by the desire for social change.[46] What these and other commentators on Schmitt have missed is the incipient theory of tactics that he presents in *The Theory of the Partisan* and how this work remains concerned with territory and sovereignty.

Returning to some of the questions that began this section, from Schmitt we find a conception of sovereignty not as a static object, but as a dynamic material practice. The partisan initiates the claim to space through deploying extralegal tactics. Whether or not the democratic subject is pluralist does not matter—what is central is establishing a clear enemy that is potentially and actually challenged. Such a claim to space is mutually exclusive with respect to the enemy. The sovereign claim to space, which is mutually exclusive in its demand for control, is simultaneously ongoing. Or in other words, a movement can both present a program for claiming to control space while at the same time engaging in concrete practices to defend a particular way of life.

The Landless Movement's tactics—as a combination of *pau* and *prosa*, or of extralegal and legal action—illustrate how the movement simultaneously works inside and outside of the state. Its "insider" status arises from the regular negotiations with government officials and acceptance of public policies. These legal ways of interacting with the Brazilian state make the MST and its allies similar to many movements in Brazil and elsewhere; what sets it apart is the use of extralegal tactics, in particular land occupations of large private and public estates. Extralegal tactics give the movement its status as practicing a form of resistance that is "outside the state." When considered with respect to Schmitt's discussion of the partisan, the movement organizes to defend certain spaces and people from what it defines and represents as threats to economically impoverished populations and the environment. Opponents include large, unproductive landowners, agribusiness corporations, and certain government actors. This is where we find the Landless Movement's evolving friend/enemy distinction. The movement's tactical arsenal makes it, at once, in and out of the Brazilian state. Tactics create opportunities for the movement to engage in conflict, as well as for its organizations to reaffirm its own distinct political project in spaces that it claims to control.

The extralegal nature of revolutionary political action also pervades organizational development, namely, in the capacity for movements to provide order and govern. An early account of what can be considered radical social movement governance is found in Lenin's work on what he termed the "dual power." Writing shortly before the 1917 October Revolution, Lenin noted how the worker-council mode of governance, or soviet, arose alongside of, and took power from, the post-czarist provisional government.[47] "Seizing power" did not occur in occupying a government building but in increasing the involvement of participants in the administration of services also provided by state authorities:

security, education, and so on. Service administration and execution involved democratizing economic and private affairs, such as housing policy, poor relief, pension distribution, preschool administration, orphan care, and theater management.[48] Increasing participation in service provision and representation directly opposed the liberal democratic state, which only periodically held elections, and institutionalized a public/private divide that left the control of economic matters to private actors. This focus on organization and order-providing qualities shows signs of governance, or as Jameson notes in his appropriation of the concept of dual power, "power moving in networks which people turn to for practical help and leadership on a daily basis."[49] Even in establishing order, the manner of policy administration challenged prior social relations, economic interests, and political elites. The early soviets show how governance can be resistance; or in other words, in dual power we find the creation of organizations that claim space and transform social relations.

Similar to Lenin, contemporary radical democratic theorists Antonio Negri and Enrique Dussel find constituent and constitutive power at work in a radical project of organization building.[50] In "constitutive power," initiatives encourage popular participation in state services where it was previously absent. Negri calls such attempts to increase social participation in cultural, political, and economic life "absolute process."[51] In opposition, we find already-existing legal and bureaucratic structures, and normative principles that are not subject to collective debate or contestation—examples of what is termed "constituted power." Concrete examples of constituted power appear in thinking of and institutionalizing economic and/or familial affairs as private, and thus as primarily apolitical. This later quality, especially in liberal democracies, is premised on the generally accepted division between the public and private. Such principles are reinforced by various institutions, for example, the police or congress, which have the final authority to pass laws and/or regulate social relations. What counts as constitutive power varies country by country because of the many different institutions that exist, formally and informally. Constitutive power opens and claims spaces for further debate, discussion, and interaction within and through the institutions where we find constituted power. Similarly, the work of feminist theorists, for instance Sonia Alvarez's work on Brazilian democratization, also notes how private affairs can be politicized.[52] The concept of constitutive power complements the discussions of how the private can be made public, going further by emphasizing additional forms of political action that challenge the distinction between public and private authority.

Dussel, Negri, Lenin, and Schmitt focus our attention on how extending democratic practices into services under the domain of the state count as revolutionary. Such movements challenge state power by opposing the institutionalization and bureaucratization of a public/private divide. In so doing, they are making concrete attempts to control space and people—what is best understood as sovereignty. Schmitt's "partisan," with its explicit claim to space and thus to sovereignty, is akin to Lenin's understanding of the dynamics of dual power. Lenin's and Schmitt's theoretical insights contribute to how theorists of food sovereignty have conceived the dynamics through which movements seek to democratize food production. One way to democratize production is to claim space, and in so doing abolish prior modes of governance through constructing more participatory alternatives that reorganize economic, political, and cultural relationships. Additionally, dual power retains the standard meaning that such practices are transitionary and dynamic. Dual power does not acknowledge a specific time horizon for "revolutionary completion." Without visiting spaces that the Landless Movement claims to govern, analyzing its documents, or speaking with members and leaders, it could appear that the movement's embrace of public policies means that it is participating within policies created by Brazilian government. It may seem that the movement is showing a form of participatory democracy or even collaborating with official authorities.[53] At best this is a partial understanding of the movement's goals, organization, tactics, and past and present governing practices. The movement is best considered a case of revolutionary resistance, from its use of tactics to the organizations that it develops to attempt to govern affairs in certain spaces.

The concept of revolutionary contention that I use to chart the Landless Movement's mode of resistance differs from, yet also builds on, other more commonly held conceptions. Theda Skocpol's definition of revolution, with its focus on "basic transformations in social structure and political structure," is exemplified by the actions of the MST and its allies in the services it claims to administer.[54] Akin to this centrality of "transformation" is Hannah Arendt's focus on the modern definition of revolution as a force in motion that liberates people to produce something that is "novel."[55] Charles Tilly's work is also helpful in this regard, mainly in his characterization of dual power as a process, or prolonged "revolutionary sequence."[56] The Landless Movement shows that reaching a "revolutionary outcome," or what Tilly sees as the point when one government replaces another, is not required for building a transformative project. Eric Selbin's comparison of revolutionary movements in Latin America also makes a distinction between revolutionary institutionalization and consolidation. Institutionalization, according to Selbin, is when a revolutionary movement reconstitutes state power, while consolidation involves movement adherents "not only embracing the revolutionary project in words, but in deeds."[57] Or in other words, when revolution institutionalizes, it ends. What I argue is that the Landless Movement has spent decades consolidating and expanding its revolutionary project without institutionalizing it. The two processes—expansion and consolidation—are not mutually exclusive and occur simultaneously as well as at different moments. This was especially displayed from 2002 to 2016, when the movement organized under the auspices of a government that dedicated more resources to the movement's objectives.

Other research on the MST and its various allied organizations that have led the decades-long struggle for agrarian reform in Brazil reads Gramscian concepts of hegemony, political society, and the organic intellectual into the movement's political project.[58] This scholarship is helpful for noting the extent to which the movement engages in preparation *and* direct engagement. One problem with the Gramscian approach is the persistent, if not implied reliance on a liberal form of the state/movement interaction. What the MST's mode of resistance displays is neither a form of political action that "connects" civil society with the state, nor "a space where society organizes the state." Jameson recommends a turn to Lenin and dual power given that the Gramscian distinction between ideological and practical political work has lost its applicability in a post-Cold War world.[59] In following Jameson, as the Landless Movement reveals, practical political action and ideological, or cultural, struggle, are inextricably connected in the movement's mode of revolutionary political action.

Revolutionary political action works inside, outside, and through the state to construct an alternative. This complements the discussions of food sovereignty that argue that effective actions must be national in character. Or in other words, in working through the state, government institutions potentially become a vehicle, but not the end, for social transformation. In constructing alternatives, the state is superseded, and with that the distinction between public and private is erased. Extralegality, as derived from Schmitt's discussion of irregularity and political action, better captures the nature of the MST's signature action—the land occupation—as well as the movement's tactical repertoire in general. The framework for understanding the movement's offensive and defensive characteristics, as well as their relationship to the Brazilian legal order, is further elucidated by combining Schmitt's and Lenin's thoughts on tactics. Furthermore, dual power and the difference between constitutive and constituted power show how radical resistance is not only about increasing participation in particular

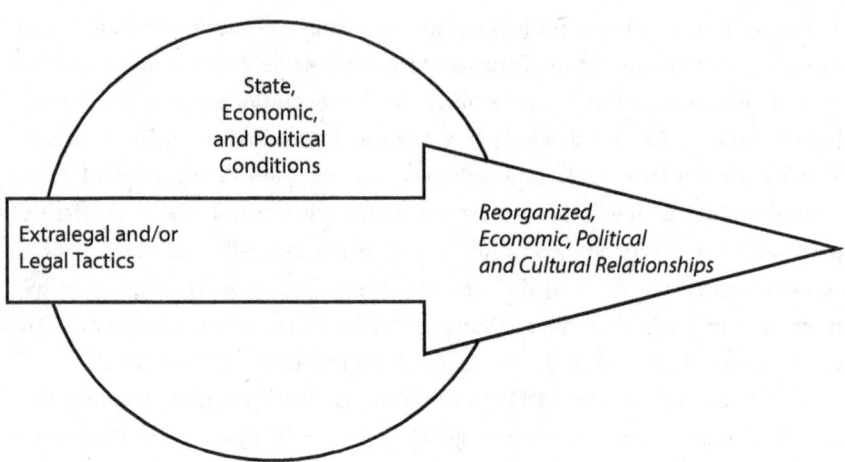

FIGURE 1 Diagram of revolutionary resistance.

policy areas. An increase in participation must dismantle state structures, or as we derive from Dussel and Negri, drive constitutive power through constituted forms of power in the abolition of both.

Another point concerning the nature of the Landless Movement's resistance involves the idea of autonomy. Since its formative years, the movement has claimed to act autonomously from state authority and capitalist production practices. Some have claimed that the MST is radically "autonomous," existing entirely adjacent to state structures of authority, indicative of a movement that is "changing the world without taking power."[60] The Landless Movement's many complex, regular interactions with state authorities—for example, demanding public policies from local and federal governments—problematize such oversimplifications of autonomy. My framework provides a novel approach for understanding how the movement works, at once inside and outside of the Brazilian state.

What has been missing in studies of the Landless Movement is a conceptual focus on the nature of its resistance and an explicit analysis of the contradictions that characterize how the movement relates with the Brazilian government. Wendy Wolford and Angus Wright, when describing movement practices, almost lament that "MST activists find themselves caught up in traditional politics, because this is the most effective way to get things done."[61] I see the movement's engagement with "traditional politics"—especially public programs offered by the Brazilian government—as a key tactical choice that contributes to the development of revolutionary resistance. Tarlau's recognition of different modes of engagement with authorities clarifies the seemingly contradictory means through which the movement engages its opponents. Complementing her work, the framework I construct with Lenin, Schmitt, and Negri foregrounds the revolutionary character of the movement's tactics and forms of organization. Also, following Wolford's work, I see the movement's identity work as integral in the construction of revolutionary subjectivities.

The Landless Movement—which the MST is the dominant member of, but which also includes religious organizations, small farmer movements, and labor unions—challenges the Brazilian government over *who* and *what* has authority in providing services and *how* it is exercised. By weaving together insights from Lenin, Schmitt, Negri, and Dussel, I provide a way of understanding the nature of the movement's resistance, its tactics, and ultimate political project. Reading the Landless Movement as such also contributes to how we ought to conceive of revolutionary dynamics in general and the current state of certain Latin American social movements. For example, conflict between the government and the movement has developed over the administration and execution of agrarian reform policy. Land occupations trigger reactions from the police, judges, and bureaucrats in various ministries. Educational struggles, likewise, have continued to the present day. In 2010, the Ministério Público (MP; Public Prosecutor's Office) in Rio Grande do Sul shut down movement schools for supposedly endangering children.[62] Regular conflicts show continued and collective resistance, qualities that are incompatible with mutual-benefit societies or groups acting in the absence of state presence. The Landless Movement's form of resistance touches precisely on policy areas that are simultaneously the concern of government. In building and proliferating its form of revolutionary resistance, the movement works simultaneously within and against the state to build alternative forms of political, economic, and social organization.

WHEN THE TIME (AND CONDITIONS) ARE "RIGHT," IN BRAZIL AND ELSEWHERE

External, nonmovement factors are just as crucial as agency for the process of revolutionary political action. Or in other words, and to paraphrase Marx's statement from the "Eighteenth Brumaire," movements create the conditions within which they mobilize, but not in the way that they chose. Movements exist within, represent, and reorient a world of which they are necessarily constituted. Revolutionary political action is a manner of deploying tactics that joins space and representation within the historical development of any given society. In offering a way to conceptualize external elements that movements engage, some theorists use the notion of political opportunity structure (POS).[63] Even as the research on fields, networks, and kinds of opportunity offer nuanced ways to think about nonmovement factors, many studies remain unclear on how to conceptually differentiate "political" conditions from others.[64] In fact, everything is usually equally deemed "political," including parties, corporations, the police, and contests over legitimacy.[65] This lack of precision runs the risk of providing ad hoc explanations for the outcomes of resistance. Or in other words, every time we see collective action, it is possible to attribute its success and/or origins to *some* external factor that can be called political.

I propose differentiating kinds of conditions to address this problem, breaking nonmovement factors into state authority, government institutions, and economic relationships. Conditions are structures—defined as relationships between different actors, and of which social movements are part—that constrain, direct, and produce action.[66] Analyzing structures features beliefs such as legitimacy, as well as more concrete elements like public policy expenditures and labor markets. Government conditions, for instance, include the presence or absence of allies, the level of legitimacy of a particular administration, and regime type—liberal democracy, authoritarian, and so on. Government is not the same as the state—administrations come and go with coups and elections. Dilma's government in Brazil was not the same as Lula's, while the Brazilian state did not cease to exist with the transfer of power in 2011.

What differentiates the state from government is sovereignty. When analyzing sovereignty, the focus is on how authority is claimed over and through a distinct people in a certain territory. This leads us to understand how space is appropriated, divided, and claimed. Max Weber's oft-cited definition of the state—a human community that claims the monopoly of force through a specific territory—calls attention to discerning how people are related to one another, and to space.[67] Central to how I analyze state authority in relation to sovereignty is whether the claim to control a certain space and people is uniform, or rather, uncontested. As revolutionary movements illustrate, governments are not the only actors that may claim sovereign power. Still other actors can contest ultimate territorial authority—families, businesses and corporations, and rival factions within government. What matters in the analysis of state conditions is if authority claims are in dispute or not.

Different from government and state conditions, economic conditions involve the production and distribution of goods and services. Economics draws our attention to labor markets, employment levels, and wealth inequality. Most social movement theorists, chiefly the proponents of the political opportunity structure concept, either neglect a discussion of economic factors, or simply lump them into the overly vague notion of "political." Special attention to economic factors is crucial for analyzing the Landless Movement, namely for the movement's development through different economic eras, which Delgado has delimited as the periods of conservative rural modernization (1965–83), the first global adjustment crisis (1983–93), the neoliberal surge (1994–99), and relaunching of agribusiness strategy (2000–2005).[68] Such macrolevel depictions of economic factors have impacted the movement's trajectory, as well as more microlevel elements, such as the recruitment of different kinds of workers—for example, sharecroppers, day laborers, displaced small producers, the unemployed, and self-employed people from the urban informal sector.

Analysis of these three specific conditions—state, government, and economic—helps clarify the dynamics of the unfolding of revolutionary contention, in Brazil and elsewhere. Opportunities exist when movements mobilize people and deploy tactics to take advantage of unstable, precarious conditions. When political actors deploy extralegal tactics, and potentially legal forms of action when state, government, and economic conditions are destabilized, then we ought to see revolutionary political action develop. Such destabilization may occur independently of a movement's actions, or as a result of them. As I use the term, opportunity does not exist as an objective entity independent of action, but instead is produced from a movement engaging in tactics to exploit the instability of state, economic, and/or government conditions.

An analysis of state conditions leads us to evaluate the nature of authority over people and territory, searching out if claims are contested. James Scott's discussion of mapping and grids in *Seeing Like a State* illustrates how analyzing state conditions involves documenting who lives in certain spaces.[69] In Brazil, as well as in much of the Americas, this entails tracing the historical dynamics of colonial and postcolonial development. In fourteenth-century Portugal, the Lei de Sesmarias (Law of Land Grants) established that land must be worked productively, and if it was not, it could be distributed to people who would. The motive behind the law was to incentivize landowners to address a food crisis, as well as provide tribute to the king—a sixth of an owner's profits was due to the king, hence the name of the law.[70] This also became a way to promote Christian expansion into territory previously occupied by Muslims, who at the time were being driven from Portugal.[71] The Sesmarias had two roles—the one, strictly economic, and the other based on expanding the reach of European cultural and economic norms.

The Sesmarias became the basis for organizing colonial territorial authority in Brazil. Within fifteen allotments, the territory that would become known as Brazil was divided among Portuguese nobles (*capitães donatórios*). Subsequent *cartas de sesmaria* became the standard practice for distributing land in the colony. Each letter detailed various responsibilities of the subject/recipient, detailing the manner of passing land to others, the nature of agricultural production, and the size of the grantee's space.[72] The letters issued specific directives and sanctions for each land holding. Regardless of the differences, the imperative was to develop exportable commodity crops like sugar and tobacco.[73] The territory demarcated was extensive—usually several thousand square miles[74]—and poorly measured. Governing the actual allocation and roles for each holding proved next to impossible, with proprietors frequently expanding their territory without official permission and the land's inhabitants regularly violating the officially sanctioned behavior.[75] In assessing this system, James Holston considers it overly bureaucratic and contributing to the creation of an ad hoc mode of governing land distribution and organizing territorial authority.[76]

Brazilian political independence in 1822 did not fundamentally alter the dynamics of land titling and state power. The major piece of legislation to have an impact on land tenure was the 1850 Lei de Terras (Land Law), which dealt with the administration of *terras devolutas*. Article 3 of the law establishes that land is considered *devoluta* when it is not public land, an original *sesmaria* allocation, or privately claimed with title. The term *devoluta* comes from the Portuguese word *devolver*, or "returned." The idea is that space claimed without legal authorization was to be given back to the newly formed, independent Brazilian Empire (1822–89).[77] Besides creating the legal term, *terra devoluta*, the 1850 Land Law established the means to measure and acquire property. Specifically, the law established that areas could be acquired by sale and the price determined at public auction. The proposed unit of measurement for demarcating properties was set at increments of fifty *braços* (arm lengths).

The Land Law gave landed elites the means to control acquisition of territory instead of enabling small-scale squatters and newly arriving immigrants to obtain land. Pricing lands was usually done at the discretion of large property owners in a certain region, with immigrant communities ultimately working on land instead of owning it.[78] Furthermore, the territory acquired was not purchased in neat parcels. Often, the space incorporated into production by large-scale landowners was not surveyed. The dynamics of territorial acquisition and sovereign development in Brazil, as well as in United States, which will constitute most of our attention in the conclusion, was far from peaceful or democratic. In fact, the rampant corruption and violence surrounding land policy in nineteenth-century United States parallels events in Brazilian history.[79] The mapping technologies, however, were different. While in the United States a grid system predominated in areas acquired by land speculators, railroad companies, and mining interests, in Brazil extensive surveying technologies were never part of a state project.

Mapping has been, and remains, one cause of territorial conflict and crises of authority in Brazil. Large landowners acquired land and retained it through a process that became known as *grilhagem*. *Grilhagem* is derived from the word for cricket—*grilho*. It is claimed that forged titles were placed in desk drawers with crickets that would nibble at the edges of documents, giving the semblance of deterioration that presumably came with age. With or without crickets, the extensive practice of falsification left various areas throughout Brazil with multiple parties claiming ownership. In effect, owners would expand territorially without purchasing a particular area that others also claimed. While the practice of further subdividing and selling parcels illicitly was already commonplace during the colonial era, the practice became more widespread following the creation of a land market with the 1850 legislation. Disputing ownership became part of the dynamics generated by *grilhando terras*, as squatters, rural workers, and Indigenous communities routinely challenged the legitimacy of titles claimed by large proprietors.

At various times during and following Brazil's colonial era, distributing and delimiting space has been disputed. When the conflicts are local, or small scale, then the matter can be easily dealt with—either by local landowners or by government officials. For most of the country's history, this took place when landowners and tenants, sharecroppers, or squatters periodically entered into conflicts.

The matter is different when movements organize to challenge well-established systems of territorial authority on a scale beyond isolated areas. Challenging already-accepted means to demarcate territory, as well as maintain those divisions, strikes at state sovereignty. The colonial and postcolonial state features this perpetual vulnerability. Other conditions—government and economic—are also crucial for the unfolding of revolutionary processes. Yet state conditions, not to be conflated with government institutions, draw our attention to space, people, and authority in a different fashion.

Government is not the same as the state. The Brazilian government, especially since the time of the Landless Movement, has changed in multiple ways. Even before the movement, for most of the twentieth century Brazilian governments oscillated between liberal democratic rule and authoritarian governments led by military or authoritarian leaders. The government regime most relevant when considering the Landless Movement's origins was Brazil's military government that lasted from 1964 to 1985. The changes in government conditions brought by the military coup on April 1, 1964, profoundly affected, in a negative way, the plans, projects, and hopes of many social movements. The coup hit the union movement particularly hard. Anthony Pereira notes how over 300 union leaders were killed, jailed, and/or sent into exile in 1964.[80] Maria Alves claims that 452 organizers were removed from their posts in the initial "clean-up operation" led by the military government.[81] Particular alarming events included what happened to the union organizer Gregorio Bezerra, who before being jailed was tortured in public. Meanwhile, the already-weakened Peasant Leagues were effectively disbanded when many of their leaders, Francisco Julião being the most important, were sent into exile. In southern Brazil, the remaining members of Movimento de Agricultores Sem Terra (MASTER; Movement of Landless Farmers)–a direct predecessor of the MST and which we will return to in chapter 3—were similarly jailed or exiled.[82] One sizeable group moved to Paraguay, and another escaped to live clandestinely on the Nonoai Indigenous Reserve in the state of Rio Grande do Sul. Politicians who were movement allies also faced repression—Governor Brizola and President Goulart went into exile initially into Uruguay. Governor Arraes, after eleven months in jail, was finally granted asylum in Algeria.

Decrees and actions by the military government in the 1960s made it difficult to organize resistance in any form. Institutional Acts 1 and 2, the former issued seven days after the coup and the latter in 1965, concentrated decision-making power in the executive, selectively eliminated the electoral mandates of politicians affiliated with movements, and created an electoral college with the purpose of providing the military the ability to create the rules concerning succession. Later in 1965, Complementary Act 4 within Institutional Act 2 forced every then-existing political party to reorganize, resulting in the formation of two—the legal opposition Movimento Democrático Brasileiro (MDB; Brazilian Democratic Movement) and the pro-military Aliança Renovadora Nacional (ARENA; National Alliance for Renovation).

The decree that had the most impact was Institutional Act 5 (AI-5), issued in 1968, which initially granted the military government the power to silence the wave of student and worker unrest. AI-5 allowed the military government to close congress, cancel electoral mandates, suspend political and civil rights, fire any public official, declare a state of siege without impediments, confiscate private property, and legislate through decree. The institutional acts were accompanied by wage controls and additional legislation that essentially prohibited strikes. The violent removal of the union movement's more outspoken, critical leaders from power left labor, especially the Confederação Nacional dos Trabalhadores na Agricultura (CONTAG; National Confederation of Workers in Agriculture), in a state of shock. This was compounded by a variety of institutional changes that generalized repression and removed any left-leaning allies from positions of influence in government. Government conditions had changed radically, disrupting and then eliminating the main institutional sources of support for the revolutionary movements that were active in the 1950s and early 1960s.[83]

The period of what became known as *abertura* (opening) in the late 1960s signaled a significant shift in government conditions. New political parties were allowed to organize, and social mobilization by nonstate actors, in both rural and urban areas, was increasingly allowed. With the new constitution passed in 1988, the Brazilian government officially assumed the institutional dynamics of liberal democracy. Such a form of government allows for free and fair elections, while also promoting and privileging the institution of private property.

Government conditions within Brazil are also characterized by federalism. Federal systems, as opposed to unitary constitutions, grant significant executive and legislative powers to subnational levels of government. In Brazil, while the national executive must officially decree each expropriation of property for redistribution, state-level governments have considerable power in allocating resources for agricultural production and educational purposes. In fact, most decisions concerning education policy are made by state and municipal governments. Brazil's federal nature—as will become especially relevant for our discussion of revolutionary consolidation and development in chapter 5—has also led to different responses to the Landless Movement's actions. In fact, strategically, the movement has at times opted to work with certain national-level authorities, while at other times with state governments. Movement success has often been linked to the nature of the institution at a certain level of government, as well as to the political party in power. How subnational units of government affect the mobilization of the Landless Movement is a relatively underresearched dynamic of the movement.[84] I address this shortcoming in subsequent chapters, which is made possible by my conceptual differentiation between state, government, and economic conditions.

Besides state and government conditions, economic factors have been central to the development of the Landless Movement. Historically, following the abolition of slavery in 1888, European immigrants gradually replaced the slave workforce in the south and southeast—especially in São Paulo, Paraná, Rio Grande do Sul, and Rio de Janeiro. Between 1880 and 1903, approximately two million Europeans arrived in Brazil, mainly from Germany, Italy, Portugal, and Spain, Ukraine, Russia, Lithuania, Hungary, Armenia, China, and Korea, followed by a second wave of over two million people from Italy, Poland, Russia, and Romania from 1904 to 1930.[85] Settlement companies, in addition to forming settlements, moved families to live and work on large plantations. Italians, for example, were the most numerous immigrant group to arrive and then work on the plantations on the eve of the twentieth century, composing close to 70 percent of the workforce on plantations throughout the state of São Paulo.[86] In the northeast, the majority of former slaves became sharecroppers and tenant farmers. Economic relations in rural areas, particularly with respect to the rural labor, involved large landowners ceding usufruct rights to various populations without providing former slaves and immigrants definitive private property rights.

Immigrants lived within the social relations that characterized Brazil's many latifundios. Before and after the 1850 Land Law, large-scale latifundios or fazendas dominated Brazilian rural life. The owners of these operations widely used *grilhagem* to acquire property and expand their plantations. Defining the latifundio, especially as it existed during the twentieth century, in terms of size or economic activity would be overly reductionist. Latifundios were institutions that blurred the boundaries of politics, economics, and the state. Especially before the Great Depression in the twentieth century, latifundios were hierarchically organized and nearly self-governed. Even though Brazil was nominally administered by a centralized government, large landowners established near exclusive control over their particular parcels of earth. Control included the lives of the people who lived there. Until 1881, local officials were elected directly by the people, who later voted for provincial and national leaders. Reforms in 1881 and later in 1889 extended suffrage to literate men, yet during the period of the First Republic (1889–1930), large-landed proprietors from the states of São Paulo and Minas Gerais used fraud and force to ensure their control over political parties and local affairs.[87] Internally, plantations hosted urbanlike centers with pharmacies, theaters, and general stores, with landowners in charge of distributing land and even officiating marriages.[88] The plantation, wherever it was present in Brazil, fractured sovereignty between government and economic authorities.

Economic and political transformations during the twentieth century challenged the nearly autonomous existence of latifundio society. Economic transformations concerning labor relations began during the 1930s. José da Silva documents two distinct periods of industrialization—the first between 1933 and 1955, which he calls "restricted," and the latter, "heavy" period that occurs from 1956 to 1966.[89] During the first period, Brazilian agriculture and life on the plantation were "opened." This occurred as the result of two processes. First, production began to incorporate inputs produced from outside the plantation. Seeds, fertilizers, and machines such as tractors began to appear in the first half of the twentieth century. While it is true that the military regime in the 1970s promoted more industrialized, monocultural styles of production, the "opening" of the latifundio really began decades earlier. Meanwhile, government institutions began to intervene separately from landed interests. Getúlio Vargas came to power in 1930 after the economic shock left landowners requiring extensive outside assistance to stabilize the coffee industry. His administration strengthened controls over coffee production and pricing to prevent overproduction, while also introducing extensive labor legislation as part of the Estado Novo (New State).[90] Labor law went only as far as the plantation gate. The creation of the corporatist state with a series of laws in the early 1930s, and finally with the Consolidação das Leis do Trabalho (CLT; Consolidation of Labor Laws) in 1943, granted the right to organize, among other rights, to workers. The application of rural labor law, however, was at best sporadic. Still, industrialized goods and economic policy became an ever-growing part of plantation life.

The destabilizing effects of industrialization on labor and the latifundio were compounded by the Estatuo do Trabalhador Rural (ETR; Rural Worker Statute) in 1963. This law made union formation legal, as well as offered protection for workers from arbitrary dismissal, and an eight-hour day, among other long-sought rights. In effect, the ETR raised the cost of rural labor, prompting landowners to further mechanize and eliminate sharecropping arrangements. It is during this time, the 1950s, not the 1960s or 1970s, Biorn Maybury-Lewis notes, that the large landowners experienced a "changing mentality." At mid-century, instead of focusing their energies on preserving the myriad of social relations on their fiefdoms, plantation owners opted to focus on commercial agriculture and cut back the numbers in the permanent rural workforce.[91]

Incorporating technology into agricultural production was not a night-and-day change, but took decades to develop. In Paraná, coffee production according to the sharecropping arrangements was already in decline when a series of destructive frosts hit in the early 1960s.[92] Beginning in the 1940s and continuing through the 1950s, many coffee planters in the southeast began to adopt labor-saving technologies when they entered the dairy, beef, and orange juice industries with the assistance of government subsidies and technical support services.[93] Other regions, particularly in the northeast, witnessed similar technological transformations. Owners who decided to plant more land and use new technologies on sugar plantations began to eliminate the need for certain classes of workers, as well as the quarters for the laborers and their families. The paternalistic relations characteristic of latifundio society were ending.[94] The changing labor relations and urbanization trends show that many individuals, across various regions in Brazil, were experiencing the destabilizing effects of changing economic relations.

Historically, economic, state, and government conditions have facilitated or inhibited collective action. What is just as important is how conditions interact with a movement's tactics to produce opportunities and the persistence of organized contention. Opportunities are short-lived, periodic episodes of conflict generated from movements deploying their tactics that potentially lead to negotiations, a change in government, and new policies, as well as potential retreat and defeat. My work on conditions and opportunities draws attention to differences between state, government, and economic factors. Narrating how tactics interact with conditions emphasizes the contingent, dynamic nature of social movement activity. Theorists of revolutionary action, such as Theda Skocpol, Joel Migdal, and Lenin, also analyzed how changes in economic relations or the breakdown of state authority structures helped contribute to social transformation.[95] Building off this prior work, I isolate kinds of conditions and how they intersect with legal, illegal, and extralegal tactics.

Periodic efforts to establish territorial authority, as in the Lula-era efforts to map territories in the Amazon in the Territórios da Cidadania (Territories of

Citizenship) program, have been effective in stabilizing state power and weakening revolutionary efforts. Such government-led projects to stabilize state power contrast with others, such as the military governments increasing instability in the late 1970s, which further exposed the Brazilian state's vulnerable property rights regime. Efforts to decentralize political power that began during the military's transition benefitted various actors besides the MST, such as the Central Única dos Trabalhadores (CUT; United Workers' Central) and the Partido dos Trabalhadores (PT; Workers Party).

The policies and effects of neoliberal restructuring also disrupted state, government, and economic relations. I am not the first to conceive of how neoliberalism impacted social movement resistance. Ruth Collier and Samuel Handlin, for example, note that political and economic changes led to an increase in movement activity on the continent.[96] Deborah Yashar connects budget cuts and state weakness to the emergence of Indigenous movements in the Andes.[97] Economic, state, and government instability due to neoliberal restructuring in the 1990s was principally seen in the growth of the urban informal economy. The Landless Movement, as I show, adapted its use of occupations and encampments to involve actors from the informal economy. Other actors that initially in their existence had radical, transformative aspirations and projects, such as the PT and the CUT, did not make the adequate tactical adjustments to continue revolutionary contention. Current challenges encountered by the MST and its allies, particularly involving recent divisions in the movement and a drop in land occupations, can be traced to changes in stabilizing nonmovement conditions that came during the Lula and later Dilma administrations (2002–10 and 2010–16). The movement has made tactical adaptations, remaining active extralegally through organizing collective, anti-capitalist efforts via production support policies. While still transformative, this newer accumulation-of-forces stage of the MST is not about extending revolutionary resistance, but consolidating its efforts in spaces already claimed.

THE LANDLESS REVOLUTION BY THE NUMBERS

Discussions of the Landless Movement often begin with a reference to its size. Its claim of mobilizing over one and a half million people is regularly mentioned in books, articles, and by the movement and activist supporters. At first, these figures may be considered inflated. In fact, they are not very exaggerated, especially if we take into consideration that the MST and its allies have been active for three decades, and that as of 2015, there existed 9,255 agrarian reform settlements where close to one million families live.[98] Even though numbers are unavailable for which settlements have resulted from the MST versus the actions of other movements, given that the total number of settlements pre-MST was 67, the vast majority of the families can be attributed to the MST.[99] We need to remember that the movement began with thirty families who decided to occupy the Macali and Brilhante ranches in Rio Grande do Sul in 1978.[100] According to Gabriel Ondetti, after the movement slowly grew throughout the 1980s and early 1990s, a mass "take-off" in terms of membership occurred in the late 1990s/early 2000s, when positive press coverage of massacres of landless workers garnered public sympathy, international outrage, and additional government resources.[101] These figures show an immense movement that is engaging in revolutionary political action. What differentiates the Landless Movement from other examples of revolutionary resistance, such as in Cuba or Nicaragua for instance, is not some qualitative aspect, but the number of people who have been involved.

The MST, also, has worked closely with various other movements and organizations over the course of its development. The landless revolution includes the Confederação Nacional dos Trabalhadores na Agricultura (CONTAG; National Confederation of Workers in Agriculture), the Conferência Nacional do Bispos do Brasil (CNBB; National Conference of Brazilian Bishops), the Comissão Pastoral da Terra (CPT; Pastoral Land Commission), as well as other movements like the Movimento dos Atingidos por Barragens (MAB; Movement of People Affected by Dams), and the Movimento dos Pequenos Agricultores (MPA; Movement of Small Farmers), many organizations led by Indigenous communities, and groups of Afro-descendants, known as the Quilombolas. Despite the plurality of actors, the transformational political project occurring in Brazil was initiated by and is primarily led by the MST. In fact, as I discuss in later chapters, movements like the MPA owe their emergence to the MST. Others, such as CONTAG, began to also engage in extralegal action and coordinate more closely with the MST only after the latter movement showed a potential to create social transformation. For these reasons, the MST is at the center of this book's narrative. Yet, this collection of movements and organizations, together, forms the singular actor known as the Landless Movement.

We can better discern the nature of participation within the MST if we break down membership by area of involvement. Such figures, especially for occupations and encampments, are limited because they were not cataloged by different social movements until 2000. Despite this slight problem in the organization of the data, we can still document a large movement with active participants dividing their time between certain sectors. These figures also indicate that there is active and passive participation within the ranks of the MST's million or so adherents.

In Brazil, the centerpiece of agrarian reform policy is the settlement, which is composed of redistributed land and certain social programs that provide resources, such as housing credits, for new participants. Both academic studies and official reports indicate the MST's high level of success. Sergio Leite, who conducted the most in-depth study of settlements to date, finds that if not for MST pressure post-1985, the increase in settlements would not have taken place.[102] Likewise, comparison with other democracies reveals the near unparalleled advances in land reform due to MST pressure.[103]

We can identify the number of MST occupations and encampments since 2000—the first year with data that accounts for the different members of the Landless Movement. In comparison with other movements, MST occupations and encampments are at 51 percent and 49 percent of the total instances, respectively. Similarly, the number of families mobilized stands at a total of 562,115 in land occupations, with 388,160 of them—63 percent—organized by the MST. If we conservatively assume that each family has two members, then the number

TABLE 1 Figures According to Particular Services (2000–2015)

AGRARIAN REFORM	EDUCATION	ECONOMIC DEVELOPMENT
Responsible for over half of the ~9,200 settlements in Brazil. Since 2000, has mobilized over 388,160 families in occupations and 88,369 families in encampments. Over one million people mobilized around land access.	~20 schools under movement control and over 2,000 built by the government but controlled by the Brazilian state. Annually runs ~25 courses in postsecondary institutions for movement members. Delivered the movement's own instruction to between 400,000 and 500,000 people.	Created 49 collective production cooperatives with 2,229 families participating, as well as 32 service cooperatives with 11,174 members and 7 more cooperatives that deal with credit and other activities. Helped thousands of producers receive benefits from public policies and transition to agroecological production techniques.

Sources: INCRA 2016; CPT 2000–2014; Plummer 2008; de Carvalho 2006.

of people organized in occupations alone by the MST has been over a million. However, this does not mean that millions of people remain active after gaining land or that people become active participants in other areas. The movement has also mobilized the largest number of families in encampments, with over 58 percent of the total number of families being affiliated with the MST, or 88,369 families out of a total of 146,295 between 2000 and 2014. From these numbers, and given that twenty-three other movements have at one time or another organized land occupations, encampments, and settlements, the MST dominates this service when compared to its allies in the struggle for agrarian reform. The movement has essentially redefined agrarian reform, given the near moribund status of efforts pre-1985.

The movement also boasts impressive numbers in education, claiming to have pressured state authorities to construct 2,250 schools where over 350,000 people have learned to read and write, with another 350,000 people currently studying all kinds of subjects from geography to agroecology, taught by 4,000 movement-trained teachers.[104] Despite a relatively low number of settlement elementary and high schools, MST gains are more apparent in the implementation in various states of the *escolas itinerantes* (itinerant schools) in encampments.[105] At their peak in Rio Grande do Sul (1998–2009) and Paraná (2002–15),[106] a total of fifteen schools attended to roughly one thousand students each year per state.[107] Success is also seen in the movement's experiments with secondary education, particularly with technical schools, where in 2010—one year where we have specific numbers from the movement and the state—roughly 40 percent of high school age students attending rural technical schools were affiliated with the MST (10,058 students affiliated with the movement out of 24,465 total students).[108] Since 1985, movement-affiliated high school students have attended thirty-one different spaces under movement direction.[109] The number of Landless Movement students and schools shows that the movement's success rate is low in comparison with agrarian reform. Still, if we compile the numbers from various sources, it appears that around 400,000 or 500,000 people have been part of MST education through the 1980s, 1990s, 2000s, and 2010s.

While the movement flaunts its collective, successful cooperatives as illustrative of an alternative mode of economic development, many have succumbed to heavy debt and bankruptcy. In one interview, I was told that only around 5 percent of the hundreds of cooperatives initiated in the 1980s and 1990s continue.[110] In the same interview I was told that "without cooperatives, the settlements cannot survive," indicating current problems faced by the movement in creating a collective form of economic production. As a result, the movement has emphasized agroecological production techniques, with currently around 5 percent of movement members applying such production approaches. Agroecological practices, which I document more in the next chapter, emphasize small-scale production without the use of chemicals, often in decentralized groups. If compared with the standard tally for movement membership—1,500,000 people—about 75,000 people are involved in the policy area of economic development.

Another measure for movement involvement in economic development is the number of families benefitting from state policies for small-holder, typically organic, agricultural production. From numbers available in 2009 and 2010 in the Programa de Aquisição de Alimentos (PAA; Food Acquisition Program), the percentage of finances went from 8 percent to 12 percent (R$28,699,236 of R$363,381,941 to R$44,643,666 of R$379,735,466), while the percentage of participating families in settlements went from 7 percent to 11 percent (7,444 of 98,340 families to 10,440 of 94,398). We can extrapolate from these numbers—because we know that roughly 50 percent of land occupations and encampments in Brazil are under the Landless Movement's influence—that thousands of movement families participate in these public policies.

CONCLUSION: REVISITING THE NUMBERS OF REVOLUTION

These figures concretize the Landless Movement's actions. They also show how the movement has actual, specific gains in individual policy areas. These numbers draw our attention to the movement's mobilization of membership into certain services also provided by the Brazilian government. Such mobilization within policy areas, and concomitant acceptance of government resources, does not mean that the movement adheres to dominant economic and political practices. As I detail further in the next chapter, the MST and its allies revolutionize the services they take, or occupy. As I document, the movement's revolutionary form of resistance is in the nucleos that democratize state services by challenging the institutionalization of a public/private divide. In this fashion, the movement takes state power, not in armed insurrection, but by reappropriating public programs to claim space in ways that conflict with status quo norms and rules. The movement's revolutionary actions challenge state power and vie for control, while simultaneously challenging and transforming dominant economic, political, and cultural practices.

This chapter also provides the theory and concepts that reappear throughout this book to explain revolutionary contention. In building off the work of others, I theorize revolutionary resistance as a form of collective action that features extralegal and potentially legal modes of engaging political and economic elites. Revolutionary political action works in, against, and through state power to produce alternative organizations that contest already-existing political, economic, and cultural relationships. In this conceptualization, revolutionary modes of action abolish the institutionalization of a public and private power, especially within liberal democratic states. Revolutionary struggles can unfold within liberal democracies, and when they do, they erase public and private distinctions in transforming social relations. How this kind of transformation has unfolded in Brazil is the focus of the remainder of the book.

The main argument in this book is that the use of legal and extralegal tactics interacts with propitious external conditions to produce revolutionary resistance. This book's contribution lies not only in offering a new way to conceptualize the Landless Movement and explain its development, but also in providing a way to understand revolutionary political action in general. I present the movement's mode of revolutionary resistance as a way to organize political, economic, and social life that challenges the current neoliberal orthodoxy that privileges individualized, market-oriented practices.

In revisiting the Landless Movement's origins, my study highlights a nuanced attention to kinds of conditions and the dynamics of intra- and cross-movement learning. To understand how the movement has developed, and its current challenges, we need to trace how it has changed over time. Attention to origins—especially their contingency—is central because the Landless Movement, as the largest social movement active in Latin America, tends to be heralded as a model. Reappraising the movement's early efforts reminds us of its difficulties and the extreme sacrifice of the first members and leaders. Brazil's landless revolution has been decades in formation. Simply because armed guerrillas were not present does not make it any less transformative or radical.

2

THE REVOLUTION IN EDUCATION, ECONOMIC DEVELOPMENT, AND AGRARIAN REFORM

AGRARIAN REFORM BY OTHER MEANS

"VAMOS, LÁ!" (LET'S GO, OVER THERE!) At the crack of dawn, I was startled awake in my hammock by these words from a young MST activist. He was going hammock to hammock, sleeping bag to sleeping bag, waking up the couple hundred people who had occupied a space and encamped in front of the INCRA (Instituto Nacional de Reforma Agrária; Institute for Colonization and Agrarian Reform) government office where we had spent the night. Just two days before, I had joined a march to demand agrarian reform in the state of Pará. Others had been marching for seven days, spending nights in public parks or on movement settlements that were on the way. When I first entered the march, I asked some people where we were going. To my surprise, no one knew. On the second day, I again asked a few of the marchers about our destination. I gathered from various conversations that we were going to Belém, the capital city in the state of Pará, but still, no one provided details. I first thought this was because I was not a movement member. For any movement, some stranger—especially a gringo—asking questions could be viewed with suspicion. Later, however, I found that many people truly did not know the endpoint. We were on a march, and agrarian reform was the goal—that was all that mattered. Ultimately, we arrived at, and then occupied, INCRA's headquarters in the state. Fortunately, one family loaned me a hammock. While eating supper—with a plate and fork also provided by my impromptu host family—I found one movement leader and asked what we were doing the next day. She shrugged her shoulders, smiled, and said, "Sei lá cara, ninguém sabe, vamos ver" (Man, I don't know, no one does, we'll see). After three hours of sleep, my hammock was shaken, I woke up, and found that we were going to occupy the MDA offices to demand debt relief.

The secrecy I experienced throughout the march was intentional. The logistics of land occupations led by the MST and its allies are similarly concealed, mainly because of worry that infiltrators would obtain and communicate relevant details to the movement's enemies. Occupations usually take place late at night, when dozens or sometimes hundreds of people load buses for destinations known only to a handful of organizers. When families reach their stop—typically a large ranch or farm of an unaware landowner—the people squat there for months, often years. Immediately after "taking" the land, the families set up black-tarp tent communities known as the *acampamentos* (encampments). Members live in these spaces with few tangible resources, having unreliable access to water, food, and sanitation. In the face of such adverse conditions, the occupiers show a surplus of ingenuity when building nascent communities with whatever prior knowledge they possess. From providing security in group-based patrols, to dedicating spaces to religious buildings and sporting events, movement members carry out a de facto form of agrarian reform by claiming to control these spaces according to new, transformative economic, political, and cultural uses. Even though official expropriation and the legal recognition of *assentamentos* (settlements) characterize government agrarian reform policy, the movement already implements an alternative version from the moment member families occupy land.

Land occupations destabilize monocultural, agro-export economic production, entrenched patterns of unequal land ownership within Brazilian agriculture, and standard government agrarian reform practices. Simultaneously, occupations, along with establishing encampments and managing relations in settlements, show complex organizational and order-providing dynamics. At times, the movement works with state authorities on various matters related to occupations. It is common to find INCRA representatives offering Landless Movement leaders "tips" on which lands to occupy and negotiate with movement leaders over which families will gain land and where. Landless Movement practices display well-organized, systematized efforts, not only in their grassroots version of agrarian reform, but in various other services such as education, health care, and economic development. What unifies their actions across these diverse services, or policy areas, is a common revolutionary form of resistance. The movement works in, against, and through the Brazilian state to transform cultural, political, and economic relationships in certain spaces. In this way, the Landless Movement, with the MST as one of its largest and most provocative members, forces us to seriously consider the meaning of the movement's claim to "sovereignty" in the demand for food sovereignty.

In this chapter, unlike in the others, I detach the movement's governing structure—the *núcleos de base* (nucleos) and the internal, pyramid-like organization otherwise known as the MST's *organicidade* (organicity)—from my explanation of movement development. Tactics and external, nonmovement conditions occupy my focus in chapters 3, 4, and 5. This chapter, also, focuses exclusively on the internal dynamics of the movement instead of comparing its actions with past or present movements and processes. This allows us to understand how the MST's governing structure exemplifies a revolutionary form of organization. I document precisely the transformations that the MST has implemented, as well as particular setbacks. The MST, especially in this chapter, is central given that most other small farmers, rural workers, and labor union members of the Landless Movement ultimately participate in the organizations that were first created and managed by the MST.

Most studies of the MST and its allies document specific policy changes, for instance, in education or economic development, without classifying the movement's mode of resistance. My account differs by foregrounding that what runs through each change is a revolutionary form of contention, as I theorized in the previous chapter. Additionally, most of the evidence used to document the movement's mode of organization comes from ethnographic, participatory methods, drawing from field notes and interviews. Sue Branford and Jan Rocha's classic study of the MST, *Cutting the Wire*, and Angus Wright and Wendy Wolford's well-known *To Inherit the Earth* also feature reflections from activists.[1] My use of ethnography differs by locating precisely—in activists' words and conduct—the meaning and practices of revolutionary political action.

To direct the analysis, I highlight Landless Movement governance in education, economic development, and agrarian reform. I selected these three different services because each clearly impinges on areas where the Brazilian state also claims authority. This discussion illustrates how the MST and its allies create an alternative to state power and dominant economic, political, and cultural practices. Following especially Antonio Negri and Enrique Dussel's insights in this regard, we can locate the movement's alternative when its practices oppose a separation of public from private affairs and the bureaucratization of service provision. Challenging the public/private divide means extending debate and deliberation into seemingly apolitical "private" issues that involve economic and/or family matters. The Landless Movement contests bureaucratization by opposing divisions that grant officials in formal institutions the exclusive privilege of designing and executing policy. Revolutionary change erases the state/society binary. This is not to claim that the movement has no hierarchical qualities or promotes some kind of unadulterated equitable system of service provision. At various points in this chapter, I show how the movement has encountered problems related to economic mismanagement, gender inequality, and centralization. These challenges coexist, often awkwardly, with the radical changes accomplished by the Landless Movement in its cultural, economic, and political transformations of relationships in particular spaces.

I describe what is known within the MST as the *mística* before I analyze the movement's practices in agrarian reform, economic development, and education.[2] In addition to the nucleo form of governance, the MST's practice of the mística cuts across the various areas of movement involvement. The mística is a ritual conducted by movement members that is sometimes composed of songs, poems, and/or videos. The ritual often features prominent Landless Movement symbols, past leaders, and/or grievances. While the MST was the primary movement to initiate the mística, other members of the Landless Movement also take part in it when in the areas that the movement claims. Foreign, non-Brazilian allies, likewise, usually join the místicas if they are at movement schools, encampments, or events. I include a discussion of the mística in this chapter because it is the primary vehicle through which the organization of revolutionary cultural elements is materialized.

The MST's organizational and governing dynamics have been critiqued in decontextualized ways. For example, Zander Navarro describes the movement's organization as authoritarian without explaining what this means.[3] In the popular Brazilian press, specifically the center-right publication *Veja*, MST education has been likened to religious fundamentalism in the Middle East.[4] In an interview I conducted with a former Brazilian secretary of education, who on occasion, often begrudgingly, worked with MST leaders, I was told that the MST was part of the "backward left" that is "absolutely ideological . . . really, out of this world."[5] My approach is to first understand and interpret rather than rush to judgment. I balance my own perspectives with those of movement members and leaders, as well as those of opponents. I claim neither that the MST's mode of governance is the realization of some utopian dream nor a totalitarian nightmare. My analysis intends to describe the nature of revolutionary governance with its successes, failures, and obstacles.

PRACTICING A REVOLUTIONARY CULTURE: THE *MÍSTICA*

The MST's revolutionary resistance cultivates a movement-centered identity in addition to challenging the state's manner of designing and executing services. Movement leaders and activists go to great lengths to intentionally organize this identity in what is known as the *mística*. Most movement activities, including children's school day and national level meetings of leaders, begin with songs, chants, and theatrical displays of MST symbols. Místicas usually start with the *grito de ordem* (call to order). The *grito* features a certain phrase used in marches or protests, for example, *patria livre! venceremos!* (free country! we will succeed!), or *reforma agrária, cuando? agora!* (agrarian reform, when? now!). Místicas often involve the MST's flag, references to past—usually deceased—leaders or members, and common movement demands such as policies that would promote agroecology or land redistribution.

Such cultural, identity-creating activities are far from unique to the MST. Identity cultivation has long been recognized as a pillar of social movement activity. In addition, theorists have found that identities are acquired in struggles with opponents, allow actors to attribute blame to an antagonist, assist groups in differentiating between friends, allies, and enemies, and help leaders craft strategies.[6] Maggie Thayer's study of Latin American feminist movements notes how activist networks and organizations consolidated a coherent political identity even as inequalities within the movement grew.[7]

The MST's cultural work in the místicas has many, if not all, of these qualities. João Pedro Stédile, one of the movement's founders and member of the *direção nacional* (national coordination), recognizes how the mística produces hope and solidarity among members.[8] A relatively early description of the practice's importance mentioned in the MST's *Jornal dos Trabalhadores Rurais Sem Terra* (*JST*; Journal of the Rural Workers) tells how "the mística helps keep members committed to the struggle.⁹ The call to order resonates with participants by penetrating into the masses and orienting their actions."¹⁰ In the same publication two years later, the ritual is defined

> not as something external, but a feeling we all have for the collective that strengthens our participation and helps us improve our practices. The *mística* can be defined as that joy or emotion [*gosto ou sabor*] we feel when we participate in MST actions. It strengthens our trust in the organization, the masses, and our future.¹¹

The liberation theologist and MST ally Leonardo Boff characterizes the mística as "the collection of profound feelings, grandiose visions, and strong passions that strengthen people and that inspire them to confront challenges. The mística is sociopolitical and utopian."¹² Another longtime member of the MST's national coordination, Ademar Bogo, has regularly explained in MST publications since the 1980s how the mística helps members deal with personal vices, serves as a propaganda tool, and inculcates socialist values.

The místicas I observed in encampments were the most organized and disciplined when compared with similar practices in other movement spaces. In one encampment where I stayed, once a week everyone lined up single file to sing the movement hymn (and not the Brazilian) while leaders reported on events and upcoming demonstrations.¹³ In encampments, one usually sees more MST imagery than Brazilian. Entrance points typically are demarcated by the movement's flag and guarded by members who are wearing the movement's easily identifiable red shirts and hats. The impression one receives, from this extensive material proliferation of symbols on shirt, hats, and flags, is that one is entering a territory under the MST's control rather than the government's. Identity construction is embedded in the physical space that the movement occupies. The sovereign claim to space makes the movement's identity materially part of most facets of daily life.

Becoming part of the movement, living the "Sem Terra" identity, is a revolutionary cultural change that features repeated efforts to promote the movement at the expense of potential rivals. Even though the mística and MST symbolism appear at many events and sites, their role in encampments is especially salient because many people in these spaces are new recruits. No matter their previous occupation or beliefs, living in an encampment is an MST rite of passage where participants learn to identify first and foremost as "Sem Terra."¹⁴ During my research, I met former small-store owners, rural wage laborers, displaced small farmers, and recovering drug users who became active participants in the MST. The movement, in its daily and routine identity work found in the mística, productively channels prior beliefs and practices through its own symbolism. Roseli Caldart emphasizes this point in how

> the landless bring different ways to see the world, understand life, conceive of relationships, as well as prejudices.... [W]ith whatever are their individual pasts, [the movement] constructs a new identity, from a person without land (*trabalhador sem a terra*) to a landless worker (*trabalhador sem terra*), and later Sem Terra, which is an identity rooted in organization building and collective resistance.[15]

What is also emphasized in the identity is its uniformity—it is Sem Terra, not Sem Terras. The MST's identity and cultural work privileges collectivity over plurality.

In another encampment that housed a movement-run school, I was told how the children learn the movement's hymn as part of their mística activities. In addition to cultivating a sense of belonging to the movement, the incorporation of the MST's hymn was used to teach the alphabet.[16] In yet another mística—one in which I was recruited to participate—a group of women who were studying early childhood education spent days making cardboard cutouts of the individual letters of *reforma agrária* (agrarian reform). In the performance of the mística, one member stood in the middle of a room, announced a letter, and then read a statement connecting the letter to other practices promoted by the MST: for example, "A, also is in agroecology, which we promote so that healthy, sustainably produced food is grown, free of poisons." While the statements were read, each of us entered the room single file with our individual letters. We then stood side by side in a line to make the words r-e-f-o-r-m-a a-g-r-á-r-i-a.[17] This mística, I later discovered, was filmed and later broadcast by a local news affiliate.

The precise content of the místicas includes clear divisions between movement allies and foes, as well as references to particular demands and historical figures. Many of the místicas I observed every day during the month I stayed at the MST school, Instituto Educar (Educate Institute), showcased deceased revolutionary icons. Such figures included the Argentinean-Cuban leader of the Cuban Revolution, Che Guevara, as well as Carlos Marighella, who theorized urban guerrilla warfare in Brazil before being killed in combat in 1969, and Soviet educator Anton Makarenko. Another mística highlighted the music of the

FIGURE 2 A mística at the tenth annual Jornada de Agroecologia, in Curitiba, Paraná. Movement members are imitating labor-intensive seed sifting and cleaning techniques.

Chilean singer-songwriter-activist Victor Jara, who was killed by the Pinochet regime in 1973. Most of Jara's lyrics focus attention on economic inequality, class struggle, and exploitation of rural workers by large landowners.

To further make manifest the rural worker/producer identity, místicas often also involve seeds, farm tools, and food. The meanings connected to these items present the idea that movement members are the main agents involved in growing food, not only for themselves but for all Brazilians. Large landowners and agribusiness corporations are represented in the místicas as ultimately unproductive actors who exploit rural people and pollute the earth. This repetitive work on identity formation cultivates a common, collective sense of belonging and antagonism towards real, concrete opponents, a division that Schmitt would consider constitutive of the "friend/enemy" distinction. What permeates the practices of Sem Terra identity construction is a thorough politicization of social relations, as individuals from various walks of life, and who may not have had strong political identities before joining, organize to recognize one another collectively with a common antagonist.

FIGURE 3 The second picture shows students at an MST elementary school beginning their day with the movement hymn and a little exercise.

It is hard to verify if místicas are effective in producing their intended cultural changes. I observed people who were very impassioned during the ritual, while others seemed to be simply going through the motions. I also noticed that older members practiced the mística differently than their younger counterparts. Longtime members who were enrolled in a training course on cooperative management that met every day conducted místicas only two times a week.[18] At the course, the leaders would read a poem and others would listen in silence. This contrasted with the everyday presentation of the mística by elementary and high school-age students, who often spent hours, sometimes over the course of days, in preparation. Místicas at large events, such as the yearly Jornada de Agroecologia (Journey for Agroecology) or national meetings, involve days of planning, music performed by live bands, and intricate, almost parade-like processions. Depending on the place, sometimes a simple poem, song, or on occasion, the presentation of a YouTube video, sufficed. Some have noted that MST identity is far from unitary despite the mística. Conflicting perspectives on the meaning of land and politics coexist within the movement's ranks.[19]

Still, what the mística does create is a space within which movement symbols and practices dominate. Whether or not members actively participate in the ritual, the phrases, images, songs, and other actions are always connected back in some fashion to the MST. Alternative, even competing identities may coexist, but are organized by the MST's incessant identity work to create a clear "us" and "them."

REVOLUTIONARY POLITICAL ACTION IN THE DETAILS: THE *NÚCLEOS DE BASE*

The movement's claim to space is not limited to identity work. In fact, transforming social relations within a particular area also includes the practice of an alternative mode of governance. The political change characteristic of the MST's revolutionary resistance is found in the movement's *núcleo de base* (nucleo, or group) form of organization, otherwise known as its *organicidade* (organic structure). The MST introduces this mode of administration in "taking" or vying for the control of a service that is simultaneously claimed by the Brazilian government. Through nucleos, the movement asserts a claim to design and manage services in various policy areas, for example, education, economic development, and agrarian reform, which are simultaneously the prerogative of state power. While central to the MST, this style of governance has been adopted and practiced by the other groups in the Landless Movement. Nucleos exist within each of the movement's sectors and levels, from the local encampment to the national level of coordination. Each small group has ten to twenty people and is ideally led by one man and one woman who are elected for two-year terms. Nucleos decide on matters by consensually approving, critiquing, deliberating, and planning actions.[20] Nucleo governance cuts through all of the movement's actions, which in the following sections of this chapter I further specify in the movement's practices in the areas of education, economics, and agrarian reform.

Nucleos came from members' participation in the religiously oriented Comunidades Eclesiais de Base (CEBs; Ecclesiastical Base Communities) and the Brazilian military government's (1964–85) failed settlement projects that were promoted in the Amazon. While CEBs provided early movement leaders and members a sense of group decision-making and action, failed settlements and direct contacts with earlier social movements in the 1950s made landless families aware of agrarian reform. The nucleo form of administration later became documented and analyzed in internal movement documents.[21] Wright and Wolford also see the Church influence and presence of CEBs as constitutive of the MST's origins.[22] What is omitted from their analysis is how the CEBs were an incipient form of organization that the MST fused with INCRA settlement plans. This mode of governing affairs may appear similar to how Communist parties and governments were organized, what is known as democratic centralism. The reality is that Brazil's Communist parties, the PCB and PC do B,[23] which based their internal organization on democratic centralism, were not involved in the early days of the movement's emergence and even opposed the MST's more direct-action tactics.[24] Together, these three qualities—INCRA settlements, the CEB groups, and early trial and error—composed the foundation for the MST's alternative, revolutionary mode of resistance. In chapter 3, I further detail how for many organizers and families, the experiences of failed agrarian reform settlements and involvement within the CEBs coalesced to produce an incipient form of revolutionary governance and claim to space.[25]

While the practice of revolutionary contention in the MST's nucleos challenges the state's institutionalization of a public/private division, the movement has encountered problems. Some movement leaders, while I was in Brazil, told me frequently of their worry that the embrace of public policies had led to a decrease in collective action and a narrowing of movement practices. The dynamics of working through state power has ambivalent effects on the movement: while on the one hand, participation periodically drops, on the other hand, members gain access to additional resources. Also, even as nucleos exist throughout the movement, the national coordination has been led by many of the same members for decades. For instance, João Pedro Stédile has been in the national coordination since he helped found the movement in the 1970s. Similar contradictions have been noticed in other movements that promote radical democracy, such as the Zapatistas, which Subcomandante Marcos helped create and within which he retains disproportionate influence.[26] Another, more persistent challenge to the Landless Movement's revolution is the reinscribing of more traditional gender roles within their organization. Given these issues, the MST has recently made it a priority to *retomar os assentamentos* (regain control of the settlements) and other areas where participation has become a concern. This is part of the MST's current strategy to accumulate forces, which I discuss in chapter 5. Despite these problems, the nucleo form of revolutionary governance is an ideal that actually exists.

OCCUPYING THE SCHOOLS: REVOLUTIONARY EDUCATIONAL GOVERNANCE

The revolutionary mode of governance displayed by the nucleos is exemplified in Landless Movement education. No matter the school—elementary, secondary, or postsecondary—administrators, students, and teachers debate, evaluate, and decide on everything from who cleans the classroom to how to incorporate agroecology or the history of slavery into a course. This structure is described in movement documents as "ascending and descending democracy." Within schools, students in each class form nucleos that elect coordinators to represent their group. From these elected coordinators, classes by grade then chose other leaders to speak for everyone when in meetings with the school's administration. The same nucleos that elected representatives at the classroom and subclassroom level monitor and execute the decisions made by the administration.

As discussed in the pedagogical statement of the MST's sole private high school, the Instituto de Educação Josué de Castro (IEJC; Josué de Castro Educational Institute),[27] "in ascending democracy, each nucleo debates and makes proposals at each level . . . [while] decisions that are ultimately decided upon are implemented, and responsibilities distributed for execution, in descending democracy."[28]

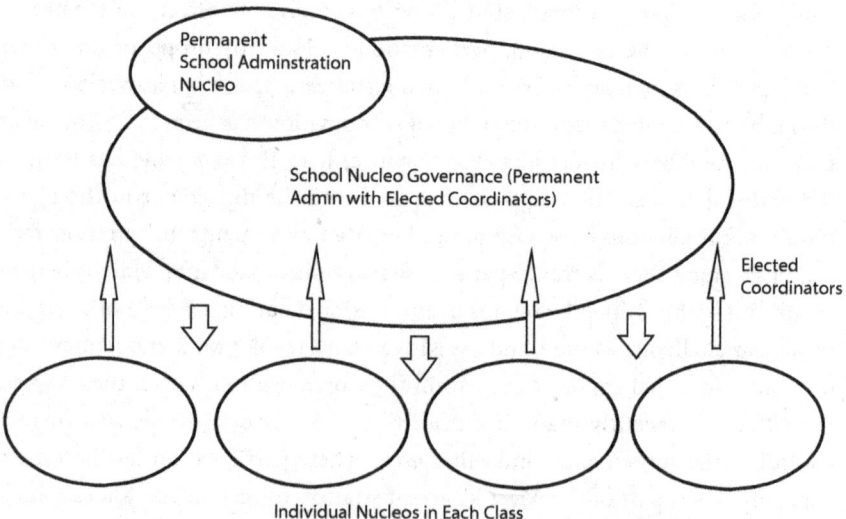

FIGURE 4 Ascending and descending democracy in MST schools.

Every high school I visited in São Paulo, Paraná, and Rio Grande do Sul organized daily mealtime preparation and cleanup with different nucleos. Study times and many in-class assignments were also coordinated by groups. In Instituto Educar, I became a member of one nucleo, participated in classes as a student, assisted in a class project on local agricultural production practices, served breakfast, and helped in the daily farm chores where students practiced agroecology techniques. My participation in management activities included periodically meeting with all nucleo leaders and the school administration. At one meeting, the topic concerned how to organize the school's day-to-day maintenance during *semana santa* (holy week) when many students returned home.[29] Elementary students also form nucleos, but are more dedicated to raising issues for classroom discussion and school cleaning. Rebecca Tarlau, who attended and actively participated at the MST's IEJC for two weeks, shares similar details on the small-group mode of decision-making.[30] The school's permanent administration may appear as a set of governing elites—perhaps indicative of Negri's or Dussel's understandings of constituted power. Actually, these administrators function more like custodians. The administration assumes the daily maintenance and security of the school when the students return home or are engaged in noncurricular activities, leaving governance when school is in session to the students.

Ascending and descending democracy provides students many different ways to participate in decision-making. By allowing individuals to express concerns and problems in the "ascending" phase, the structure decentralizes implementation and design-making by distributing responsibilities throughout each school's student body. In the "descending" phase execution is shared by many members, rather than remaining with a few. The active involvement of students in both phases democratizes the design and execution of educational policy. There is no permanent bureaucratization of certain administrative roles for particular individuals or groups.

Disciplinary actions in schools show similar dynamics. Every school, for example, prohibits alcohol consumption. While I was at one institution, a student was expelled by the administration after repeated violations. The school's permanent administrators at this time called a series of meetings with the students to explain what happened. While providing discipline, the administration explained its actions to the students and asked for input. At the same school, a stolen item was returned after pressure brought by schoolwide meetings. Periodically, all the students at the school were assembled to discuss the problem of stealing. Everyone was told that whoever had stolen the item should leave it in the school basement. After multiple meetings, and through playing on guilt, the object was found without anyone claiming responsibility.[31] Living and abiding by collective rules and norms means that one is subject to dismissal and expulsion by the group. Group discipline shows movement-created order, but equalizes the administration of punishment throughout the membership. Rather than creating a separate institution, or entrusting punishment to an outside force, discipline in MST schools is carried out by the student population. School governance politicizes education by involving students collectively in daily management and organizational activities.

Certain elementary schools also show a collective, community form of discipline, but one that is not related to punishment. In the movement's *escolas itinerantes* (itinerant schools), which are legally recognized public schools that exist in encampments, families contribute food for the school's daily snack. While there is nothing forcing families to donate, this "voluntary contribution" improves the families' reputation within the movement. Members increase their chances to be positively recognized by the movement leadership by regularly contributing to movement schools. Specifically, members provide food, repair buildings, and monitor student performance, in addition to other activities. Reputation is important because encampment leaders select who gets land and where based on movement participation. MST leaders then relay this information to the government when negotiating who gets land. In this sense, families are disciplined for not actively participating in movement activities. The point is that the MST uses a state service—agrarian reform—to incentivize and discipline members to contribute provisions for movement schools. This shows a hierarchical relationship between movement leaders and rank-and-file members.

These practices have led many scholars of the MST to believe that the movement is best considered an actor that "mediates" between state and society.[32] Scholarship on service provision in other social movements and nongovernmental organizations has noted how actors can work with partners in government institutions to serve marginalized populations.[33] The term "mediation," however, only partially captures the movement's actions. By collectivizing discipline, the MST is placing schools under community control instead of simply acting as a conduit for service delivery. Moreover, it is true that the MST "partners" with the Brazilian state in certain ways, particularly by adhering to certain curricular guidelines and contract agreements and accepting resources. Neither "mediation" nor "partnership" fully captures the MST's interactions with official authorities because the movement's practices of coordinating punishment, instilling a distinct cultural identity, and setting up nucleo forms of governance produce forms of organization that rival state sanctions and proscriptions. The movement is using public policies to deliver education as it sees fit, as well as to proliferate its mode of organization and identity throughout its claim to control social relationships in a specific area. The movement is not an accessory of state authority or the Brazilian government, but is working in, against, and through the state in the effort to create an alternative.

The MST alters service provision in yet other ways. For example, the regular use of the Freirian concept of *temas geradores* (generative themes) democratizes lessons in schools.[34] When asked to provide an example, one teacher told me how the content of his classroom discussions came from students' own understanding of the encampment's needs, which at one time concerned access to water and at another time the need for literacy.[35] At a movement school where early childhood educators were receiving training, teachers analyzed how standard Brazilian nursery rhymes, for example, "Escravos de Jó" (Jo's Slaves), could be used to teach history and geography.[36] The motive was that abstract lessons dealing with history and geography often do not resonate with children. Working with children on the meaning of slavery concretizes not only the African continent, but the historical, political, and economic relations between Brazil and Africa. Generative themes allow students to make their own education by using local practices to shape instruction. The themes also enable movement teachers to incorporate issues such as class struggle and exploitation into instruction. As with community control in school discipline, students lay claim to their classrooms through directing their own lessons.

Another way the movement extends participation, or rather, democratizes education, is through what is known as the *pedagogia de alternância* (alternating pedagogy). In alternancy, students regularly go back and forth between their homes and the school over the duration of a course—usually between two and three years. Typically, students oscillate between spending three months at school, *tempo escolar* (school time), and three months in their encampment or settlement, *tempo comunidade* (community time). Alternancy allows students to remain updated on developments at home and incorporate into their studies the needs of the places where they live. During a visit at a movement high school in Paraná, I was told by students how they learn "what it means and how to live in the collective" so that they can later "take that [knowledge] back to the settlements to practice."[37] The nucleos are stronger in schools, as the movement's ability to accompany students in certain settlements and encampments has been at times poorly enforced.[38] The schools, therefore, also function to strengthen the MST's nucleo system throughout the movement.

Alternancy, moreover, connects the tangible needs of students' communities with movement objectives. For their Trabalho de Conclusão de Curso (TCC; Final Course Project) students elaborate projects that benefit a cooperative or a group of families from their respective communities. TCCs are common in secondary schools in Brazil. In MST education, they have this added community-focused element. Examples I discussed with students included an organic milk operation, a distillery for liquor production, and a community garden for a settlement school.[39] Themes that orient entire courses at ITERRA (Instituto Técnico de Capacitação e Pesquisa da Reforma Agrária; Technical Institute for Capacity-Building and Research for Agrarian Reform) also arise from outside the school. Every Técnico em Administração de Cooperativas (TAC; Technician in Cooperative Administration) course—which in 2011 while I was conducting my fieldwork was in its tenth iteration—has featured different needs considered essential to the MST, such as training movement members in health care or in settlement design. Instead of emanating from government elites, the content discussed and learned in courses arises from perceived movement organizational needs.

The MST's educational project challenges the Brazilian government's manner of designing and executing education policy. Law 9394/1996, otherwise known as the Lei de Diretrizes de Bases da Educação (LDB; Law of Educational Directives), decentralizes pedagogical autonomy to state-level and municipal governments. Article 26, however, still ensures uniformity in instruction through promoting a single, national curriculum.[40] The LDB recognizes rural education—where the MST inserts its pedagogical project—as "distinct" and "particular," ultimately intending it to "complement" dominant, centralized directives. The place of rural education is clear; alternative education projects are welcome as long as they are subordinate to government direction. Brazilian educational policy has historically favored schools in urban over rural areas, and tended to promote rural education only as a way to professionalize technical skill sets.[41] Furthermore, the Ministério da Educação e Cultura (MEC; Ministry of Education and Culture), through its administrative organ—the Conselho Nacional de Educação (CNE; National Council of Education)—and in collaboration with state and municipal secretaries of education, has the ultimate authority to govern educational policy.[42] The composition of the CNE by mainly actors from civil society seems to show a permeable, democratic institution. MEC still bureaucratizes education policy because it permanently arrogates decision-making power. MST education presents a rural alternative that challenges MEC's permanent institutionalization of decision-making power and historical urban bias. It also shows both an offensive and defensive posture with respect to the Brazilian government—on the one hand, the movement attempts to defend rural education, but on the other, the MST's educational project contests entrenched hierarchies and practices.

My time in Instituto Educar, and in other secondary and primary schools, illustrates how the movement contests the bureaucratization of service provision. Constituted power, for Negri and Dussel, exists when decision-making practices concerning policy execution is divorced from social participants. Bureaucratizing service provision erects a barrier between institutions that create and execute policy and the social actors that receive it. The MST nucleos in school administration demonstrate an alternative, what Negri would consider indicative of "absolute democracy." Particularly in ascending and descending democracy, as well as in how the movement connects nonmembers to schools, democratic practice pervades the design and execution of education policy. New themes and courses constantly emerge, not in a top-down but bottom-up manner. Or in other words, student and nonstudent movement members decide on educational goals and the manner in which to execute them. Even in discipline, the MST facilitates a means to disseminate community control over education. The Landless Movement's alternative is found in challenging not only who or what has control over people and territory, but also how that control is exercised.

The transformational objectives of the Landless Movement's educational project have encountered significant barriers. First, stubborn gender inequalities characterize many of the movement's actions. Others have also documented the continuation of more stereotypical gender roles in the MST overall.[43] In education, we see this in the disproportionate number of women involved in educational activities. From my own experience, one training course for early childhood education that I attended hosted close to fifty teachers, none of which were men. Two years later, a seminar that I attended on generative themes set up by the University of Londrina and the MST in the state of Paraná was also almost entirely attended by women. The MST has attempted, at each level, to ensure that each nucleo is led by one man and one woman. Despite this attempt at parity, the overwhelming majority of participants in the area of education remain women. This contrasts with economic production and cooperative management, which shows the opposite ratio. A second challenge involves state finances. As evidenced by opposition from the Ministério Público (MP; Public Prosecutor's Office) and the Tribunal das Contas da União (TCU; National

Audit Court) between 2009 and 2011, the Landless Movement's use of public programs to contribute to their project can be disrupted through allegations of misuse and corruption.

Brazil's federal system of governance has also posed problems for the movement's revolutionary practice of education. In São Paulo state, the MST and its allies have never succeeded in gaining resources for or acknowledgement of primary or secondary education, while in Rio Grande do Sul, movement gains were thwarted when the Crusius administration (2006–10) brought into power public officials who ended collaboration with the movement.[44] When I spoke with one movement activist in the Pontal do Paranapanema region of São Paulo state, I was told how "the materials in settlement schools are often printed and distributed by agribusiness, promoting the use of pesticides and so on. And the director of education in the area, when he hears that we are with a social movement, doesn't even want to talk or listen."[45] The director of pedagogy in the Pontal, where there are over one hundred agrarian reform settlements with schools, had never heard of Educação do Campo (Education of the Countryside).[46] Individual allies within government can promote the movement's efforts, while opponents can close doors, for years in some cases.

In chapter 5 I document further how the movement has navigated opposition from state-level elites, as well as from government institutions such as the TCU. I also show in that chapter how the movement's efforts in education—through politicizing members with the Sem Terra identity and organizing people in the nucleo style of governance—became central to efforts to oppose agribusiness firms' attempts to promote a form of rural education that privileges capitalism, capital-intensive modes of farming, and individualism. As the analysis in chapter 5 will also detail, the movement's existence during the Workers' Party administrations of Lula (2002–10) and Dilma (2011–216) was not one of decline. Instead, especially by showcasing changes in education and economic production practices, the movement made significant efforts to consolidate its revolutionary mode of resistance.

COOPERATIVES AND AGROECOLOGY IN THE MST'S ALTERNATIVE ECONOMIC DEVELOPMENT

We also find the nucleos in movement-organized cooperatives, as well as more generally in the MST's mode of economic development. Most designs and examples of cooperatives have been initiated by the MST, with the other groups that compose the Landless Movement also privileging collective forms of production and food sovereignty. One of the clearest examples of the movement's economic vision appears in the *cooperativas de produção agrícola* (CPAs; agricultural production cooperatives).[47] Since the late 1980s, the MST has considered the CPA its "superior form of cooperation."[48] Every CPA—totaling forty-nine, with 2,229 participating families[49]—has the same guiding rules and encourages similar kinds of economic democracy. One CPA I visited, the Cooperativa de Produção Agropecuária Nova Santa Rita (COOPAN; Cooperative of Agricultural Production in New Santa Rita), works with thirty families.[50] These families divide production into different areas, or sectors, rotating between pork, dairy, and rice production. Each sector periodically meets to discuss what they will produce and need, which is then communicated to the entirety of the cooperative general assembly for debate and approval. Sectors—in the same nucleo design of MST schools—make decisions concerning how to distribute and administer resources. In this group-based division of labor, spending and buying priorities are subject to debate within and across the cooperative's different areas. A porous division of labor also characterizes each group, as no formal requirements force members to remain in one specific area. Salaries are divided equally between members, with deductions for personal consumption coming from their monthly pay.

The way the MST's cooperative design challenges private property reveals how family life is subject to democratic practice. In the CPAs, member families' houses are shaped in a circle, known as the *agrovila*, with a communal garden, kitchen, and school. Collective organization—not just of eating, but housing—characterizes the division of land that belongs to the cooperative. Families have individual houses, but production and socialization spaces are not privately demarcated. Families decide collectively who will prepare lunch for everyone, while breakfast and dinner usually take place within people's homes. In the cooperatives, seemingly private matters such as living arrangements and meals are subject to debate and discussion; or in other words, they become politicized in the movement's collective project. In the MST's cooperatives, a clean and clear separation of public from private is erased. Absent is the subordination of social actors to centralized, expert decision-making in bureaucratized government institutions.

Another cooperative experience similar to COOPAN is Cooperativa Nacional de Terra e Vida (CONATERRA; National Cooperative of Land and Life), which is better known by the brand name of its seeds, Bionatur. Only one other

MST cooperative—COAPVI in Paraná—operates fully free of chemicals. It is more common for movement cooperatives to have individual sectors that operate according to agroecological principles, for example, COOPAN and its rice production. Bionatur's structure differs from CPAs like COOPAN because the former's nucleo organization is dispersed throughout the state of Rio Grande do Sul rather than remaining in one settlement. The cooperative buys a certain percentage of the seeds from their members to sell to the Brazilian government and private actors. Programs such as the Programa Nacional Alimentar Escolar (PNAE; National School Food Program) and the Programa de Acquisão dos Alimentos (PAA; Program for Acquiring Food) have become central to efforts by the movement to develop economically, especially during the Lula and Dilma administrations, assuring markets for small farmers' produce. Instead of rejecting these public programs, MST leaders encourage movement members to sign up and participate. As with their practices in education, the movement works simultaneously within and through these programs to construct a form of economic development that is opposed to both the current neoliberal orthodoxy and capitalism in general.

Bionatur is central to the MST's development of a revolutionary mode of economic development because it focuses on promoting biodiversity instead of profit acquisition. One way that the cooperative promotes biodiversity is by placing limits on the quantity of specific seeds purchased from members. Bionatur guarantees a market for a producer, but one that is restrained. The intention behind this rule, I was told, is to challenge monocultural production.[51] Neoliberal policy prescriptions, especially in agricultural production, promote specialization in one crop in the name of comparative advantage.[52] The logic of comparative advantage and monoculture remains apparent in programs promoted by the state institute, the Empresa Brasileria de Pesquisa Agropecuária (EMBRAPA; Brazilian Enterprise for Agricultural Research). EMPRABA's focus on plant genetics and improvements in land and water use helped open Brazil's midwestern region—*o cerrado*—to agribusiness expansion and export agriculture.[53] Bionatur's limit on purchases provides producers a reliable source of income, but not one that they can exploit without end. The theory of comparative advantage promotes accumulation without restrictions. Furthermore, Bionatur is a "social business," which means that losses are socialized, or assumed by all members, rather than falling on the shoulders of separate individuals.[54] Through Bionatur, MST displays an organization that demonstrates an alternative to deregulation and unlimited accumulation.

Bionatur's diffuse nucleo structure also connects biodiversity to economic planning. Usually comprising five or six growers, each nucleo has one lead coordinator and an MST-affiliated extension agent who communicates with all the groups in a region. Because Bionatur works with growers in multiple areas, different kinds of seeds can be grown that are unique to specific regions.[55] With their extension agents, the cooperative directs producers to focus on certain seeds rather than others. When I was visiting the cooperative in 2011, a drought had resulted in one area losing most of its seed production. Coordinators met with producers to reassure them that despite their losses they would receive new seeds the following year to begin again. The cooperative would acquire seeds from areas that had not experienced the drought and then redistribute them to farmers who had lost their production. Bionatur's nucleo structure facilitated its ability to plan future harvests, assure member well-being, and continue production. As in the movement's work in education, the MST's mode of governance is simultaneously offensive and defensive in nature. Its offensive qualities are found in the challenge to neoliberal prescriptions and agribusiness. Defensively, the movement claims to protect life and small-farmer modes of production. Such a manner of governing space and production clarifies the meaning of sovereignty that is integral to the movement's demand for food sovereignty.

Also connected to the concrete practice of food sovereignty, MST-led initiatives in agroecological production outside of cooperative ventures democratize and localize production practices. The MST's technical assistance cooperative, Cooperativa de Serviços Técnicos (COPTEC; Cooperative of Technical Services), specializes in disseminating agroecological production technologies among nucleos in settlements and encampments. While I was in Rio Grande do Sul I attended a regional workshop led by COPTEC technicians. Shortly before visiting a production site of one farmer, COPTEC technicians led a presentation to the nucleo—an assembly of producers numbering close to twenty-five—about permaculture and land use. The discussion centered on how producers can acquire knowledge of their specific sites, including the location of water sources, the nature of soil quality, and the layout of the terrain. They were told that "they, too, were to do research. That everyone can research, not only people with college degrees."[56] COPTEC workshops train producers on how they can make their own decisions, collectively, concerning what and how they grow. In Paraná, the MST has implemented a particular form of training called *o dialogo dos saberes* (dialogue of knowledges). As with COPTEC's efforts, nucleo members are trained to grow their crops according to agroecological

FIGURE 5 Agroecology training course and cooperative. A COPTEC technician shows an overhead on permaculture to regional agroecology nucleo.

methods. While the promotion of agroecology is a nationwide imperative for the MST, the efforts in Paraná and Rio Grande do Sul were the only two state-level projects that I became aware of while I was conducting my fieldwork in 2010 and 2011.

MST production is not limited to cooperatives and agroecology. Many families participate in neither, opting to produce for their own consumption according to a mix of conventional and agroecological techniques. This is permitted, somewhat hesitantly, by movement leaders. I was told in one interview with a longtime leader that it was a problem that certain members used conventional farming techniques. This showed that the movement was "losing control over the settlements" owing to the growing presence of salespeople selling conventional seeds and pesticides to members who were becoming "small agribusiness farmers" (*agronegocinho*), betraying the movement's intended push for agroecological, sustainable practices.[57] To overcome individualism and isolation, MST leaders have attempted to encourage acts of cooperation, such as sharing tractors or tools.[58] This smaller, more localized form of cooperation is

FIGURE 6 A slaughterhouse located on an MST settlement, part of a collectively administered cooperative, COOPTAR. The administration and operation of the CPAs, including the slaughterhouse in the case of COOPTAR, is collective. Tasks and salaries are shared equally among all members.

not as sophisticated as the CPA, but is intended to generate further communal practices over time.

Various scholars describe the relatively recent promotion of agroecological production as indicative of the MST's "peasant" nature. One danger in characterizing the MST as a "peasant" movement is to reduce its economic activities to subsistence.[59] Or in other words, actors primarily engage in production to satisfy needs. Leandro Vergara-Camus, for instance, believes subsistence farming is central to the MST's economic project and anti-capitalist alternative to neoliberalism.[60] He is correct to note how MST production attempts to decommodify production inputs and use nonmarket means to develop. The mistake is to overemphasize the nonmarket nature of the movement's production practices. In fact, many of the MST's successful cooperatives and agroecological production practices embrace state-supported markets created through public programs such as the PNAE and PAA. Besides this omission, we ought to recognize that the movement's alternative economic development features the production of collective modes of production, innovative agroecological techniques, and new forms of conducting business. If the peasantry is defined as producing only for immediate needs and subsistence farming, then the MST defies this oversimplification.

The MST democratizes economic development. This normally conceived of "private" activity is subject to the same nucleo form of administration that we find in the movement's efforts to govern education. Especially in housing, the MST makes private or even intimate matters such as eating arrangements part of debate and discussion. In subjecting private life to public decision-making, the private/public distinction disappears. The limits to democratic practice identified by Negri and Dussel, particularly the institutional separation of decision-making from social actors, are fundamentally challenged in the everyday practices found in the MST's brand of economic development. Furthermore, group decision-making practices within cooperatives show a fluid division of labor. This mode of organizing production challenges the bureaucratization of decision-making by refusing to reserve certain decision-making roles in special institutions. The movement's actions can be understood as creating dual power given that the MST extends democratic control to nearly all facets of economic activity in certain geographical spaces.

The movement's efforts in economics, however, have not been uniformly successful. More than in education and agrarian reform, the movement's initiatives in economic development have encountered obstacles. Initial movement-led efforts to form collective modes of production in the form of the cooperatives, especially in the 1980s, were uniformly applied to every settlement created by the MST. The imperative to collectivize nearly every facet of economic life through cooperatives alienated members who preferred to work individually. Moreover, at the end of the 1990s, many production cooperatives were in crisis economically.[61] A principal reason for problems in the movement's economic project—past and present—has been debt. State-financed credit programs in the 1990s distributed large sums of money to agrarian reform beneficiaries with few strings attached. The main credit program for agrarian reform beneficiaries, the Programa de Crédito Especial para a Reforma Agrária (PROCERA; Special Program for Agrarian Reform Credit), existed from 1985 to 2001. Resources dedicated to its execution tripled from R$89 in 1995 to R$250 million in 1998, and the movement encouraged families to sign up. In chapter 5, I document how the movement faced its economic crisis, adopting and politicizing agroecology in the process.

Despite such efforts, insolvency continues to plague rural producers—some of whom are in the movement, and some of whom are not. Some studies claim that insolvency reaches rates of 15 to 30 percent in certain municipalities.[62] In 2013, President Dilma pardoned 80 percent of PRONAF debts (Programa Nacional de Fortalecimento da Agricultura Familiar; National Program for Strengthening Family Farming) owed by beneficiaries and discounted other indebted producers upward of 65 percent.[63] The number of PRONAF participants has remained low while contract amounts have risen over time, suggesting that those producers already with assets benefit more than those that lack machinery and other capital goods.[64] That the government pardons and regularly restructures debts should be worrisome, not only to the producers, but also to those who believe that these programs are the gateway to eradicating hunger and rural poverty.

The MST's mode of economic development is revolutionary despite certain setbacks. Similar to movement efforts in education, in areas where the movement initiates its economic projects, nucleos refuse to permanently delegate decision-making to certain bureaucracies. Private affairs are subject to debate and dialogue, or rather, are politicized in the movement's claim to control space. The movement's efforts in economic development, with respect to credit programs and public policies, show how MST and its allies work in, against, and through state power. More so than in education, the movement's project challenges neoliberal orthodoxy by favoring collective decision-making practices over individualization, as well as state support for economic action instead of deregulation or privatization. State-led economic development is conceived of as primarily spurred by offering top-down credit policies with limited to no social participation. While the movement encourages members to accept credits and access public programs, the key to understanding the movement's mode of economic development lies in how collective decision-making practices blend with the movement's claim to transform social relationship in a particular space. To evoke sovereignty is not to claim to exist purely autonomously from others. Rather, revolutionary political action posits a sovereign claim to transform political, economic, and cultural relationships in a certain area. Such a form of contention exists at once as a set of practices and mode of organization, as well as in the realm of representation that postulates a clear "us versus them."

REAPPROPRIATING LAND: THE NUCLEOS OF AGRARIAN REFORM GOVERNANCE

In agrarian reform, *small-group* governance is clearest in the encampments the MST and its allies establish immediately after occupying land. According to the Comissão Pastoral da Terra (CPT; Pastoral Land Commission), a nongovernmental organization that emerged in the mid-1970s during the Brazilian military government and a longtime Landless Movement ally, the MST alone has mobilized 562,115 families for land occupations and 88,369 families in encampments since 2000.[65] For the Landless Movement, agrarian reform begins long before de jure recognition of the encampment. From the moment the land is occupied, nucleos are created, each with different tasks that correspond to movement sectors,[66] including health, education, production, and culture. Considered together, the nucleos provide the general governing structure for encampment affairs. Both occupations and encampments, as I mentioned in the previous chapter, are central to the movement's extralegal set of tactics. Occupations and encampments also show organizational dimensions. Or rather, while on the one hand they are practices that disrupt certain relations of authority, on the other, they display administrative structures for coordinating member actions.

Requirements for belonging to a nucleo are minimal, even nonexistent. In one encampment where I lived, identifying land for production and preparing it was organized by various families, many of whom had no prior experience in agricultural production.[67] In another, the requirement for participation in the education nucleo was having children. Their primary work involved finding transportation for children to the municipal school and guaranteeing that the children were well received.[68] In two other encampments in different states—Paraná and Pernambuco—I participated in nightly patrols that ensured security, especially if families needed to be notified in case of a police (or private security) eviction.[69] Regardless of region or state, as well as activity, I found similar small-group administration with minimal knowledge requirements organizing encampment affairs. Nucleo participation, in this regard, democratizes land access and management.

Reappropriating land with the knowledge that each individual brings to the encampment challenges the mode of territorial acquisition promoted by Brazilian government institutions. Only INCRA officials are legally sanctioned to conduct studies that ascertain levels of economic productivity and verify if a particular property is suitable for expropriation. Furthermore, recent efforts have been made to track and document land with GPS technologies to classify all properties in Brazil. This practice provides elites with privileged, exclusive information that erects a barrier between representatives of state authority and social actors, like the MST, who lack data. INCRA is also responsible for distributing initial credits for houses and production—known as *créditos de fomento* and *créditos de instalação* (formation and installation credits)—that distribute material resources (to be repaid at a later time) to families once they have usufruct rights. The actual de jure act of expropriation is sealed with an executive decree. The MST's conduct of agrarian reform distributes roles between different nucleos in the encampments, as well as in certain settlements. As in Paulo Freire's understanding of dialogue and knowledge, the members are all experts (or seen as capable of becoming so) in a variety of ways, from providing security to leading meetings. A "lack" only exists from the standpoint of government authorities, who consider the execution of agrarian reform policy to depend on credit, expert knowledge, and decrees.

There is also a disciplinary side to agrarian reform governance. Problems within encampments like stealing, fighting, and drinking usually result in movement leaders expelling rule-breakers after discussing the issue in assembly with the rest of the encampment.[70] Some encampments and settlements have completely banned alcohol following incidents.[71] Individuals become subjects trained to form groups, work together, and punish one another, with movement leadership prepared to step in only if necessary. This, as also displayed in MST schools, is in contrast to the state form of discipline that is rooted in a separate, "public" institution, namely, the police. Government police are usually called for larger crimes such as murder.[72] The movement's promotion of its own security in encampments challenges granting complete authority to government police forces. The discipline is supplied by groups themselves, without particular knowledge requirements that could subordinate social actors to government elites. The claim to transform relationships in a certain area recasts educational, economic, as well as disciplinary modes of conduct.

Discipline is also seen in the movement's incipient tax system. While visiting one encampment in the state of Paraná, I was told that families in the encampment each pay a R$3 contribution per month to the movement, while others who do not live in the settlement but who want land pay R$90.[73] The contribution is often coupled with a service charge—for example, attendance at protests and political trainings or activities to manage the encampment, such as security patrols. These kinds of charges are typical of MST actions throughout Brazil.[74] In another visit to an encampment in São Paulo I was told that such activities earn potential land reform beneficiaries "points."[75] MST leaders use a ranked order of encamped families when negotiating with INCRA over who gets, or rather, who deserves land and where. This practice is referred to in movement documents on encampment management as the *sorteio* (raffle). The raffle grants the movement control over the land at the center of agrarian reform policy. Schmitt would see these practices as also indicative of the movement's attempt to claim space—for the MST, taking area means detailing and controlling the procedures surrounding access.

In addition to encampments, occupations are central to the Landless Movement's revolutionary resistance. The apparent spontaneity of occupations belies months of door knocking where organizers recruit families from rural workers and people who live in the urban periphery for what is sometimes called a *festa* (party).[76] The location of occupations is shrouded in secrecy, with the destination known only to a few leaders. For example, in one occupation, not of land but of a government building, I was never told the destination. When I asked other members where we were going, I found that many were just as confused.[77] Secrecy constitutes a rule or procedure, regularly practiced in organizing occupations. In a sense, it centralizes decision-making in the hands of a few movement leaders. This feature is temporary, however, as occupations involve many families in actual reappropriation.[78] I participated in one occupation of a large ranch during my time in Brazil. Briefly before we arrived, we were directed where to go and how long to wait. We were also told that the length of time we would stay would be based on the police's reaction.[79] As I came to realize, the particular occupation that I was a member of was used to test if the police would react violently or not. I also found that the people participating in this occupation were from the MAB (Movimento dos Atingidos por Barragens; Movement of People Affected by Dams) and MTD (Movimento dos Trabalhadores Desempregados; Movement of Unemployed Workers), or rather, while the action was led by the MST, the occupation featured members of other groups from the overall Landless Movement. Surveying CPT documents on land occupations shows that such coordination between allies in occupations and marches, especially over the last ten years, has become commonplace.

The initial acts following the actual taking of a certain parcel of land include preparing the area for production and constructing tents. These efforts serve both symbolic and practical goals: on the one hand, families need to live somewhere and grow their food, while on the other hand, the movement legitimates their occupations by demonstrating their use of previously unproductive lands. The Brazilian Constitution of 1988 and the Estatuto da Terra (Rural Land Statute) of 1964 sanction expropriation when owners violate labor, environmental, and productivity regulations. Together, these criteria establish a certain area's productivity.[80] The point is that working the land immediately after an occupation is how the Landless Movement shows authorities its version of productive land use. Leading occupations and setting up encampments challenge the large landowners and agribusiness firms that the movement claims are breaking particular laws or contaminating the environment with pesticides. What is defended, following Schmitt's thoughts on the "partisan," is the Brazilian legal order and the environment. Constructing tents presents to authorities that communities—not individual proprietors—should live in the space in dispute.

I observed the movement's nucleos system at work in the aftermath of the land occupation in which I participated. After three days in an encampment, and a day of negotiations with the police and INCRA officials, movement leaders decided to leave. While I could leave, and return to a neighboring settlement where an MST family was waiting for me, the majority of the families had no place to go. Most formed another encampment on the side of the road, near the farm that was previously occupied, but on a space that a different rancher permitted. Later, I found that this too was negotiated by MST leaders. Immediately after arriving at the new space, the small groups divided their time between digging holes, setting poles, and placing the black tarp over pieces of wood. Before I could offer any help, the nucleos had already built the tents and moved on to other projects.[81] In reality, my help, most likely, would have been more of a nuisance than a form of assistance. In another roadside encampment, this time in the state of Pernambuco, I was told that a group of approximately three dozen families had been evicted seven times from a large ranch. Movement leaders also told me that the land was unproductive. This situation in the northeast was dire given the scarcity of water. Families at this site set up cisterns to collect water and relied extensively on church food donations to survive.[82] As Gabriel Ondetti notes in his study, this practice of encamping on the side of the road—*na beira da estrada*—became more popular with the MST in the 1990s.[83] On the one hand, an advantage of this form of encampment is mobility. Families, when located on roadsides, can easily move to new sites. On the other hand, one drawback is that encamping on the side of the road places individuals in a precarious position. Instead of encamping on a friendly rancher's farm, or on an MST settlement, movement opponents and the police can harm the occupiers with near impunity.

The nucleo style of administration, where we see the opposition to bureaucratization and an institutionalized public/private divide, is apparent in MST-style agrarian reform. Encampment affairs, including discipline, are socialized among participants. Low knowledge requirements keep decision-making within the movement's ranks, while countering the Brazilian government. Minimal knowledge prerequisites and drawing on the know-how of members equalizes participation in movement governance. Not only the content but the form of official agrarian reform policy is challenged by the MST. INCRA has been conceived of as a weak institution staffed by various officials who believe in agrarian reform and who also are willing to help movement initiatives.[84] Regardless of the personnel's own beliefs, standard practices surrounding expropriation and redistribution in agrarian reform policy still features top-down qualities. The Brazilian state's bureaucratization of agrarian reform is challenged by movement nucleos in the encampments and mass occupations. Private affairs, like alcohol consumption, are also subject to movement debate and decision-making. In a way, movement nucleos resemble Lenin's soviets. How they operate resembles his analysis of dual power. According to Negri and Dussel, such an effort to include participants in a way that is prohibited by authorities is indicative of constitutive power. As seen in both education and economic development, the MST works simultaneously in and against the state to transform political, economic, and cultural relations in particular spaces it claims.

One concern I often heard from MST leaders was that participation changed, if not declined, after many families acquired land. Or in other words, the movement's contentious activities are alive and well in occupations and encampments, but not in settlements. *Trabalhar no coletivo* (work and live collectively) was what I often heard opposed to *individualismo* (individualism). Within the MST, this is known as the difference between *a luta pela terra* (the struggle for land) and *a luta na terra* (the struggle on the land).[85] I was told by one of the MST's agricultural technicians how encampments and settlements that developed a rigorous and well-planned nucleo format were more likely to remain cohesive, produce economically, and stay affiliated with the movement.[86] This view was confirmed by all my visits to cooperatives, where I found that the decision to collectivize production was agreed on by families while they were encamped. Despite this concern, it is hard to verify if participation drops on settlements, or if it actually changes. Some of the most revolutionary actions by the MST occur in schools and cooperatives—sites mainly on settlements.

One matter that the movement has to address is abandoned settlement plots. Neither INCRA nor the Landless Movement likes to admit that some agrarian reform beneficiaries do not remain on the land they acquire. According to Ariovaldo Umbelino de Oliveira, close to 233,000 parcels were abandoned and then reclaimed by the state during Lula's administration.[87] It is hard to blame the Landless Movement for settlers abandoning their lots, despite flaws in the movement's early collectivization strategy. A government report from the state of Piauí cites the lack of infrastructure as a contributing cause of abandonment.[88] Another report on settlements in Mato Grosso found poverty and a lack of credit as primary reasons.[89] Similar stories and challenges have appeared in other states. When pressured by the Brazilian Senate to be more transparent, in 2014 INCRA published on its website a list of abandoned plots on various settlements in multiple states.

Mainly external with respect to the Landless Movement, changes in government conditions due to neoliberal policy prescriptions can be traced to settlement abandonment. At the core of this is the set of policies that constitute *emancipação* (emancipation), the name bestowed by the FHC administration in the 1990s for the approach to agrarian reform policy that would "free" or emancipate settlers from INCRA's oversight, programs, and policies. Government support is intended, from the emancipation perspective, to create self-sufficient, individualistic proprietors who eventually own their land and exist independently of social programs and services.

Since its mid-1990s origin, emancipation has been opposed by the MST. The movement's goal is to create settlements where families have usufruct rights, not definitive title that would allow individual families to sell their land.[90] The movement opposes land sales and insists that title ultimately remains with INCRA, rather than with the individual families. Living on government-owned land removes the ability of movement members to individualize land holdings though sale or rent. This gives the movement a way to retain members because sales could enable individuals to leave the movement by selling their land. By refusing the right to alienate property, the MST places a barrier for members to exit the movement, while also keeping the government as a target for complaints. The idea that the movement converts itself into a "permanent ward" of the government is only a brief concern during the initial two to three years following de jure recognition. It's at this time in settlement development that credits and loans for houses and production implements are distributed.[91] After the distribution of these resources, however, interaction with the government is minimal.

Residing on public land with usufruct rights also connects the MST and its allies to the state for reasons other than to acquire resources. In a sense, the movement uses the state to progressively subject territory to movement control—which I will argue in the subsequent chapters is indicative of the movement's tactical orientation. It also clearly reveals the movement's intention to work in, against, and through state power to construct its alternative. Also, included within the movement's goal to democratize the control of land is the proposal that more people should have the ability to acquire and control space, which opposes the position that territory can be accumulated without end by private actors.

CONCLUSION: THE REAL AND IDEAL NATURE OF THE NUCLEOS

This chapter shows how the nucleo form of governance, which is the MST's creation yet has also been adopted and practiced by others in the Landless Movement, constitutes a revolutionary form of social movement political action. My focus has been on illustrating the revolutionary nature of the Landless Movement's efforts in three areas: education, economic development, and agrarian reform. In addition to the nucleo form of governance, the cultural work of the mística cuts across all movement activities in the spaces that are claimed. In the areas analyzed in this chapter, nucleos challenge the bureaucratization of service provision and the strict division between public and private affairs. The movement's opposition to bureaucratization is apparent in how group administration democratizes service design and execution. The institutional divisions between private and public life, likewise, are challenged in the thorough democratization of economic management and seeming apolitical affairs like housing. Instead of privileging individuality or profit acquisition, the movement builds its alternative mode of governance on the principle of collective cooperation. My elaboration of the movement's claim to space, and transformation of political, economic, and cultural relations, contributes to how we think of its practices as constitutive of food sovereignty.

Nucleos are not perfect. Throughout this chapter, I have mentioned various challenges—some resulting from the MST's own errors—faced by the movement. I analyze such challenges, obstacles, and innovations more in chapter 5. Despite problems, the movement's political project resembles the kind of revolutionary governance analyzed in Lenin's description of dual power, Schmitt's understanding of the partisan, and Negri's and Dussel's theorization of constitutive power. It does not always function in uniformly the same way. Differences become apparent within the movement, especially when comparing the slightly more hierarchical nature of agrarian reform governance with its counterparts in economic development and education. The concepts provide novel ways to think about the exact nature of the Landless Movement.

The attempts to categorize the movement's resistance are relatively few. Wolford classifies the movement as a case of "de facto participatory democracy."[92] The allusion here is to other cases of participatory democracy, which include the experiences of *orçamento participativo* (OP; participatory budgeting) that developed in various Brazilian cities in the 1980s and 1990s. This implicit comparison, however, applies only to the movement's efforts in agrarian reform. I agree that there are new modes of participation in both examples, yet with key differences. Principal among the ways that the OP and the Landless Movement differ is that in cases of participatory budgeting redistributive policies are already decided on prior to the participation of social actors. Or rather, in each state, individuals accept that a certain percentage of the state budget will be discussed and allocated. The MST's actions, obversely, leave open the questions of what to redistribute and how much. Elsewhere, Vergara-Camus describes the MST as a new form of peasant rebellion.[93] Despite recognizing a certain novelty in their resistance, he does not clearly differentiate between rebellion and revolution. Fernandes conceives of the Landless Movement as a "social-territorial movement."[94] This idea is similar to how I analyze the movement's resistance in light of theorists of revolutionary movement organization and governance. The analysis in this chapter makes clear that the Landless Movement's style of resistance is revolutionary given the emphasis on transforming cultural, political, and economic relationships within certain spaces, which takes place simultaneously with the movement's concerted efforts to erase the distinction between state and society.

Defining the movement, and reading its mode of political action as explicitly revolutionary, is not simply an academic exercise. It provides ways for us to see and understand its mode of political action. The concepts used in certain definitions at once reveal and conceal certain elements. This point will become even clearer in the next chapter when I analyze the movement's tactics. Legal and extralegal tactics, initially developed in the early stages of MST activity, later became perfected by movement leaders. Along with propitious conditions, these internal and external factors explain how the MST and its allies have revolutionized economic development, agrarian reform, and education for decades.

3

WORKING WITH THE PAST

Incorporating Public Policy, Religion, and Prior Movement Tactics

PRECARIOUS, EARLY ORIGINS

"EVERYTHING JUST SCREAMED PRECARITY (*tinha precariedade gritante*), I mean, there were no roads, no schools. And we were there, some people encamped for five or six years, totally isolated, away from the city . . . and the mud!"[1] This description came not from a longtime MST activist, but from an ally who regularly volunteered with the movement in the 1980s and 1990s. I listened to similar stories from others—other allies and movement members—who told me of their passion and sacrifice, especially when relating experiences from the movement's infancy. What made a few of these conversations intriguing was that government officials also expressed their commitment to agrarian reform and the movement's efforts. On one such occasion, I met an INCRA official who was on the verge of retirement. He recounted significant moments from his more than three-decade career with INCRA, which began in the 1960s. After the interview, he grabbed my arm and practically dragged me over to a map of the state of Rio Grande do Sul to point out the sites where he had personally worked. One of the projects involved thousands of families, many of whom were displaced owing to the construction of the Passo Real Dam in the late 1960s. "Let me tell you, if there hadn't been the occupation, things would probably be the same there now," he stated, shaking his finger at the map. "Before [the occupation], things just went back and forth, INCRA, Annoni, INCRA, Annoni, INCRA, Annoni. We were getting nowhere."[2]

The two comments quoted above—the first from a past movement ally, and the second from a retired INCRA official—reveal how the Landless Movement has incorporated nonmovement actors into its struggle, as well as how the movement has endured times of extreme uncertainty. Many studies of the movement refer to its size, emphasizing that it has mobilized over one and a half million people throughout twenty-three of Brazil's twenty-six states. An inspection of government figures reveals that the estimates are not exaggerated. As of 2016, close to 9,300 agrarian reform settlements exist in Brazil. Before the MST's emergence, there were only 67.[3] Yet, to focus solely on the movement's size and accomplishments hides its precarious origins. Some of the first occupations that are traced to the movement's emergence in the southern states of Rio Grande do Sul, Paraná, and Santa Catarina involved only dozens of families. The thousands of people who would later engage in occupations and live in encampments during the formative years in the 1980s experienced violent evictions at the hands of government and private actors, as well as extensive delays over land acquisition. Before the MST's first national congress in 1984, there were multiple actors without a single organizational structure to coordinate activities. As a matter of fact, it is difficult to speak of one movement, let alone the "MST" and the "Landless Movement," in the late 1970s and early 1980s.

In this chapter, I unpack the dynamics of the Landless Movement's early development in southern Brazil. While acknowledging the various other studies that have documented the movement's emergence, my account provides crucial nuances. Wendy Wolford locates the movement's "official genesis story" in three factors: the collapse of the Brazilian military regime, agricultural restructuring that displaced certain populations, and assistance provided by preexisting social networks.[4] Gabriel Ondetti privileges the Brazilian military government's gradual easing of political controls and incipient democratization as the primary catalysts of mobilization.[5] Miguel Carter focuses less on propitious external conditions and more on the centrality of religious ideas.[6] While I agree with these accounts in part, I argue that to understand the birth of the movement's revolutionary mode of resistance, we have to further understand the intersection of weakening nonmovement conditions, public policies, and lessons learned from past episodes of contention.

To complement these studies, I highlight the contingent process of learning—especially with respect to how early organizers and families incorporated lessons from past movements and public policies. When I claim that the movement has incorporated certain elements into its style of contention from others, I am not only referring to coalition formation. Or rather, as will become clearer in this chapter, by "incorporation" I mean the appropriation of specific ways of engaging authorities. Capturing contingency requires tracing the histories of events and practices to observe change over time. Toward this aim, and given my ethnographic focus, I work with the reflections of members, allies, and government officials, as well as with movement publications from the 1970s and 1980s. Such publications, principally the *Boletim Informativo da Campanha de Solidariedade aos Agricultores Sem Terra* (Landless Farmer Solidarity Campaign Informative Bulletin), which later became *O Jornal dos Trabalhadores Sem Terra* (*JST*; Journal of the Landless Workers), have received scant attention from most scholars of the movement.[7] Such a variety of sources enables an analysis of the overall social context that is not confined to the viewpoints of leaders.

As I document in the first part of this chapter, organizers and families in the late 1970s and early 1980s studied and learned from past movements. In the second section, I discuss how activists began to conceive of legal forms of engagement. The third section focuses on the history of the rural settlement—how it was at first a technique for domesticating dissent, and then later transformed into a movement demand. The other additional element that was vital in the movement's emergence was the Catholic Church, specifically the CEBs (Comunidades Eclesiais de Base; Ecclesiastical Base Communities). I analyze in the fourth section how the CEBs spread a decentralized, small-group model of administering affairs among rural communities, while also emphasizing economic matters and cooperation in production. The fifth and sixth sections of this chapter shows how the movement's revolutionary tactics and organizational development had been consolidated when member families were settled in 1982 at Nova Ronda Alta. Later, seminal actions at Fazenda Annoni in 1985 display how movement tactics and forms of organization were in operation, as well as already in an early phase of revolutionary consolidation.

While this chapter highlights the actions of the various organizations and movements that compose the Landless Movement, the central focus is on the MST. I chart at points in this chapter the trajectory of other actors in the movement—CONTAG, the CPT, and various groups that later become MAB—to document their respective forms of resistance. One of the most thought-provoking qualities of the MST has been the movement's ability to reinvent itself over its three decades of existence, even as it retains certain core features. Paramount to the movement's consistency has been its manner of combining extralegal and legal tactics, as well as develop its nucleo style of governance. In adapting the works on tactics, revolution, and democracy from Schmitt, Lenin, Negri, and Dussel, we can understand the movement's political action as working through the state to claim control over particular spaces, while also abolishing the institutional divisions between private and public life. Throughout the movement's history, there has been a series of subtle, yet crucial alterations made to its revolutionary form of contention. The chapter shows how the MST did not invent its tactical and organizational repertoires, such as leading land occupations or establishing settlements. Instead, the movement incorporated and adapted such past practices in the process of creating its own revolutionary form of political action.

EXTRALEGAL ACTION AMID STATE AND ECONOMIC INSTABILITY

Many consider the two-year encampment at Encruzilhada Natalino in the early 1980s as a turning point in what would later become known as the MST. One organizer, Darci Maschio, claimed that the press coverage of the encampment "pulled at everyone's heart strings, making the general population sympathize with the families suffering."[8] João Pedro Stédile, one of the movement's founders, notes that the encampment was of "historical importance."[9] Carter's study of the encampment postulates that its impact on the Brazilian Landless Movement, including the MST and its various other allies, was similar to the effect that the 1955 Montgomery bus boycott had on the U.S. civil rights movement.[10] Along with these comments, testimonies, and memories, a monument now stands at the place where the encampment took place to commemorate the events.

Some studies of the MST, in documenting the movement's origins, present the reasons for the families' early actions as if they were self-evident. For example, Wright and Wolford describe the actions chronologically, noting how various families were driven from the Nonoai Indigenous Reserve in the late 1970s, then occupied the Macali and Brilhante ranches and later encamped at Encruzilhada Natalino, to subsequently gaining access to land with the Catholic Church's assistance at another site, which became known as Nova Ronda Alta. When referring to this period, Wright and Wolford write that for organizers and families "it seemed logical to begin there [in the south]."[11] Branford and Rocha, similarly, document events during the formative years in the 1970s and 1980s as a seamless sequence.[12] In explaining their own motives, the families who encamped at Encruzilhada Natalino stated in their first issue of the *Boletim Informativo da Campanha de Solidariedade aos Agricultores Sem Terra* that they occupied land and requested settlements because "as farmers, we think we have a right to obtain land to grow food for ourselves and for people in the cities."[13]

After one pauses to reflect on the expressed motives of the movement's first participants, the ostensibly simple statement raises more questions than answers. In the first place, why did the people who organized in 1981 demand settlements? What made them even believe that encampments would lead to land redistribution? It is true that many families who decided to occupy land and form encampments displayed determination and resolve. Strength of will, however, does not tell us why occupations, per se, were chosen and why

FIGURE 7 An encampment from the early stages of the movement. While I am unsure of the exact date that the photo was taken, I believe the encampment dates from the 1980s. Photo from the MST-CEDEM archive, a public collection of Landless Movement documents, photos, and other materials donated by researchers and social movements, São Paulo.

FIGURE 8 Black tarp tents located in an encampment in Paraná state, 2011. Notice that the manner in which the movement occupies and encamps on disputed territories has essentially remained the same for over three decades.

settlements were demanded. Why not engage only in protests or marches? The history of Brazilian rural contention, even during authoritarian regimes as Cliff Welch details in his study of unionization, is full of dedicated families and leaders organizing letter-writing campaigns, demonstrations, strikes, and other tactics.[14] We are still left with the question: how did the sequence—occupation, encampment, settlement—enter into the activists' minds as the viable trajectory of action?

Placing the movement in historical perspective begins to answer these questions. Instead of arising spontaneously, the land occupation tactic was learned from prior movements. The most relevant movement that immediately preceded the MST was the Movimento dos Agricultores Sem Terra (MASTER; Movement of Landless Farmers). In the north of Rio Grande do Sul, prior to the 1964 military coup, MASTER leaders targeted Fazenda Sarandi, one of the largest farms in the state—at roughly 26,000 hectares—and which was under the ownership of absentee Uruguayan nationals. These owners, similar to many others throughout Brazil, possessed titles of dubious legality. Given these factors, as well as the level of rural poverty in the region, the local mayor of the city of Nonoai, Jair Calixto, believed the space susceptible to expropriation and redistribution.[15] Calixto did not work alone. Another politician from Rio Grande do Sul, Milton Serres Rodrigues, also became influential in the formation of MASTER, as did João Machado dos Santos (known as João Sem Terra), who was a local political organizer for the left wing of the Partido Trabalhista Brasileiro (PTB; Brazilian Labor Party), and the Partido Comunista Brasileiro (PCB; Brazilian Communist Party) leader, Ari Saldanha. MASTER would remain closely connected to the PCB and PTB for the entirety of the movement's short existence.

Calixto and dos Santos had the idea to occupy Fazenda Sarandi. The PTB was in control of the government at this time in the state of Rio Grande do Sul, under the leadership of Governor Leonel Brizola. Having worked on the Brizola campaign and meeting Calixto, the organizers felt that Brizola would support forms of political action based on specific elements that were present in the 1947 Rio Grande do Sul State Constitution. Especially of note was article 174, section 1, which reads that "the state will combat unproductive property either by taxation or expropriation." Initially, and after recruiting a group of interested people, families targeted and occupied parts of Sarandi. After physically taking the area, the people remained on the land as a way to consistently pressure the governor to carry out the constitution's expropriation clause. It is claimed that MASTER quickly grew and eventually organized around 100,000 people at Sarandi, as well as on other large estates, in occupations and encampments during its four-year existence.[16] After it was shown that land occupations were effective in terms of mobilizing people to demand land redistribution in Rio Grande do Sul, others such as the Peasant Leagues in northeastern Brazilian states such as Pernambuco took notice and began launching their own version of the tactic.[17]

Leading occupations and forming encampments provided a way for the movements to claim space. The tactics constituted "new forms of pressure" that were "worker-led offensives."[18] The "newness," as well as encouragement by leftwing politicians affiliated with the movements, gave the tactic legitimacy. It is hard to document, precisely, how social relations were reconstituted within the movement encampments, especially because each movement lasted for only a few years—MASTER for just a few years in the early 1960s, and the Peasant Leagues, from the mid-1950s until the early 1960s. Still, the tactic posed a direct challenge to existing economic relations by forcing redistributive measures. It also presented movements as protagonists in forwarding government policy, which was often left to landowners and other economic elites. Furthermore, other sites, not only Fazenda Sarandi in the north of Rio Grande do Sul, appeared suitable for redistribution.

Land occupations and encampments during the time when MASTER was organizing were characterized by a general legal ambiguity, highlighting the tactic's extralegal quality. At the root of this ambiguity is the confusion, or rather, juridical gray area, relating to the meaning of a land occupation. The Brazilian penal code (*codigo penal*) of 1940 states that trespassing with the intent of stealing, and in groups of two or more people, is illegal (trespassing with the intent to steal is known as *esbulho possessorio*, article 161). The actors who perpetuate such acts also have names—*quadrilhas*, or gangs, which are criminal organizations that intentionally steal property and/or objects. Also in the penal code, we find the concept of invasion (*invasão*), which is defined as stealing private property by a group. The landowners at Sarandi challenged the government, refused to cede their land, and entered into court battles to protect their ownership claim. To support their argument, they referred to the Brazilian penal code. Yet occupations, especially in the 1960s, began to be considered as different from invasions. Essentially, they are not indicative of stealing because ownership claims are unclear. Redistribution, furthermore, is not indicative of robbery if government representatives establish legal means to redistribute territory. More so at this time than before, these newer actions—occupations—begin to be acknowledged, and accepted, by certain elites as something other than invasions or acts of trespassing. Land occupations and encampments, on the one hand, appeared like acts sanctioned by government authorities. On the other, organized "takings" of land seemed to certain economic and political elites to be clear violations of the penal code and the right to private property. This ambiguity continues to give occupations and encampments their extralegal quality.

In Rio Grande do Sul, Ildo Meneghetti won election as governor in 1962 after Brizola went to serve as a representative in Congress. Land expropriations were halted, and the police and military were ordered to disperse the encamped families throughout the region. After the 1964 military coup, the authorities further repressed rural and urban activists. It is difficult to overemphasize the impact of the military government's use of torture, repression, and censorship, not only on rural actors, but urban movements as well.[19] Many participants in MASTER fled to the nearby Kaingaing Indigenous Reserve in the municipality of Nonoai. Indigenous authorities initially allowed people to enter, but the close to 1,500 families who became squatters on the reserve were later evicted in the 1970s. Some of families relocated to urban areas, others were resettled by the state government near the southern municipality of Bagé, while still others were sent to settlements in the northern state of Mato Grosso. At the state level, and then federally, the coordinated use of force silenced radical efforts, showing how government conditions were unified in opposing social movement action.

Many of the evicted families, around two hundred, remained unsettled and effectively homeless in the area surrounding Nonoai in the late 1970s. What made this group somewhat special when compared to many other impoverished, economically marginalized people throughout Brazil was their past political activity. Most notably, the group contained many of the same people who had participated in MASTER's occupations and encampments. Far from wandering lost in the countryside, certain individuals still mulled over the possibility of occupying land. One evicted farmer, Osvaldino Rodrigues de Freitas, was quoted as saying that he "had learned [during his days in MASTER] that one receives land only when it is occupied (*a terra so consegue invadindo*)."[20] What kept the occupation and encampment tactics alive were the very same families who had used them prior to the rise of the military government. Or rather, the practice of extralegal political action led by MASTER persisted in activists' memories. Thus, the two hundred families who were evicted from the Nonoai reserve in Rio Grande do Sul, instead of initially organizing a demonstration for land or marching to the capital, decided to occupy the nearby Brilhante ranch and remain there in an encampment for a few months. They were later evicted in 1978.[21]

For the duration of the 1970s, state conditions became increasingly unstable in the north of Rio Grande do Sul. At this time, Fazenda Sarandi was the subject of much debate and dispute. Sarandi had been subdivided during the 1960s, with various parts remaining large estates. Two separate farms emerged—Macali and Brilhante—with another area purchased by Ernesto Annoni in the 1960s. By the 1970s, three separate large estates were carved out of Sarandi—Macali, Brilhante, and Annoni. MASTER participants in the 1960s had been promised land in this area, but had been denied in 1962 and then forced into silence. In addition to other claims to the area by businesses, the construction of the Passo Real Dam in the early 1970s led the military government to begin negotiations to expropriate land for an additional six hundred displaced families.[22] The state agency in charge of administering agrarian reform, INCRA, slowly began the process of relocating the six hundred families, but was stopped in 1974 when landowners initiated a legal process that questioned the state's authority to expropriate. As a longtime INCRA official told me about the area, not only was there a constant back-and-forth with Annoni and the government concerning ownership, but also properties were periodically given to families "totally irregularly, there were lots of squatters (*posseiros*), but no one had title."[23] Large stretches of territory in the north of Rio Grande do Sul were characterized by unstable territorial claims, showing a weakness in state authority and an ad hoc manner of distributing property.

Such problems with territorial, state authority and sovereignty were by no means confined to Rio Grande do Sul. Just a few kilometers north of Sarandi in the municipality of Campo Ere in the state of Santa Catarina, various members of the Taborda family had been engaged in a dispute among themselves since the 1950s over thousands of hectares. The internal family disagreement was further complicated by INCRA's expropriation of certain areas, with documentation of exactly where, how much, and from whom contested.[24] Ownership of the property was disputed by government authorities and family members, as well as by dozens of sharecroppers who lived on the adjacent Fazenda Burro Branco—a large operation also under the ownership of various Taborda family members. Still elsewhere, farther to the north in the state of Paraná, the construction of the Salto Santiago Hydroelectric Power Plant and Dam in the late 1970s displaced over forty thousand people.[25] Similar to the processes unfolding

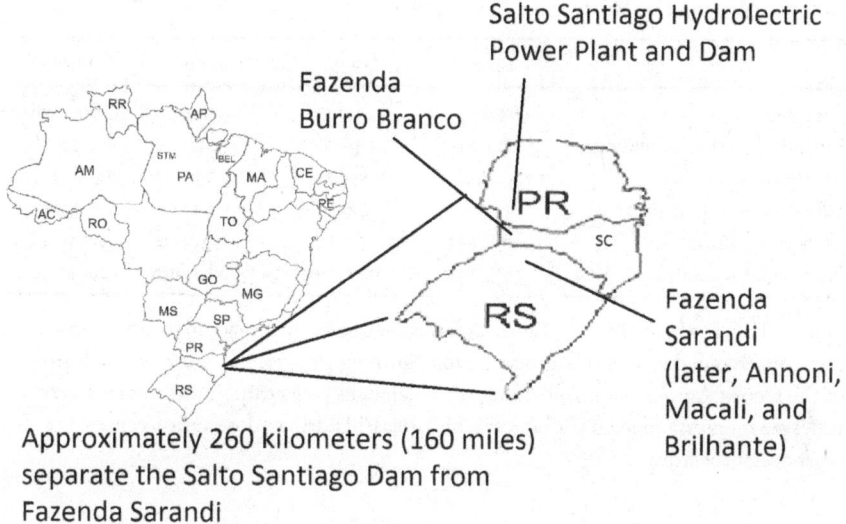

FIGURE 9 Rural conflicts, southern Brazil: late 1970s to early 1980s.

with the Passo Real project in the state of Rio Grande do Sul, various families' livelihoods were disrupted. Large-scale public works projects, state intervention, and family squabbles throughout this strip of land connecting Rio Grande do Sul, Paraná, and Santa Catarina made state authority claims to control and administer territory particularly unstable.

Additionally, economic conditions were destabilized with the changes in seed technologies, pesticide use, and mechanization that began in the 1950s and then accelerated throughout the 1970s and 1980s. Sugar operations in the northeast saw dramatic changes. Increased fertilizer use, as well as the availability of subsidies to purchase other inputs and land made rural labor markets more precarious and mobile.[26] Soy production, which tends to be capital- rather than labor-intensive, displaced various rural families in the south and southeast, while the sharecropping arrangement known as the *colonato* became completely extinct by the end of the 1970s. These changes in labor markets did not result so much in proletarianization—the development of an urbanized workforce that regularly relies on wages to survive—but in depeasantization.[27] Depeasantization does not refer to a stable way of life, or manner of economic production, but rather to how rural workers lose one way of economically ensuring their existence without finding an alternative. The displacement of the families

TABLE 2 Agricultural Production, 1970s–1980s

	1970	1975	1980	1985
Tractors	165,870	323,113	545,205	665,280
Hectare per tractor average	204:1	130:1	105:1	94:1
Workers	17,582,089	20,345,692	21,163,735	23,394,919
Workers per operation	3.57	4.07	4.1	4.03
Owner operators	2,932,245	3,077,561	3,233,320	3,539,189
Nonowner operators	1,786,139	1,781,249	1,7439,968	2,031,712

Source: IBGE, *Censo Agricola, Censo Agropecuario*, 1970, 1975, 1980, 1986. The Censo Agricola changed to Censo Agropecuario beginning in 1970. For more on the history of the Censo Agropecuario, including the challenges concerning measurement over time, see memoria.ibge.gov.br/sinteses-historicas/historicos-dos-censos/censos-agropecuarios.html.

throughout various regions, in the northeast and the south principally, illustrates instability in labor relations, or rather, in economic conditions.

CHANGING POLITICAL CONDITIONS, THE EMBRACE OF LEGAL TACTICS, AND THE MILITARY

Economic and political legitimacy were interconnected in the Brazilian military government's claim to govern. When economic policies were bearing fruit and inflation was under control, the regime garnered a kind of legitimacy, if not complacency, among the growing middle class in the early part of the 1970s. While not necessarily enjoying active popular support, Brazil's military regime survived due to targeted repression, managed elections, extensive censorship, and steady economic growth.

During military rule, CONTAG, which emerged shortly before the coup d'état as a result of rural syndicalization efforts,[28] saw its leadership and functions change significantly. After its more radical leaders were replaced, many of its member unions became service-providing agencies that jettisoned novel, potentially transformative forms of resistance. The ETR (Estatuto do Trabalhador Rural; Rural Worker Statute), which was passed on the eve of military rule in 1963, allowed unions to collect funds from a 1 percent tax on commercialized agricultural goods to fund social welfare programs such as medical services.

Similar, seemingly pro-rural union legislation was promulgated by the military government. For instance, 1967 saw the creation of the Fundo de Apoio ao Trabalhador Rural (FUNRURAL; Rural Worker Support Fund), which ensured medical, dental, and retirement services for rural workers. In 1971, access for rural workers to social services was enlarged and simplified with the creation of the Programa de Assistência ao Trabalhador Rural (PRORURAL; Program for Rural Worker Assistance). Because of these laws, CONTAG became the main organ in charge of administering the newly formed set of social services for its union members.[29]

Various CONTAG member unions maintained throughout the military period a certain level of opposition, despite government oversight and the fear of repression. Instead of uniformly acting in a completely subordinate manner to the military elites, some unions were more autonomous and less subservient to the military government.[30] First, many of the more contentious unions repeatedly called on the national government to uphold and respect workers' civil, political, and economic rights.[31] Second, these unions also continued the call for agrarian reform that social movements had made before the military took power in 1964. Overall, the unions sought to protect the right to collective bargaining, as well as the concrete material benefits for rural workers, that had been delivered before and during military rule. Absent from their engagement with authorities, however, were the extralegal occupations and encampments the social movements conducted in the 1960s. Striking as a tactic to pressure for change, due to the extensive and oppressive labor court system of the CLT, was virtually unusable. Many of CONTAG member unions kept agrarian reform on the political agenda, but did not promote deploying direct action tactics to demand or carry it out.

Any claims to legitimacy made by the Brazilian military began to erode in 1973 when the first of two oil shocks, and the ensuing abrupt rises in oil prices, led the government to begin to accrue large amounts of debt to continue purchasing foreign oil for its developmental program. While not initially a problem, steady GDP decline and increased indebtedness led to high levels of inflation by 1980.[32] In addition to having what appeared to be a failed developmental model, the military government was caught deliberately misreporting wage statistics in 1977. This contributed to the reactivation of the urban labor movement, which began in that same year as its "wage recovery campaigns." Also, in 1978, Institutional Act 5, which essentially had suspended political and civil rights, was revoked. Sensing their loss of support, in 1979 the military government issued the Novo Lei Organica de Partidos Politicos (Party Reform Bill) to control the reintroduction of parties and so increase the military's chances of uninterrupted succession.[33] Such liberalization efforts were part of the regime's policies of *distensão* (decompression). Decompression was part of the overall plan known as *abertura* (opening) to slowly and gradually allow more participation in government from civil society and new political parties.

Political conditions at the subnational, state level were also destabilized. Both the administrations of Sinval Guazzelli (1975–79) and José Augusto Amaral de Souza (1979–83) were receptive of movement demands in Rio Grande do Sul. Despite belonging to the political party that supported the military government—ARENA (Aliança Renovadora Nacional; National Alliance for Renovation)[34]—both governors were open to redistributing land in order to settle the recently displaced families in the state. The Guazzelli administration provided families transportation to areas within Rio Grande do Sul to await settlement.[35] The subsequent governor, de Souza, on various occasions met with activists about the possibility of settlements and redistribution. One religious leader, Padre Arnildo Fritzen, who followed the expulsion from the Nonoai reserve and short-lived occupation of Fazenda Brilhante in 1978, rented a bus to take the displaced farmers to meet with the governor. This attempt to negotiate for land was decided on by the families because previous failures made it clear that they had to build support with people in and out of government who could represent them. After a somewhat storied exchange between negotiators and the governor,[36] the families returned to encamp at Fazenda Brilhante. Meanwhile, a worker within the state government—João Pedro Stédile—used his position in the office of the Secretary of Agriculture to gain official approval for the encamped families to harvest and sell corn raised at Macali and Brilhante. Political conditions were changing as allies were found within government administrations.

In helping to craft the incipient movement's tactical repertoire, Stédile emphasized the importance of a precise manner of working with political leaders. Stédile and other organizers studied prior social movements such as MASTER and the Peasant Leagues to understand their challenges and problems.[37] When the primary organizer of the Peasant Leagues, Francisco Julião, was in exile in Mexico, Stédile had a series of meetings with him to learn about the league's successes and failures. Stédile later recalled that Julião believed that the Peasant Leagues erred by becoming too connected to political parties, failing to create its own leaders, and remaining particularly a regional and not a national organization.[38] Fritzen's and especially Stédile's actions reveal, in their working with the hundreds of landless families who were encamped at Macali and Brilhante, how certain legal tactics—namely, entering into negotiations with politicians and seeking resources—became part of the movement's tactical repertoire. Additionally, not every mode of legal interaction was promoted, with running candidates in elections expressly eschewed.

Meanwhile, state conditions, especially on distinct sites in the late 1970s and early 1980s, remained unstable. The ad hoc, bureaucratic nature of colonial and postcolonial territorial administration that involved imprecisely mapped land grabs undergirded the entire country. Nowhere was this more visible than in the north of Rio Grande do Sul, where government actors, certain powerful families, unorganized peasant farmers, and now, the incipient Landless Movement, were making claims for space. Economically, small-scale producers and peasants were displaced—deproletarianized—due to changes in the agricultural economy and large public works projects. Furthermore, the legal nature of the land occupations and encampments had not changed since the 1950 and 1960s. Past activists from MASTER knew this. Thus, after gaining potential support from government elites, organizers and families practiced extralegal land occupations and encampments to claim space. Finally, government changes nationally and at the subnational, state-level offered the possibility for political mobilization and alliance formation. In learning about and combining legal and extralegal actions, activists took advantage of unstable conditions and created the opportunity to continue mobilizing.

TO THE AMAZON (AND BACK): SETTLEMENTS, COLONIZATION, AND INCRA

Some of the families who were expelled from the Nonoai reserve in 1978 stayed in Rio Grande do Sul, while others were sent to the Amazonian region of the state of Mato Grosso. This experience was not the first instance of a planned rural settlement in Brazil. Other projects were initiated during Getúlio Vargas's administration (1930–54) with the intention to disperse immigrants and thus avoid the formation of "cultural enclaves."[39] Overall, the settlement policies from the 1930s to the 1960s were sporadic. From São Paulo to Pará, families were relocated onto public lands to "diminish the threat—real or potential—that 'surplus' workers posed."[40] Multiple government ministries were involved in the creation of rural settlements during this period, including the Ministério do Trabalho (Ministry of Labor) and the Ministério de Agricultura (Ministry of Agriculture). In 1953, the Instituto Nacional de Imigração e Colonização (INIC; National Institute for Immigration and Settlement) was created, with the primary function to settle poor, primarily urban and/or immigrant populations in rural areas. From 1941 to 1944, seven separate settlements were created,[41] while in 1956, eight were established. Those inaugurated in the 1940s were somewhat evenly distributed throughout the country, with the settlements created in the 1950s located in the northeast to target areas where social movement activity was growing.

The creation of settlements became central to the military government's efforts in agrarian and national security policy. Shortly after the military coup, in November of 1964, the military government decreed the Estatuo da Terra (Rural Land Statute). The text of the law seems strikingly left-wing and popular. First, the statute openly elucidates the conditions for land redistribution. Second, instead of requiring that the Brazilian government pay market value for expropriating property—a stumbling block in prior initiatives—the government would compensate owners with government bonds (*títulos da dívida agrária nacional*). The legislation also sanctioned new institutions to carry out the project—the Grupo Executivo da Reforma Agrária (GERA; Agrarian Reform Executive Group), the Instituto Brasileiro de Reforma Agrária (IBRA; Brazilian Institute for Agrarian Reform), and the Instituto Nacional do Desenvolvimento Agrário (INDA; National Institute for Agrarian Development). In addition to these agencies, other, more regionally focused entities were enlisted, including the Superintendência do Desenvolvimento Econômico do Nordeste (SUDENE; Superintendent of Economic Development in the North East), the Superintendência do Plano de Valorização Econômica da Amazônia (SPVEA; Superintendent of Economic Valorization Plans in the Amazon), the Comissão do Vale do São Francisco (CVSF; Commission of São Francisco Valley), and the Superintendência do Plano de Valorização Econômica da Região da Fronteira Sudoeste do País (SUDOESTE; Superintendent of Economic Valorization Plans for the Southeast Border Region).

In actual practice, instead of leading to a wide-sweeping change in agrarian relations, the Rural Land Statute encouraged redistribution through a series of planned settlement initiatives (*colonização*) in certain regions and priority areas (*áreas prioritárias*). This differs from standard agrarian reform legislation that was enacted in various Latin American countries during the twentieth century.

From Cuba to Ecuador, agrarian reform measures established certain usually productivity- and size-based criteria for expropriation, dividing the entire state territory into "reform" sectors and exempted "nonreform" areas.[42] In Brazil, the various regional agencies targeted the Amazon, the northeast, the San Francisco Valley, and the southeast. A subsequent decree approved action in the priority areas. These areas included sites in the states of Pernambuco, Rio de Janeiro, Rio Grande do Sul, and the Federal District.[43] Such sites, for example, the Alto Uruguai in Rio Grande do Sul, were targeted for their high levels of poverty and past histories of organized conflict that were led by movements such as MASTER and the Peasant Leagues.

The military's land redistribution efforts culminated in 1970 with the merging of IBRA and INDA into INCRA, as well as the launching of the Plano de Integração Nacional (PIN; National Integration Plan). After visiting the drought-stricken lands of the northeast—the home of the recently demobilized Peasant Leagues—General Medici spoke to a crowd of northeasterners, telling them that the government would take "*homens sem terra para uma terra sem homens*" (people without land to a land without people). PIN, which was issued through decree 1106, initiated the construction of the Transamazonia highway and shifted resources to infrastructure projects and settlement schemes in the northeast and the Amazon. To focus efforts, the military regime also launched a series of targeted development and migration programs—the Programa de Redistribuição de Terras e de Estímulo à Agro-indústria do Norte e do Nordeste (PROTERRA; Land Redistribution and Agroindustry Stimulation Program for the North and Northeast) in 1971, the Programa Especial para o Vale do São Francisco (PROVALE; Special Program for the São Francisco Valley) in 1972, the Programa de Pólos Agropecuários e Agrominerais da Amazônia (POLAMAZONIA; Programs for Agricultural and Agromineral Exploration in the Amazon) in 1974, and the Programa de Desenvolvimento de Áreas Integradas do Nordeste (POLONORDESTE; Program for the Integrated Development of the Northeast) in 1974. While the various priority zones throughout Brazil would receive attention from the Medici and later military governments, the Amazon from the early 1970s onward was especially targeted.

Furthermore, the military government extended subsidies for further mechanization and technological improvement. Large-scale operations benefitted, as the government did not promote redistributive efforts in either income or land.[44] EMBRAPA (Empresa Brasileria de Pesquisa Agropecuária; Brazilian Enterprise for Agricultural Research) was created to help develop plant technology, while PLANALSUCAR (Programa Nacional de Melhoramento de Cana-de-Açúcar; National Plan to Improve Sugarcane) began an overhaul of the sugarcane industry in the northeast. Meanwhile, the displacement of rural workers who used to live on plantations and the industrialization of large-scale monocultural operations that began in the 1940s/1950s continued. Gervásio Rezende notes how these three factors—cheap credit, improved technology, and increased labor costs—were stabilized for large-scale producers and skilled workers, while destabilizing the lives of tenant, sharecropper, or simply small-scale farmer populations.[45] Changing economic conditions benefitted the rural elites, not the historically marginalized populations in the countryside.

Within the military's plans, the settlement was a technology married to national security policy. Colonization through creating settlements was what José de Souza Martins called the military regime's "safety valve"—any potential disruption concerning land was diffused by sending groups to settlements, usually in remote areas of the country.[46] Rural settlement remained sporadic and relatively minimal, even after the passing of the Rural Land Statute in 1964. Nigel Smith, drawing on official INCRA sources, finds that by 1978, 7,764 families had participated in colonization settlement.[47] The seeming low number of participants was intentional—the military government led redistribution efforts in specific and targeted instances.

Within the context of national security, INCRA officials took their jobs seriously. Plans were devised for the organization of settlements, featuring specific governing structures that were to be implemented according to a twelve-step program. The twelve steps, in their intended order for implementation were: distribute land, plan territory, set administration organization, distribute initial credits, distribute initial production credits, build infrastructure, create means for education, administer health care, set up housing, create cooperatives, distribute another round of credits, and assist in commercializing production. Within the settlement, families were to become involved in running schools, administering health care, and establishing cooperatives. One retired official also included how "cooperation" and "self-management" were encouraged between the settlers, in addition to organizing "small groups" with specific "functions."[48]

Various officials I interviewed who had worked at INCRA during this period lived with families during the implantation and construction of settlements. Many remembered this time fondly. In one case, an official, after describing the twelve-step program, praised the military government's efforts to strengthen INCRA and lamented the institution's relative demise in terms of prestige.[49]

Other officials somewhat bemoaned how current technologies like computers had limited their ability to have face-to-face interactions with people.[50] I interviewed INCRA officials in Brasilia, São Paulo, Paraná, and Rio Grande do Sul. In each state, I made a point to interview workers who were recently hired as well as older officials. Similar to what Wendy Wolford reports in her study of INCRA, I found a high level of enthusiasm and dedication to improving the lives of rural people among INCRA officials.[51] Additionally, most, if not all, of the elder officials with whom I spoke did not seem to care if a democratic or authoritarian government was behind redistributive efforts. The commitment to land reform, rural communities, and INCRA went beyond government regime.

INCRA's settlements at this time concealed a larger social plan for the reorganization of rural life. Geographically, newly redistributed spaces would center around the *agrovila*, a circularly organized housing community. Families would live close together in individual houses. Located around the community would be local clinics, schools, religious sites, and stores. The lots where people would work were disconnected and located away from their homes. These smaller communities were to be connected to form what was called the *agropolis*, which would feature administration and security and health care services. At the apex of the settlement hierarchy was the *ruropolis*. Here, settlers would find an airport, large hospitals, banks, and communication headquarters.[52] Twenty-seven *agrovilas*, three *agropolises*, and one *ruropolis* were completed during the time of military rule.

I was told often, by both INCRA officials and movement leaders, how colonization was not agrarian reform. First, the military redistributed land in the public domain for settlement primarily at the border with neighboring states and in the interest of national security. In one interview, I was told how the state of Rondônia "was basically a bunch of settlements" created and administered by INCRA to act as a buffer against potential Bolivian aggression.[53] The settlements, such as those located in the Alto Uruguai region of Rio Grande do Sul near the Passo Real Dam project, did not share a border with a foreign country. Still, these initiatives count as colonization and not agrarian reform measures because they were created to diffuse potential political unrest as part of national security policy. Agrarian reform, unlike colonization, does not involve national security, but rather the redistribution of potentially productive farm land in one region to displaced, poorer families from the general vicinity.[54] As one longtime MST activist told me, "agrarian reform is not colonization. The settlements [in agrarian reform] are different. Agrarian reform gets into the structures of unequal land ownership (*reforma agrária mexe na estrutura fundiaria*)."[55] Agrarian reform settlements force the redistribution of the property from economic, and often political, elites.

The military's national security settlement efforts succumbed from a series of problems. Many of the people were relocated to areas with which they had little or no familiarity. Malaria, which was not an issue in temperate Rio Grande do Sul, posed acute challenges. So did the nature of the soil, which was radically different from what was found in Brazil's south. The colonization schemes were also poorly staffed and executed with respect to their grandiose objectives. Squatters from nearby regions and migrants who did not have official land claims would often informally claim land in the same areas where the relocated families were sent. The unexpected arrival of squatters and other migrants, combined with another of INCRA's policies that allowed large owners and corporations to acquire extensive stretches of territory for strictly economic purposes, led to overlapping territorial claims and periodic clashes. One of the central imperatives for the rural settlements in the military's national security program—to diffuse and calm social conflict—failed. In effect, the military government took political unrest from one area of the country and simply moved it to another.

Many families who moved to the Amazon during the 1970s, instead of remaining on the settlements, eventually decided to return to their places of origin. In one project, Terranova, which was located in the north of Mato Grosso state, close to 80 percent of the one thousand initial participants returned to their original state of Rio Grande do Sul between 1979 and 1981.[56] From the Altamira project, which was created in 1971, nearly 50 percent of the participants returned to southern Brazil, while 40 percent of participants in the Canarana project that began in 1972 also went back to their places of origin.[57] Most other settlement projects that attempted to relocate farmer families from the south to the north similarly ended in failure, as families opted to return to their home states. The returning families arrived to find leaders and activists in the incipient stages of organizing for land redistribution—not in the Amazon, but in Rio Grande do Sul.

The families' return had various impacts. First, it directly rejected the military government's efforts in the late 1970s/early 1980s to settle people in colonization programs. The offer of land in the Amazon lured people in the early 1970s who may have otherwise mobilized for political change in the south. Yet, instead of gaining access to land in new areas, returning families demonstrated that the military's colonization scheme was characterized by disease, mismanagement, and persistent conflict. Many families expelled from the Nonoai reserve and who would encamp at Encruzilhada Natalino in 1981 returned from failed efforts in the Amazon.[58]

Once returned, they would tell others that the colonization programs were failures. This led many to wonder: could land redistribution take place, not in some state where families had no familiarity, but in spaces that they knew? Returning families began with the belief that this could and should happen. The people returning from the Amazon brought with them experiences in settlement organization. Even in failed or poorly administered projects, the individuals acquired lessons from their experiences within *agrovilas*. They had participated, in some sense, in incipient administrative projects in INCRA's settlements. Settlements and *agrovilas* had potential, just not in the Amazon. Families would incorporate into their own demands and vision for agrarian reform the notion of constructing settlements that they gained from their experiences in the Amazon with INCRA.

The demands of the families at Encruzilhada Natalino in the early 1980s, as found in the *Boletim* message from 1981, begin to make sense in light of the history of the rural settlement. Settlements became part of early organizers' vision of change from the adaptation and development of colonization programs throughout the twentieth century. Families' direct experience with settlement administration in the Amazon, as well as their close collaboration with various INCRA officials, contributed to how organizers demanded land redistribution in the south of Brazil. Last but not least in piecing together the organizers' early tactical repertoire, land occupations, as learned from past movements, became central to the demand for agrarian reform settlements.

FAITH, ECONOMICS, AND UNITY: INCORPORATING THE CHURCH INTO THE MOVEMENT

Mobilization in the early 1980s had little coordination beyond the isolated sites where families were organizing. Occupations of large estates were taking place simultaneously in Rio Grande do Sul, Paraná, and Santa Catarina. Extralegal and legal tactics were learned and adapted, often from past struggles. The goal—to redistribute land to form rural settlements—resulted from interactions with INCRA. Activists also acquired three additional lessons during these formative years: first, how to practice a decentralized, participatory mode of organization to govern affairs; second, the importance of cooperative economic production; and third, the dynamics of scaling up and unifying across regions.

Decentralization, which was part of INCRA's settlement design, was further emphasized by the Catholic Church. The need for extensive, decentralized participation came from the religiously oriented Comunidades Eclesiales de Base (CEBs; Ecclesiastical Base Communities). In Brazil, as well as throughout Latin America, the CEBs' origins can be traced to the Second Vatican Council (1962–65) and the meetings of Catholic bishops in Medellin (1965) and Puebla (1979). As opposed to the Church's traditionally organized, hierarchical structure, the CEBs were "a new Church experience" that promoted direct interpersonal relationships, increased fraternity, and mutual help. Practically, this meant the "active presence of the lay person in the work of evangelization . . . in the absence of the priest."[59]

It was not only about *how* to evangelize, but also *what* was in the content of the message. Parishes around the continent were encouraged to confront poverty, hierarchy, and violence. The idea of the "preferential option for the poor," a term coined at the Puebla Conference of Latin American Bishops in 1979, was intended to draw attention to poverty and promote work with economically marginalized populations. These three general themes did not lead to uniform change around the continent. In fact, more radical appropriations and practices became standard in Brazil, Nicaragua, Chile, and El Salvador.[60] In these cases more than others, the challenge to hierarchy included an embrace of struggles that sought to promote decentralized, participatory ways to challenge poverty.

In Brazil, the grassroots, religiously inspired CEBs developed as the military government persistently repressed and censored student groups, unions, and social movements.[61] One result was the formation of the CPT in 1975. The CPT emerged primarily in the south and northeast of Brazil, working on rural labor issues.[62] Whether individuals were actually religious or not, many people became involved in the CEBs and the CPT because other chances for mobilization were closed off by the military regime and the restrictions from IA-5. With other avenues for politically conscious actors restricted, the CPT and the CEBs had the mission "to set up meetings meant to resolve community problems, particularly economic issues."[63] Giving preferential option to the poor, besides helping marginalized communities organize, meant especially in Brazil exploring "hands-on" actions to directly confront material needs.

The collective, decentralized mode of participation practiced and encouraged by the CEBs and the CPT became part of the practices of early landless activists, first in southern Brazil. Not only was the CPT active there, but many key leaders who would remain influential in the MST—João Pedro Stédile, Darci Maschio, Ademar Bogo, among others[64]—were active in these organizations in Rio Grande do Sul. In the early days of the Encruzilhada Natalino encampment, Father Fritzen helped adapt the CEBs to the nascent movement for agrarian reform by helping to organize the encamped families into small groups to administer basic encampment needs and affairs.[65] In the earlier encampments, and later settlements, the Church's influence also became manifest in the idea of promoting collective land cultivation. This was based in the religious imperative of treating fellow members and "creation" with respect.[66] These changes promoted by the Catholic Church connected a form of organization with an incipient mode of organization and administration. Because of the Church's presence, collective administration was joined with economic production.

The Church assisted still other groups of landless families to mobilize in distinct, less confrontational ways. On the border of Rio Grande do Sul and Santa Catarina, on the Rio Uruguai, various hydroelectric dam projects were in development. Eletrosul—the Brazilian state-owned enterprise in charge of preparing spaces for construction—engaged in campaigns to convince people to leave. With the help of the CPT in 1979, a counter-campaign began to show that the government was "misinforming" residents about the project.[67] This mobilization of displaced farmers, as well as union activists and religious organizations, formalized various Comissões de Atingidos (Commissions of the Affected) in the south and in other areas of Brazil where similar public infrastructural works were in development. Various organizations then developed, which included CRAB (Comissão Regional dos Atingidos por Barragens; Regional Commission of the Affected in the South), CAHTU (Comissão dos Atingidos pela Hidrelétrica de Tucuruí; Commission of the Affected by the Tucuruí Dam), and CRABI (Comissão Regional dos Atingidos do Rio Iguaçu; Regional Commission of the Affected Near the Iguaçu River). These organizations engaged in protest but were principally concerned with informing the public of the nature of the public works projects and the need to resettle people who had been displaced. The actions of these groups, which are included in the overall movement that was emerging at this time, did not feature more confrontational, direct-action tactics.

One additional role played by the Church at this time was in unifying many of the diverse groups that were demanding land redistribution. In the late 1970s in Brazil periodic conflicts over land access were plentiful. The CPT helped coordinate the formation of various groups between 1979 and 1982 in Rio Grande do Sul and Paraná.[68] Coordination meant providing a network for actors to connect and see their struggles in light of one another. Religious organizations also allowed activists to think in terms of new identities to orient their political struggles. Before the MST's first official meeting in 1984, the CPT hosted various regional and national-level meetings to bring together leaders involved in land and labor disputes. These spaces provided places to forge a common identity and disseminate common tactics, which included how to lead occupations and encampments.

The CPT and the CEBs were not neutral observers. The focus on decentralization and economic injustice colored the incipient movement's debates and discussions. The organizers in the late 1970s did not compete with Brazil's Communist parties, either the PC do B or PCB, to mobilize the families that were occupying land in southern Brazil. On various occasions in the early 1980s, PCB leaders actually expressed opposition to the land occupation tactic and the MST.[69] Conspicuously absent from the list of actors who acted in solidarity with the encamped families at Encruzilhada Natalino were any organizations or parties with "Communist" in their name. At this time, in the formative years of the Landless Movement, Communist parties were silent owing to a combination of internal ideological disagreements[70] and repression from the military government.

At this historical moment, Church actors permitted and encouraged the development of legal and extralegal tactics. Leaders helped organize legal marches and negotiations, while also either participating within or encouraging families to conduct land occupations and also organize collective forms of economic production. Moreover, the Church had an essential monopoly over coalition-building efforts, without competition from other parties to organize the families in the emerging Landless Movement.

FROM ENCRUZILHADA NATALINO TO ANNONI, AND BEYOND

The combination of legal and extralegal tactics—negotiations and occupations, respectively—was put to a test at the Encruzilhada Natalino encampment after some, but not all, of the families in the region received land on the Macali and Brilhante ranches in 1979. Initially including only a couple dozen families, the encampment became the temporary home for hundreds of families from around the region.[71] The site was in one sense strange because rather than occupying a particular ranch or plantation that could be expropriated, the families occupied an intersection that did not belong to a private owner and could not be redistributed. This helped the families make their demand for land because the road was not an option for settlement and space had to be found elsewhere.

Government agents attempted to divide and co-opt the families at various times over the encampment's two-year existence. At the center of the government's efforts was Sebastião Curió, who led the successful counterinsurgency campaign against the PC do B's armed insurrection in the Amazon from 1972 to 1974.[72] Before Curió's arrival at the end of July 1981, the state police force (*policia militar*) frequently harassed the encamped families. The encampment was also infiltrated by officials from the Departamento de Ordem Política e Social (DOPS; Department of Political and Social Order), the military government's official political police force.[73] Government forces attempted to divide and manipulate the families by propagating among the occupiers the idea that there existed "true" and "fake" landless families.[74] Candy was offered to children and land in the Amazon was promised. Physical force was also used. On various occasions the police invaded the encampment, burnt the makeshift tents, and attacked individuals. Curió continued many of these practices.

The federal government's intervention lasted the month of August, resulting in the military's effective withdrawal from the area later in 1981. The reason for the mobilization's success—at least in terms of remaining united—is found in part with the families' preparation. Prior to the decision to form the encampment, Fritzen recognized the need to organize the families not only ideologically, but also according to certain roles. Specifically, he noted the need to form "committees" that were divided into areas like "health, food, hygiene, and negotiation."[75] What also helped the occupiers to remain resolute were their frequent marches and negotiations with government elites. Religious imagery and vigils were constant, engendering a powerful ideational force that bound the hundreds of families together. One of the most powerful and enduring symbols for the emerging movement from the encampment was a large cross. To emphasize the sacrifice and desperation of the people involved in the action, a handkerchief was tied to the cross for each child who died during the encampment.[76] Once Curió departed, the state government of Rio Grande do Sul once again had to deal with the mobilized families. Church and labor allies strengthened their solidarity campaign with other emerging movements and allies, as well as facilitated discussions between INCRA and officials in the state government.

The mobilized families and their allies benefitted from weakened state and government conditions. There were other military efforts at this time to confront potential conflicts in individual, targeted areas. The GETAT (Grupo Executivo de Terras do Araguaia-Tocantins; Executive Land Group of Araguaia-Tocantins) was created by the military government in 1980 to quiet mobilizations where the PC do B was active at the end of the 1960s. In this area, foreign mining interests had been and remained crucial to the military government's economic development plans. The military's political and economic legitimacy, as they were connected, determined where the government launched its periodic national security operations. The north of Rio Grande do Sul did not feature similar mineral resource wealth and was therefore not considered a government priority when compared to Araguaia. State conditions remained vulnerable in both the Amazon and in Rio Grande do Sul. The use of force to support business interests in Araguaia stabilized state territorial authority at that site, while in Rio Grande do Sul, the mobilized families took advantage of the state's vulnerability, a relative lack of government attention, and instability in labor relations.

The encampment at Encruzilhada Natalino was vital for land struggles in the south for various reasons. First, it brought many different people into the movement, including sharecroppers, wage laborers, and families who had left the countryside to work temporary jobs in cities. With the arrival and swift departure of Curió, the encampment drew statewide, if not national, exposure. This showed that a movement was possible and could challenge the military regime. The occupation also demonstrated how land redistribution was possible in Rio Grande do Sul. According to Wagner, of the six hundred or so families who were at Encruzilhada Natalino at its apex, one third quit, another third eventually gained land at other spaces in the state, and the last third went to another site that became known as Nova Ronda Alta.[77] Specifically, 162 of the remaining 200 or so families would receive land at Nova Ronda Alta in 1982. This settlement did not directly result from direct action tactics used to pressure the government to redistribute land, but instead emerged after religious allies, principally the CNBB (Conferência Nacional do Bispos do Brasil; National Conference of Brazilian Bishops), purchased a property. Even though buying land detracts from the call for agrarian reform—to force land redistribution— the acquisition promoted the growing movement. The president of the CNBB at the time, Dr. Ivo Lorscheiter, stated that the ease with which the purchase took place illustrated that redistribution was possible in the south.[78] Again, and despite the failed settlement schemes in the Amazon, the military government attempted to direct rural families to participate in colonization programs. Nova Ronda Alta illustrated how developing settlements in the south was a better option for displaced rural people.

The experience at Nova Ronda Alta displayed a fully developed, participatory governing structure. Participant descriptions of life on the early settlement include one of the first systematizations of nucleo, or small-group, governance. The settlement's two hundred or so families were organized into and governed by seven groups that were democratically elected. The nucleos together were called the *assembleia do povo* (people's assembly), which was further subdivided into groups dedicated to collective gardens, animal maintenance, transportation, sanitation, and other services.[79] Frequent reports on the nucleos, and Nova Ronda Alta, are found in early editions of the *Boletim Sem Terra*. In one, the newsletter documents a visit from French union leaders to the site, as well as how the area's local mayor allowed the families to fish on a nearby lake.[80] Over the course of those two years, the newsletter presented "news" on the settlement in a special section, featuring a man with his back turned to readers, carrying a scythe and casting a shadow in the shape of a cross—a reference to Encruzilhada Natalino. In total, there were thirty-seven references to visits, meetings, production, and daily life in Nova Ronda Alta in the monthly *Boletim* from 1982 to 1984. In development at Nova Ronda Alta was a revolutionary claim to territory that dramatically restructured political, economic, and cultural relations by abolishing the distinction between public and private power.

Lessons in the use of legal tactics, particularly with respect to accessing public schools, were also gained by certain individuals at the provisional settlement at Novo Ronda Alta. Two women—Salette Campigotto and Lucia Webber— regularly met and negotiated with government officials in the office of the Secretary of Education in the municipality of Ronda Alta. Campigotto had been a teacher in public schools in the area since 1978. After roughly two years of meetings with local officials, the school that had been informally in operation in the Nova Ronda Alta settlement became officially recognized as public in 1984.[81] While a public institution, the teachers were from the settlement. Teachers had to abide by certain curriculum requirements and would receive pay, but retained the prerogative over pedagogical decisions. Organizers began to understand the strategic role of education within the movement at this point. Pressuring

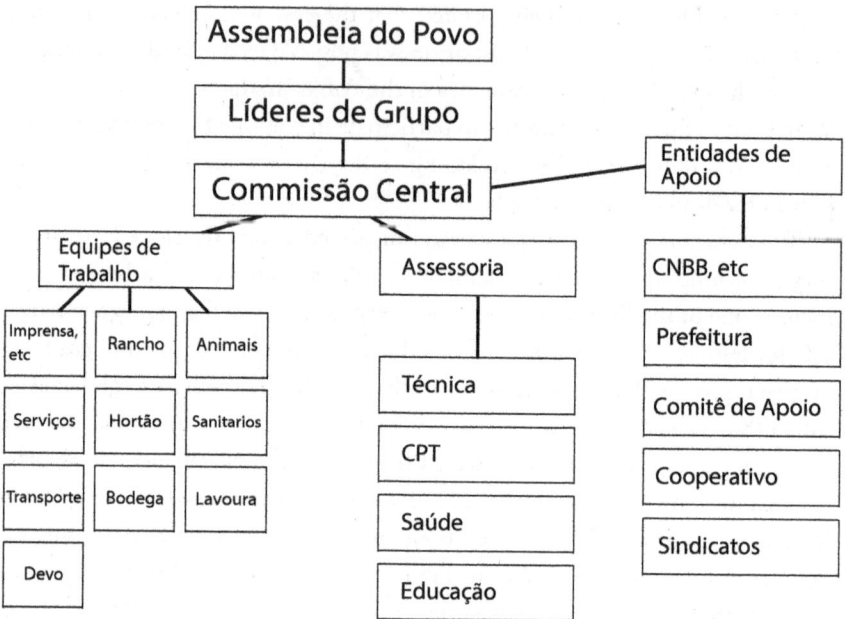

FIGURE 10 Nucleo and assembly diagram of Nova Ronda Alta's organization. *JST* 1982. Every edition of *JST* is publicly available online, through the MST-CEDEM online database.

for schools entailed the recruitment of entire families, instead of only single men who tended to participate more in the occupations and encampments.[82] In addition to being a right found in the constitution, schools were a way to mobilize entire families.

Simultaneously, the movement's identity and cultural work were developing in a way to clearly differentiate Sem Terra from large landowners and government opponents. The Church's early role in identity creation was pretty clear—when encamped at Encruzilhada Natalino, the cross that the families created became an object that represented sacrifice and commitment. Once families arrived at Nova Ronda Alta, biblical language was used to describe the site—for example, calling the site *a terra prometida* (the Promised Land).[83] Meanwhile, the movement was crafting a more combative identity. The principal target was the large-scale latifundios. In an early MST newsletter, under the subheading "massacre" and above a list of deceased rural organizers, the movement claims that the latifundio has "declared war on rural workers.... They [the deceased organizers] lost their lives fighting for all Brazilians."[84] Besides being represented as violent and war-making, latifundios were connected to government favoritism and export agriculture.[85] Additionally, in their early demands for agrarian reform at Encruzilhada Natalino, movement leaders and rural union organizers claimed that their struggle "was a just way to access land, part of actually carrying out what is found in the Constitution and the 1964 Land Statute."[86] In the encampment, families studied and referenced the Rural Land Statute to legitimize their actions, simultaneously impugning large landowners and the government. The movement represented itself as the primary actor upholding the law, while the government and latifundio were guilty of breaking it. A stark divide, between friends and enemies, was crystalizing in movement symbols and discourse.

While participants were testing and perfecting nucleo governance at Nova Ronda Alta, early movement leaders were taking up still other organizational issues. Many movement organizers met to discuss the prospects of formalizing a movement that would act independently of its religious allies. Already in the early 1980s, many leaders noticed that the Church's influence needed to be limited. Darci Maschio notes how periodic conflicts with Church leaders led to a division concerning larger strategic goals.[87] Organizers met in 1983 to discuss formalizing a movement, which officially would take place in 1984. The 1983 meeting established that the occupation would be the central tactic used by the movement. The 1984 meeting would give the movement its name, O Movimento dos Trabalhadores Rurais Sem Terra (MST; Landless Rural Workers' Movement). The Church, particularly the CPT and its many religious leaders, would remain influential allies. From this point on, however, direction came primarily from the movement.

Another transformation at this time occurred with respect to how land occupations were utilized. While the conduct of occupations had already been altered from their use by MASTER in the 1960s, in the mid-1980s the tactic began to test opponents and provoke elites to act. In a demonstration of these newer attributes, leaders organized an occupation of the Estação Experimental da Secretaria da Agricultura do Estado de Rio Grande do Sul (Experimental Station of the Secretary of Agriculture, Rio Grande do Sul), which is located near Fazenda Annoni in the north of Rio Grande do Sul. The occupation drew the attention of the local police, and the families were forcibly removed. As part of a plan, the families then began an encampment on a nearby farm in the municipality of Erval Seco, while movement leaders negotiated with the

Rio Grande do Sul state government over the families' eventual settlement to other areas in the state.[88] What took years to develop at Encruzilhada Natalino, namely occupying and then encamping at a certain locale to pressure elites to find another space for redistribution, took less than a year to accomplish at the Estação. This test proved that political and economic elites could be pressured to negotiate through well-planned and organized occupations.[89]

ANNONI, THE CONSTITUTION, AND CONSOLIDATING REVOLUTIONARY POLITICAL ACTION

The next, more significant act began with the occupation of Fazenda Annoni in 1985. Similar to what happened at Encruzilhada Natalino, the events that would unfold defined the MST's course for years and placed the movement on the national stage. It was no surprise that this fazenda would become the target of the MST's actions. The area had already been identified by movement allies and leaders as the best place to settle the families who encamped at Encruzilhada Natalino. INCRA's prior involvement in the area and the history of disputes concerning the areas of the former Fazenda Sarandi revealed a zone where state authority was weak. Agrarian reform was becoming political in the Schmittian sense—the sides of conflict were being drawn as collectives became aware of their differences. On the one side were large landowners and the national security state, while on the other were the MST and its allies. A relaxation of censorship by government elites, as well as the persistence of extralegal mobilization, contributed to this clarification of antagonism.

One document in particular—*Caderno de Formação n1* (Training Notebook #1)—captures the degree of the movement's work at this time in drawing a distinction between itself and its opponents. In addition to its newsletter, the MST began to publish a series of *cadernos* (notebooks) on everything from how to manage a school to the meaning of the Bible. These materials were for use in movement schools, as well as by leaders in encampments to introduce new adherents to the movement. Training notebooks, particularly, are oriented around organizing techniques and how to inculcate the movement's identity. The first half of Training Notebook #1 details the MST's history—from the first occupations at Macali and Brilhante to the first national congress in 1985. Besides reminding readers of the movement's history, another section lists various kinds of workers as Sem Terra, including sharecroppers, tenant farmers, squatters, small property owners, and rural wage laborers.[90] In the second section of the document, entitled the "Conjuntura Nacional" (National Conjuncture), it reads: "in our society, in Brazil, we are divided into two main groups or classes. On the one side, there are workers who live from their work and salaries . . . on the other side is the bourgeoisie who have capital and live from exploiting workers. . . . The bourgeoisie controls the state and uses the government to continue to exploit workers."[91] At this moment in the movement's existence, the leadership felt the need to clarify the sides of the struggle and represent their respective identities.

Two national events were taking place at the same time as activists were occupying and encamping at Fazenda Annoni: the passing of the Plano Nacional de Reforma Agrária (PNRA; National Plan for Agrarian Reform) in 1985 and the beginning of the Constitutional Assembly in that same year. Concerning the latter, the military government negotiated a peaceful transition from power in 1985 by allowing for the indirect election of a civilian leader, Tancredo Neves.[92] Neves fell ill shortly after the election and died. The vice president, José Sarney, attended the inauguration in Neves's place and then served as president until the first direct presidential election was held in 1989. In 1984, the two legal parties—the oppositional PMDB and pro-military PDS—planned for the drafting of a new constitution. On June 28, 1985, Sarney officially convoked the Assambleia Nacional Constituente (ANC; National Constituent Assembly) and set the date for the initiation of debates on its content for January 31, 1987.

The ANC became the subject of controversy immediately, mainly because participation in drafting the new constitution was limited to the legalized political parties. Organizations from civil society were not involved. Many such organizations were active in the Landless Movement, and provisions dealing with agrarian reform took up a central place in the ANC. Interest in agrarian reform was not confined to organizations in the emerging MST and their allies in southern Brazil; one survey published in the periodical *Jornal do Brasil* (Journal of Brazil) in 1987 found that 38 percent of Brazilians considered agrarian reform the most important issue for discussion in the ANC, with 46 percent of respondents believing that education was the first priority and 40 percent believing income inequality was paramount.[93]

The other national event, the creation and passing of the PNRA, was also of special concern for the MST and its allies in 1985. Unlike the ANC, within which the movement could not directly participate, the MST directly proposed and helped craft sections of the PNRA. The PNRA was a blueprint to establish national and regional plans with specific deadlines and objectives. The formulation of a PNRA was originally part of the 1964 Rural Land Statute. In 1966, the first PNRA was issued with decree 59.456. Yet, various projects from the 1966 PNRA were only partially, if at all, begun. Many of the sites, such as in the Alto Uruguai region of Rio Grande do Sul, were designated as priority zones in the 1966 PNRA for agrarian reform projects. With the exception of a few areas located around the country, the military government focused its attention on settlement plans in the Amazon. In 1985, unlike in 1966 when MASTER and the Peasant Leagues had already been demobilized, a new PNRA would be considered legitimate because the social movements demanding agrarian reform could participate. The new PNRA was decreed in October of 1985. That such a document was drafted with social movement input shows how more open political conditions intersected with the desire of movement leadership to participate within government institutions.

Then, on October 29, 1985, 150 buses from twenty-five different cities in Rio Grande do Sul took approximately six thousand people to occupy the Fazenda Annoni. The occupation was intended to get the attention of state officials from Rio Grande do Sul and the federal government, and to show the need to deal with land issues at that particular space that had been in dispute for decades.[94] While that occupation was under way, multiple others began throughout Rio Grande do Sul and Brazil. In fact, forty-two encampments of over twelve thousand families were established in eleven states.[95] Occupying Annoni while also working in multiple other sites allowed the MST to surprise and overwhelm government forces. Or in other words, deploying the extralegal tactic during a time of political instability and in a space where state authority was contested gave the movement an opportunity to grow. Meanwhile, a delegation was sent to Porto Alegre to persuade both the police and representatives in the office of the Secretary of Agriculture to allow the families to remain. The legal tactics of negotiating and meeting with political authorities were also displayed in a march of allies that totaled around fifty thousand people in 1986. Shortly after, in 1987, some families began acquiring titles. In that year, 35 families were settled in Annoni, while around 250 were taken to other areas in Rio Grande do Sul. Only in 1993 would the remaining 500 or so encamped families officially receive land.

Tactically and organizationally, the MST's political action at Annoni displayed what theorists of revolutionary contention would call consolidation, or as Eric Selbin notes, the revolutionary project is present in symbols, identity, and practices.⁹⁶ What was incorporated from the failed settlements in the Amazon, learned from past movements and religious organizations, and practiced at Nova Ronda Alta had become standardized among its membership. The families at Annoni were organized into health, hygiene, water, public relations, press, and cultural nucleos. The movement organizational dynamics had now grown to include groups meant to deal with external actors and more social, cultural concerns.⁹⁷ One nucleo decided to work and live entirely collectively. In what became COOPTAR (Cooperativa de Produção Agropecuária Cascata; Cascata Agricultural Production Cooperative), a couple dozen families decided to collectively manage land and inputs. At both Nova Ronda Alta and Annoni, the settled families—in collectives and individually—began to publicly sell, advertise, and promote their production.⁹⁸ Such displays not only served to show how agrarian reform was viable, but how the movement's adaptation of the Catholic Church's emphasis on collective economic production was materializing. By the mid-1980s, the Landless Movement had developed its tactical repertoire to such a degree that it could export it to other regions of the country.

The MST and its allied groups were not reconstituting a state form of claiming and administering territory, one based on distinguishing private from public authority, or bureaucratizing the exercise of sovereign power. Years before the LVC emerged and grounded its demand in the concept of food sovereignty, the MST and its allies were engaging in forms of resistance that claimed space to transform economic, political, and cultural relationships. Food sovereignty began to gain traction among radical rural movements in the 1990s and 2000s. The MST's manner of combining revolutionary contention with the sovereign, mutually exclusive claim to space shows how it was a movement that embraced food sovereignty before the LVC formalized and introduced the demand to a global audience.

The movement's consolidation of revolutionary political action challenged entrenched political and economic hierarchies. Unequal patterns of land ownership were directly contested, as were large landowners who were either investing in capital-intensive modes of production or simply choosing to let their land lie fallow. The Brazilian national security state sought to protect private property, both of foreign and domestic actors. The MST and its allies challenged the government's police forces and the institution of private property. Resistance also took place through various government institutions. Settlements, which had been an anti-movement technology used by the military government, became incorporated into the MST's struggle for agrarian reform. Mobilizing through government to construct an alternative meant adopting one mode of settling land and subsequently transforming it. Also, the PNRA granted the emerging movement legal justification for its demands, in addition to the Rural Land Statute from 1964. The former, however, included no explicit references to the legal nature of land occupations. As a result, land occupations retained their extralegal quality, while also giving the movement the chance to take the offensive by surprising landowners and government representatives. During this early moment of revolutionary consolidation, at a local level in southern Brazil, people from a variety of areas and who had been previously employed in different occupations were acquiring a new, more confrontational identity.

CONCLUSION: WHY THE SOUTH? (AND WHY NOT THE NORTHEAST?)

This chapter documents the emergence and early development of the MST and some of its key allies, with a particular focus on developments in southern Brazil. The initial organizers and families learned and adapted tactics from past movements that were active in the 1950s and 1960s. Failed INCRA settlements and the Catholic Church provided a means for the incipient movement to develop during the military regime's managed transition. As seen in the organizations developed at Nova Ronda Alta and Annoni, the movement had begun to consolidate its revolutionary practice of a decentralized, participatory manner of administering services. Many of the services—health care, education, security—were also provided by the Brazilian government. By leading occupations and encampments, the movement demanded those services in areas where the government was ill prepared to provide them. The families claimed space, defending it and themselves from police violence and economic exploitation. Throughout the territories that were claimed, the new Sem Terra identity, forms of collective production, and a decentralized mode of governance materially transformed prior social relations in ways that abolished institutionalized divisions between public and private power. In the early 1980s, we see the Landless Movement consolidate its form of revolutionary political action—not institutionalize it by reconstituting state forms of authority—in localized regions. At each of the key points referred to in this chapter—Encruzilhada Natalino, Nova Ronda Alta, and Annoni—the movement drew clear distinctions between friend and enemy, opened up opportunities for negotiation and further mobilizations, as well as engaged in organization building. By the mid-1980s, the MST was expanding its then consolidated form of revolutionary resistance throughout southern Brazil.

In the northeast, a wave of rural contention also developed during this time period, but not featuring the use of land occupations and the demand for settlements. Instead, rural workers went on strike. When rural workers were leading land occupations in Rio Grande do Sul, Paraná, and Santa Catarina, their northeastern counterparts—also with religious allies—went on strike on sugar plantations. Both the south and the northeast had long histories of rural resistance, with the Peasant Leagues—one of the movements claimed by the MST as a source of inspiration—emerging in Pernambuco. The regions were also witnessing rural displacement throughout the era of the Brazilian military government owing to the advance of capital-intensive forms of agricultural production. State, economic, and political conditions appeared virtually identical in both regions. Still, the first orchestrated efforts for agrarian reform in the region would take place in 1987, at Fazenda Projeto 4045 in the state of Bahia. Then, after a short period of relative calm in rural contention, in 1989 the Engenho do Complexo de Suape was occupied by MST activists. These activists were not from the northeast originally, but actually from the south—Jaime Amorim from Santa Catarina being one of the most central. The northeast would later become a stronghold for the movement, but only in the late 1980s and 1990s. This raises the question—why did the MST first emerge in the south and not the northeast?

The analysis of tactical and organizational development developed in this chapter explains why the Landless Movement emerged first in southern Brazil instead of elsewhere. Gabriel Ondetti also asks this question, arguing that the movement emerged in the south because of an easing of political repression and already-existing social networks.[99] While I agree with Ondetti's assessment, there are a few missing elements. First, what becomes apparent after tracing the contingent development of MST's tactical repertoire and organizations is the role of activists with distinct forms of knowledge from prior movements. Most centrally, in Rio Grande do Sul, settlers continued the history of MASTER, bringing into the MST the land occupation tactic as a means to pressure authorities. In Pernambuco, there was no equivalent to the Nonoai reserve in Rio Grande do Sul where members of past movements who had led land occupations, such as the Peasant Leagues, could escape to wait out the military regime. It is true that the regions featured different populations, with immigrant populations dedicated more to family farming in the south while descendants of slaves inhabited the northeast. Economically, the northeast was also dominated by sugarcane operations that resembled factories.

Economic and demographic differences, however, do not determine tactical and movement development. This is shown not only in the Landless Movement's growth in the region, especially in the 1990s, but also in acknowledging that past movements such as the Peasant Leagues successfully organized families to take land and create encampments. The practice of leading land occupations and creating encampments had a history in the region. What was lacking was continuity; or rather, what actually differentiates the south from the northeast, in terms of catalysts for the emergence of the Landless Movement, is the persistence of activists. In the Pernambuco, after his exile, the former left-wing governor of the state, Miguel Arraes, returned in 1979—not to help coordinate land reform initiatives, but to run for political office in the newly formed PMDB. Francisco Julião would also return to Brazil—but in 1991. In the south, activists kept the occupation tactic alive in their memories when they took refuge on the Nonoai reserve, and then had a chance to practice it once the military government began to break down.

A second crucial difference across the regions involves the Amazon. In Rio Grande do Sul, not only did former members of MASTER keep the memory of the land occupation tactic alive, but scores of displaced families who ventured into the Amazon returned to the region with stories of failed settlements. When they returned to Rio Grande do Sul, they were keenly aware of INCRA's efforts to create settlements. This return of families from failed settlement projects did not occur in the northeast. With past MASTER members and their tactical knowledge, the returning families decided to claim territory in their home state. The occupation-encampment-settlement trajectory of political action came into being in the south first, given the confluence of public policy and past movements. Revolutionary political action is not determined by activism solely, or by economic conditions. Rather, as is shown by comparing movement development in the south and northeast, it is a combination of the two.

Concluding this chapter with this brief discussion of the differences in the northeast and south serves a variety of objectives for studies of contention. First, collective action does not emerge spontaneously, but draws on long histories of prior resistance. Understanding how resistance unfolds requires tracing the histories of collective action. Leaders and organizers use, as well as adapt, lessons learned from this history. Families and organizers in the late 1970s did not copy the way in which MASTER led occupations or the way that INCRA developed settlements. Rather, the movement learned and adapted past actions for mobilizing within its historical reality. In the case of settlements, organizers actually took the settlement technology, which was at the time intended for national security purposes, and transformed it into one of its principal demands. In its emergence, as well as in its subsequent years, the Landless Movement made history, but not always as it wished or in circumstances that were entirely under its control.

4

MOBILIZING THROUGH NEOLIBERALISM

Revolutionary Persistence and Decline

NEW ADVERSARIES AND CHANGING CONDITIONS

IT WOULD BE AN understatement to describe the developments within Brazilian society during the 1980s and 1990s as eventful. Unprecedented mass mobilizations, led by the newly formed CUT (United Workers' Central), PT (Workers Party), MST (Landless Workers Movement), and other organizations, demanded direct elections (Direitas Já!) in the early 1980s. Strike activity and the proliferation of factory councils developed in response to restrictive labor laws, wage stagnation, and economic mismanagement. The twilight of military rule saw the drafting of a new constitution. Exorbitant rates of inflation left citizens wondering and worrying about the price of everything from bread to bus fare. Protests over a corruption scandal were mounted against the first directly elected president—Fernando Collor de Mello—in 1992. His resignation was followed by the administration of Fernando Henrique Cardoso (FHC) (1994–2002), who continued and deepened various neoliberal policies that dramatically reorganized politics and economics. Then, in 1995 and again in 1996, massacres of protesting landless activists left dozens dead, drawing domestic and international attention. The MST, along with other longtime landless allies such as the CNBB (National Conference of Brazilian Bishops) and CONTAG (National Confederation of Workers in Agriculture), led large demonstrations—the most exceptional being the 1997 march on Brasilia—to demand an end to impunity, new public policies, and land redistribution. In 2002, Luiz Inácio Lula da Silva—one of the principal leaders of the Direitas Já campaign—became president.

Such definitive events in Brazilian society took place against the backdrop of the extended processes of democratization and neoliberalization. Brazil became a paradigmatic case of "democracy with adjectives," which refers to the country's combination of free and fair elections and high levels of police violence and human rights violations. The 1990s was also a time when postmilitary political and economic institutions gained legitimacy.[1] Cardoso was the first democratically elected president to complete a term, and then gain reelection, after the military left power. Liberal democratic institutions, having emerged in the 1980s, were becoming consolidated. The FHC administration also initiated various social policies, namely Bolsa Escola (School Fund), which was expanded, renamed, and consolidated during the Lula government (2002–10) as Bolsa Familia (Family Fund). Economic institutions were innovated. With Cardoso's Plano Real, which he developed when serving as the minister of finance in the Itamar Franco administration (1992–94), inflation became manageable and a new currency—the real—was introduced. Wide-sweeping privatizations of state-owned enterprises, in steel, petrochemicals, and fertilizers, began during the Collor government (1990–92) and continued with the FHC administration. The partial privatization of the oil industry in 1997, which targeted Petrobras, opened gas and oil markets to potential foreign investment while also sparking union protests that were thoroughly repressed.

Similar changes during the 1990s around the continent resulted in a general decline and deradicalization of collective action. This trend in contentious political action not only in Brazil but around Latin America prompted Susan Eckstein to ask in the epilogue of *Power and Popular Protest: Latin American Social Movements*, Where have all the movements gone?[2] Many movements ceased conducting disruptive activities when liberal democracy offered formal options for participation. Sonia Alvarez noticed how neoliberal reforms led to professionalization in the feminist movement, which contributed to fragmentation and the marginalization of radical actors.[3] This tendency to isolate certain voices was checked by networks that promoted a collective identity.[4] The growing environmental movement, similarly, persisted throughout the 1990s via the formation of nonprofit organizations and its cooperation with government elites to develop public policies.[5] When confronting the changing conditions brought by democratization and neoliberalization, the PT and CUT steadily deradicalized.

This did not mean complete demobilization. The labor movement remained active in the 1990s, but in a more defensive manner. The PT, in a similar fashion, became ever-increasingly focused on winning elections instead of promoting and developing a revolutionary transformation of Brazilian society.

Scholars such as Theda Skocpol would predict such a trend, noting how the advent of liberal democratic structures of authority tends to spell the end of revolutionary movements. The MST and its allies, as this chapter makes clear, bucked the tendency. The movement's growth was seen in the movement's membership, the number of successful land occupations organized, and the land redistributed. In fact, the Cardoso administration—the same government mainly responsible for the institutionalization of neoliberalism in Brazil—redistributed more land than any other government. Moreover, as the movement grew, it retained the central qualities that make the Landless Movement a revolutionary actor—the claim to collective sovereignty to transform political, economic, and cultural relations within a certain space at the expense of state power. As Ivo Poletto notes, three actors—the Landless Movement, CUT, and the PT—arose at the same time in history and even with the assistance of the same religious allies.[6] Despite their common beginnings, each actor followed different paths as liberal democracy institutionalized and neoliberal restructuring unfolded. Explaining how the Landless Movement maneuvered the changing conditions brought with these two processes and remained involved in simultaneously expanding and consolidating its mode of revolutionary political action, while comparable actors did not, is the main concern of this chapter.

In six sections, this chapter focuses on the rise and decline of revolutionary contention during the late 1980s and throughout the 1990s. At this time, the MST remained the primary movement leading transformative changes in Brazilian society within the growing coalition of actors and allies that is known as the Landless Movement. I compare the practices of the CUT, PT, and MST to explain how the latter movement remained a force for transformational economic, political, and social change, while the CUT and the PT became more domesticated. The first section illustrates how these other actors also embodied revolutionary forms of action, analogous to the Landless Movement's combination of legal and extralegal tactics. Each of the three actors also claimed space to transform cultural, political, and economic relationships, most notably in the 1980s. In the second section, I show how neoliberal restructuring and the institutionalization of liberal democracy changed the conditions for collective action. Changes to the economy brought by neoliberalism especially weakened the labor movement's ability to consolidate revolutionary political action. The third section's focus is on how different state, government, and economic conditions interacted with each actor's tactical repertoire. We find that the CUT and PT, in response to different structural changes, adapted their tactics in ways that led to deradicalization. The MST and its allies did not face the same conditions. Furthermore, as I note in the fourth section, the movement adapted its repertoire of extralegal and legal tactics during the 1990s in ways that enabled its consolidated revolutionary project to expand. The fifth section returns to a comparison of the rise and fall of revolutionary contention across the three actors analyzed in this chapter, while the sixth section firmly establishes how the Landless Movement's mode of revolutionary resistance directly challenges the depoliticizing effects of neoliberal restructuring.

Few studies of the Landless Movement have documented the movement's ebbs and flows. Wendy Wolford's account notes differences in the movement regionally, but not over time.[7] Other studies focus on new conceptual ways to understand the movement's actions.[8] Gabriel Ondetti's study stands out in emphasizing the role of government in either facilitating or impeding mobilization. In the 1990s, he notes, the movement's growth was due to particular incentives offered by land occupations and the new constitution.[9] My explanation differs in two ways: first, by explicitly comparing the Landless Movement with other active movements in Brazil, and second, by providing an alternative theory with nuanced concepts that highlights the revolutionary nature of the movement. Comparing the CUT, PT, and the Landless Movement shows that we need to understand how tactics interacted with changing state, government, and economic conditions. Appealing to and using laws have been integral to the Landless Movement's tactical repertoire since the movement's origins. In the 1990s, the movement perfected and improved these tactics. In particular, the MST managed to adapt to the emerging neoliberal order and development of liberal democracy in ways that other actors could not. The Landless Movement, led by the MST, devised ways to politicize neoliberal reforms in ways that allowed the movement to expand its revolutionary form of political action. Similar to what was described in the previous discussion of the movement's incorporation of past policies and tactics, the MST and its allies mobilized through neoliberal policy to continue to claim space and transform social relations.

THE MST WAS NOT ALONE: REVOLUTIONARY UNIONS AND POLITICAL PARTIES

The CUT, PT, and MST were each calling for and practicing revolutionary change in the 1980s. From the MST's land occupations and encampments to CUT-affiliated unions organizing factory commissions and demanding fundamental changes to the labor code, these actors were mobilizing people in ways that challenged how Brazilian politics and economics had been organized for most of the twentieth century. In Brazil, as well as elsewhere, revolutionary slogans are never in short supply. The actual organizing of people to effectively participate in transformative, contentious modes of action, not just briefly but over time, is rare. Examining developments in Brazil during the 1980s helps us understand the dynamics of revolutionary transformation by focusing not so much on the demands, but on the concrete practices of these three individual actors.

Like the MST, the CUT and the PT formalized in the early 1980s. The MST's official founding congress was in 1984, with the CUT's taking place in 1983. While no single event is considered the formal starting point for the PT, meetings and discussions among workers, intellectuals, and politicians began in earnest in 1979. The 1980 drive to obtain legal recognition, on the heels of the military government's new law that regulated political parties in 1979 (A Lei Organica dos Partidos Politicos; Organic Law of Political Parties, Law 6767) prompted activists to mobilize people on a mass scale throughout Brazil. The MST, PT, and CUT allied with organizations affiliated with the Catholic Church, such as the CPT (Pastoral Land Commission), while many of their members often participated in the CEBs (Ecclesiastical Base Communities).

For the CUT, this connection between social actors and the urban-based working class promoted the development of what is known as "social-movement unionism." Definitive elements of this mode of unionism include participatory democracy, political autonomy, and societal transformation.[10] Concretely, CUT-affiliated unions defied the Brazilian labor code that had been on the books since Vargas's Estado Novo originated in the 1930s. Various elements of the legislation severely constrained the labor movement. For instance, the Vargas-era labor code allowed for the removal of certain leaders who were considered political or disruptive. Also, the labor law's *unicidade* clause prohibited union formation at the workplace, forcing unions to represent workers throughout abstract geographical areas. The Brazilian labor code configured political and economic relationships between members of the labor movement and government for decades.

Concerning revolutionary forms of organization, the labor movement promoted the formation of factory commissions. In São Paulo, worker-led commissions decentralized decision-making within factories and challenged the prevailing authoritarian factory culture and manner of dismissing employees.[11] The CUT's demand for autonomy encapsulated the intention and practice to create such decentralized, worker-managed unions. In effect, the commissions were decision-making organs that were independent of both already-existing political parties and government institutions. Furthermore, factory commissions, akin to the MST's occupations and encampments, were claims to space. For the labor movement, the space claimed was the factory. The formation of commissions directly challenged the Brazilian labor code and the government that enforced its mode of recognizing unions. Attempts to control production at the factory level also struck at state authority, given the defiance of the labor code's *unicidade* provision. Leaders and members collectively, through commissions, sought to revolutionize cultural, political, and economic relations.

The PT also sought transformative changes. Just as the MST inherited the CEB's style of organization, the PT also developed small-group decision-making processes. Small groups had the principal objective of sending local representatives to higher levels in the party. Party nucleos were to develop everywhere, including the workplace and the neighborhood. Like the CUT's social movement connections, the PT's nucleos intended to break down and transform already-existing political and economic divisions in society. Despite initial challenges with the military's legislation, the party found a way to "superimpose" its decentralized, grassroots nucleo structure onto the government's official regulations for political parties.[12] This entailed that in addition to meeting the requirements of the 1979 law, the PT included further requirements to generate a more democratic, participatory internal organization. The party's transformative claim to space was in the various areas where it mobilized and incorporated social actors into its ranks. The party had this revolutionary quality: while following the legal requirements then in place, it worked through them to build an alternative in specific areas.

Early union mobilization began in a repressive, heavily regulated environment in the late 1970s. The military government's vulnerability became apparent in economic problems, including the regime's announcement in 1977 that it had manipulated inflation statistics from 1973 and 1974. After learning this, workers in the São Bernardo do Campo Metalworkers' Union began a wage recovery campaign. This mobilization, given that it was not exactly a strike, had an ambiguous quality. Authorities allowed the campaign to continue. Later, when strikes were led—and authorities became involved—the unions managed to maneuver the police and military forces by stopping and starting their actions around the time frame set by the Brazilian labor courts.[13] Strikes, per se, were heavily regulated and essentially illegal. The way the labor movement led and organized them revealed an extralegal quality by evading legal sanctions.

The strike waves in 1978, 1979, and 1980 built off of economic and government instability. Taking advantage of the military government's political vulnerability that came from its admission that it had manipulated inflation stats, workers began mobilizing in the industrial ABC region—the cities of Santo André, São Bernardo do Campo, and São Caetano do Sul—in São Paulo state. São Bernardo especially occupied a privileged position in the overall Brazilian economy. At the apex of the wage pyramid, and the center of the military's industrial development strategy, the workers could take greater risks when compared to other unions from sectors of the economy that were not government priorities. The formation of unions in factories and the direct targeting of employers were unprecedented. The military was "temporarily stunned into inaction," while the employers who were losing money with workers on strikes opened negotiations and agreed to demands in 1979.[14] This success created further opportunities for mobilization, as workers continued to organize large strike assemblies to debate and decide on their course of action.

Unstable economic conditions contributed to the destabilization of the military government's legitimacy throughout the second half of the 1970s. Central to the military government's economic project was wage suppression, which was complemented by incentives for foreign direct investment and the repression of any organized resistance from workers. At this time, balance of payments problems ensued when imports exceeded exports and the uptick in oil prices caused the price of imports to rise. To counter this problem, the military government took out foreign loans without altering their import-heavy industrialization policy. Economic surpluses turned into deficits, which the military government addressed through printing money, thus causing inflation. Extralegal tactics, in the form of striking at the workplace, helped make these economic conditions into an opportunity to build alternative organizations and continue subsequent mobilization.

The 1980s were a time when both the PT and CUT grew. The passing of the new law regulating political parties was the latest change in the military government's process of *abertura* (opening). Effectively disbanding the two officially recognized parties, the government sought to change the party system in a way that would destabilize opposition forces. The PT, despite having to file officially and follow strict legal protocols to participate in the 1982 elections, managed to amass enough support to receive provisional recognition. At this time, the party claimed over two hundred thousand members, from various radical left-wing groups, unions, neighborhood associations, and religious organizations.[15] Many of the radical currents present in its membership were opposed to the Stalinist, more vanguard, and hierarchical PCB (Brazilian Communist Party), which chose to remain connected to the PMDB (Brazilian Democratic Movement Party).[16] Meanwhile, unions mobilized over three million workers in a variety of strikes and factory occupations in 1979.[17]

Throughout the 1980s, union mobilizations continued to challenge dominant political, economic, and cultural structures. Striking for higher wages contested the government for its policy of price indexing. Challenging the legitimacy of the labor code continued, with the organization of factory commissions and demands for union independence. As a result, CUT representatives helped to enshrine in the 1988 constitution special provisions to guarantee union autonomy from government intervention. For the PT, disappointing results from elections in 1982 were followed by greater electoral successes in the mayoral contests of 1985 and 1988, and the presidential election of 1989. Cultural changes were promoted by the CUT and the PT in their emphasis on autonomy and authenticity. These actors were claiming "the right to have rights," affirming a new, contentious identity rooted in an amplified understanding of citizenship that stood in opposition to status quo modes of conduct.[18]

State conditions at this time were also unstable, but not in the same way as found in rural areas. First, rural to urban migration continued throughout the military regime. Urbanization was not a new phenomenon, but by the 1970s the flow of people to large urban areas such as Recife, São Paulo, and Porto Alegre was beginning to cause concern among governing elites. Most importantly for our understanding of the state, many of the new urban inhabitants were living on the urban periphery, in areas without formal property rights.[19] While this was an economic issue given the precariousness of labor markets and resource inequality, the trend also presented a problem for state authority because government authorities lacked the ability to track where people lived. In addition, international creditors weakened the Brazilian government's claim to sovereignty. The government in the 1980s attempted to limit capital controls, but ultimately refrained because of the need for foreign loans and World Bank aid.[20] The effect of oil prices, which particularly hurt the military's industrialization goals, also shows how the government's ability to claim sovereignty over affairs within the Brazilian territory was weakened. State sovereignty was weakened by domestic and international factors.

Both the PT and the CUT were challenging, with the support of millions, political, economic, and social relations throughout Brazilian society. *How* these actors practiced their resistance—in terms of their tactics, namely of the extralegal variety—was just as important as the alternative organizations that emerged. Along with the MST, these three actors deployed innovative tactics that created revolutionary political action by working in and through the state to transform culture, politics, and economics in certain areas. Each actor had to navigate, within ten or so years of their emergence, neoliberal restructuring *and* democratization. These changing conditions would impact their tactics, as well as the prospects for the persistence and consolidation of their respective revolutionary modes of political action.

NEOLIBERALISM, DEMOCRATIZATION, AND THE CONSTITUTIONAL CONVENTION

The changes brought by neoliberal restructuring and the development of liberal democracy are often conflated. With phrases like "free markets," political and economic processes are sometimes equated in popular discourse. The logic is that if capitalism is freedom, then non-capitalism must be *un*freedom, tyranny, despotism, and so on. In the early 1980s, Milton Friedman issued a ten-part video series—*Free to Choose*—proclaiming precisely this point: that freeing markets from government oversight leads to personal and economic prosperity. The end of state socialism in the Soviet Union and Eastern Europe apparently confirmed Friedman's project. In these regions, new political parties emerged and competitive elections took place following mass protests, while state-owned enterprises were privatized, prices indexes ended, and financial markets liberalized. These changes took place during what Samuel Huntington calls the "third wave of democratization," which was also spreading throughout Latin America.[21] Liberal democracies replaced authoritarian governments. Governments began to feature competitive elections, the toleration of public manifestations of discontent, and initiatives to institutionalize the rule of law. Neoliberalization and democratization, generally, took place at the same time. The processes characteristic of each, however, are distinct.

Throughout the continent, the development of neoliberalism occurs in two time periods. The first, commonly referred to as the "Washington Consensus," began in the late 1970s in countries like Chile and Argentina and extends from the early 1980s to the mid and late 1990s in Mexico, Brazil, and elsewhere. The subsequent "post-Washington Consensus" continues to the present day. The division is rooted in differences between macroeconomic reforms focused on privatizing state-owned enterprises, reforming monetary policies, and removing import tariffs,[22] and other subsequent efforts grounded in promoting local actor participation in social programs and granting greater autonomy to national governments to craft development strategies.[23] Jamie Peck and Adam Tickell summarize this shift as "rollback" versus "rollout" neoliberalism,[24] with the shift a direct response to perceived failures by elites who oversaw the first round of reforms. "Rollback," contrary to "rollout's" more macro approach, involves micro, or localized, practices meant to cultivate individual entrepreneurship and responsibility. From Mexico to Argentina, principally in the 1980s and 1990s, people and markets were "freed" from government regulations.

The Brazilian experience offers various insights for understanding the unfolding of democratization and neoliberalism. With respect to democratization, the political party law in 1979, while attempting to privilege the regime's representatives, was also motivated by the military's goal of managing growing civil unrest. The repeal of AI-5 in 1979 restored civil liberties, and direct elections for state governors were permitted in 1982. Since 1964, the military's electoral college had ensured through indirect elections that a military officer would retain executive power. This changed when a civilian—Tancredo Neves—was selected to succeed João Figueiredo in 1985. Neves's death shortly after his election led to José Sarney assuming power; Sarney was a member of the military government's Partido Democratico Social (PSD; Social Democratic Party). At this time, even as the military's 1967 Constitution was in force, it was also widely considered illegitimate because the administration granted itself the power to suspend it. Such a government opening and legitimacy crisis made the debates concerning a new constitution—from both the left and the right—notably intense and protracted in the mid-1980s.

The resulting 1988 Constitution, along with direct elections for the president in 1989, heralded the efforts to restore the institutions characteristic of liberal democracy. For unions, the new constitution removed interference in their internal affairs. It did not make any significant changes to the principal of *unicidade*, or the union tax, which channeled resources to recognized unions for the administration of social services. The document institutionalized a series of decentralizing government initiatives, most notably instituting municipal, state, and national-level councils (*conselhos*) in various policy areas. Councils, however, were not created in macroeconomic policy, or in economic matters more generally. As a demand from more left-leaning actors, such as the PT, the decentralized councils were to function as consultative organs that involved government and social actors in the crafting and development of social policies in areas such as education and health care.

Debates over agrarian reform were particularly heated during and after the constitutional convention. In the 1980s, the principal law concerning agrarian reform remained the 1964 Rural Land Statute. The statute sanctioned expropriation, with payment in government bonds, when a property owner violated the law's social function clause (*função social*). To adhere to the social function clause, an owner would have to actively display a concern for social well-being, respect labor laws, and practice natural resource conservation. Despite the existence of these de jure conditions for expropriation, which it would seem could be mobilized by left-wing actors, landowners remained confident that their property was protected. Specifically, the military's use of repression and colonization schemes assured large landowners that their interests were protected.

These dynamics changed with the relative instability brought about by the return of civilian rule, as well as with Sarney's Programma Nacional de Reforma Agrária (PNRA; National Agrarian Reform Plan) in 1985. The PNRA promised to redistribute a little over 43 million acres to 1.4 million people. Worse for landed interests, the decree recognized the legitimacy of the 1964 Rural Land Statute without the military government's national security regime's politically and economically motivated periodic repression or colonization efforts into the Amazon. Property again appeared vulnerable, due to the underlying problems in state authority that date from Brazil's colonial and postcolonial property regime.

As a way to respond to movements such as the MST that were leading occupations throughout much of Brazil's south and southeast, large landowners formed their own organization, the União Democrática Ruralista (UDR; Democratic Rural Union). Central to the UDR's mission was exerting pressure on the Constitutional Assembly delegates and intimidating rural workers. At the time of the UDR's emergence, its spokesperson, Senator Ronaldo Caiado, claimed to have organized over six thousand members.[25] The organization's major achievement in the 1988 Constitution was enshrining that productive property could not be redistributed (article 185). The UDR's actions outside of the Constitutional Convention challenged any coordinated support for agrarian reform, often violently. One of the organization's leaders from the northern state of Acre, Darcy Alves, was tried and convicted for the 1988 murder of rural union activist Chico Mendes. While not exclusively linked to the UDR, violence on the part of rural landowners remained fairly constant throughout the period of redemocratization, resulting in reducing the number of people who mobilized for agrarian reform after the new constitution was passed in 1988.[26]

While the social function clause became part of the articles within the constitution concerning agrarian reform, large landowners used violence and promoted the inclusion of other articles that established barriers to expropriation. What the 1988 Constitution enshrined, thus, was a series of liberal democratic institutions—free and fair elections, with limited intervention in economic affairs and productive private property protected.

Legal changes brought with the constitution touched on, but did not effectively change, the extralegal nature of land occupations and encampments. In the constitution we find that the executive retains the privilege to redistribute land. Also, only land considered latifundio—not small or medium-sized operations—and that is not serving its social function can be subject to agrarian reform measures. What classifies a property as latifundio remained the same

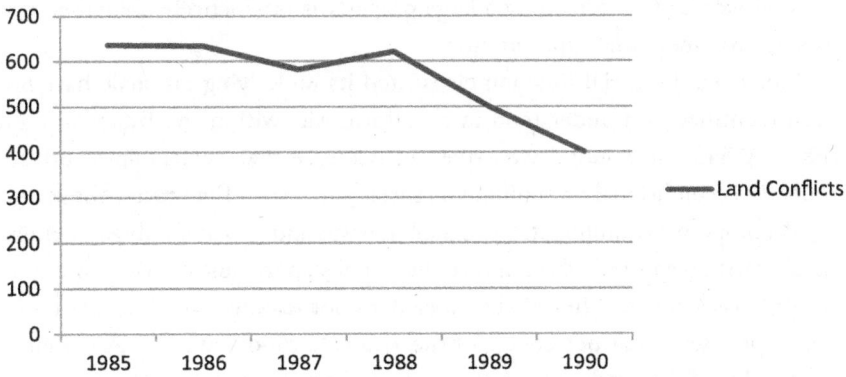

FIGURE 11 Land conflicts, 1985–1990. CPT, *Conflitos no Campo*, 1991.

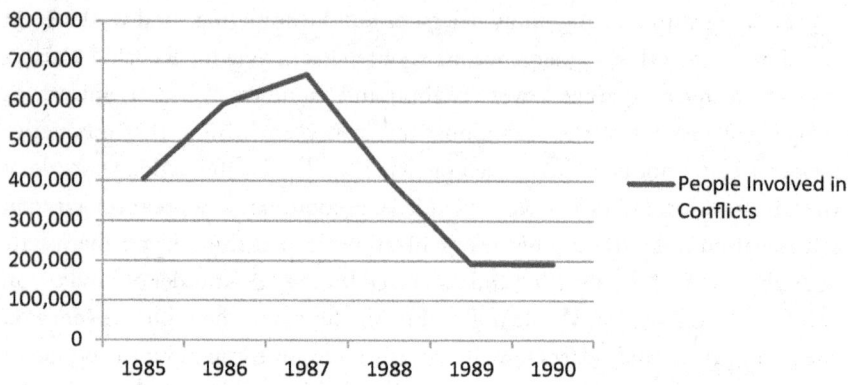

FIGURE 12 People involved in conflicts, 1985–1990. CPT, *Conflitos no Campo*, 1991.

as in the 1964 Rural Land Statute. In that law, latifundio is primarily defined in terms of size—varying between municipalities, according to the unit of measurement known as *modulo fiscal* (fiscal module). According to the statute, properties over one hundred fiscal modules—on average this means a property with thousands of hectares—qualify. The constitution relies on the Rural Land Statute for the size criteria, adding a few other stipulations to the social function clause. As listed in article 184, an owner must rationally and adequately use a property, as well as respect environmental and labor laws. Precise requirements concerning rational and adequate use for a particular area are later specified in Law 8629/1993. According to this law, which was passed over seven years after the constitution, at least 80 percent of an operation must be in production. Or in other words, if 80 percent of a large property is productively used, then it is exempt from potential expropriation.

Moreover, the social function clause and its underlying rationale have not been identified and understood in a uniform way within the Brazilian legal order. A São Paulo judge even ruled in one case that ownership of private property is conditional on fulfilling its social function.[27] The process for verifying if a property is fulfilling its social function was and remains ambiguous, most notably with respect to who can take the initial step to indicate which property requires assessment. After all, territory does not feature signs that notify the public precisely what percentage of the area is in productive use. An attempt to liberalize the procedure for expropriation, Decree 2250 from 1997, states that nongovernment actors may "indicate to federal authorities" (*indicar ao órgão fundiário federal*) which lands to expropriate. Still, even with such additional legislation, how one can "indicate" is left unspecified.

Redistributive efforts initiated by the Sarney administration were negligible. The government expropriated only 748 properties between 1985 and 1989. The administration met 6 percent of the PNRA's family targets and 10 percent of the land that was also planned for expropriation. The MST, during this time, concentrated much of its efforts on remaining on the Annoni ranch in Rio Grande do Sul. Given the press attention and focus of the movement's actions, Annoni became synonymous with the MST. The early years of democratization were a mix of successes and failures for the MST and its allies, plagued by entrenched battles on ranches, with landowners, and in government. On the one hand, the political conditions looked favorable for mobilization because of the retreat of the military. On the other, the constant threat and use of violence by social actors such as the UDR routinely repressed rural worker mobilization.

CHANGING ECONOMIC CONDITIONS AND REPRESSION DURING NEOLIBERAL RESTRUCTURING

Sarney was in office at the time of the Constitutional Convention, as well as during the demise of Brazil's state-centered development model. Inflation remained a problem in the new democracy. From 1980 to 1990, the annual rate of inflation was 529 percent, with 1985–89 averaging 980 percent.[28] Sarney's three economic plans—Plano Cruzado 1, Plano Cruzado 2, and the Plano Verão—provided momentary stabilization, which was then followed by increased periods of economic instability. Wage and price freezes, followed by the introduction of a new currency, the cruzeiro, failed to address economic instability. The CUT was particularly active at this time because of the negative effects of inflation on working-class people's incomes. Through the 1980s the union movement grew in terms both of membership and strike activity. From 1985 to 1990, the number of strikes quadrupled, going from 927 to 3,943, and the number of participants jumped from over six million to twenty million.[29] The era has been considered the CUT's "golden years," as high inflation, wage freezes, and low unemployment provided favorable economic conditions for the labor movement's growth and expansion.[30]

Neoliberal restructuring begins during the administration of Fernando Collor de Mello in 1990. With the Plano Collor, tariffs on foreign goods were eliminated and privatizations began of state-owned enterprises in the steel, petrochemical, and fertilizer industries.[31] In agricultural policy, Collor ended price-fixing policies for particular crops and cut investment subsidies.[32] Privatizations targeted the public sector, including businesses such as Petrobras and the Caixa Econômica. During the military government, public sector industries in agriculture, technology, and infrastructure, among others, were used not only to integrate and industrialize Brazil, but also to accumulate large quantities of foreign debt. These state-owned enterprises also became a place for distributing political patronage in the form of employment. By Collor's election, almost half of all Brazilian state-owned enterprises were reporting losses.[33] Cuts that began during the Collor administration continued through the following Franco era (1992–94) and the first mandate of FHC (1994–98).[34]

Accompanying neoliberalism's "rollout" were various tactical measures introduced by government authorities against radical political actors. For example, the Collor administration became known for calling on individual CUT leaders to negotiate as a way to create divisions within the labor movement, using the labor courts to declare most strikes illegal, and expressing support for the less-radical, pro-government union, Força Sindical (Union Force).[35] The Collor government used already-existing institutions to incorporate and domesticate the more radical elements within the labor movement. For the MST, repression took more overt and violent forms. Members at this time report the extensive use of wiretaps to collect information on activists, infiltration of movement encampments and settlements by police forces, and the arbitrary arrest of various activists.[36] The difference between how the government engaged with the MST and the CUT shows a more forceful, if not repressive, approach with rural movements. Furthermore, only twenty-eight properties were expropriated during Collor's time in office. The movement for agrarian reform was at a virtual standstill as a result of this brief, yet focused attempt to stifle popular mobilization. Collor's impeachment for corruption scandals destabilized the government in 1992, which led to a reprieve from government repression.

Neoliberal restructuring continued with further privatizations during FHC's first term (1994–98). One of the main actions at this time was the continued, focused attempt to privatize the oil and natural gas sector. The constitution reserved special protections dating back to the Vargas era for the industries within this sector, specifically Petrobras. Anticipating the privatization, workers at Petrobras planned a strike to oppose the government's attempts. Once initiated, the FHC administration paid special attention to how the strike was perceived by the public, citing the past successful privatizations in the early 1990s of Embraer and Usiminas to mobilize the general public in its favor.[37] This helped the government gain legitimacy for their actions and create divisions within the union's membership. Other actions taken by the government included purchasing oil stockpiles from foreign companies so that supply would not be disrupted during the dispute and preparing substitution workers for the strikers who walked the picket line. Various refineries were occupied by troops, and thousands of strikers, among them various labor leaders, lost their jobs. Breaking the thirty-two-day strike was considered a major accomplishment for the continuation of the neoliberal project. Specifically, opposing the union showed the degree to which the government would openly confront the public sector and embrace privatization.[38] It also led to changes in the Brazilian Constitution, whereby Petrobras's monopoly in the petrochemical industry ended after the government's carefully planned and executed campaign.

The effects of neoliberalism were disastrous for the CUT and more radical elements in the labor movement. First, the privatizations of public sector firms created unemployment. In the 1980s, unions had more leverage against the state-owned enterprises and private businesses when there was little to no fear of job loss. This changed with FHC's privatizations. As a result, the character of strikes changed—from more offensive actions in the 1970s and 1980s that surprised elites through leading general strikes and promoting councils, to defensive practices oriented around keeping wages steady and returning workers to their jobs.[39] Second, economic stabilization from FHC's monetary policy negatively affected the labor movement's selection of targets. For the unions, inflation was a double-edged sword—on the one hand, high inflation hurt economically marginalized sectors of a population who lacked access to foreign currency and were more dependent on domestic industry. This generated an interest among union membership for inflation to end. Yet, inflation facilitated union mobilization and confrontation. During the time of hyperinflation in the 1980s especially, unions regularly led strikes for wage increases to counter the effects of inflation. The CUT, and other unions, kept their membership mobilized and focused on attacking government policies that were failing. FHC's Plano Real removed this economic condition from engagement. Starting in 1994, inflation fell 40 percent per month to 10 percent in 1996. Without this destabilizing economic condition that also weakened government legitimacy, the labor movement lost a target and a guaranteed way to mobilize its members.

Another change in economic conditions that was not directly a result of FHC's policies, but still deleterious for the labor movement, was the introduction of labor-reducing technologies. In the banking sector—which contained some of the CUT's more combative unions—new technologies removed the need for tellers. The steel industry also incorporated technological innovations in the 1990s that led to a decrease in union membership. During this time, the percentage of Brazilian workers in the formal sector dropped from 56 percent to 42 percent, contributing to the rapid growth in the informal, nonunionized sector.[40] On various fronts, the labor movement saw economic conditions present a series of difficulties. The stabilization of economic conditions—in cutting inflation, adopting labor-saving technologies, and privatizing the public sector—changed movement tactics, away from offensive, more extralegal action and forms of organization to defensive modes of contention.

A DIFFERENT STORY: NEOLIBERALISM AND REPRESSION IN THE COUNTRYSIDE

The international context during and following the Petrobras strike showed how the Brazilian state's claim to sovereignty was weak. Neoliberal restructuring, especially in its rollout phase through the early and mid-1990s came as a result of the U.S.-inspired and promoted Washington Consensus. The need to suppress the strike was thus related to the Cardoso regime following a set of policies that originated outside of Brazil. Meanwhile, for Brazil to pay off the large foreign debt it had accrued during the 1970s and 1980s, the government required periodic loans from the IMF. In 1998, this led the government to propose further cuts to multiple social programs.[41] International actors, in the examples mentioned above, hindered the Brazilian government's ability to control certain policies. State conditions remained contested and unstable throughout the 1990s owing to the persistent vulnerability of territorial authority. The MST, on various occasions, used its tactical repertoire to exploit this vulnerability.

Economic conditions in rural areas during the early years of FHC's government differed from urban developments. The 1995–96 agricultural census marks the first time that the total number of people working on farms *decreased* in absolute terms—with 23,394,919 people registered in the 1985 census and 17,930,890 in 1996. Rates of people working per operation also continued to fall

TABLE 3 Agricultural Production, 1980s–1990s

	1985	1995
Tractors	665,280	799,742
Hectare per tractor average	94:1	62:1
Workers	23,394,919	17,930,890
Worker per operation	4.03	3.69
Owner operators	3,539,189	3,393,946
Nonowner operators	2,031,712	1,232,512

Source: *Censo Agricola, Censo Agropecuario*, 1985, 1995–1996.

during this time, from 4.03 in 1985 to 3.69 in 1996, owing to the increased use of fertilizers and capital goods in agricultural production. From 1990 to 2000, the total consumption of fertilizers would increase from over three million tons used in 1990 to six million in 2000, while acreage used for grains remained for the most part constant (thirty-five million hectares in 1992 and thirty-eight million in 2000).[42] The fall in worker per operation shows how trends that began during the military government, in terms of an increase of investment in capital-intensive sectors of the agricultural economy such as soy cultivation, were continuing. Thus, agricultural transformation and development continued to displace people throughout the 1990s.

What is particularly relevant for our analysis of economic conditions are the figures of nonowner operators. The people in this category tend to occupy the exceptionally marginalized rungs of the rural agricultural hierarchy—sharecroppers, tenant farmers, and so on. In 1985, there were over 2 million people in this category, falling to around 1.2 million by the mid-1990s. This decrease prompts the question: where did the nonowner operators go? Again, looking at the census, we find that they did not become farmers. That the number of proprietors *fell* during this time—from 3,539,189 in 1985 to 3,393,946—shows that more people did not acquire land titles. What is most likely, especially given historical demographic trends in terms of rural to urban migration, is that this population left the countryside for the urban periphery. Or rather, in the midst of technological change, changing labor relations in rural areas remained precarious, perhaps more so.

Regarding political conditions, the government's management of conflict in the countryside differed when compared to urban areas. Conflicts that parallel the Petrobras strike in 1995, at least in terms of impact on movements, include the events surrounding two massacres of protesting landless workers in the states of Roraima and Pará. While the FHC administration delicately orchestrated the confrontation with urban labor movement, in rural Brazil the government was far less strategic. In both actions, police forces opened fire on protesters, killing dozens. What took place in Pará, near Eldorado das Carajás, was recorded and broadcast domestically and internationally. It even spurred the creation of a sympathetic Brazilian soap opera, *O Rei do Gado* (King of the Herd). Shortly before the events, FHC dismissively labeled the MST as part of an "archaic Brazil" that was an impediment to "modernity."[43] Following the events at Eldorado dos Carajás, and the public outcry, Cardoso responded by calling the events "unacceptable." Still, instead of personally visiting the site of the conflict, the minister of justice, Nelson Jobim, was sent. Cardoso was later criticized for stating that "the events took place in Pará, but were not indicative of greater trends in Pará" (*no Pará, mas não do Pará*). Using "*no*" instead "*do*" was an attempt to localize and regionalize the conflict, or in other words, downplay its significance. Whereas the FHC administration carefully planned its actions when engaging labor unions in the petrochemical industry, with the MST and agrarian reform, the government showed little initial concern.

The reality was that these massacres were not isolated events, but actually part of a general increase in conflicts over land and resources. Over the course of the 1990s, we see an upsurge of conflicts over territory, from approximately 300,000 in 1993 to 700,000 in 2000. The number of people involved, likewise, tripled over the course of the decade. Also during the 1990s, the MST became entrenched in states such as Pernambuco, and initiated systematic efforts to

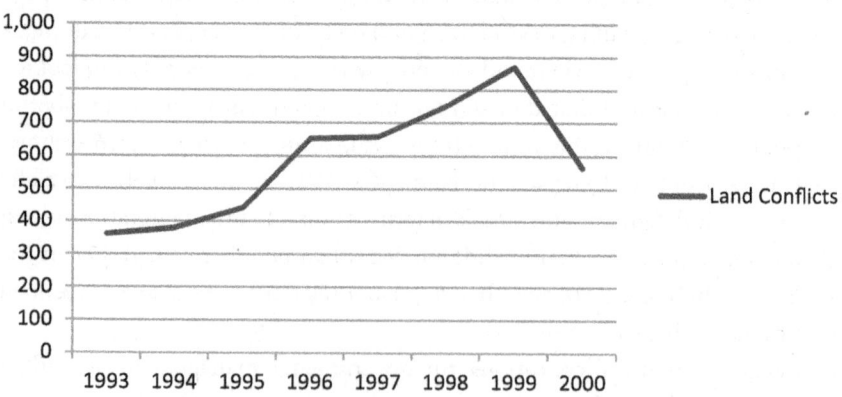

FIGURE 13 Land conflicts, 1993–2000. CPT, *Conflitos no Campo*, 2000.

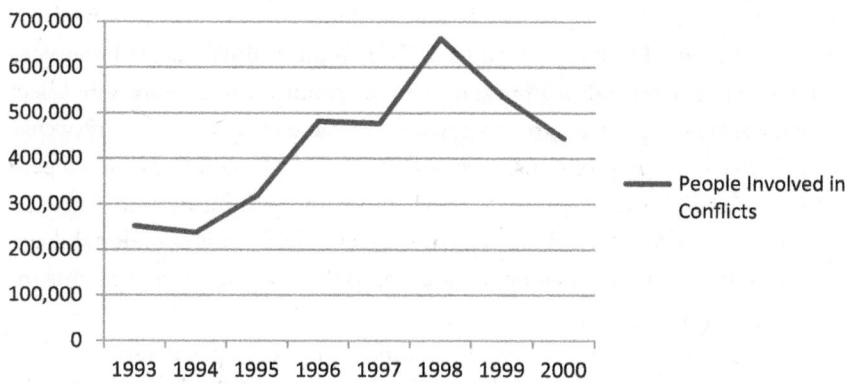

FIGURE 14 People involved in land conflicts, 1993–2000. CPT, *Conflitos no Campo*, 2000.

expand into the Amazonian states of Pará, Maranhão, and Tocantins.[44] At this time, more than before, the movement's revolutionary project expanded in territorial reach throughout Brazil.

What makes the particular acts of repression—principally by nonstate actors—different from the 1980s was how it was covered in the media. As Ondetti emphasizes, media coverage "indirectly" led to the increase in mobilization and calls for agrarian reform.[45] Movement actions in the early 1980s in Rio Grande do Sul most notably were also covered by a variety of media sources. Events such as the occupation and encampment at Encruzilhada Natalino generated sympathy for the incipient movement, while coverage remained relatively local. Coverage of the mid-1990s massacres, besides the favorable soap opera, reached more Brazilians, as well as international activists. Shortly after events in the 1990s, international solidarity groups—known as the Friends of the MST—sprung up throughout the United States and in various European countries. Continuing to this day, these organizations host activists and facilitate the collection of funds for the MST.

NEOLIBERALIZING THE AFTERMATH OF REPRESSION

Protests and public outcry after the massacres led to a series of new programs and redistribution efforts. The Lumiar project, for example, featured a new, decentralized approach to providing technical assistance for small producers.

Social actors, many from the MST and its allies, were trained and involved. The World Bank, through the Cédula da Terra project, also dedicated resources to financing a decentralized program where families would peacefully select areas for acquisition, then agree to purchase the land over the course of twenty years. New education programs, such as PRONERA (Programa Nacional para Educação na Reforma Agrária; National Program for Education in Agrarian Reform), were also initiated. Media coverage and public response destabilized government conditions, opening institutions to the demands of movements for changes in the countryside.

Many of the changes in political conditions that took place during FHC's second mandate (1998–2002), while addressing some of the Landless Movement's demands, also mark the transition from "rollout" to "rollback" neoliberalism. The intent to neoliberalize agrarian reform became central to the FHC administration's general statement on problems in the countryside, featured in the document *Reforma agrária: Compromisso de todos* (Agrarian Reform: Everyone's Commitment). This change in agricultural policy, which favors the *agricultor familiar* (family farmer), simultaneously displaces the *camponês* (peasant). To create policies for the family farmer, a new institution was created—the Ministério de Desenvolvimento Agrário (MDA; Ministry of Agrarian Development). In one interview with an MDA official who works in the FHC-created Secretário de Agricultura Familiar (SAF; Office of the Secretary of Family Farming), I was told how the MDA's targeted credit and loan policies were intended for "family farmers, you know, like what you have there in the United States."[46] Others in INCRA would use "farmer" (in English) to distinguish between Brazilian "peasants" and the supposedly superior U.S. "farmer."[47] In what the government called the Novo Mundo Rural (New Rural World), every small producer was to receive the same treatment by "integrating agrarian reform beneficiaries into family farming."[48] To "integrate," the already-existing credit policy for agrarian reform beneficiaries, O Programa de Crédito Especial para a Reforma Agrária (PROCERA; Special Program for Agrarian Reform Credit), tripled from R$89 million in 1995 to R$250 million in 1998.

The language—expressed by both INCRA and MDA officials as well as found in the *Compromisso* and PRONAF criteria to receive credit—depicts agricultural production by the family-farmer-as-business as superior to peasant ways of producing and as a goal of government policy. "Integration" is a step on the path toward creating "efficient," market-oriented economic producers. Agrarian reform policies, and credit, work as instruments in the state-led effort to localize neoliberal restructuring, encouraging a market-oriented ethic, or culture, among recipients. Experts, from officials in the MDA to INCRA, administer and deliver these credits to agrarian reform beneficiaries, along with the knowledge and ethic of family farming.

PROCERA was later eliminated when agrarian reform beneficiaries were absorbed into the already-existing credit policy for small producers known as the Programa Nacional de Fortalecimento da Agricultura Familiar (PRONAF; National Program for Strengthening Family Farming). The practices constitutive of PRONAF further sought to instill neoliberal conduct at the microlevel. First, families that are agrarian reform beneficiaries receive credit that they are expected to repay. The goal is to promote business proprietorship and an ethic of entrepreneurial responsibility. To qualify, recipients must meet certain group-based requirements, divided according to gender, age and, most importantly, income. According to the Brazilian Central Bank, one of the primary providers of PRONAF credit, the program is meant to "stimulate profit-generation by improving the application of technology and the use of a family's labor."[49] Echoing the Central Bank's goals, the Banco do Brasil (Bank of Brazil) adds that PRONAF is supposed to "insert family farming into the agribusiness production chain."[50] The allusion to responsibility fuses market principles and imperatives—the pursuit of profit—with the family, fashioning the latter out of the former. Despite the group-based classification system, the focus is almost entirely on individuals: the overwhelming percentage of recipients have been individuals (98 percent between 1999 and 2004), with little to no money given to or contracts signed with cooperatives or group associations (2 percent), or devoted to projects for infrastructure.[51] Such subjects, whom van der Ploeg calls "agricultural entrepreneurs," are supposed to exist fully within the capitalist exchange economy.[52]

Another of the FHC administration's attempts to neoliberalize agricultural policy involved land titling and redistribution. The efforts became known as *emancipação* (emancipation). Its goal—which some call neoliberal because of an emphasis placed on privatization—is for families to pay back the government for the property and any credits they received.[53] The idea is to "free" or emancipate families from INCRA's oversight, programs, and policies. This notion is also found in the constitution (article 189), where it is stated that titles for recipients will last ten years. What specifically will happen after this time is not explored. In 2001, FHC attempted to place limits on titles by specifying that *titulos de concessão* (TCs; concessionary titles) would be held for ten years, which would then become *titulos de dominio* (TDs; definitive titles). With TCs, families can use the land and receive government support without the right to sell or rent the property. Gaining a TD enables the sale and rent of land, but also requires that people purchase the land and repay any credits they received for housing or economic production. Government support is intended, from the *emancipação* perspective, to create self-sufficient, individualistic proprietors who eventually own their land and exist independently of social programs and services.

EXPLAINING PERSISTENCE AND DECLINE: ADAPTING TACTICS TO CHALLENGE NEOLIBERALISM

The end of the military government, advent of democratization, and rise of neoliberalism decreased centralized state repression and promoted decentralized approaches to policy. Neoliberal restructuring led to a rise of urban unemployment and increased the size of the informal economy, while also stabilizing monetary policy. Decentralizing political power was supported by left-wing unions and parties that mobilized during the transition away from military rule and during the drafting of the 1988 Constitution. This potential, or even unintentional, combination of neoliberal policy imperatives with democratic principles is what Dagnino calls the "perverse confluence."[54] The danger is for social actors to promote policies in the name of decentralization and participation, which seems to connote empowerment, but ultimately contributes to economic processes that exacerbate inequality and marginalization. A comparison of the PT, CUT, and the MST, as well as the growing Landless Movement, illustrates how the latter actors managed in the 1990s to extend their revolutionary mode of political action while avoiding the danger of conflating neoliberalism with democratic practice.

For the PT, signs of deradicalization were already present in the early 1980s. Focusing more on winning elections through mass appeals, the party began in the mid-1980s to drop its more combative class-based rhetoric with references to the more inclusive, amorphous middle class.[55] Additionally, as neoliberal policies advanced, many of the party's more radical constituencies were depleted—principally the CUT. The party's nucleos and internal structure, however, remained in existence, which allowed the PT to retain a formal kind of mass-party organization that could adapt to the changing beliefs of its membership base.[56] Retaining this relationship, while promoting internal democracy, has also been connected to the party's recurring corruption scandals. Specifically, the mass, working-class membership tends to lack the ability to make significant monetary contributions. This led, according to Wendy Hunter, to the party periodically using illegal means of financing.[57] The PT's ensuing scandals—one of the most notable being the *mensalão* corruption scandal that was uncovered in 2005—revealed a political organization that had become accustomed to using illicit means to forward a legislative agenda. Similar practices plagued the Dilma administration until her impeachment and removal in 2016.

The principal government condition that impacted the PT's revolutionary resistance was electoral politics. From its beginning, the PT sought to gain legitimacy through participating in elections. Elections, per se, were not the problem. What posed a significant challenge to the party's more radical elements was the series of legislative hurdles and requirements to register. The military government's 1979 party reform, specifically, required the organization to publish a manifesto, program, and statutes, with copies sent to the Supreme Electoral Tribunal for approval. The law established rules that parties needed to follow regarding meeting minutes, times for campaigning, and enrollment. These external, government conditions for party formation led the PT to rush its recruitment during the 1980s and rely more on the legally prescribed decision-making organs instead of its own, extralegal nucleos.[58] Internal democracy remained integral to the party, yet social ties and representation in spaces outside of government were neglected. Extralegal qualities of the party were gradually eliminated. Illegal actions continued until scandals exposed the party's financing practices. Altering its message, losing radical members, and favoring more legal forms of organization contributed to the PT electoral success, as well as its deradicalization.

Government and economic factors were also at work in the CUT's decline. Early in its development, the Brazilian labor movement, with the CUT as its most active union, showed tactical ingenuity similar to the MST with its factory sit-ins and commissions. Its early strike actions and campaigns in the 1970s were new and extralegal in nature, mainly because of their legal ambiguity. Yet changing economic conditions—particularly the end of inflation—removed one of the union's principal targets. The substantial increase in the informal economy also decimated the labor movement's membership. Throughout the 1990s, the union embraced defensive tactics to protect gains instead of unleash new actions. It dropped its social movement connections and avoided attempts to organize in the growing informal sector.[59] Strikes became routine and the movement's extralegal practices stopped.

Government structures that negatively impacted the CUT included the already-existing corporatist labor code. Initial calls by certain currents in the labor movement for greater independence and autonomy were incorporated into the 1988 Constitution. Aside from removing state oversight into internal affairs and prohibiting the government's right to remove leaders, many of the core elements of Vargas's CLT (Consolidation of Labor Laws) remained unchanged. The union tax and social welfare provisions divided radical union leaders, who were in favor of more autonomy, from others who wanted to work within the status quo government institutions. While initially challenging the territorial-based method of union formation by launching occupations and demanding factory-level unions, various leaders gradually accepted *unicidade*. Challenging this principal was initially a way to defy state power—territorial control and authority included how labor was recognized and where. Over the course of the 1990s, the CUT dropped appeals to socialism in favor of social democracy, cut down on strike activity, and standardized the way it negotiated with government and business.[60] Tactical and organizational development led the union into predominantly defensive, less revolutionary action.

The effects of neoliberalization, directly for the CUT and indirectly for the PT (due to their once heavy union membership), caught both actors off guard and weakened their radical potential. Electoral politics—principally the need for registration to enter elections and the adoption of a middle-class identity to appeal to voters—curtailed the PT's revolutionary project. Revolutionary contention works simultaneously inside, outside, and through state power. Building dual power, not to participate in the state, but to work through it to transform culture, politics, and economic, for these actors ended in the embrace of legal tactics and forms of organization.

The Landless Movement interacted with state, government, and economic conditions differently, and in ways that contributed to the extension of the movement's revolutionary political project. The main method through which the movement interacted with the state remained the land occupation and encampment. Agrarian reform became enshrined in the constitution, even with the protection of productive property. In 1993, law 8693 was passed, which the 1988 Constitution required in order to specify the productivity criteria for expropriating properties. While the law established production requirements, the nature of land occupations and who can indicate which land to redistribute remains opaque. Unions, both urban and rural, have specific criteria about how strikes can be conducted and in what industries. Land occupations, even despite additional criteria established in new laws passed in the 1990s, remain without detailed regulations. Assailing and engaging state conditions remained possible as the new laws concerning occupations did not take a clear position on the legality of the movement's tactical repertoire. Meanwhile, the holdings of large landowners were not effectively catalogued or measured.

The MST and its allies did not have to engage already-existing political institutions. Unlike the PT or CUT, which had to confront legislation pertaining to political parties, or labor unions, the movement lacked a set of institutions with which leaders had to interact. To form and organize, the movement did not need to submit to government authorities any documentation concerning its membership. The Landless Movement never had to write up bylaws, which would later be assessed. There was no "social movement tax" or guaranteed social service privileges that resulted from government recognition. Union legislation was extended to rural workers through the Estatuo do Trabalhador Rural (ETR; Rural Worker Statute) in 1963. The military further incorporated rural unions into the corporatist state. Throughout the military government, CONTAG continued the demand for agrarian reform. CONTAG was also the primary entity, along with the CNBB, to pressure delegates at the Constitutional Convention for agrarian reform. Still, the union itself, especially in the 1980s and 1990s, was hesitant to engage in any direct-action practices focusing on redistribution. CONTAG and the CUT would flirt with using the land occupation tactic in the late 1990s, but only after the MST demonstrated the tactic's effectiveness. The unions' forays into agrarian reform, however, have never matched the MST in terms of people mobilized or spaces acquired.

Other, new movements emerged at this time to join the MST and help compose the growing ranks of the Landless Movement. In 1997, thousands of small farmers who owned land, with the assistance of longtime MST ally Father Sergio Görgen, helped found the Movimento dos Pequenos Agricultores (MPA; Movement of Small Producers).[61] Similar to the MST, the MPA would engage in land occupations to call attention to the need for special credit for small farmers and demand land redistribution. Their flags are one clear sign of the connection between the MST and MPA—both are red, with similar iconography.

The MPA also practices the mística at movement events. In like manner, the various regional commissions that originally emerged to oppose the military government's large public works projects came together to officially form the Movimento dos Atingidos por Barragens (MAB; Movement of People Affected by Dams). Meanwhile, feeling that women were underrepresented in these movements, various leaders helped organize in 1995 the Articulação Nacional de Mulheres Trabalhadoras Rurais (National Organization of Rural Women Workers).[62] Unlike MAB or MPA, this latter group features overlapping membership with other Landless Movement member groups. The MPA arose with MST leadership, while the MAB would gradually learn and use the MST's trademark land occupation tactic when making its demands. Despite their differences, each movement followed the MST's lead in terms of cultural or identity work, tactics, and overall goals.

The government institution that is most often the target of the Landless Movement's actions is INCRA. Compared to the CLT and party legislation, INCRA, and agrarian reform policy in general, was more destabilized throughout the 1980s and 1990s. The institution experienced high rates of turnover in leadership during the implementation of various neoliberal policies. Rolf Hackbart was the longest serving president in INCRA's modern history, from 2003 to 2010. Before Hackbart, Sebastião Azevedo served from 2001 to 2002, Francisco Orlando Costa Muniz from 2000 to 2001, Raul Jungmann from 1996 to 1999, Xico Graciano and Brazílio de Araújo Neto split the post in 1995, and Osvaldo Russo was president from 1993 to 1995. INCRA's national leadership is in charge of developing more conceptual directives, as well as the budget, for state-level agencies. The lack of consistent leadership at the national level hurt the government's ability to promote and implement coherent policies. Following the military government's use of INCRA for disastrous and unsuccessful settlement schemes, Sarney created the Ministério Extraordinário para o Desenvolvimento e a Reforma Agrária (Extraordinary Ministry for Development and Agrarian Reform), with INCRA enclosed within it, to undertake the ultimately unsuccessful PNRA in 1985. This was an institutional demotion because during the military regime INCRA was directly connected to the executive. In addition to its loss in stability and prestige, discussions of completely dismantling INCRA began in 1987, with a decree issued that actually abolished the institution entirely. Later, in 1989, INCRA reemerged. The Landless Movement's primary government interlocutor was in an almost constant state of flux during the time when the movement was growing and expanding.

While INCRA—and thus government conditions—were destabilized, the neoliberalization of agrarian reform policy made rural areas more vulnerable and susceptible to movement tactics. The national security state of the military government never had what could be called a strong presence in rural areas, instead engaging in sporadic repressive actions in select areas. The neoliberal state initially ignored rural areas by focusing on urban issues and actors, then briefly bolstered certain policies when compelled into action. FHC's emancipation policies, which cut resources to rural programs, further weakened state conditions through eliminating resources. It is true, as Sue Branford argues, that FHC's expansion of agrarian reform policies ultimately had the opposite effect of its intended goal, namely, that instead of co-opting movement leaders, additional resources provided the movement with the lesson that pressuring the government can yield results.[63] Furthermore, such gains must be placed in their respective historical and institutional context. Or rather, only by comparing the institutions, such as INCRA, with those that other movements, such as the CUT and the PT, interacted with, can we fully understand the dynamics behind the Landless Movement's expansion during the 1990s.

Just as crucial a factor in the movement's expansion was that while Brazil's growing informal sector presented challenges to the CUT, the MST turned the deproletarianized, urban underemployed into an opportunity. Movement organizers began encamping near urban areas, and then demanding settlements in the general vicinity to recruit people who lived in the urban periphery.[64] One MST settlement, Comuna da Terra (Commune of the Land), which was established near the city of São Paulo at the end of Cardoso's time in office, resulted from this tactical adaptation. When I visited the Comuna, multiple connections to urban life were manifest. One MST leader with whom I stayed woke up every morning and got her children ready for the bus that took them to school, which was located in the city. When I asked the organizer why she joined the movement, she stated, "I used to work at Ford. Then I was laid off and decided that I didn't want to sell my labor-power anymore."[65] Her comment indicated not only her previous employment in urban industries, but also a Marxist-inspired interpretation of events. The husband of another family I stayed with could not spend the night in a bed because he had slept for years on city sidewalks in São Paulo. In one of the newer encampments in Paraná, I met a small business owner who had recently lost his corner store in bankruptcy and a retired librarian who struggled to make ends meet. I am unsure exactly how many people with urban roots were organized by the MST. Still, these anecdotes show that the movement has made concerted attempts to recruit from the urban periphery over the past couple decades. Showing dynamics similar to the

MPA's emergence, another landless—actually "roofless"—movement, known as the Movimento dos Trabalhadores Sem-Teto (MTST; Homeless Workers Movement), emerged to claim urban areas for housing after witnessing the MST's successes.[66]

Before, for much of the 1980s, occupations and settlements were located in more remote, rural areas. In the 1990s, MST leadership, by adapting its tactics to changing conditions, took advantage of the rise in urban informality to persist and grow by recruiting more people, many of whom had not been mobilized by the movement. The movement's revolutionary mode of political action expanded at this time, in terms of new members and territorial reach, as well as through involving new demographics. The movement's actions also spurred the formation of an urban counterpart, which grew, but never reached the same scale as its rural equivalent. By organizing in and near cities, the MST and its allies organized the people whom the labor movement did not. The same economic condition that was a liability for the labor movement was turned into an opportunity for the Landless Movement.

REVOLUTIONIZING LAND TITLES, CHANGES IN IDENTITY, AND NEW CHALLENGES

The MST's political action involving settlements and titling shows the movement's ability to politicize neoliberalism and further develop its revolutionary manner of resistance. The MST's goal is to create settlements where families remain with usufruct rights instead of definitive property title, or in other words *titulos de concessão* and not *titulos de dominio*. Living on government-owned land with usufruct rights removes the ability of movement members to individualize land holdings though sale or rent. This gives the movement a way to retain members, because sales could enable individuals to leave the movement by selling their land. The political component of this demand is to make all land public and thus challenge the development of private property. Success, in this regard, is apparent in the movement's efforts to confront *emancipação*. In one interview with an INCRA official, I asked about the dynamics of emancipation. When asked if the government had been successful in issuing definitive titles, the official laughed at me. He then pointed to stacks of boxes that contained definitive title application forms that were sent to MST members and returned blank.[67] Similarly, I was told of the lack of progress in privatizing settlements in São

Paulo state, where only one settlement was referenced.[68] Extralegal occupations open particular sites, encampments and settlements, to alternative practices in politics, economic, and culture. In opposing private property, and resisting definitive titles, the movement keeps the spaces it has claimed.

Efforts were made to introduce a counter-neoliberal element to the movement's identity. Movement publications throughout the 1990s show a continued Manichean division rooted in class divisions. The MST began to refer to their collective production cooperatives as "on the political front against neoliberalism,"[69] and the role of their schools as to "oppose the anti-humanist values represented by capitalism in its neoliberal variety, specifically individualism, consumerism, and egotism."[70] In instructions, movement teachers were encouraged to work into their lesson plans "how religions in the past have been integral for liberation or complicit in justifying the neoliberal project."[71] The MST's health sector recognized that "FHC's neoliberal project is leaving the Brazilian people without the means to live a dignified life. . . . His project wants to commodify everything, including health care."[72] Considering the struggle in these stark terms recalls how Schmitt conceives of the friend/enemy distinction created in political action. This identity work is further seen in the movement's representation of the neoliberal project as "marginalizing of agriculture, especially of small producers and the demand for agrarian reform"[73] and "impossible to humanize because it has no heart."[74] Especially in the movement's training manuals, the "us/them" division is made explicit. Comparing these statements with those from the movement's identity work a decade earlier shows a continuation in terms of class, but also a greater degree of complexity by the inclusion of health care and education into the movement's counter-neoliberal project.

The repression, as well as the nature of the government's response to the massacres in 1995 and 1996, displayed weak government conditions. Shortly after videos of the massacres were released and public outcry grew, the movement organized its mass 1997 march on Brasília. Demanding agrarian reform, and with mass public support, the movement pressured the government to create public policies in education and agricultural production. Beginning during the FHC administration, we find what Antonio Negri and Enrique Dussel would call practices illustrative of constitutive power. Following the protests, more people became included and active participants in a series of public policies from which they were previously excluded. By engaging the government at this time, the MST, along with its coalition of religious allies and rural union leaders, claimed more public policies for the movement to attempt to control. As with their appropriations and adaptations of the settlement technology that had initially been created by INCRA, the movement would take education, economic development, and other policies in new directions in the 1990s and after.

The movement also benefitted from a general approval by civil society. In a 1997 survey conducted by the Confederação Nacional da Indústria (CNI; National Confederation of Industry) and the Instituto Brasileiro de Opinião Pública e Estatística (IBOPE; Brazilian Institute of Public Opinion and Statistics), 77 percent of respondents answered yes when asked if the MST was legitimate in demanding land for rural workers. The results, however, were not in favor of every aspect of the movement—62 percent of respondents also felt that landowners should have ultimate say on who can access their property. Three years later, the movement's public support remained high, but was waning. When asked in 2000 if the movement was legitimate, 63 percent of respondents answered in the affirmative. Most importantly, 91 percent thought that the MST should not occupy land and use "violent" means.[75] Despite falling support in the late 1990s, the MST outplanned the administration by cultivating widespread public support and mobilizing the people who were adversely affected by the changing economic conditions in occupations.

Conditions, especially during FHC's second term, began to change in ways that did not favor the MST's revolutionary mode of contention. First, the government passed Portaria-MDA 62, March 27, 2001, and Medida Provisória 2.183–56, August 24, 2001, which prohibited the government from expropriating for two years any land involving a land occupation. Furthermore, the government ended certain public policies, such as Lumiar, which various Landless Movement members had used for technical assistance for production matters, settlement design, and resources. FHC also attempted to dissuade people from organizing land occupations by creating a mail-in method for landless peasants to acquire property. As a result of these changes, state conditions were strengthened. The alternative means to apply for land, as well as the prohibition on expropriating land in occupations for two years, protected the Brazilian state's weak land tenure regime from attack. Public opinion also began to turn against the Landless Movement, with people starting to equate land occupations with violence.

The turn in public opinion and the end of certain public policies revealed a growing opposition to the MST and its allies. Economic conditions remained somewhat favorable for the Landless Movement during this time, as unemployment remained high and technical changes continued to displace rural people.

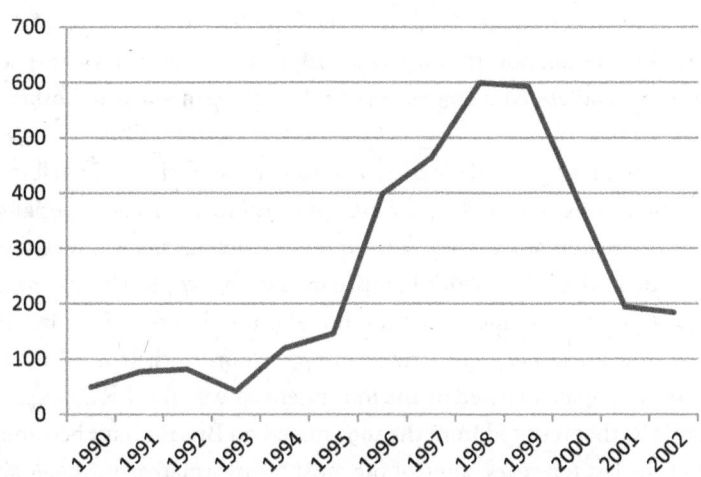

FIGURE 15 Land occupations, 1990–2002. CPT, *Conflitos no Campo*, 1990–2002.

Land occupations, which increased during the 1990s owing to the movement's tactical innovations and ability to take advantage of media representations of the two massacres, decreased because of coordinated political opposition from the FHC administration.

CONCLUSION: ANTI- OR POST-NEOLIBERAL CONTENTION?

Laying out how different kinds of conditions—state, economic, and government—interact with particular tactics allows us to see how during the 1990s the MST created opportunities to expand its mode of revolutionary political action, in terms of membership and territorial reach. As during the period of the military government when the movement emerged, the Landless Movement found ways to retain as well as adapt its tactical repertoire. The comparison with the CUT and PT provides a disciplined analysis with other movements, which could have developed in a similar fashion but did not. This chapter's findings on the nature and persistence of the Landless Movement complements other research, mainly through its additional conceptual points, comparisons with other actors, and greater focus on the dynamics of neoliberal restructuring. Occupations have always provided certain kinds of incentives for movement members, before and after the FHC government. Analyzing the different array of structural conditions, and then noting how they interact with tactics, offers a newer explanation for how the Landless Movement persisted and expanded while other actors declined.

That the MST and its allies experienced a period of what Eric Selbin would call revolutionary expansion during FHC's government is ironic, especially given that the movement is an outspoken critique of neoliberalism. Many of the innovations made in the movement's identity incorporate explicitly anti-neoliberal rhetoric. What the movement's actions reveal is the ability to mobilize through neoliberal policies rather than strictly in opposition to their implementation. Lumiar, for example, was used by the movement, as was also PRONAF. Educational projects that resulted from the 1997 march on Brasília have become, especially over the last ten years, some of the most transformative movement efforts. Instead of avoiding government, the movement engages it in various ways. This is a defining quality of their mode of revolutionary contention—building alternatives within already-existing political, economic, and social relations by working both inside and outside the state. Unlike its contemporaries that also emerged at the conclusion of military rule, the MST shows how revolutionary resistance can persist and even grow during democratic transition and consolidation, as well as during seemingly adverse economic conditions.

The nature of the movement's resistance is both anti- and post-neoliberal. In many of its demands, the MST challenges privatization and the development of private property. Neoliberal agrarian reform encourages privatization and the Landless Movement's alternative challenges it. The MST and its allies also propose and enact concrete alternatives. From cooperatives to schools, the movement shows ways to mobilize people in a post-neoliberal manner. The "post" quality is seen in community, collective forms of production and management. Its origins date to before neoliberal restructuring in Brazil, which should not limit our focus on the movement's revolutionary project. Rather, and as will become clearer in the next chapter, the movement's earlier objectives have continued and further developed through working within and against particular government policies and changes brought by neoliberal restructuring.

5

DILEMMAS AND CHALLENGES WHEN CONFRONTING AN "ALLIED" GOVERNMENT

THE PT IN POWER: FRIEND, ENEMY, OR SOMETHING ELSE?

LUIZ INÁCIO LULA DA SILVA'S election in 2002 caused concern among international investors and some segments of the domestic population. This was the same politician who in an interview in the early 1980s spoke openly about anticapitalist action and the PT's radical organization.[1] Just a year and a half before his election as president, Lula stated that a PT government would lead "a real agrarian reform" through "expropriating large estates," while also claiming that "the IMF doesn't work to help our country, but only certain creditors."[2] Many worries were assuaged with Lula's selection of the conservative businessman José Alencar Gomes da Silva from the Partido Liberal (PL; Liberal Party) as his running mate. Lula would later issue "a Carta ao Povo Brasileiro" (Letter to the Brazilian People) to emphasize dialogue and cooperation with economic elites. Throughout the 1980s and 1990s many of the more transformative elements within Lula's rhetoric and the PT's organization had been lost. Still, on the eve of his election in 2001, some domestic and international elites were distressed about what a national-level PT government would do.

From the perspective of the Landless Movement, it is difficult to clearly and simply characterize the nature of the Lula and subsequent Dilma administrations. On the one hand, various public policies—PNAE and PAA, for instance—which directly support small rural producers, including many movement members, were granted significant resources. INCRA also became stable and more dedicated to financing development initiatives on settlements. On the other hand, Lula would redistribute less land than the previous FHC government. Dilma Rousseff, prior to her impeachment and removal in 2016, was criticized by the MST and its allies for her administration's seeming unwillingness to expropriate land.³ Production support programs have grown, but other government actions aimed at directly challenging monoculture and large-scale operations have not received priority.

Additionally, during both Lula and Dilma's time in government, the number of land occupations initiated by the Landless Movement steadily declined. Occupations and encampments continued, yet pale in comparison with 1990s levels, as well as compared with the early years of the Lula administration. According to the CPT, an approximate 66 percent decrease in occupations took place from 2004 to 2015.⁴ In 2011, the cover of the Brazilian newsmagazine *IstoÉ* read "O Fim do MST" (The End of the MST), accompanied by a story that included a series of melancholic comments concerning the future of the movement from longtime activists.⁵ In the same year, a group of fifty longtime leaders left the MST over disagreements on tactics and philosophy.⁶ The Brazilian newspaper *O Estado de S. Paulo* noted that the MST celebrated its thirty-year anniversary in 2014 at a time when areas expropriated by the Brazilian government for redistribution were at historically low levels.⁷ Within the MST, a concern among leaders led to the issuing of two *cadernos de debate* (notebooks for debate) in 2009 with the expressed goal of addressing perceived internal weaknesses and Brazil's changing external, nonmovement conditions. Within these notebooks, we find the notion that the movement used to define the nature of its resistance during the PT administrations—the *acumulação de forças* (accumulation of forces).

I argue that instead of conceiving of the time when the PT was in power as one of defeat, decline, or retreat for the Landless Movement, we ought to recognize how the accumulation-of-forces stage features the persistence of revolutionary contention, but primarily consolidation. Revolutionary consolidation, in the way I have been using the concept throughout the book, emphasizes strengthening a movement's project in terms of identity, demands, and in practice. As I argued in chapter 3, the movement emerged and consolidated its mode of revolutionary political action, even if only in certain spaces, in southern Brazil in the 1980s. The movement's expansion, which continued into the 1990s—in terms of new members and geographical space—simultaneously involved the growth and adaptation of central elements of its revolutionary political project, namely the combination of extralegal and legal tactics to claim space and transform social relations. During Lula and Dilma administrations, through incorporating new kinds of legal maneuvers and adapting the movement's trademark extralegal mode of conflict, the movement again engaged in revolutionary consolidation. The difference from previous eras is that the movement did not expand into new areas, or include new demographics. Consolidation more so than expansion took place while the PT was in power owing to a combination of changing state, economic, and political conditions.

Demonstrable efforts by the Landless Movement at consolidation can be seen in the connections between the movement's plans for economic development and education, which in many ways have been spearheaded by the MST. The Landless Movement's efforts in education have served as a means to prepare rank-and-file members for future conflicts and as a catalyst for direct confrontations with local, state, and federal opponents. The movement's consolidation efforts during the PT governments drew attacks from new antagonists, notably in special government institutions. Agribusiness elites, which have long been considered the enemies of the movement, also began engaging on the terrain of educational battles in addition to conflicts over land. Efforts to implement the MST's pedagogy into public schools generated new forms of struggle and movement-led ways to defend itself. Such conflicts illustrate how the dynamics of agrarian reform have changed in Brazil during the years when the PT was in power.

The Landless Movement has remained a force calling for, practicing, and demanding revolutionary social transformation. Seminal studies on the Landless Movement document its origins, as well as internal organization, while later scholarship has analyzed the increase in its interaction and cooperation with the Brazilian government.[8] These latter scholars recognize that such interaction has led neither to demise nor to profound internal divisions. In complementing these studies, I add that the Landless Movement's form of revolutionary political action has become further consolidated during this time, and in certain ways even stronger.

This chapter charts the more dilemma-ridden period of the Landless Movement's existence in six sections. In the first, I begin with how the movement at the end of the 1990s was encountering problems on settlements and in economic production. The movement, to address difficulties in its economic development project, began to reorient its actions toward agroecology, as I detail in the next section. It also developed innovative uses of public policies that reveal a continuation and adaptation of its extralegal tactical repertoire. The fourth section of the chapter covers how the PT changed government conditions for the Landless Movement. In the next section, I analyze what is known as the movement's shift to accumulate forces. I especially foreground how this newer stage of the movement touches on economic production through working more with education. Then, I compare the movement's efforts in the area of education in two states—Rio Grande do Sul and Paraná. I focus on its attempts to build and strengthen as different state-level movement groups have learned from one another over time. This section concretizes the movement's accumulation-of-forces stage, illustrating how lessons for engaging movement enemies developed over time and eventually became part of national-level tactics. It also reveals how the movement during its accumulation-of-forces phase has found new antagonists. The chapter ends with an analysis of how government, economic, and state conditions during the PT regimes were, overall, unfavorable for the expansion of revolutionary political action.

PROBLEMS IN THE SETTLEMENTS

"You know, if the cooperatives fail, so do the settlements."[9] I was quite shocked when I heard this statement. Not only was its content surprising, but a longtime MST member who had spent years working on economic development had said it. On another occasion, while driving between settlements to meet with members and discuss cooperatives, another leader told me roughly the same thing. I was asking about how the cooperatives were organized, their history in the region, and if there were any problems. Previously, I had read some studies that documented how many cooperatives were bankrupt, or continued but with serious debt problems. So, I figured that discussing economic matters with movement leaders was, at best, a sensitive matter. Understanding the measures that the MST was taking to deal with such problems in production was one of the original reasons I chose to research the movement, especially in the south of the country. I wanted to approach the issue with delicacy, not wanting to appear as if I was searching for movement weaknesses or rubbing salt in the movement's open wounds. Yet, again to my surprise, a movement member spoke frankly when I asked about any "issues" with economic production—"Oh, you mean the crisis? Yea, there's been problems and families have left. Some felt that what the movement promised them, like, didn't happen."[10]

That a member called the moment "a crisis" was surprising, especially because most often Landless Movement allies and members present the movement's collective cooperatives and settlements to visitors as indicative of success. The rationale for showing off its accomplishments is fairly obvious: the movement wants to present its mode of economic production and organization as a successful alternative to the contemporary Brazilian status quo. Instead of large-scale ranches and farms that specialize in one activity, the movement emphasizes the relevance of and potential for smaller, less chemically dependent operations. Rural communities, likewise, are intended to grow with schools, clinics, and soccer fields functioning in spaces that were once occupied by a few families, a couple hundred cows, and/or thousands of acres of soybeans. Instead of seeing the city as the future, the countryside is represented—both to visitors and new movement recruits—as the place for enrichment and development. Knowing

FIGURE 16 COOPERAL, regional cooperative. The building in the background, which was purchased with PROCERA credits, was not operational when this photo was taken. The adjacent consumer cooperative remained in operation, selling mainly basic consumer items such as soap, rice, and candy, with few products produced locally and/or by the MST.

FIGURE 17 COPTIL. This CPA retained a dozen or so members after collective projects ended in the 1990s. The picture shows an effort by one group of families to organically grow eucalyptus seedlings for transplant and then sale.

this, I was struck by these leaders' candor, and that their descriptions were based on issues in the states of Rio Grande do Sul and Paraná—two of the states where the MST and its allies have been mobilizing for decades.

While traveling, I slowly became more aware of problems in the movement's proposed form of economic production on agrarian reform settlements. Visits to a few cooperatives revealed significant variation in success. Some, like COANAL (Cooperativa Agrícola Novo Sarandi; New Sarandi Agricultural Cooperative) had become defunct and mired in debt, whereas others, like CONATERRA (or Bionatur) were engaging in innovative nucleo forms of agroecological seed production and development. COPAVI in Paraná produces entirely according to agroecological production techniques, with such a demand for its produce that people are hired periodically throughout the year. Meanwhile, while visiting COPTIL (Cooperativa de Produção e Trabalho Integração; Cooperative for Integrated Production and Work) in the extreme south of Rio Grande do Sul, I was told that the initial collective production plans had failed and that the remaining member families rarely coordinate activities. In the same interview where I was told that cooperative survival was connected to the very existence of the settlements, I was also told that only 5 percent of members participate in collective production units.[11] Individual cases—from Rio Grande do Sul to Ceará—are, in fact, exemplary of a transformative, revolutionary project that movement leaders have designed, promoted, and consolidated for decades. However, when paired with the case studies of particular successes the overall figures show a complicated, troubled history of movement development full of starts, stops, setbacks, and adaptations.

The challenges facing the movement, economically and otherwise, must be placed in the appropriate economic and government context. When the Lula administration was entering power, the MST faced internal and external problems. At the same time that the previous Cardoso regime initiated a series of legal obstacles to land occupations and public opinion began to turn against the movement, the movement's system of cooperatives was manifesting problems. One internal assessment noted that most cooperatives were plagued by debt and mismanagement.[12] Both of these issues had deep roots in the movement's proposals and in some public policies. For instance, the main credit policy for agrarian reform beneficiaries before PRONAF, PROCERA, existed from 1985 to 2001. Resources dedicated to PROCERA tripled from R$89 to R$250 million in 1995 and 1998, respectively. What posed a problem was not the increase of available money per se, but the incentive structure found within the policy. PROCERA incentivized the formation of groups by dividing funding opportunities into *tetos* (ceilings) 1 and 2.[13] To receive Ceiling 2 resources, which were double Ceiling 1 amounts, a person had to form a group to request credit. MST encouraged members to form cooperatives to receive the additional resources.[14]

Problems began to emerge after many members with poorly framed plans received credits. At one cooperative, I was told that in the 1990s families intended to engage in monocultural production of commodities like corn and soy. The goal was "to be like the big ones, you know, like the large landowners."[15] According to other MST assessments, this sentiment was dominant in many cooperatives.[16] It is hard to fault movement members for these objectives given that their knowledge of production came from working on large-scale operations.[17] The 1996 Agrarian Reform Census shows that the vast majority of movement members occupied nonmanagerial positions within large-scale operations.[18] Members who received credit referred to this period as a time of "easy money" because initial restrictions and requirements for obtaining credit were lax.[19]

As a result, cooperatives debt-financed many of their assets, but without the knowledge of how to develop sustainable business plans. Debts mounted while early cooperatives were outcompeted by more successful, well-established large producers. Thus, by the end of the 1990s, many members were leaving cooperatives and attempting to farm alone.

An additional planning conundrum unfolded in collectivization efforts. Early movement plans for settlement development called for communal living, uniformly applied. The idea was that property, production, responsibility, and profits would be shared equally. Every family mobilized by the movement, instead of receiving individual lots, was to live on land that was held and administered in common. Then, with this common, undifferentiated land mass, families were to form collectively administered production cooperatives. This kind of arrangement, in fact, is what visitors see when they visit many of the MST cooperatives that have remained—COOPAN, COOPTAR, and COPAVA, to name some of the best known. In effect, the movement mobilized people to engage in collective production, deemphasizing if not actively discouraging individualized forms of production and living. One unintentional result was resentment among certain families that continues through the present day. Members who wanted to work individually actually stopped participating in movement actions.[20] I was told in the southwest area of Paraná, outside of the city of Rio Bonito where there are many large settlements, that organizing members into cooperatives was difficult because many "felt burnt" (*sentiu queimado*) by the failed cooperative attempts. Some families on the settlements remained affiliated with the MST, but were reticent to offer their time or money to what they considered potentially risky activities.

POLITICIZING AGROECOLOGY: TACTICAL INNOVATION, CHANGES TO IDENTITY, AND INTERNAL DIVISIONS

In the early 2000s, movement leaders began to devise ways to address the crisis in the cooperatives and settlements. A period of extended debate ensued in what I was told was called the movement's "transitional period."[21] One result was the embrace of agroecological production. In addition to favoring labor-intensive forms of production, this mode of agricultural production attempts to mirror natural processes instead of dominating them, and replacing purchased inputs, for example, seeds, feed, labor, with what is found locally and/or on an operation itself.[22] Occupying land to secure it for families, develop production, and sell any surplus have been movement objectives for decades. Adopting an agroecological mode of production, in a sense, is a continuation of these earlier movement practices. One difference, however, is that the embrace of capital- and chemical-intensive farming is explicitly rejected. Emphasizing agroecological methods decentralizes production through sustainable production technologies, in line with the Landless Movement's demand to break up large estates. Beginning in earnest and accelerating throughout the 2000s, leaders focused on and planned to confront the problems in economic production by coordinating individual and group transitions to labor-intensive technologies, like permaculture, and away from mechanization. The plan was to free members from the imperatives of large-scale production, which often require the purchase of implements and accompanying debt and dependency.

An additional reason for the Landless Movement appropriating agroecological production is explicitly political. In championing agroecology, the movement is simultaneously challenging corporations that promote the use of chemicals in production, the adoption of genetically modified organisms (GMOs), and industrialized agriculture in general. The explicit embrace of agroecology has prompted activists to lead various occupations of territories owned by multinational corporations. Two of the most high-profile instances are the 2006 occupation of a site owned by the multinational seed corporation Syngenta, in the state of Paraná, and another of the Brazilian company Aracruz, in Rio Grande do Sul. Technically, these occupations were of productively used land—if understood strictly as the use of 80 percent of a particular space. The MST, however, believes that such an interpretation of the constitution's social function clause is now incorrect and too narrow. The reasoning is that multinational firms, their promotion of industrialized agriculture, extensive use of chemical inputs, and in some cases their alleged use of space in the public domain[23] violate the social function clause's environmental section and what constitutes "rational use." One MST leader justified the movement's occupations of sites owned and used by agribusiness firms by stating:

> The action that took place, for example, in Aracruz, was precisely for the purpose to highlight to society the issue of land productivity. Right there in the constitution, it is written that land has a social function to produce and produce also food. Large multinational companies today in Brazilian agriculture are, in addition

to establishing more large landowners (latifundios), abusing the environment, not respecting water, and not addressing social problems that exist in Brazil like hunger.[24]

In these actions, the movement expands the criteria for deciding which properties should be expropriated. As with prior adaptations, the movement has changed how tactics are used and deployed. The land occupation tactic, during both the Lula and Dilma regimes, has retained its extralegal status within the Brazilian legal order. The central ambiguity concerning who can use it and under what conditions, allows for such an adaptation, which the MST and its allies have employed to confront agribusiness firms in new ways.

Over the course of the 2000s, the politicization of agroecology has meant more direct and indirect attacks on transnational agribusiness firms. It has also led the MST to consider new forms of designing settlements and conceptions of its own economic identity. In encampments, leaders were to teach families that "mechanization and the use of chemical inputs were capitalist practices and not appropriate for our nature . . . agroecology has to orient our practices. We have to find ways to teach members to become proficient in such practices for the development of a new form of economic production and a new social subject."[25] Before the occupations in 2006, in 2003 participants marched to a local area where ten acres of transgenic soy was planted, and burned it to conclude the movement's annual Jornada de Agroecologia conference.[26] In 2005, the Venezuelan government, the Federal University of the state of Paraná, and the MST dedicated space at the Contestado Settlement for the Escola Latino-Americana de Agroecologia (Latin American School for Agroecology), which has the express purpose to "work with peasants and construct a new technological matrix that opposed the conservative, transnational alternative provided by agribusiness."[27]

Other actors in the Landless Movement followed the MST's lead. For example, MAB adopted slogans such as *agua e energia não são mercadorias!* (water and energy are not commodities!) Similar to the MST's identity work with agroecology, MAB organizes its members to perceive private businesses and foreign companies as its principal opponents. MPA has explicitly adopted agroecological production, along with its concomitant identity that identifies multinational agribusiness corporations as its opponents. This movement has also, following the MST, begun to issue training manuals that are intended for its own members. Two notebooks, issued in 2014 for the MPA's national congress, feature prolonged discussions of agroecology, critiques of the developmental policies promoted by the Brazilian government, the role of women in the movement, and the importance of agroecology.[28] Together, the MPA, MST, and MAB, along with various allied student and religious organizations such as the Pastoral da Juventude Rural (PJR; Rural Youth Ministry) and the Movimento de Pescadores e Pescadoras Artesanais (MPP; Movement of Artisanal Fishers), form Brazil's regional organization of the transnational movement, La Via Campesina (LVC; The Peasant's Way). During the PT government, with the MST in the lead, these various LVC-affiliated movements have contributed to the spread of the Landless Movement's demand for agrarian reform to actors outside of Brazil.[29]

The LVC's demand for food sovereignty has become a regular demand explicitly made by the MST and its allies. The MST's first direct reference to the concept in its publications occurs in the mid-1990s, when the movement commented on how other international LVC groups were organizing protests at a United Nations' meeting on food security.[30] Even though there are only six references to food sovereignty in MST publications from 1995 to 2000, from 2000 to 2012 we find 123 discussions of the term. The nature of activities that fall within the purview of food sovereignty range from promoting decentralized, de-commodified forms of using resources in food production to regular organized protests against the influence of agribusiness corporations in international summits organized by the United Nations.[31] One story from a 2014 edition of *Jornal Sem Terra* that documented events from the thirteenth annual Jornada de Agroecologia (Journey of Agroecology), which is a multiday workshop on the politics and practice of agroecology that is hosted by the Landless Movement, directly connects the MST's own history to the concept of food sovereignty. In the account, one MST activist who gained land and who had adopted agroecological production methods stated that "it's important to keep and exchange seeds. It's even better to know that the seeds were produced in areas that people fought for in order to have food sovereignty."[32] The movement's first explicit use of the concept of food sovereignty was by the LVC in the 1990s. Still, members of the MST understand that the movement practiced the fundamentals of food sovereignty, notably in the claim to space, well before the LVC introduced and globalized the term.

The political incorporation of agroecology, as practice and identity, has led MST cooperatives to scale down and professionalize. In some cases, such as COOPTAT (Cooperativa de Produção Agropecuária dos Assentados de Tapes;

Cooperative of Agricultural Production in Tapes), members decided to transition to agroecological production and sell their larger equipment that had been purchased with PROCERA credit, whereas others, such as COANOL, stopped operation after declaring bankruptcy.[33] The movement also focused on "regional reference points," or rather, special cooperatives, for example, COOPAN in Rio Grande do Sul and COPAVI in Paraná, which concentrated their energies in terms of training members in production and finance.[34] Unlike with past attempts to fit every settlement into a "one-size fits-all" collectivization model, only a few sites are selected for special attention. The movement has also recruited technicians and experienced practitioners from the Mondragón cooperatives located in the Basque region of Spain to teach members how to manage finances and organize production in Sergipe and Paraná.[35] Instead of a unilateral agreement, the course is an exchange between the Basques and the MST that is intended to last at least ten years. Professionalization and scaling back are still within the overall goal of full collectivization. The difference is that since the 2000s, the efforts are more focused and directly planned.

The many different experiences—individual peasant plots, collectively organized cooperatives, and efforts to practice agroecology—do not always exist harmoniously within the MST's vision of rural production. Historically, there have been intense and fruitful debates over differences, including the 1985 national congress on whether or not families who receive land should remain in the movement. In agricultural production, however, tensions create problems, specifically through the competing identities of peasant, *colono*, and worker. First, multiple movement documents note the existence of a peasant consciousness, not as something to cultivate, but as something to be replaced by a worker sensibility. One training document notes that the "worker" overcomes certain "ideological behaviors" that characterize "emerging classes like the peasant and artisan."[36] Echoing this sentiment, in one interview I was told how "the mentality of the *colono* is limited . . . it needs to be trained to produce."[37] Peasants and *colonos* are considered easily susceptible to manipulation, isolated, and reactionary. The nature and existence of the peasantry has been debated extensively in academic circles, chiefly in recognizing its connection to revolutions, economic development, and transnational mobilization.[38] In the most minimal sense, the peasantry is considered a rural actor, usually engaged in semi- or noncapitalist forms of production. Regardless of the acknowledgment in some scholarship of an apparent connection between peasants and revolution, various MST training manuals emphasize that this form of production, and any accompanying forms of identification, should be superseded.

Other movement materials and practices directly contradict the emphasis on transforming peasants into workers. In fact, the MST and its allies privilege a peasant form of production in their annual agroecology conference events. The event is by no means small. At the tenth conference, which I attended, workshops were attended by over four thousand people. Production practices that were addressed included everything from beekeeping to smoking meat.[39] The production technologies encouraged throughout the conference were oriented around creating peasants who independently produce. Conference participants also receive a publication documenting peasant production techniques and specific illustrations of agroecological best practices. Contradictions in identifying who is the subject of MST agricultural production have led to internal movement disagreements over the use of resources. In one case, I was told that efforts to standardize agroecological techniques outside of Paraná in movement training centers, while initially embraced, ended after leaders decided to focus energies on other sectors of the movement.[40] The Carta de Saida de Nossas Organizações, which was signed by fifty leaders from the MST, MAB, and MTD who decided to leave the Landless Movement in 2011, stated that such economic improvement efforts distracted the movement from more radical forms of engagement.[41]

THE PT IN POWER AND THE LANDLESS: A STRONGER MOVEMENT, OR DOMESTICATION AND DECLINE?

Lula's election in 2002 improved conditions for the movement and provided time to deal with its difficulties. First, shortly after assuming power the government stopped applying the Medida Provisória issued by FHC that prohibited expropriating occupied properties.[42] This signaled to the Landless Movement that the new government was committed to agrarian reform in some capacity. Another change involved financing. INCRA's budget for various agrarian reform policies—including funds for officials' salaries, disappropriating land, education, and credit—grew exponentially.

INCRA also changed its guiding directives and leadership. Concerning directives, officials appointed during the center-left Lula administration explicitly

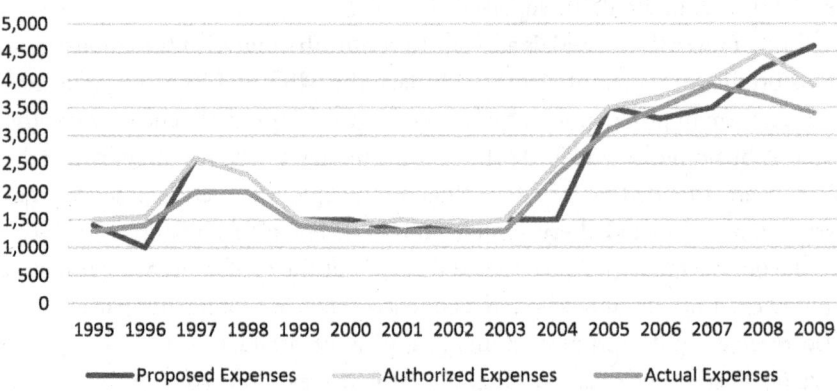

FIGURE 18 Evolution of INCRA's budget, 1995–2010. (Initially estimated expenses are in pink, blue shows authorized expenses, and teal displays actual expenses.) INCRA 2010.

rejected the concept of emancipation that characterized FHC's plans. In what was called *consolidação* (consolidation), the emphasis shifted from trying to "free" families from public policies to building adequate infrastructure and production capacities. Consolidation also deemphasizes the impetus to form individualized, private landholdings. Focusing on infrastructure and development means that prior to issuing titles, priorities include building roads, making viable economic production, and establishing working sanitation systems.[43] The credits distributed, as well as the land, have been considered during the last ten years *fondos perdidos* (lost funds), meaning that families who have received resources are not expected to repay.[44] During the Dilma administration INCRA continued these practices, changing law 8629/1993 in 2014 to remove explicit time frames for when families are supposed to receive definitive ownership of particular parcels of land. A separate government institution, the Tribunal das Contas da União (TCU; National Audit Court), has taken issue with the relaxation of emancipation by pressuring INCRA to force families to purchase land and repay any loans they receive.[45] Rather than coherent or unified, the government's position on agrarian reform, especially concerning titling, is disputed.

Public programs that favor small farmers received additional resources from the PT governments. The monetary resources given to Brazil's school lunch program—PNAE—were greatly increased from 2003 to 2010. PNAE guarantees that a certain percentage of the food served at schools within a municipality comes from family farms (*agricultura familiar*). PNAE has grown from R$1 million to R$4 million (US$450,000–1,800,000) from 2002 to 2014, serving over forty-three million children.[46] Also in 2003, law 10.696 created the PAA. Like the PNAE, the PAA targets small-scale producers, especially indigenous people, agrarian reform beneficiaries, fishers, Afro-descendants, and others. Through the PAA, small-scale farmers can sell their produce to the government in the event of poor market prices, as well as use institutions to direct food to underserved, marginalized communities. From numbers available in 2009 and 2010 for the PAA, the percentage of finances went from 8 to 12 percent (R$28,699,236 of R$363,381,941 to R$44,643,666 of R$379,735,466), while participating families in settlements went from 7 to 11 percent (7,444 of 98,340 families to 10,440 of 94,398). We can extrapolate from these numbers—because we know that roughly 50 percent of land occupations and encampments in Brazil are under MST influence—that thousands of Landless Movement families access these public policies. Branford notes that such an increase presented the movement with some "difficult choices," namely for not carrying out deeper redistributive measures, while at the same time it improved access to resources, in terms of production support policies, when compared to previous governments.[47]

The mode of interaction that the MST has encouraged with respect to these policies has extralegal qualities, but not in the same way as land occupations. I was told by the director of the MST's confederation of cooperatives, CONCRAB, that the plan is to foment agroecological production practices among debt-burdened, and in some cases insolvent or bankrupt, producers.[48] If farmers, individually, are insolvent, then they cannot legally access any production support programs. This poses a problem for the movement, especially because creating an alternative mode of economic production is critical to the MST's revolutionary vision and success. As a way to subvert the problems posed by insolvency, MST leaders have recruited insolvent members into the successful cooperatives. Any functioning cooperative, as an entity, can access the public program, with some of its members—some of whom may be experiencing bankruptcy—indirectly receiving credit or access to markets as well. Concrete examples include selling vegetables to neighborhood schools in Rio Grande do Sul via these social programs, where insolvent, yet active, members affiliate with productive cooperatives that access PNAE.[49] The MST's ultimate goal is to challenge private property and facilitate collective modes of production.

The extralegal quality of the movement's tactics and form of organization is also seen in how these actions have been interpreted by government actors. At the federal level, various congressional inquiries (Comissões Parlamentares de Inquerito, or CPIs) in 2002, 2005, and 2010 targeted the MST and cut resources that were intended to finance movement educational and economic initiatives. The opposition cites alleged criminal behavior, which it defines as the misuse of public resources to promote violence and spread of an anti-democratic ideology.[50] A central claim is that the MST uses public resources to strengthen the capacity for illegal land invasions (*esbulho possessorio*) through forming criminal organizations (*quadrilha*). Given that an invasion (not occupation) is an illegal act, opponents of the MST's political project claim that the movement and various of its leaders are breaking the law, particularly the clauses of the constitution that enshrine productive property and the sections of the penal code that prohibit trespassing and stealing. None of the allegations have been confirmed or proven. Still, the CPIs resulted in a periodic suspension of public programs that later resumed. Neither illegal, nor legal, recruiting members with economic difficulties superimposes these revolutionary objectives onto public programs with the goal of creating alternative modes of economic production through their cooperatives that stand in stark opposition to neoliberal forms of economy.

Increases in resources and programs during the Lula administration did not lead to harmonious relations with the Landless Movement and the PT. After Lula won the presidency in 2002, the MST and its allies engaged in a series of occupations and actions to pressure the administration. Despite issuing a second Plano Nacional de Reforma Agrária (PNRA) in 2004, as Lula's time in office went on it became clear that the government was not going to implement a wide-sweeping land redistribution program. Over time the government was criticized for resettling people on abandoned plots in already-established settlements rather than expropriating new sites. According to Oliveira, close to 233,000 parcels were abandoned and then reclaimed by the state during Lula's administration (2003–9).[51] The Lula administration, ultimately, distributed less land to fewer families than FHC.

Some in the Landless Movement, across the coalition of actors, saw the increase in resources as an opportunity. PAA and PNAE offered assured markets for cooperatives and individual producers on settlements. While I was attending a MST-run high school, one day was devoted to a COPTEC technician explaining to the youth how to register producers for PRONAF when they returned back to the settlements.[52] I had spent weeks at the school, and this session was by far the most boring. Neither the students nor the COPETC technicians really showed an interest or passion in the program. At one point, the technician even noted that in the past, accessing and understanding public policies were not important. At the yearly conference of Bionatur agricultural extension agents and cooperative members, in a breakout group on the PAA, MST leaders emphasized that the program was one of the main reasons why the cooperative persisted throughout the drought. Some movement training manuals and newsletters, like those that appeared in 1995 encouraging members to use PROCERA, continued to praise public policies and government support for small-scale production.[53]

Government conditions during the PT governments have been favorable for movement attempts to consolidate its claim to space, but less so for the attempt to expand into new territory. The rapid increase of members and settlements that took place during the FHC years were indicative of the movement's successful expansion. Such growth, however, also revealed the MST's limited capacity to adequately train and include new recruits. As I was told by one activist who had recently retired from movement affairs and who was active principally at the national level during the 1990s, the MST's growth had resulted in the movement "losing control of the settlements.... People, businesses, whatever, now come and go as they please. Agrobusiness sells seeds to people, they are becoming small agribusiness (*agronegocinho*)."[54] The movement's claim to space and attempt to transform relationships was beginning to be seen as endangered.

The revolutionary element of the movement's actions, especially when the PT was in power, is found in the attempt to regain control of particular spaces by fortifying the movement's political, economic, and cultural projects. This does not mean that the MST and its allies have demobilized. What we see is a tactical shift, especially with respect to land occupations and conventional protest. The Landless Movement's consistent ability to mobilize participants is apparent in the number of demonstrations that have been organized for agrarian reform. The movement has conducted over 58 percent (1,354 out of 2,326 total actions) of the demonstrations calling for agrarian reform since 2002. These figures do not include land occupations, but practices like marches and traffic blockades. What stands out when comparing demonstration and occupation trends is their reversal. A steady decrease of land occupations has occurred simultaneously with an increase in agrarian reform manifestations. Also, while occupations have remained steady for the last five years, they have not resulted in encampments. Or rather, occupations have apparently turned more into protest actions than direct claims to acquire territory and pressure the Brazilian government

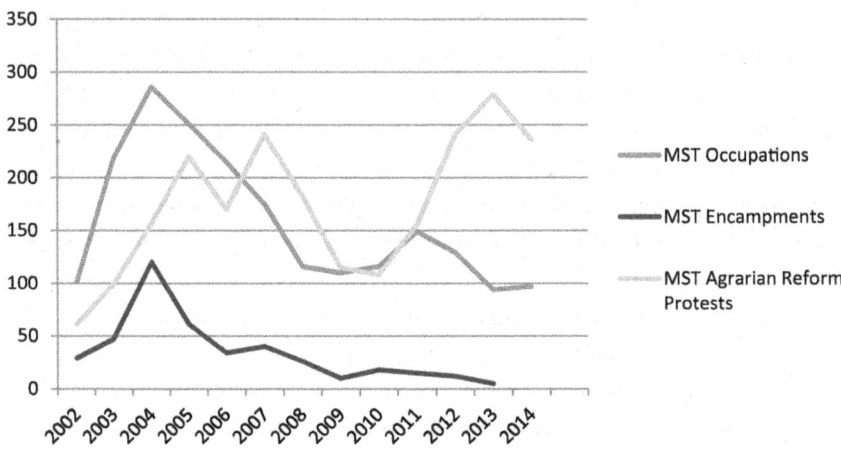

FIGURE 19 MST-led occupations, encampments, and protests, 2002–2015. CPT, *Conflitos no Campo*, 2002–2015.

to redistribute property. The occupations, for example, of Syngenta's and Aracruz's sites, were not aimed at expropriation. Instead, the occupations serve to highlight what MST activists claim is a mode of economic production that is harmful to the environment and rural communities.

CONSOLIDATING REVOLUTIONARY CONTENTION, NEW STRUGGLES, AND *ACUMULAR FORÇAS*

The changes that occurred within the Landless Movement during the Lula and Dilma administrations, from divisions within its leadership to the embrace of agroecology, are constitutive of what certain leaders have deemed the movement's accumulation-of-forces phase. Various documents, especially those since 2008, explain the reasons and goals for this new moment in the movement's history. In 2009, a few MST leaders took the initiative and issued two *cadernos de debate* (notebooks for debate) on the direction of the movement. In the first—*Os desafios daluta pela reforma agrária popular e do MST* (Challenges Facing the Struggle for Agrarian Reform and the MST)—the movement recognized how opposition from large landowners and the Brazilian government has changed, especially with Lula's election in 2002. "The agents of repression," it is claimed, "have begun to use other spaces and other facets of the state."[55] The government institutions identified include the MP and the TCU, while the CPIs are noted as the primary means to halt movement efforts. "We must confront," it reads in *Os desafios*, "such challenges to building political and economic forces in our settlements and encampments. It is understood that the struggle for agrarian reform today is a process of accumulating forces."[56] Echoing the concern of longtime activists about the presence and growth of *agronegocinho* on settlements, training manuals and published materials for internal circulation offer strategies for regaining control over space in movement-led initiatives.

In addition to new kinds of challenges from the Brazilian government, agribusiness firms have initiated programs that directly counter the Landless Movement's efforts in education. The nongovernmental organization the Associação Nacional de Defesa Vegetal (ANDEF; National Association for the Defense of Vegetation), with members Syngenta, Bayer, Basf, Dupont, Dow, and Monsanto, have launched their own rural education campaign in direct opposition to the movement's Educação do Campo. Known as Educação no Campo (Education in the Countryside)—notice the subtle shift from "do" to "no" in the agribusiness version—one purpose is to distribute educational materials in schools that emphasize the safety of pesticides and progressive nature of large-scale agriculture. In 2014, ANDEF began a partnership with fifty elementary schools in São Paulo state. For this effort, the organization created a cartoon mascot—Andefino—a white man in a green shirt and blue jeans, often pictured in fields and with animals. In one set of materials, *Boas práticas agrícolas no campo* (Good Agricultural Practices in the Countryside), Andefino lays out how pesticides control the spread of pests and outlines "dos" and "don'ts" when handling chemicals (2011).

ANDEF has the support of the government's public health regulatory agency, the Agência Nacional de Vigilância Sanitária (ANVISA; National Health Surveillance Agency). ANVISA conducts research and publishes findings on a variety of issues pertaining to public health, from the potential effects of tobacco use to problems arising from cosmetics. The agency is governed by a four-member board—three pharmacists and one rural extension agent. Concerning agriculture, ANVISA has issued eight publications on appropriate pesticide use, how to identify when one has been poisoned, and pesticide residue in food.

One publication, *Trilhas do campo* (Countryside Pathways) presents the agency's program, the Programa de Análise de Resíduos de Agrotóxicos em Alimentos (PARA; Program for the Analysis of Pesticide Residue). The document begins noting how "Brazil is the world's largest consumer of pesticides," and how given this fact, "store owners and purchasers who sell food must themselves discern whether or not a food item contains the appropriate level of pesticides. . . . Caring for our health is everyone's responsibility."[57] In claiming that "everyone is responsible," consumers and wholesale purchasers are represented as the regulators, which removes the burden from the chemical industry and large producers, and presents pesticide use as part of daily life. Without Andefino, but still utilizing cartoonlike figures to appeal to youth, ANVISA's *Cartilha sobre agrotóxicos: Série trilhas do campo* (Notebook on Pesticides: Countryside Pathways Series) lays out the appropriate practices when working with chemicals (2011). Directions detail how to handle pesticide poisoning and store and transport chemicals. Using chemicals in agriculture is again depicted as natural—not as integral to a form of production that benefits certain companies and large-scale producers. Five of the nine sources in this *cartilha* are from ANDEF.

The other sources in this ANVISA publication are from SENAR (Serviço Nacional de Aprendizagem Rural; National Service for Rural Learning) and CNA (Confederação da Agricultura e Pecuária do Brasil; Brazilian Confederation of Agriculture and Livestock).[58] Through SENAR, the CNA has launched initiatives throughout rural elementary schools with its own notebooks for students that detail how to grow vegetables, maintain tractors, and access credit. In CNA's Escola Viva (School Alive) program, created in 2009, affiliated technicians and teachers visit families to improve production capacities while also tutoring children. Other efforts to promote agribusiness include SENAR's high school and postsecondary education initiatives. In partnership with MEC, another program—the Programa Nacional de Acesso ao Ensino Técnico e Emprego (PRONATEC; National Program for Access to Technical Education and Employment)—targets high school age youth. From 2011 to 2014, this program graduated over ninety thousand students.[59] How PRONATEC depoliticizes students is apparent when one reviews its core courses. Students select from sixty-four different classes while enrolled in the PRONATEC, ranging from beekeeping and tourism to artisanal Indigenous crafts and tractor driving.[60] Missing are classes on politics, history, or culture. The identity promoted in PRONATEC is strictly based in economic production and individualized forms of conduct.

ANDEF, ANVISA, and SENAR privilege an identity based in agribusiness production techniques. Nowhere in their materials are nontechnical elements of rural life present. Students are taught to view themselves as individuals, not as part of an organization or movement. Furthermore, the emphasis on chemical inputs benefits agribusiness companies—the CNA is led by large landowners who specialize in crops that require pesticides. Standard practices encouraged by government and economic elites favor a narrow understanding of economic production that perpetuates inequalities and hierarchies.

In the face of these changing programs from enemies that challenge the Landless Movement revolutionary project, the accumulation-of-forces stage entails a shift toward consolidating the movement internally. The movement's second notebook in the series, *Para debater os desafios internos do MST* (Debating the MST's Internal Challenges), brings up a series of internal issues, which include over-centralization, a lack of creativity among the rank and file, excessive attention to economic matters, and an overall lack of learning, debating, and reflection.[61] Internal consolidation means fostering the capacity of members to develop their abilities to critique and assess themselves, as well as the MST. It also means improving the movement's outreach efforts. In a separate MST pamphlet that focuses on the organization of settlements, members are encouraged to consider that they serve the movement "not only in a strict economic sense . . . but also as a space for building popular power and counter-hegemony in order to communicate with society and other workers."[62] In another document, *A constituição e gestão de iniciativas agroindustrias cooperativas em areas de reforma agrária* (The Constitution and Management of Agroindustrial Initiatives by Cooperatives), movement leaders from Paraná document the successful practices of cooperatives with the goal of "contributing to the process of regaining control over cooperation and cooperatives in agrarian reform settlements."[63]

Economic development remains important, as the movement intends to broaden how production is conceived. Relations on settlements need to be strengthened, not only for the sake of the families who live there, but also as a way of recruiting members from the urban periphery in the future. Urban people have been one of the MST's targets for recruitment, growing in numbers during the 1990s. The embrace of agroecology is intended to show that rural life is not entirely about machines. Instead, the promotion of healthy life and work on settlements is an intentional display and additional tactic for recruitment. If there were a sudden rise in unemployment because of a new economic crisis, or dismantling of Bolsa Familia, then the countryside might reappear as a relatively better option for people than living in the urban periphery.

A second critical element in the accumulation-of-forces period is the effort to create a new leader—what is called the *técnico-militante* (militant-technician).

Creating the movement's leaders from its own ranks, rather than relying on outsiders, has long been a staple of the MST's mobilizational model.[64] Since the movement's formative years in the early 1980s, dozens of training manuals have been produced and used by movement leaders to educate new recruits and members on the reasons for demanding agrarian reform, how to organize meetings, and how to conduct land occupations. While producing the militant-technician is a continuation of these dynamics, the emphasis is different. For this kind of leader, the movement requires official, usually formal training, in addition to commitment to the MST. In a description of the IEJC's pedagogical project issued in 2004, the school's goals include offering professional and high school education, and the training of militants and technicians for work within the movement.[65] Another description of the MST's professional training courses states that they "help form militant technicians who are capable of influencing and organizing practical issues in settlements, as well as providing political and technical assistance."[66] At the MST's Escola Milton Santos (Milton Santos School), which specializes in promoting agroecology in the state of

FIGURE 20 Part of a painting on a wall of the Milton Santos School, outside of Londrina, in the state of Paraná. It reads, "Only we poor people can have a pedagogical debate on true politics. You are in a school that was built with the hands of workers."

Paraná, when I asked what it means to be a militant-technician, I was told by one student that in addition to receiving instruction about agroecology, they were "learning how to work and live collectively, with the idea to take this back to where we live."[67] MST schools teach skills to the students, such as agroecological production techniques, while also promoting and consolidating the movement's revolutionary collective form of organization.

Education, particularly, has received more attention since the end of FHC's governments and throughout the MST's accumulation-of-forces phase of contention. The movement's focus on education is not new. The first school administered by MST leaders emerged in the early 1980s in Rio Grande do Sul.[68] Demands for access to education increased throughout the 1990s, culminating in a national march in 1997. Then, the first Encontro Nacional de Educadores da Reforma Agrária (National Meeting for Educators in Agrarian Reform) took place in Brasília. At this time a coalition—featuring CONTAG, CNBB, and the MST—demanded educational policies oriented around rural life. One result was PRONERA.

Beginning with resources for one class in adult literacy, PRONERA has increased to finance at the secondary and postsecondary level over twenty-five courses over the last ten to fifteen years in areas such as history, medicine, and cooperative management. In 2010 alone, over ten thousand students who are Landless members participated in courses funded with PRONERA resources. Social movement membership is also required to participate in the courses, which has grown to include members from MPA, MAB, and newer movements like the MTD. Before PRONERA, the movement's educational project did not have an official name. The first reference to Educação do Campo occurs in *Por uma educação basica do campo* (Towards a Primary Education of the Countryside), a manual published by the movement to disseminate the debates from the first national conference on rural education in 1998.[69] While the Landless Movement has always been concerned with education, Education of the Countryside explicitly starts in the late 1990s.

Conceived of from the outside, without analyzing the Landless Movement's plans and strategy, these changes might seem to connote a certain kind of pacification. From the perspective of the MST and its allies, however, the dynamics of movement/government relations illustrates how revolutionary resistance has adapted over time. The movement's plans reveal a coordinated attempt to consolidate its membership base. While land occupations have subsided, the movement still deploys extralegal actions through using public policies and programs for its own internal, collective development. On occasion this has generated accusations of stealing, but without any practices actually confirmed as illegal. The Landless Movement continues to claim particular spaces and to deepen its project of transforming cultural, political, and economic relationships. It does this through superimposing its mode of organization, whether in economic production or education, onto certain public policies. Spaces that have been claimed are now being reclaimed and strengthened, through vying for control over government policies and training a new generation of movement activists.

LEARNING AND LEGISLATION IN PARANÁ, RIO GRANDE DO SUL, AND AT THE FEDERAL LEVEL

A focus on the dynamics of Landless Movement's educational project shows how the accumulation-of-forces period remains contentious with respect to certain authorities, while also serving the movement's newer goals and objectives. Focusing on practices in particular states, furthermore, shows how the movement has learned over time from its own past actions. While the movement is active in twenty-four of Brazil's twenty-six states, the many commonalities in Paraná and Rio Grande do Sul—particularly in agricultural economies and settlement patterns—allow an illustrative, experiment-like comparison. The original members in both states were displaced small farmers—from large-scale public dams in Paraná and evictions from Indigenous reserves in Rio Grande do Sul. This contrasts with many in the movement's membership base in states such as Pernambuco who were former wage laborers in the sugarcane industry, or in the Amazonian state of Pará, which has a particular history of internal migration and indigenous activism. Concerning mobilization in Pará, Gabriel Ondetti and colleagues found that while the MST is active, its achievements—in terms of occupations and settlements—are significantly less than the rural labor union, FETAGRI (Federação dos Trabalhadores e Trabalhadoras na Agricultura; Federation of Agricultural Workers).[70] Furthermore, what makes a comparison of activities in Rio Grande do Sul and Paraná revelatory is that the MST has a long history in these states, emerging in these states at roughly the same period in the late 1970s/early 1980s. The MST has also promoted various innovative educational projects in each state, including elementary, secondary, and postsecondary experiences. ITERRA, for example, is found in Rio Grande do Sul, while Paraná has four separate schools that serve high school–age and older movement member students. Despite the commonalities between the MST and its allies in these two states, scholarship on the movement has tended to neglect comparing their trajectories, either focusing on single case studies, or documenting similarities and differences between efforts in other regions that omit Paraná.[71]

In terms of numbers of students, the movement has been successful in both states. Thousands of Landless Movement members, children, and allies have participated in movement schools in Rio Grande do Sul and Paraná. During their time in Rio Grande do Sul (1998–2009) and Paraná (2002–15), the MST's itinerant schools served roughly a thousand students each year per state in a total of fifteen schools.[72] The highest number of students attending schools in Paraná was 1,255, which was spread among ten encampments in 2010.[73] Concerning secondary and postsecondary education, we can turn to PRONERA numbers. In 2010 and 2011, there were approximately 220 high school–age movement members attending classes in Paraná and 280 in Rio Grande do Sul.[74] At ITERRA, every TAC (Técnico em Cooperativismo; Technician in Cooperativism) course, which in 2014 was in its fourteenth iteration, usually graduates 30 students.[75] Additionally, between 1990 and 2004 in normal education, the MST reports graduating ten classes with between 30 and 50 movement-trained teachers in each class.[76] Other courses at the postsecondary level also train movement members in their pedagogy, specifically the *licenciatura em educação do campo* (undergraduate course in countryside education), with over a hundred students enrolled in 2010.[77]

Understanding the role of the Landless Movement's participation within the public programs in each state helps us analyze the differences between the movement's practices in general. The *escolas itinerantes* (itinerant schools), which first appeared in the southern state of Rio Grande do Sul in 1996, were initially authorized by the Conselho Estadual de Educação (CEE; State Educational Committee).[78] Instead of being permanent sites of instruction on settlements, the itinerant schools were mobile and followed encamped families in the event of eviction. The roles for the MST and the state Department of Education are specified in the 1996 *parecer* 1.313, which granted the schools government authorization.[79] In 2003, Paraná's CEE legalized itinerant schools in *parecer* 1.012. In each state, the Department of Education supplies financial and physical materials for the schools, while elaboration and execution of the pedagogy remains with the movement, as does the selection of professors and the majority of evaluating procedures. While the associated "base school" handles the pedagogical elements for the itinerant schools, a separate nongovernmental organization (NGO) administers the flow of material resources from the state to the individual schools.[80] In Rio Grande do Sul, the NGO was Instituo Preservar (Institute for Preservation), and in Paraná, the Associação de Cooperação Agrícola e Reforma Agrária do Paraná (Association of Agrarian Cooperation and Agrarian Reform of Paraná).

Similar dynamics are found in the movement's efforts in secondary and postsecondary education. While the itinerant schools collaborate with state-level departments of education, MST high schools receive support from the federal government. Working within the network of *institutos federais* (federal institutes) in each state, movement leaders certify their courses and issue diplomas. Similar to the kind of agreement found between the movement and governments in the *pareceres*, the MST establishes contracts with the different regional institutes that demarcate movement and institute roles. When I asked the director of the Instituto Federal–Sertão, which has a contract with the MST's Instituto Educar in Pontão, Rio Grande do Sul, about their relationship, I was told there had never been any problems in the years of collaboration. The technical nature of the relationship was discussed, with the director telling me how Educar fit within the Federal Institute's own mission of offering improved technical training for rural people that began during the Lula administration.[81] Financing comes through the periodic distribution of PRONERA resources, while the implementation of pedagogical decisions and managing of day-to-day course activities is the responsibility of specific universities or private places of instruction and the movements involved.[82]

The MST's use of legal, public programs provides resources and legitimacy. When I asked why the movement in Rio Grande do Sul first chose to work with government, I was told how "students were learning to read and write [in nonofficial, movement schools], yet had nothing to prove their skill levels. When they went to state schools, they had to take tests, many times having to repeat grades."[83] The need was quite practical—students, to enter formal public schools, had difficulties with paperwork. The primary concern for parents was that their children would not have continual access to education, mainly because of the precarious dynamics of living in marginalized rural areas and regularly engaging in contentious movement activities. Leaders learned of this concern, and then sought a practical solution. By taking on the administrative responsibility, the movement could also offer its own distinct pedagogy. Concerning the movement's relationship with public authorities overall, I was told that the movement's educational goal is to "ensure access to education."[84] Claiming education as a right means that the movement's members cannot be excluded, which gives the demand for and practice of MST education legitimacy.

Despite similar dynamics and rationale for working with the government, movement actions differed greatly at the subnational level. In Paraná, MST leaders and various Department of Education officials in Paraná created a series of legally binding documents to promote Education of the Countryside. In 2010, the Paraná government issued *pareceres* 117/10, 743/10, 1011/10, while the state secretary of education formalized *resoluções* 3922/10 and 4783/10 and *instruções* 27/2010 and 001/2010.[85] This flurry of legislative activity ranges from formally recognizing the legitimacy of Education of the Countryside in certain elementary schools (*parecer* 117/10) to listing the required classes that movement-affiliated teachers must take to work in schools (*instrução* 027/10).

Similar legislative work did not take place in Rio Grande do Sul. While one *parecer* sanctioned the itinerant schools in 1996 in Rio Grande do Sul, concomitant *resoluções* and *instruções* did not follow. Instead, the movement banked on the government's Constituente Escolar (Constituting the School) program, which actively involved social actors in crafting school directives and rules.[86] The program was heralded as a "process of popular participation in the direction of public policies" and was believed to be a way "to strengthen control over the state."[87] While the program succeeded in generating conferences and meetings, it did not result in legislation. When the ally Dutra government of the PT left power in 2002, Constituente Escolar also ended. The movement, in both states, sought collaboration with the local governments. The key difference was that in Paraná, the Landless effort became quite intertwined with government officials and laws.

Why was the movement far more active in subnational legislative activity in Paraná than in Rio Grande do Sul? Part of the answer is found in external, nonmovement government conditions. Germano Rigotto of the PMDB became the governor of Rio Grande do Sul after Dutra. His government ended Constituente Escolar and increased scrutiny of movement involvement in education. While I was interviewing MST members in Rio Grande do Sul, I was told that his government did not directly oppose the movement but did place more reporting requirements on movement schools and cut funding. Still, it was after the Rigotto administration that external factors changed dramatically. From 2006 to 2010, the Landless Movement faced a concerted effort by the Ministério Público to end the movement, repression from the state-level government of PSDB governor Yeda Crusius, and hostility from the secretary of education. The then secretary of education, who periodically negotiated with movement leaders, told me that the MST was part of the "backward left" that is "absolutely ideological . . . really, out of this world."[88] The *escolas itinerantes* (itinerant schools), which are mobile schools located in encampments where families await land title, were closed in Rio Grande do Sul in 2008 when the MP issued a TAC—*termo de ajustamento de conduta* (conduct readjustment statement)—requiring that the state Department of Education end its partnership with the MST.[89] Meanwhile, the Crusius government repressed rural and urban movements, leading to a federal investigation into the administration's heavy-handed tactics.[90]

In Rio Grande do Sul, the MP was expressly opposed to the MST. One leading MP official described the movement as "terrorist," employing tactics "similar to those used by guerrillas in the Vietnam War," and with children in schools "never learning to read or write anything but the name Karl Marx."[91] This statement reflects the beliefs that led the MP to initiate its campaign to eradicate the MST. The ministry sought to "declare the MST illegal," in the name of "protecting children" from the movement's alleged "disruption of public order" and "use of public resources for criminal behavior."[92] Declaring the movement illegal involved denouncing it as a terrorist organization, which sanctioned the arbitrary arrest and detention of members, the increased use of force during protests, and demarcating various areas as "off-limits" to mobilization.[93] One MST leader in the state claimed that the repression led many members, particularly in the area of education, to either quit or devote their energies elsewhere.[94]

In Paraná, government conditions were more favorable. Roberto Requião became governor in 2003. While a member of the PMDB, Requião had a reputation for favoring movement objectives and demands. As one movement described, "Requião was different. His government was like a united front, with many parties and allies. And he made an agreement with movements that if elected, he would carry out their ideas."[95] Among the movement ideas that the administration supported was education for rural areas, as well as placing a ban on the export of GMOs from Paranaense ports. The administration also appointed key officials in the state government who regularly met and negotiated over policy issues. His approach differed greatly from the prior Jaime Lerner government (1995–2002), which, as other scholars note, was known for violently repressing social actors.[96]

Government conditions, while crucial, provide only a partial explanation for the differences in movement actions in the two states. In 2002 leaders in Paraná went to Rio Grande do Sul to learn about how the movement interacted with public officials to establish schools in encampments. As I was told by movement leaders, "we went to learn how the schools functioned, how they were organized. We copied them. We also went with some people from the government."[97] Later, after repression unfolded in Rio Grande do Sul, movement leaders and government officials in Paraná saw the need to protect their gains in promoting Education in the Countryside. In 2008, in the midst of the movement's struggles against the government in Rio Grande do Sul, the MST published *Escola itinerante do MST: História, projeto, e experiencias* (The Itinerant School of the MST: History, Project, and Experiences). As stated in the document's opening, its "principal objective" is to "disseminate the experience of the movement's work in education for reflection and to translate the history of MST schools for members in other states."[98] One ally who worked in the state government mentioned how at the end of the Requião administration, he made a concerted effort to discuss and formulate laws with Indigenous and Landless movement leaders.[99] A former member of the MPA who became part of government similarly mentioned how for fear of what took place in Rio Grande do Sul, the movement favored laws and created new routines. Specifically, I was told that "by the last years of the government, the government and the movement had learned. Things became routine. Like, when we needed buses for events, and we had over 60 events in 2009 and 2010, the government would provide."[100] The reason why the movement engaged in legislative work in Paraná is attributable not to external conditions, but to how movement leaders and allies learned from the repression that happened in Rio Grande do Sul.

The use of legislation for self-defense and protection for the movement to consolidate its gains was incorporated into its tactics at the federal level. Similar to what occurred in Rio Grande do Sul—but not with the same degree of violence—congressional inquiries, the CPIs in 2002, 2008, and 2010, periodically cut the movement off from resources. Movement leaders began to protect themselves from the potential pernicious results of these investigations by codifying their educational project. Particularly relevant is Resolução 1 CNE/CEB from 2002, which recognizes Education of the Countryside and that rural life requires a special form of education featuring social movements. Commenting on the resolution, one movement leader emphasized that it is "an instrument that the movement uses to assert the right to education, as well as something that gives people an increased sense of self-esteem."[101] From 2002 to 2015, twenty of Brazil's twenty-six states passed similar resolutions that recognize the legitimacy of Education of the Countryside.[102]

Two other actions at the federal level are noteworthy—one during the Lula administration and the other while Rousseff was in office. The first, decree 7352, made PRONERA a public policy (*política pública*) in 2010. When I asked movement leaders in Brasilia about the meaning of the decree, I was told that it functions as a "legal impediment in case someone challenges [the movement's actions]. Programs (*programas*) do not have this kind of protection."[103] What this means is that even if government authorities choose to defund PRONERA, they still must debate it yearly. As a program, and not a public policy, PRONERA could simply have been ignored and cut without discussion in government.

The action concerns the status of settlements. Since the 1980s, the movement has proposed that families who acquire land should remain with usufruct title (*titulo de concessão*) instead of definitive title (*titulo de dominio*). Granting definitive title allows members to rent and sell their land. The movement argues that the government should first provide extensive infrastructure investment over the course of many years before definitive titles are even considered. Government actors, especially since the 1990s, have promoted definitive titles as a way to cut government spending. For years, definitive titles have been resisted. When I asked one INCRA official about his ability to convince families to accept definitive titles, he pointed over his shoulder to boxes of titles sent to MST members and that were returned blank.[104] Similarly, I was told of the lack of progress in settlements in São Paulo state, where people in only one settlement had accepted definitive titles.[105] One problem for the movement was the stipulation within the Brazilian Constitution that stated that upon receiving land, families should receive definitive title. Government actors, such as the TCU, repeatedly called upon the movement and INCRA to begin to follow the law or face sanctions. After repeated meetings and negotiations with the government, the movement succeeded in 2014 in having this requirement for definitive title removed.[106] In this example, the change in law protected settlements from potential division, as well as the schools and training centers found therein.

Despite these tactical maneuvers to protect and consolidate the movement's revolutionary projects, interaction with governments has not always yielded success. When I spoke with one movement activist in the Pontal do Paranapanema region of São Paulo state, I was told that "the materials in settlement schools are often printed and distributed by agribusiness, promoting the use of pesticides and so on. And the director of education in the area, when he hears that we are with a social movement, doesn't even want to talk or listen."[107] This was corroborated in my interview with the director of pedagogy in the Pontal—where there are over one hundred schools on agrarian reform settlements—who had never heard of Education of the Countryside.[108] While in São Paulo, the Landless Movement has never succeeded in gaining resources or acknowledgement for primary or secondary education, in Rio Grande do Sul, movement gains were thwarted when the Crusius administration (2006–10) brought into power public officials who ended collaboration with the movement. Tarlau's research on the failures in these states highlights the barriers to movement growth placed by government elites.[109] Still, political conditions and the movement's legal mode of interaction are ways to understand the Landless Movement's work in education. Instead of mobilizing state and society, the movement mobilizes *through* public policy to demand and construct an alternative mode of organizing politics, economics, and culture.

The accumulation of forces, spearheaded by the MST in its efforts to consolidate the Landless Movement's educational project, emphasizes the use of legally binding documents and legislation to provide the movement material resources, legitimacy, and autonomy. At the core of the movement's efforts is a paradox that Sidney Tarrow draws our attention to regarding social movement contention: contentious political action destabilizes order while simultaneously requiring actions that stabilize it.[110] Or in other words, continuing practices of disruption must be coordinated by some organization. In addressing this paradox, the Landless Movement has increasingly regularized its actions internally and with respect to government institutions. At first glance, this seemingly removes its capacity to act independently of the state, endangering the Landless Movement's very existence as a social movement. Analyzing the movement's practices reveals a different set of dynamics. In fact, the Landless Movement's autonomy is sheltered by state protection more than ever during the accumulation-of-forces phase of resistance, allowing the movement to consolidate its revolutionary mode of resistance in certain spaces and adapt to changing political, state, and economic conditions.

The newer opponents to the movement, the MP and TCU for instance, differ from the large landowners and police forces that movement members encountered in the past. Taking account of these differences has led the movement to seek legal protection. Interacting with these new challengers to the movement's project has also required a different kind of leader—the militant-technician, someone who has formal training and also remains committed to the MST. The experiences in Rio Grande do Sul illustrate how autonomy without legislative support weakens the movement's efforts. In Paraná, the MST learned from the experiences in Rio Grande do Sul. The movement planned differently in Rio Grande do Sul, where movement leaders chose informal means of engaging with government leaders and engaging in more direct-action confrontations. As a result, the movement's efforts were undone more easily in Rio Grande do Sul than in Paraná. Lessons have also been learned at the national level, as seen in 2010 when the movement supported and encouraged the government to issue the decree that recognized Education of the Countryside. The practice of MST education is contentious, but not like the movement's land occupations and encampments.

LEARNING AND CONSOLIDATION DURING LESS FAVORABLE CONDITIONS

An analysis of state, economic, and political conditions helps explain why the movement sought to learn and consolidate, as opposed to engaging in more direct confrontations with political and economic elites. With respect to the economy, especially during Lula's time in office, there have not been significant signs of disruption or instability. Inequality—not in terms of land ownership, but income—has improved with the PT in power, decreasing from 59 points in 2002 to 52 in 2014, according to the Gini coefficient.[111] In other words, since 2002 approximately forty million people have become middle class, with thirty-five million people lifted out of extreme poverty. Social programs like Bolsa Familia (Family Fund) have been, at least in part, credited with removing extreme poverty from the Brazilian landscape. During FHC's time, the MST mobilized the growing urban periphery. While the PT was in power, this base of potential support was turning more to the government for assistance. Furthermore, the industrialization of agricultural production continued, but not at rates seen in the 1970s, 1980s, or 1990s. The numbers of both owner and nonowner operators remained basically unaltered throughout the 2000s. What also increased during the PT's time in power was the productivity of export agriculture: in 2002, export agriculture accounted for over US$25 billion in sales, while in 2010 that number grew to US$76 billion.[112] Fertilizer use, likewise, showed an increase during the 2000s, accompanied by a slight expansion in the number of hectares used in export agriculture. Similar to trends in the 1990s, large-scale agribusiness operations have deepened capital investments—that is, further industrialized,

TABLE 4 Agricultural Production, 1990s–2000s

	1995	2006
Tractors	799,742	820,673
Hectare per tractor average	62:1	72:1
Workers	17,930,890	16,567,574
Worker per operation	3.69	3.2
Owner operators	3,393,946	3,946,276
Nonowner operators	1,232,512	1,229,213

Source: IBGE, *Censo Agricola, Censo Agropecuario*, 1995–96, 2006.

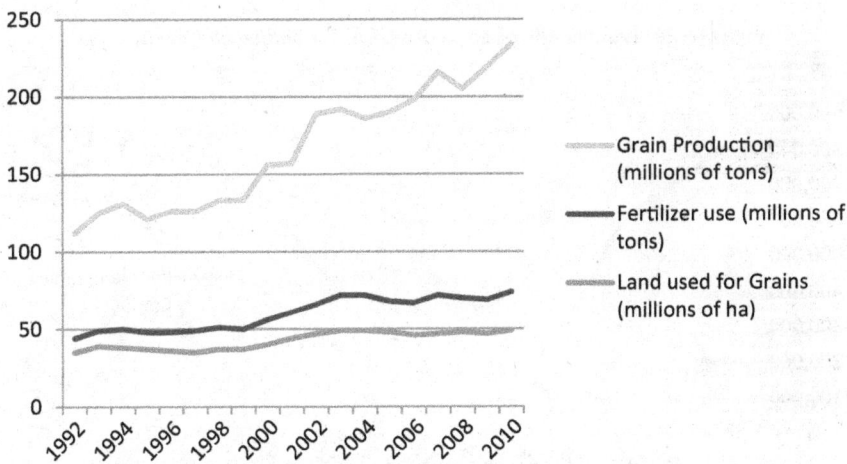

FIGURE 21 Grain production, fertilizer use, land use, 1990s–2000s. ANDA/CONCAB.

more than expanding the space in use. Taking these figures into account, we can observe that fewer people have been displaced during Lula's time than before.

State conditions—particularly with respect to territory and authority—have also changed in ways that militate against the MST's efforts to occupy and claim new spaces. First, the Lula government made a concerted effort to regularize territory in what is known as the Territórios de Cidadania (Territories of Citizenship) program. This program is dedicated to providing resources in over 120 specially designated rural areas for production support programs, public works, and land titling.[113] Lula would also repay Brazil's debt to the IMF in 2006. This did not remove deficit-spending from Brazilian politics—foreign debt to international institutions was replaced by the government's financial obligation to

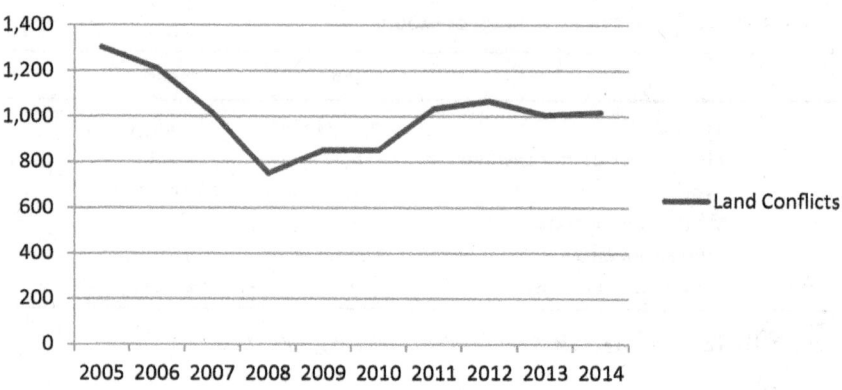

FIGURE 22 Land conflicts, 2005–2014. CPT, *Conflitos no Campo*, 2014.

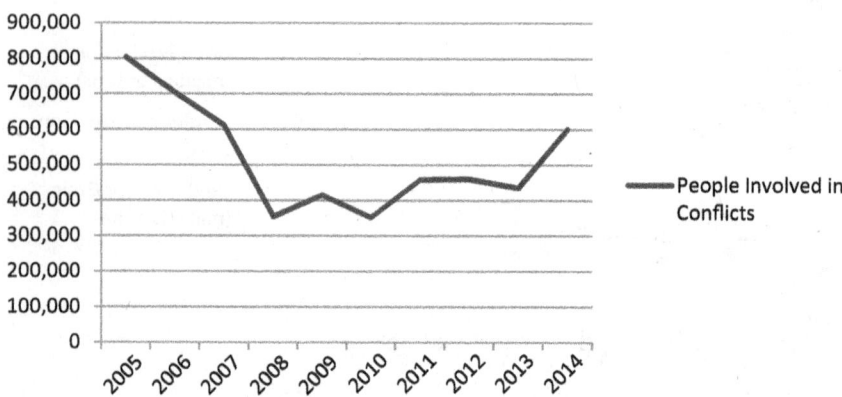

FIGURE 23 People involved in land conflicts, 2005–2014. CPT, *Conflitos no Campo*, 2014.

domestic actors. This change does mark a strengthening in state power by transferring control over government affairs to Brazilian actors, instead of remaining vulnerable to more international forces. From Lula through the Dilma administration, more people and spaces found their way onto "the grid" of state power, or to paraphrase James Scott's work, the state is "seeing" more people and where they live.[114] Such practices strengthen state power over territory and people, making use of the land-occupation tactic more difficult, if not unnecessary, when attempting to acquire space.

Conflicts over land and resources have remained constant, while showing a slight decline during this period. Land occupations have decreased as mobilizations demanding agrarian reform have increased.

Unlike in the 1990s, however, there has not been a single event to capture the public's attention or generate an outcry for agrarian reform. In fact, the coverage of the MST's occupation in 2009 of the large orange operation owned by the Cutrale corporation, especially a video of activists running over trees, portrayed the movement more as a criminal actor bent on destroying property instead of redistributing it. Similar to what occurred during the end of Cardoso's administration, public feeling about the MST has been increasingly critical. One survey done in 2009 by the CNA and IBOPE found that over 92 percent of the public believed occupations were illegal, 75 percent thought that the MST should find other means to acquire property, and 57 percent held that the MST had strayed from its original purpose.[115] Without public support, the movement's ability to receive more public programs and land has been limited. Despite the movement's identity work to represent its actions as legitimate and a defense of the public, as well as the environment, opponents have found more effective means to depict the MST's practices as illegal.

CONCLUSION: FROM THE STRUGGLE ON THE LAND BACK TO THE STRUGGLE FOR LAND?

While the movement's revolutionary mode of resistance has always been concerned with what happens after gaining land, its practices have been increasingly occupied with postoccupation struggles. In what is known as the *luta pela terra* (struggle for land) phase of the movement's actions, the focus is on pressuring private landowners and the Brazilian state to redistribute land. Equally as crucial for the movement is the post–land occupation phase of the Landless Movement's transformative, revolutionary project—what is known as the *luta na terra* (struggle on the land). At this step, the movement's energies shift to developing the territory its members receive. Here we find coordinated attempts to provide education for members and develop production cooperatives, among other practices intended to ensure that families remain on their newly acquired land. While the PT was in power, during what has been identified by the MST as the time to accumulate forces, the struggle on the land took on new dimensions. The movement's actions in this newer phase have a dual quality: on the one hand, they attempt to build capacity for future actions by creating new leaders, revising movement practices, and gaining resources; on the other, they directly challenge dominant political and economic elites. In the face of challenges from agribusiness conglomerates and attacks from congressional inquiries, the Landless Movement's work in education and in economic production remains as much about *how* policies are executed as *who* has the power to administer.

Intra-movement comparisons show how the MST has accumulated forces in different ways. Paraná and Rio Grande do Sul are particularly illustrative sites for this kind of comparison because of their similarities. The intra-movement comparison shows one way to disaggregate social movements for social inquiry. In particular, we see how actors can learn from one another to improve how they engage and adapt revolutionary modes of contentious political action. In a sense, the movement learns from itself. The accumulation-of-forces phase of the Landless Movement's resistance has seen the gathering of resources and tactical lessons.

The terrain on which agrarian reform is taking place has undergone significant changes in the last decade. Agribusiness firms and export agriculture have grown substantially in Brazil, despite the Landless Movement's opposition. Public opinion has also turned against the movement. Land redistribution remains a central demand, while production and reproduction of rural social relations in spaces already claimed by the movement also require attention. It is true that economic production remains crucial—the accumulation-of-forces period involved a focus on cooperatives and a renewed focus on agroecology. For the struggle for land to regain prominence in the movement, new leaders, with innovative tactics and critical perspectives, may have to emerge. Rather than trusting outside actors for leadership, the Landless Movement is creating the spaces for the next generation of activists to develop. How, and if, the struggle for land again becomes viable, will be decided by the leaders-to-be who are learning in movement schools.

CONCLUSION

LESSONS FROM THE LANDLESS REVOLUTION?

Post–Workers' Party Brazil and Revolutionary
Political Action in the Global North

THE LANDLESS MOVEMENT IN A POST-PT BRAZIL

IN NOVEMBER OF 2016, as part of what was called Operação Castra, Brazilian police forces raided schools and training sites operated by the MST and arrested fourteen members for alleged illegal activities.[1] Such direct acts of repression, from the perspective of the Landless Movement, are similar to the efforts of the Collor de Mello regime (1990–92), as well as the actions of the Crusius administration in Rio Grande do Sul (2006–10). What makes the arrests particularly worrisome for the Landless Movement is that the PT is no longer in power at the federal level. Dilma Rousseff, Brazil's democratically elected president, was removed from political office in August of 2016 after accusations were made that she knowingly participated in an extensive money-laundering scheme. In the investigation known as Operação Lava Jato (Operation Car Wash—the investigation found that an actual car wash was used to launder money), Brazilian authorities uncovered a wide-reaching network where executives from the country's multinational oil and natural gas corporation, Petrobras, took bribes from politicians in exchange for setting up overpriced contracts with construction companies. The scandal, the largest in Brazilian history, saw the laundering of approximately US$15 billion. Many Brazilian politicians have been implicated. Dozens of representatives from the Brazilian Chamber of Deputies are under investigation, and a third—twenty-four—of Brazil's eighty-one senators have been connected to the scandal. Overall, over five hundred people at various levels of the Brazilian government and from political parties across the spectrum are believed to have taken part in the laundering scheme.

Despite the scandal involving practically the entire Brazilian political establishment, on the political right and left, the investigation found no direct evidence of President Rousseff's direct involvement.[2] This did not stop the Brazilian lower house, the Câmara dos Deputados (Chamber of Deputies), from voting to initiate impeachment proceedings against Dilma, 367 in favor and 122 against. Dilma was later temporarily suspended from office on May 12, 2016, after the Senate voted 55 to 22. Then, on August 31, the Brazilian Senate voted 61 to 20 to remove Dilma from the presidency. She was replaced by the acting vice president, Michel Temer of the center-right PMDB, who at one time was within the PT's coalition government. During and after her removal, mass protests—both against and in support of the Workers' Party government and its policies—periodically paralyzed Brazilian society. Central to the mobilizations on the political left is the Frente Brasil Popular (FBP; Brazilian Popular Front), which has brought together over sixty rural and urban movements, unions, and organizations. Among the actors active within the FBP is the Landless Movement.

After assuming power, the Temer administration acted quickly. In fact, the same day that Dilma was suspended—May 12—Temer issued a *medida provisória* to facilitate the executive's unilateral ability to establish concessions and public-private contracts.[3] Publicly, his administration announced privatization plans that included the natural gas industry,[4] public mail service,[5] airports,[6] and state-owned electric companies.[7] The government set March 16, 2017, as the date to auction off four airports.[8] Privatizations will continue through 2018, including concessions of some of Brazil's oil fields, railways, and ports.[9] The first actual privatization came in November of 2016, when Celg, a state-owned electricity company, was sold to the Italian company Enel.[10] The publicly traded but state-controlled bank Banco do Brasil has seen thousands of layoffs and the closing of multiple branches.[11] Temer, in an act of "institutional consolidation" amid efforts to cut government spending, moved the MDA and INCRA into the MDS.[12] This, in addition to the ongoing discussions concerning potentially opening Brazilian public land to foreign investors,[13] was a direct affront to the Landless Movement and the struggle for agrarian reform. Among other changes, members of the new governing coalition proposed to restructure Social Security by establishing a minimum age of sixty-five for men and sixty for women for accessing benefits (currently citizens begin to receive benefits after thirty-five years of work, regardless of their age), as well as to reduce the total amount of benefits that recipients may receive.[14] Such plans to privatize state-owned utilities, public land, and airports expressly defy the demands of the mobilized opposition on Brazil's political left.

The rise of Temer to power provoked the Brazilian left to rally behind the PT, not so much for what the Dilma and Lula administrations did, but out of fear that a new administration would repeal popular social programs, further privatize public enterprises, and completely end support for agrarian reform. As chapter 5 documents, the PT administrations did not directly confront agribusiness interests. One principal reason for the PT's inaction on agrarian reform is that a steady supply of foreign currency allows the government to pay off foreign debt obligations and control the value of the Brazilian real to sustain capitalist development.[15] Deeper redistributive efforts, ones that would involve further expropriation and reallocation of land, would endanger the means by which the government pays foreign financiers and stabilizes the Brazilian currency for investment. The PT's half-hearted embrace of the Landless Movement's demands presented the movement with a variety of dilemmas concerning its strategic orientation—for on the one hand, the movement benefitted from increased resources for development projects, while on the other, large-scale land redistribution did not occur. Such ambiguity does not characterize the policy proposals and actions from the Temer administration. While the PT administrations could have at times been read as allies, or even as friendly to the movement, those days abruptly ended when Dilma was formally removed from office.

For the Landless Movement, mobilizing within an environment that is hostile to its interests is not new. Over its three-decade existence, the movement has periodically been met with opposition. Well-known instances include the encounter in 1981 with Colonel Curió at Encruzilhada Natalino in the state of Rio Grande do Sul, as discussed in chapter 3, and also the massacre in the municipality of Eldorado das Carajás in 1997, which is analyzed in chapter 4 in its connection to the Landless Movement's expansion. Unlike these previous incidents of repression, especially the events during the formative years of the movement, the MST and its allies are well prepared. Protecting and consolidating the Landless Movement's revolutionary project has become central to the movement's attempts to strengthen its organization, practices of economic development, and leadership. During the PT government, the movement dedicated much of its time and energy to such initiatives in its accumulation-of-forces phase. Meanwhile, in this latter phase of consolidating its mode of revolutionary resistance, the movement continues to challenge neoliberalism—which appears to be the mantra of the Temer government. Those who claim that the movement is in decline need to pay closer attention to the significant gains made by the MST and its allies, especially while the PT was in power at the federal level. As this book illustrates, the decades of organizing and mobilization makes the Landless Movement well prepared to confront its enemies in a post-PT Brazil.

How the movement's revolutionary form of political action weathers the current moment in Brazilian history will depend on the alliances that the movement makes, as well as on the effectiveness of the Temer government. The Temer administration saw its disapproval rating rise above 50 percent early in December of 2016 as six top-ranking ministers in the government resigned because of corruption scandals and pressure from other political elites.[16] At the start of 2018, a mere 6 percent of Brazilians approved of Temer's performance in office, while 70 percent explicitly disapproved.[17] This suggests a destabilization of government conditions. The Landless Movement could take advantage of such problems for the new government by expanding its political project. Yet, the movement's participation within the FBP may require spending more of its energies on coalition-building and defense. Another possibility is that members of the FBP that previously were only tangentially connected to the Landless Movement will learn the movement's tactical repertoire and become radicalized. At the time of this writing, it is too early to forecast the future of revolutionary politics in Brazil. What can be claimed is that uncertainty is certain.

SITUATING THE LANDLESS REVOLUTION IN LATIN AMERICA'S "PINK TIDE"

Often traced to the election in 1998 of the late president of Venezuela, Hugo Chávez, a series of left-wing governments gained power throughout Central and South America over the past couple decades. In fact, except for Colombia and Mexico, Latin American countries saw the rise of strong left-wing political parties and/or governing coalitions. However, the election of Mauricio Macri from the center-right Cambiemos (Let's Change) coalition in Argentina in 2015, the removal of Dilma Rousseff in 2016, and the prolonged economic crisis in Nicolaus Maduro's Venezuela indicate that the pink tide has ebbed. Even as the leftward swing in Latin American politics is in limbo, it is widely accepted that a dramatic shift took place.

Many scholars have analyzed and conceptualized the rise of the left in Latin American. Jorge Castañeda's Manichean division between what he calls the "good" and "bad" left, which he catalogues as open versus closed and modern as opposed to backward,[18] has given rise to many critiques of that as an oversimplification.[19] In the context of the region's two-decade embrace of left-wing administrations, the Workers' Party was considered a center-left alternative to the more radical governments of Venezuela and Bolivia. This is not to claim that government-led initiatives have been inconsequential. Bolsa Familia has been instrumental in lifting millions out of extreme poverty. Thousands of new agrarian reform settlements were created during the administrations of both Lula and Dilma, as millions of dollars were dedicated to education, housing, and infrastructural programs. Still, as chapters 4 and 5 detail, the PT has progressively deradicalized since its emergence in the 1980s.

The literature documenting the new Latin American left has two faults. First, the scholarship tends to focus on governments. This is not universally true—George Ciccariello-Maher's work on Venezuela shows how social and government action may become blurred in revolutionary situations.[20] Similarly, Álvaro García Linera analyzes the productive contradictions that characterize social movement and government collaboration in Bolivia.[21] These studies are exceptional in that most scholarship subordinates social movements with respect to government. The essays in Steve Ellner's edited volume *Latin America's Radical Left*, while drawing our attention to crucial differences between Ecuador, Bolivia, and Venezuela, remain focused on recently elected presidents and the challenges they face while governing.[22] Roger Burbach and colleagues and Emir Sader do not examine social movement resistance, but instead explain the rise of left-wing administrations.[23] Steven Levitsky and Kenneth Roberts's *Latin America's Left Turn* adds Peru and Chile to the cases considered part of the pink tide, yet still draws our attention to governments and political parties in these countries.[24] Social movements, in most studies of the left-wing shift in Latin American politics, are either ignored or considered, at best, ancillary partners that follow the leadership of their respective governments.

The danger in these accounts is to reify narrow definitions concerning what is the realm of appropriate social movement political action. Implicit is the notion that the government is the seat of political power, with movements as subordinate participants whose main role is to raise demands in that nebulous, poorly defined space liberals call "civil society." This kind of thinking limits our understanding of what precisely movements are doing. What this book makes clear is that movements such as the Landless Movement express and articulate social grievances, as well as set up and administer schools and economic development initiatives. Such movements, which also include El Ejército Zapatista de Liberación Nacional (EZLN; Zapatista Army of National Liberation, or Zapatistas) and La Confederación de Nacionalidades Indígenas del Ecuador (CONAIE; Confederation of Indigenous Nationalities of Ecuador), the Argentine *piqueteros*, and others, also lay claim to space to transform political, economic, and cultural relationships. These movements use and sometimes rely on official government policies, and they invoke their constitutions when carrying out their transformative efforts. These cases, especially the Landless Movement, challenge commonsense notions about the role of social movements in society and force us to rethink the dynamics of the leftward shift in Latin American politics.

This book draws attention to the role of social movements in Latin America's left turn. Instead of taking the opposite approach by focusing on movements instead of governments, I analyze, as in Linera's discussion of developments in Bolivia, the paradoxes, contradictions, and tensions between government and social movement actors. I deepen this discussion with a focus particularly on the Landless Movement because it is the largest movement on the continent in terms of people mobilized and territorial reach (the MST in particular claims to have mobilized over one and a half million members in twenty-four of Brazil's twenty-six states). Its influence has extended into other countries, spurring similar movements in Uruguay, Bolivia, and South Africa, as well as solidarity groups throughout Europe and the United States.

One quality that unifies Latin America's pink tide is opposition to neoliberal restructuring. Sader, for example, considers current developments on the continent as best defined by various governments' express rejection of neoliberal policy prescriptions.[25] I agree that a common thread connecting leftist actors is the opposition to deregulation, privatization, monetarism, export-oriented models of development, and the elimination of social services. Such policy prescriptions also, perhaps counterintuitively, have created conditions that have benefitted certain left-wing actors. In addition to making the United States a target for attack, exemplified by Hugo Chávez's frequent denunciations of U.S. imperialism and his gift of Eduardo Galeano's *Las venas abiertas de America Latina* (The Open Veins of Latin America) to President Obama, neoliberal reforms also dismantled centralized, often repressive, authoritarian governments. Neoliberal restructuring, instead of uniformly affecting leftist movements and government, created conditions that certain actors navigated skillfully and that others failed to maneuver, which I document at length in my comparison of the MST, PT, and CUT in chapter 4.

IMPLICATIONS FOR STUDIES OF SOCIAL MOVEMENTS AND REVOLUTION

From land occupations to schools, I consider the Landless Movement's mode of resistance indicative of revolutionary political action. This book shows that Jeff Goodwin and Theda Skocpol's claim that elections spell the end for revolutionary movements requires reassessment.[26] Collectivizing production decisions, promoting small-group debate and discussion on the content of courses in various schools, performing distinct cultural rituals—the routinization of these practices directly challenges the Brazilian state's mode of organizing political, economic, and cultural life. Revolutionary contention, in the case of the MST and its allies, is not about completely freeing, or liberating, people from control. The Landless Movement disciplines its members. If objects are stolen, whether in schools or in encampments, then people are punished. Still, even in these more disciplinary functions, the movement's collective action and revolutionary mode of resistance are on display. Protests against privatizations and calls for further state spending on certain public programs show the ways that the MST and its ally movements act against the dominant imperatives of neoliberal policy prescriptions. The Landless Movement's actions and form of organization illustrate not just a denunciation of current neoliberal orthodoxy, but a way to mobilize and live beyond it.

My study, in contributing to the growing literature on Brazilian social movements and Marxist approaches to revolutionary contention, provides a nuanced theoretical and conceptual apparatus to address a long-standing debate on agency and structure. One concept from this debate is what social movement theorists call political opportunity structure. Popularized by Sydney Tarrow and others, the term highlights the nonmovement context for collective action. Recent work on fields, networks, and kinds of opportunity offers additional ways to think about external factors, yet remain unclear on how to differentiate "political" conditions from others such as economic, state, and government conditions.

"Political" factors too often mean government, and the presence or absence of allies or opponents in some formal institution. Quite simply, too much is read into what can be considered an "opportunity" and "political." Skocpol, Joel Migdal, Joseph Page, and James Scott work with a much richer conception of structure when analyzing revolutions. Some find explanatory power in international forces, while others are concerned with the destabilization of economic relations. In these studies, the state and the concept of sovereignty, as well as broader economic trends, were addressed.

I build off prior revolutionary and social movement theory, while making a few modifications. Many of the elements of the conceptual apparatus I develop come from the Marxist, Post-Marxist, and Critical Theory traditions, mainly from combining insights from Lenin, Schmitt, Negri, and Dussel. Working with texts from these authors poses its own challenges—where social movement studies leave an understanding of politics and conditions vague, the theorists on whom I draw specify their concepts in great detail. I connect their insights to formulate my definition of revolutionary resistance as the mutually exclusive claim to space and the effort to transform political, economic, and cultural relations in a way that erases the distinction between institutionalized public and private power. Schmitt, moreover, provides a way to conceive of how extralegal tactics engender opportunities. In my framework, an opportunity is rare and lasts for a short time, unlike conditions such as the state, economics, and government that persist. An opportunity is an opening for action and change, a chance that results from how a movement's tactics interact with pre-existing conditions. As structural conditions change, so does the effectiveness of tactics. Movements adapt, change, and incorporate lessons in updating their tactical repertoires.

Lenin, Negri, and Dussel provide a way to understand how state power is premised on the separation between formal institutions, which retain the prerogative to design and execute services and public policy, and actors within civil society. Revolutionary political action democratizes service design and execution. This means that services and policies are taken, or claimed, by a movement. Also, such a form of political action blurs the lines between what is considered economic and political life. Lenin saw such changes in the soviets. Negri and Dussel theorize what this means in the dialectic between constitutive and constituted power. In the case of the Landless Movement, the movement uses public policies to claim control over particular services in encampments and settlements. To democratize a policy area means involving more people directly, as well as breaking down the institutional barrier between state and society. To break down, or dissolve, the division between state and society is not the same as adding civil society to government. Revolutionary contention is about working in, outside of, and through state power. Revolutions do not add government, or political society, to civil society, but abolish both in collapsing the distinction.

The concept of revolutionary political action that I develop also embraces an understanding of sovereignty. From early twentieth-century theorists, namely Lenin and Schmitt, I take the notion of a movement that claims space in order to transform social relations. The concepts of dual power and the partisan offer a new way to consider how the Landless Movement represents itself as a single, unified actor that produces collective ways of life in certain areas. Connecting sovereignty to social movement action, additionally, connects with the growing literature on the meaning, practice, and development of food sovereignty. That the Landless Movement embraces the term, especially after joining the LVC in the mid-1990s, should not distract from the ways that the MST and its allies were claiming space throughout the 1980s. This book documents how the fundamentals of the Landless Movement's revolutionary claim to space have remained constant over time, even with periodic adaptations and innovations. My combination of the insights from Schmitt, Lenin, Negri, and Dussel contributes a novel approach to the ongoing empirical and theoretical research on food sovereignty.

The theoretical apparatus developed in this book also provides a way to conceive of the difference between state and government—a conceptual division that is elided in most social movement research. State conditions homogenize a people and the means of practicing authority throughout a particular territory. Movements are successful when they deploy their tactics where state conditions are vulnerable or destabilized. Governments are the institutions and organizations that wield state power, without being conterminous with it. Government conditions include political parties, elections, and official institutions—courts, bureaucracies, and so on. As with state conditions, government stability, as seen in a population's acceptance of the power and legitimacy of these actors, tends to disfavor the unfolding of radical movement resistance. Economic conditions also feature similar dynamics concerning instability and weakness, with the focus on labor relations, monetary policy, and the distribution of goods and/or assets. When an economy is stable, movement tactics are unlikely to produce opportunities; when conditions are destabilized and vulnerable due to rising unemployment or inflation, movement emergence and persistence have greater chances of success.

The focus on the Landless Movement as a case of revolutionary resistance should provoke readers to compare my study with more commonly considered examples of revolution, which in Latin America means the Cuban or Nicaraguan cases. While an exhaustive comparison is outside the purview of this book, it is worth noting that in Cuba, the revolutionary processes initiated by the 26th of July Movement in 1956 worked inside and outside of state power for a prolonged time to create and consolidate an alternative mode of social organization. Before and after deposing the Batista regime in 1959, revolutionary practices included land seizures and redistribution, and also expropriations of foreign assets. Expelling foreign owners entailed a dramatic and radical change that had repercussions nationally and internationally.

Such acts should not distract us from subsequent initiatives, such as the Cuban government's literary campaign, which was just as revolutionary as the moment of armed insurrection. At the end of Batista's rule, an estimated 24 percent of the population could not read or write. By the end of the 1961 national literacy campaign, illiteracy had fallen to just under 4 percent; meanwhile, various elementary and secondary schools were constructed throughout the island. The education campaign generated mass mobilization and support. Close to 270,000 people ended up participating in grassroots initiatives.[27] In March of 1959—three months after deposing Batista—the Ministry of Education devised a plan and created the Comisión Nacional de Alfabetización (National Commission for Literacy) to coordinate activities. The commission, which was headed by the Departments of Technology, Publicity, and Finance, issued two notebooks for use during the literacy campaign—*Alfabetizamos* (Let's Learn to Read and Write) and *Venceremos!* (We Will Win!). The content of these notebooks featured explicit political and ideological elements, such as land reform, the importance of cooperatives in economic production, and anti-imperialism. Each department donated modest financial support to coordinate the construction of basic infrastructure projects that would allow volunteers to travel throughout the island.[28] Implementing the campaign required a variety of organizations. These groups included the 26th of July Movement, the PSP (Partido Socialista Popular; Socialist Popular Party), students, teachers, and women's groups. From these groups would arise future technicians, supervisors, government officials, and activists.

In addition to the Ministry of Education's planning, various other government resources were mobilized. Law 680 of 1959 closed a series of private schools and established new criteria for administering public primary, secondary, and postsecondary education. Also, laws ensured that urban workers would receive their wages if they left work to participate in the campaign. Universities and secondary schools, likewise, were closed early in 1961 to contribute to the grassroots efforts. Volunteers could leave work or school without penalty. To simultaneously cut costs and generate a sense of community, participants lived and worked with the families who were receiving instruction. The transformational qualities of the campaign were accompanied by disciplinary elements. At the universities, students and faculty who would not support the revolutionary initiative were fired and/or fled to Miami to join anti-Castro forces in 1960.[29] The campaign also featured a kind of militarization. Groups were organized into brigades, and volunteers wore military-style uniforms. The language used to describe the campaign objectives frequently included allusions to battles and warfare. In the language and the uniforms, the separation between the revolutionary project and illiteracy was clearly framed as a friend/enemy distinction. Through coercion, financial support, and a volunteer spirit cultivated with militarization, the campaign confronted illiteracy and poverty by merging social actors with legal institutions and policies. The division between civil society and government was abolished.

Taking the Cuban case out of comparative perspective may lead to an overly romanticized view of the transformative changes practiced on the island and a neglect of the tensions within the revolution. Specifically, it is unlikely that expropriations, and radical social projects, could have persisted without the support of the Soviet Union. The Soviet Union in the 1960s purchased Cuban sugar en masse, essentially taking over the sugar export quota that had been previously guaranteed by the United States. From the 1960s to the 1990s, through the Soviet trade bloc COMECON (Council for Mutual Economic Assistance), Cuba was the main supplier of sugar to Eastern Bloc countries. The COMECON ensured the purchase of sugar at prices above the world average, provided the island military defense, and offered subsidized oil. With such protection and subsidies, the Cuban government devoted financial resources to social programs in health care and education.[30] Agrarian reform measures, which were extensive, changed the economic structure of the country only so much—dependency on sugar exports continued for decades, only truly changing with the fall of Soviet Union. Some see the subsequent, post-Soviet era of development as leading to Cuba's fourth agrarian reform: without subsidized oil, urban and rural producers were forced to turn to agroecological and labor-intensive methods.[31] Regardless of these post-Soviet changes, monoculture and export dependence on sugar reveal a persistent economic hierarchy pre- and post-1959.

What this brief reference to Cuba highlights is that both cases of revolutionary political action—in Brazil and Cuba—display modes of claiming territory. The Landless Movement also assumes state power, but neither with the ballot nor the bullet. Mobilizing, constantly, for control over public policies is how the movement effects radical political, economic, and cultural change in certain areas. By demanding and claiming policy, the movement organizes inside, outside of, and through the state. In Cuba, deposing Batista did lead one government to replace another. Yet, in such a change, economic dependence on the Soviet Union undergirded the subsequent efforts to transform Cuban social relations. That leads to the conclusion that revolutionary political action is not necessarily about deposing governments. In fact, removing a particular administration can take place independently of transforming political, economic, and/or cultural relationships. Simply changing governing elites is indicative not of revolution but a coup d'état. Social transformation change takes time, often years and decades. What is central to revolutionary political action is that actors claim space, and in their representations and practices transform politics, economics, and culture. This brief comparison of changes in Cuba and Brazil shows that differences between the revolutionary transformations are more a matter of degree than of kind.

AGRARIAN REFORM AND REVOLUTIONARY POLITICAL ACTION IN THE UNITED STATES?

When I was in Brazil, I had many discussions with members of the Landless Movement about the potential for similar kinds of movements to emerge and develop in the United States. Certain leaders in the MST encouraged me to share with their allies and members my understanding of agrarian reform, rural movements, and revolutionary politics in the United States. What began as informal conversations about U.S. history and politics turned into organized presentations that I delivered wherever I went while in Brazil.

After returning to the United States, I continued to consider the possibility for a similar mode of movement development to take place in the United States. I began to document current U.S. movements that have similarities with the

Landless Movement. Some of these current actors are members of the LVC and many see the need for some sort of agrarian reform in the United States. For instance, Joel Greeno of the Wisconsin-based Family Farm Defenders mentioned the MST's work on land reform as impressive and worth emulating.[32] To commemorate the life of Nelson Mandela, the Federation of Southern Cooperatives—an organization in the long lineage of African American–led operations—cited the former South African president's efforts at agrarian reform as an inspiration for developing similar efforts in the United States.[33] In an article on land policy in the United States, small farmer Bob St. Peter and scholar-activist Raj Patel called for extensive government support to help newer farmers access land and rebuild rural communities.[34] While still marginal, such debates and demands concerning agrarian reform are growing. These comments on agrarian reform, furthermore, reveal a radicalization of the North American food movement—groups are beginning to demand space, new communities, and the redistribution of resources.

Analyzing such demands from movement actors and leaders leads to a variety of questions. Is there a history of demand for agrarian reform in the United States? Did these more radical approaches to food politics emerge ex nihilo, or are there traditions that current actors can draw upon? Can these movements make such demands, even in the context of seemingly impermeable external, nonmovement conditions? What are the chances that social movements analogous to the Landless Movement can even exist in the United States?

What follows is an attempt to answer these questions. It is not meant to be a comprehensive comparison of radical forms of contention in Brazil and the United States, but rather an account of moments when revolutionary actors pressed for space in the United States. It turns out that differences between the Global South and North are fewer than many believe. Future research should continue this analysis, in both its historical and existing dimensions.

With respect to the United States, the history of territorial delimitation and acquisition shows multiple similarities to that in Brazil. The 1850 Land Law in Brazil established the public auction as the principal means of distributing property, while the U.S. Homestead Act allowed acquisition either by an occupancy condition (five years with "improvement") or by purchase (for $1.25 per acre). And also akin to the 1850 Land Law, the Homestead Act in 1862 did not result in equitable levels of property ownership—close to half of the titles issued were discovered to be fraudulent, with millions of acres of territory irregularly acquired, principally by railroad companies, mining corporations, and speculators.[35] The Homestead Act was not the only piece of legislation crafted to organize the land tenure regime in the United States. Before the Homestead Act, a series of laws known as the Preemption Acts were passed by the federal government so that squatters could gain legal title to land that people previously occupied without deeds.[36] These laws, and others dealing with swamp and desert lands, as well as water, have created a body of land legislation that has been described as ultimately "ineffective" in clarifying the nature of land tenure owing to the "numerous countervailing laws."[37] The history of land law in the United States shows a patchwork of legislation that features contradictions and the legitimization of fraudulent appropriation. As in Brazil, competing claims to ownership potentially (and in some cases, actually) involve millions of acres of territory.

Undergirding the U.S. system of property acquisition and claim to state sovereignty were the multiple legal, economic, and coercive means to dispossess Native American people. Roxanne Dunbar-Ortiz divides land acquisition throughout U.S. history into three successive stages: (1) military occupation, (2) the formation of territories under civilian authority, and (3) the official establishment of statehood as soon as white settlers outnumbered the Indigenous population within a territory.[38] Marxist scholars would consider these dynamics illustrative of primitive accumulation, or as what David Harvey has theorized as "accumulation by dispossession."[39] Both these concepts recognize that violence creates and maintains the division between one class of people who lack productive property and another who possesses it, laying the conditions for the initial and continual production of capital. This is where we find the origins of private property—an institution that separates workers and owners, and which in making this division allows owners of assets through the rule of law to perpetually acquire and amass wealth.

In the United States, the dynamics of primitive accumulation are first apparent in the way the federal government appropriated land in treaties. Especially during what Dunbar-Ortiz calls the "civilian" phase of appropriation, the federal government negotiated with Indigenous nations over the geographical limits of each power's territorial authority. As of 2016, there were over five hundred federally recognized Native tribes in the United States, with more than 370 treaties made over the course of centuries. This history of recognition has been anything but; more often than not, relations were, and in many cases remain, characterized by conflict and misunderstanding. Problems tended to accompany each treaty because colonial and postcolonial Euro-American state-builders believed that land was a commodity and thus alienable, while most Indigenous nations, in different ways, rejected such conceptions. Many nations claimed and negotiated territories that other Indigenous people inhabited, and still others forfeited their "rights," thinking that the treaties were temporary.[40] Such legal arrangements, and the concomitant confusion concerning titling, ownership, and possession, often resulted in wars and the forced relocation of Indigenous people to other areas. Additionally, at the end of the eighteenth century the U.S. government instituted what became known as the factory system. Through a system of trading posts, settlers, and traders, an exchange economy based on U.S. currency and debt was gradually established with most Native Americans.[41] Dividing and then selling territory became a means for Native Americans to pay off their debts even after the factory system became a de facto institution in 1822. This is one difference between the U.S. and Brazilian systems—the treaty and debt technologies of dispossession were the model in the United States, not in Brazil.

Still, both countries feature territorial land regimes premised on fraud and violence. Another quality in common is that actors have led innovative, radical projects to claim space because of the fractured nature of colonial and postcolonial sovereignty. While not a social movement per se, the efforts by freed slaves during and shortly after the U.S. Civil War (1861–65) were one attempt at revolutionary agrarian reform. W. E. B. Du Bois documents how slaves, once the Union army won certain battles and acquired territory, escaped plantations in droves to join Union forces and fight against the Confederacy.[42] In what Du Bois considers indicative of a "general strike," the masses of slaves who arrived at the camps of Union forces caught the Northern leadership by surprise. The accompanying confusion arose in part because President Lincoln initially proposed allowing Southern states to keep the institution of slavery if they would rejoin the Union. The Emancipation Proclamation in 1863, furthermore, did not free slaves in states within the Union that permitted slavery, for example, Kentucky, but in the South. The proclamation was principally a strategic device used to weaken the Southern economy by appealing directly to slaves to abandon the plantations. The slaves' general strike took the North by surprise because the government did not have a way to respond.

Partially to respond to the impromptu exodus of slaves, as well as to challenge the Confederacy, the Union government issued particular legal actions and directives during the war to redistribute land. In 1861 and 1862, the federal government passed the Confiscation Acts. The acts legitimized the government's reclaiming and appropriation of property—land *and* slaves. General Sherman issued Field Order No. 15 after meeting with twenty former slaves in Georgia in 1864. The field order is where the now famous reference was made to "forty acres and a mule." Such legislation allowed for, at least in principle, the permanent redistribution of land. Unfortunately for the slaves, the Confiscation Acts and field order were not accompanied by any effective means of implementation.

Government inaction during and shortly after the war did not deter former slaves from mobilizing in radical redistributive projects. Groups of self-emancipated slaves in a few areas took over plantations and began to construct small communities.[43] One of the most famous examples took place off the shores of South Carolina at Sea Island, where around forty thousand former slaves organized a community that featured its own schools, churches, and production system. A similar initiative unfolded in Mississippi on the plantation owned by the president of the Confederacy, Jefferson Davis. The organizers at this place, in claiming the plantation and transforming it, referenced the unenforced Confiscation Acts to legitimize the occupation. The debates on the agrarian question continued after the war ended. Initially, redistributing plantation land was the responsibility of the Freedman's Bureau (full name: U.S. Bureau of Refugees, Freedmen, and Abandoned Lands), which was established in 1865. In 1867, the South Carolina Land Commission was created with the express purpose of purchasing land and then redistributing it.

The period for innovative grassroots initiatives to seize territory was brief. The projects behind land redistribution quickly dissipated as Southern and Northern interests returned to the South and the demand for voting rights outweighed economic concerns in the Republicans' Reconstruction project.[44] The former slaves were driven from Jefferson Davis's plantation, and the land at Sea Island was returned to its previous owner after the Union Army forced the occupiers out in 1866. The Land Commission in South Carolina fell apart in the mid-1880s owing to mismanagement and a lack of resources.[45] Despite the end of these experiments in radical, revolutionary practices of land redistribution, thousands of black farmers gained land at this time and formed cooperatives.[46] Relatives of the farmers, including members of the Mississippi Association of Cooperatives and the Federation of Southern Cooperatives, remain active today.

Other African American–led movements carried into the twentieth century the demand for land reform. Part of the Black Panther Party's Ten Point Program included land redistribution, referencing forty acres and a mule as the standard. The Panthers, in addition to challenging police brutality by conducting their own police surveillance, made food distribution a priority in economically marginalized communities.[47] Also in the 1970s, the movement called the Republic of New Africa sought reparations for slavery and prison reform. The movement attempted to declare itself independent from the national government by creating its own nation-state out of Mississippi.[48] In different ways, these civil rights–era movements claimed space as a means of transforming race relations and radically altering the economic life of marginalized African American communities.

Other sharecropper and small-farmer organizations were also active in demanding and practicing radical forms of agrarian reform in the twentieth century. One organization that emerged during the Great Depression was the Southern Tenant Farmers' Union (STFU). At its peak in the 1930s, the organization counted over twenty thousand members.[49] Its demands included reforming the oppressive political and economic qualities of Southern agriculture, as well as agrarian reform. Among its tactics, the movement organized strikes and held mass meetings to educate its members. Strikes per se were not legally recognized until the 1930s, and only then for urban workers. The organization was rare in so far as its leadership managed to organize rural people across racial lines. Its principal predecessor, the Populists, which emerged decades before the turn of the century, had difficulty organizing across racial lines, organizing in some states white and "colored" alliances.[50] The STFU—later called the National Agricultural Workers Union—lasted into the 1960s, yet was significantly weakened with the beginning of World War II and the exodus of rural people to urban areas that was caused by the introduction of labor-saving technologies in agriculture. The organization's more radical elements—which included members such as Socialist Party leader Norman Thomas in the 1930s—were rooted out by McCarthyist, federal government repression in the 1940s and 1950s.

Principal among the STFU contributions was its radical legislation and proposals with respect to territory. At the center of the STFU's innovative legislation was the New Homestead Act, which called for a national agricultural authority to nationalize all farmland except for operations owned by people with less than 160 acres.[51] While more of a demand than an actual law, various concrete New Deal projects in the 1930s developed in response. The Farm Security Administration (FSA), for instance, arose in the mid-1930s to counter the massive rural displacement caused by the Dust Bowl. Frank Tannenbaum, who had researched agrarian reform efforts in Mexico, helped craft the directives for the FSA. One document he authored in 1934, "A Program to Develop a New System of Rural Tenure," created an $300 million endowment for the FSA to purchase and then redistribute land where "the landlord function was not serving an adequate social purpose."[52] What, precisely, was the "social" component in this legislation was left open to debate. From discussions at the time in Congress, as well as comments by Tannenbaum, we can infer that land not serving a social function was characterized by owners who engaged in exploitative labor relations and who had little or no respect for the environment.[53] In 1937, the Bankhead-Jones Farm Tenant Act was passed; it established loans for farmers to acquire land and county-level commissions that decided which land was eligible for redistribution.

The historical importance of the STFU and the New Deal–era rural legislation is debated. The STFU's New Homestead Act was rejected by many movement members as insufficient. Charles Geisler notes how the FSA's redistribution of two million acres in over two hundred areas has been considered both meager given the scale of the economic problems that characterized the Great Depression, yet exceptional given the lack—past and present—of any coherent, comprehensive redistribution project in the United States.[54] The STFU's demands and innovative use of tactics created opportunities to claim space in alternative ways.

The 1930s and 1940s saw other alternative organizational experiments in claiming space. Fully cooperative settlements began in what were called rural/urban "Greenbelt" communities, which were pioneered by Eleanor Roosevelt.[55] These communities (there were three of them), while principally initiated by the government, were public settlements where families lived in separate housing without definitive ownership or title. Or in other words, families who lived on the settlements could not sell or rent their land because the government retained ownership. Besides housing, the settlements featured cooperative supermarkets, gas stations, and bars. Pressure from the real estate industry in the 1950s forced the privatization of the Greenbelt communities, especially after they were denounced for being "communist."

Another, better-known New Deal initiative was the Agricultural Adjustment Act (AAA) of 1933. The AAA established a price-support system known as parity: farmers were guaranteed by the government to receive a final sale price for their goods, including milk, wheat, and a variety of other crops, that would be at least what the producer initially invested. In this price-support system, a series of policies were integral—from the provision of subsidized credit to guaranteeing that the government would purchase a farmer's produce if sale prices on the open market would result in a loss. The act first encountered challenges in the 1960s by the emerging agribusiness lobby; later successive federal administrations cut and reduced parity provisions. The program officially ended with President Ronald Reagan's 1981 farm bill. Even as period payments for particular crops and crop insurance programs remain central to U.S. agriculture, no program currently affects prices as much as the New Deal's parity system. Despite its dismantling, parity continues to draw the attention of farmers, mainly small-scale operators who are facing bankruptcy and mired in debt. Most importantly for the analysis of agrarian reform, it is a program that runs contrary to free market principles and that intends to provide the economic means for rural producers to remain in the countryside.

Native American movements that emerged in the second half of the twentieth century made more use of laws and treaties when claiming space for alternative, revolutionary projects. Two events are particularly relevant—the occupations of Alcatraz, briefly in 1964 and then for two years beginning in 1969, and at the Pine Ridge Reservation in 1973. The Alcatraz occupation, especially the two-year takeover, referenced the broken Sioux Treaty of 1868 (also known as the Fort Laramie Treaty) as the basis for the land claim. This treaty, between the Oglala, Miniconjou, and Brulé bands of the Lakota people, the Yanktonai Dakota, the Arapaho Nation, and the federal government, guaranteed Lakota ownership of the Black Hills. Discovery of gold drew white squatters onto the land claimed by the Lakota, resulting in disregard for the treaty's provisions and the U.S. government's subsequent seizure of the land in 1877.

Other laws passed in the late nineteenth century further used legal pretenses to dispossess tribes of territory. The Dawes Act of 1887, notably, attempted to "homestead" Indigenous people by forcing individuals to claim ownership of 160-acre allotments within federally recognized reservations. Federal treaties with Indigenous nations initially ceded land as reservations without particular divisions for families, or individuals. The Dawes Act forced the individualization of property holdings and made Indigenous people "enroll," or self-identify, as a member of a particular tribe.[56] In so doing, not only reservations, but any mode of collective or communal living was attacked. After allotment and allocation, the remaining, unclaimed spaces were opened for Euro-American settlers.

Shortly before the Alcatraz occupation, the Eisenhower-era tribal termination policy sought to fully dismantle Native American reservations and land holdings. The effort was meant to pressure Native Americans to leave their communities and spaces. As part of the policy, states were granted increased jurisdiction over territory and promoted the assimilation of Native people by encouraging relocation to urban areas. Rural to urban migration resulted, yet without the government achieving the intended goal to assimilate, integrate, and eradicate Native American nations and their demands for sovereignty.

At Alcatraz, members of various tribes asserted a radical claim to space to pressure the U.S. government to recognize Indigenous sovereignty. The occupation, which initially had mainly symbolic meaning, turned into a managed attempt to redesign political and economic relations. The space became governed by small teams, each granted particular tasks such as ensuring food, sanitations, and security.[57] In its internal organization, the seizure and encampment mirrors the MST's manner of coordinating its own form of agrarian reform. The action at Alcatraz ended in 1971 when federal marshals took the island to evict the occupiers.[58]

The Pine Ridge occupation, more so than the events at Alcatraz, showed how Native American movements have used legal maneuvers in making land claims. The occupation in 1973 gained the American Indian Movement (AIM) national recognition. The reference to the Sioux/Fort Laramie Treaty of 1868 at Alcatraz symbolically invoked every treaty made (and broken) between the U.S. government and Native Americans. The land itself at Alcatraz was claimed for the original Ohlone people, while the occupiers referenced the treaty and land claim in the name of "Indians of all Tribes." At Pine Ridge, the Sioux/Laramie Treaty of 1868 had greater symbolic and practical effect. First, the Pine Ridge Reservation was where the Wounded Knee Massacre took place in 1890. Second, instead of claiming that all land was stolen in a general sense, the occupiers used the treaty at its actual intended site of application, Pine Ridge. This more practical feature of the occupation and the use of the treaty highlighted the U.S. legal system's contradictions. Specifically, the occupation forced the government to either recognize the original treaty, and thus cede territory to the movement, or to refuse redistribution, which drew attention to how the U.S. government breaks its own laws. The treaty provided activists a legal mechanism to legitimize their demand for space, and thus for redistribution.

The occupation also took on an extralegal quality with AIM's claim to uphold a law that the U.S. government would not. In the United States, trespassing is illegal, as is the use of violence to take property.[59] Yet if the legitimacy of a title is dubious because of conflicting ownership claims, then it is difficult to discern who is stealing what. The occupiers and their demands, therefore, inhabited a juridical gray area. Similar to events at Alcatraz, violence ensued between movement members and U.S. federal marshals, resulting in dozens of wounded and two deaths. In 1974, when the occupation ended, AIM continued attempting to mobilize the Native American activists by occupying federal buildings in Washington, D.C. The mobilization at Pine Ridge, despite its repression, showed how opportunities for mobilization were created through the innovative use of legislation.

A more sustained effort took place in the Kanien'kehá:ka (Mohawk) nation in north New York State. In 1968, a dispute began over the requirement to pay tolls to use the bridge that connects Canada with the United States. To contest this, as well as make a claim to territory, the Kanien'kehá:ka evoked the Jay Treaty of 1794 to gain the right to cross the border freely.[60] Gaining momentum after this victory, their reservation became a place where the *Akwesasne Notes*—a Native American–led newspaper—is issued, as well as where schools have developed to propagate Indigenous language, values, and culture.[61]

At Pine Ridge in 2013, in a similar fashion, the Oglala Sioux invoked their own constitutional authority to claim certain areas under eminent domain.[62] This provision is in nearly every constitution around the world. Implicitly, eminent domain also undergirds the social function clause in the Brazilian, Cuban, and Bolivian constitutions because of the government's role in expropriation and redistribution. In the United States, eminent domain has been often used to take space for public works projects (e.g., highways), which have typically displaced historically marginalized communities of color.[63] A Native American tribe evoking eminent domain shows the innovative use of law for potentially transformative projects. As in events that took place thirty years earlier on the Pine Ridge reservation, the tribe is displaying how territorial authority, ownership, and property rights have deep, legally ambiguous roots in the United States.

WHAT'S NEXT?

Historically, many movements in the United States have showcased revolutionary ways to claim territory for transformative change. During the Civil War, the slaves' general strike forced the Northern government to issue legal directives that it might not otherwise have. In the period after the war, emancipated slaves worked collectively to claim space and use it productively. Ownership claims were in dispute, especially because of the destabilizing effects of the war. Yet, conditions changed and were stabilized when the federal government shifted course—passing constitutional amendments and forcibly returning property to plantation owners. The initial land seizures of particular plantations mirror the MST's land occupations and encampments. There is an extralegal quality to deploying such tactics while appealing to laws and legislative acts that were written but not implemented. The STFU also claimed space, particularly through promoting legislation that would have radically transformed land ownership. Various civil rights–era organizations also attempted to claim property and challenge economic and political inequality. As I conclude this book, the movements active near the Standing Rock Reservation to stop the construction of the Dakota Access Pipeline are referencing the broken Fort Laramie Treaty of 1868 in their demands. Even though this mobilization ended with the activists decamping after failed negotiations with the U.S. government, Indigenous activists and their allies drew attention, yet again, not only to the fractured nature of the U.S. postcolonial land tenure system, but also to how movements can claim space and initiate radical, potentially revolutionary modes of contention.

From contesting the economic institution of tenant farming to organizing small governing bodies during the Alcatraz occupation, activists have claimed space to bring about changes similar to those seen in Brazil and elsewhere. Native American activists, more so than others, have developed tactics that show the contested nature of territorial claims and sovereignty in the United States. The problems in U.S. territorial authority originated in the colonial and postcolonial style of settlement creation and reproduction. Incomplete surveys, broken treaties, and fraudulent deals with speculators characterize the historical constitution of property relations for millions of acres of land. Extralegal tactics open spaces and create opportunities for further mobilization. Such practices catch opponents off guard and challenge claims of legitimacy. This brief review of various movements that have claimed spaces for transformative cultural, political, and economic change is far from exhaustive. These instances show how the demand for agrarian reform connects to larger processes of revolutionary resistance and have a potential fertile ground in the United States.

For movements that seek revolutionary change, the MST's lessons are found in U.S. history. Land occupations are not a foreign tactic, but a mode of engagement that has a history in the United States. Also, the institution of private property in the United States, at times, has been connected to the concept of social function—similar to the clause referenced by Brazilian movements. Land, when considered in light of social function, is more than a means for profit and investment; or as Tannenbaum elaborated upon, it is something with social value. Reducing space to a strictly economic rationale is the goal of the neoliberal project.

Neoliberalism's cooptation of production has made private property into an object that is mistakenly synonymous with individual possession. The reality is that private property is a complicated, often contradictory institution of conflicting norms, practices, and ideas. It has a history—one often marked by violence and dispossession. Innovative movement tactics, from organizations active during Reconstruction to AIM, illustrate how state power and property claims can be effectively contested by mobilizing people within the inconsistencies of the institution. Tactical engagement that exposes the contested nature of space, forcing others to pick sides, is where revolutionary change begins. Politicization is more than debate and discussion; as documented by these movements throughout U.S. history and the Landless Movement, it is the material process of establishing mutually exclusive claims to govern. How, and if such developments develop, and where, is to be determined.

NOTES

INTRODUCTION

1. See Brazilian Law 8629/1993. This law provides specific criteria for expropriation. I further explain controversies concerning the legality of occupations in this chapter, and also in chapters 3 and 4.
2. It is difficult to present a complete list of every organization that is a member of the Landless Movement. Bernardo Mançano Fernandes, in his yearly studies on rural contention published as *DataLuta*, notes that over twenty-five social movements engage in land occupations as well as in protests concerning agrarian reform. Many of these movements, such as the MLST (Movimento de Libertação dos Sem Terra; Movement for the Liberation of the Landless), developed from former MST members, and have since been rejected by the MST and its core allies. Throughout the book, when I make reference to the Landless Movement, I am considering this coalition of actors that includes the MST as one member. When I refer to the MST, I am analyzing the movement's practices in isolation from the greater Landless Movement.
3. Carter, "Landless Rural Workers Movement." See also Carter, "Origins and Consolidation."
4. Wolford, "Participatory Democracy by Default"; Wright and Wolford, *To Inherit the Earth*.
5. Hammond, "Law and Disorder."
6. Mészáros, "MST and the Rule of Law in Brazil."
7. Goodwin and Skocpol, "Explaining Revolutions."
8. Ondetti, *Land, Protests, and Politics*; Wolford, *This Land Is Ours Now*.
9. Carter, *Challenging Social Inequality*, 2015.

10. Fernandes, *A formação do MST no Brasil*; Branford and Rocha, *Cutting the Wire*; Wright and Wolford, *To Inherit the Earth*.
11. Cristofoli, "O desenvolvimento de cooperativas coletivas de trabalhadores rurais no capitalismo"; de Souza, *Educação do campo*; Caume, *O MST e os assentamentos de reforma agrária*; Guhur, "Contribuições do diálogo de saberes."
12. Vergara-Camus, *Land and Freedom*.
13. Vergara-Camus, "MST and the EZLN Struggle for Land."
14. Wolford, *This Land Is Ours*, 9.
15. Fernandes, *A formação do MST no Brasil*.
16. Their recognition of this lack of synthesis prompted Goodwin and Jasper in 2014 to lead a panel discussion on the subject, held at New York University. The discussion can be found on YouTube, "Do Scholars of Social Movements Need Marxism?," youtube.com/watch?v=RmBxCICatUU.
17. Jasper, "Social Movement Theory Today."
18. Buechler, *Understanding Social Movements*, 101.
19. Laclau and Mouffe, *Hegemony and Socialist Strategy*; Ilse Scherer-Warren and Paulo José Krischke, eds., *Uma revolução no cotidiano?*; Laclau, "Os novos movimentos sociais"; Slater, *New Social Movements*.
20. For Tarlau's work, see "Education of the Countryside at a Crossroads"; "Occupying Land, Occupying Schools"; and "Coproducing Rural Public Schools in Brazil." Vergara-Camus's most succinct statement and use of Gramscian theory is found in his book *Land and Freedom*.
21. Bernstein, "'The Peasantry' in Global Capitalism"; Petras and Veltmeyer, *Social Movements and State Power*; Fernandes, "Questão agrária"; Petras and Veltmeyer, "Are Latin American Peasant Movements Still a Force for Change?"; Brass, *Peasants, Populism, and Postmodernism*; Fernandes, *A formação do MST no Brasil*.
22. This is one of the more contentious elements of the Trans-Pacific Partnership (TPP) that was debated at the time that this chapter was written.
23. Some movements cite six, others seven, principles for food sovereignty. I use the list put together by the Canadian National Farmers' Union, which can be found at nfu.ca/files/Principles%20of%20Food%20Sovereignty.pdf. A video of U.S. movements discussing the principles can be found at youtube.com/watch?v=9fYGCHoP-HY. How the Landless Movement promotes and practices these same principles is one of the underlying themes in this book.
24. I will come back to the Cuban case in the conclusion. In short, the comparison with Cuba—and specifically the unfolding of resistance organized by the 26th of July Movement and the coalition of other urban and rural organizations before and after 1959—shows parallels to the Brazilian case in terms of seizing space to transform political, economic, and cultural relations. It also reveals how such a claim to space, even with the persistence of a sugar monoculture and dependence on the Soviet Union, does not mean that revolutionary transformation did not take place. For more on sugar and revolution, see Eckstein, "Impact of the Cuban Revolution." For the work of rural and urban social movements claiming space for revolutionary transformation, see Pérez-Stable, *Cuban Revolution*; Wright, *Latin*

America in the Era of the Cuban Revolution; Abendroth, *Rebel Literacy*; Chomsky, *History of the Cuban Revolution*. For a comparative study of twentieth-century revolutions, see Wickham-Crowley, *Guerrillas and Revolution in Latin America*.

25. Shortly after Lula's election in 2002, movements organized 496 land occupations. In 2015, the CPT documented 205 (CPT 2005, 2014).
26. See Chalmers Johnson, *MITI and the Japanese Miracle*; Amsden, *Asia's Next Giant*; Evans, *Embedded Autonomy*; Woo-Cumings, *Developmental State*.
27. Ankersen and Ruppert, "Tierra y Libertad," 69.
28. I was told by individuals who had been frequently interviewed by the consulate that U.S. representatives wanted to know if the MST was "planning another Cuba." See also Viana, "Brazil—Brazil—Cablegate"; Welch, "Wikileaks, o globo, historia y EU."
29. MP official, in discussion with the author, March 15, 2011.
30. Act 1.116, Public Prosecutor's Office, Rio Grande do Sul, 2007.

CHAPTER ONE

1. MST organizer in the Sector of Education, in discussion with author, Paraná, August 5, 2011.
2. Arroyo, "A educação do campo e a pesquisa do campo."
3. Former MST state and national director, in discussion with author, outside of Miguel do Iguaçu, PR, July 12, 2011.
4. For a few of the recent reflections on Marx, Mao, and Lenin, see Nimtz, *Lenin's Electoral Strategy*; Badiou, *Communist Hypothesis*; Budgen and Žižek, *Lenin Reloaded*; Žižek, *Revolution at the Gates*; Nimtz, *Marx and Engels*. The three-volume series on Communism, *The Idea of Communism*, which is edited by Žižek and published by Verso, debates in similar, but more philosophical terms, the nature of revolutionary political action.
5. Negri's work is extensive, dating back to the 1960s. His more current popularization has taken place with the works co-authored with Michael Hardt, which include *Empire*, *Multitude*, and *Commonwealth*.
6. Alinsky, *Rules for Radicals*; Marshall Ganz. *Why David Sometimes Wins.*
7. McCarthy and Zald, "Resource Mobilization and Social Movements."
8. Bevington and Dixon, "Movement-Relevant Theory."
9. Tarrow, *Power in Movement*, 10–12.
10. McAdam, *Political Process*.
11. Tilly, *From Mobilization to Revolution*, esp. pp. 185–92.
12. See, for instance, Jeff Goodwin and James M. Jasper, eds., *The Social Movements Reader: Cases and Concepts*, 3rd ed. (Malden, Mass.: John Wiley & Sons, 2014); Jacquelien Van Stekelenburg, Conny Roggeband, and Bert Klandermans, *The Future of Social Movement Research* (Minneapolis: University of Minnesota Press, 2013); David A Snow, ed., *The Blackwell Companion to Social Movements* (Malden, Mass.: Blackwell, 2008). Past edited volumes on Latin American movements include Sonia Alvarez and Arturo Escobar, *The Making of Social Movements in Latin America: Identity, Strategy, and Democracy* (Boulder, Colo.: Westview Press,

1992); Sonia E. Alvarez, Evelina Dagnino, and Arturo Escobar, *Cultures of Politics/Politics of Cultures: Re-visioning Latin American Social Movements* (Boulder, Colo.: Westview Press, 1998); Susan Eckstein, *Power and Popular Protest: Latin American Social Movements* (Berkeley: University of California Press, 2001). The cases and approaches in Eckstein's volume draw on more structural conditions, yet still do not deal with studies and concepts developed from the Marxist tradition explicitly. The Escobar and Alvarez editions include works inspired by the post-Marxist approach of Laclau and Mouffe, which I discuss later in this chapter.

13. Bernstein, "'The Peasantry' in Global Capitalism"; Petras and Veltmeyer. *Social Movements and State Power*; Fernandes, "Questão agrária"; Petras and Veltmeyer, "Are Latin American Peasant Movements Still a Force for Change?"; Brass, *Peasants, Populism, and Postmodernism*; Fernandes, *A formação do MST no Brasil*.

14. Robles and Veltmeyer, "Politics of Agrarian Reform in Brazil." The only reference to food sovereignty and LVC is on page 176, and in passing.

15. Holt-Giménez and Altieri, "Agroecology"; Martínez-Torres and Rosset, "La Vía Campesina"; Wittman, Desmarais, and Wiebe, "Origins and Potential of Food Sovereignty"; Wittman, "Reworking the Metabolic Rift"; Rosset. "Food Sovereignty."

16. Agarwal, "Food Sovereignty"; Windfuhr and Jonsén, "Food Sovereignty."

17. Rosset, "Food Sovereignty and the Contemporary Food Crisis"; Rosset, "Food Sovereignty and Alternative Paradigms"; Rosset and Martínez-Torres, "Rural Social Movements."

18. Patel, "Food Sovereignty."

19. In academic scholarship, more of the focus has been on Schmitt and his connections to the Nazi party. Most scholars recognize his theories as right-wing and authoritarian, but question whether his political theories were explicitly anti-Semitic. For studies on Schmitt, his personal politics, and his rehabilitation by radical democratic theorists, see Müller, *A Dangerous Mind*; Balakrishnan, *The Enemy*; Scheuerman, *Carl Schmitt*; Mouffe, *Challenge of Carl Schmitt*.

20. Jameson, *An American Utopia*; Nimtz, *Lenin*; Žižek, *Lenin Reloaded*.

21. Butler, Laclau, and Žižek, *Contingency, Hegemony, Universality*; Mouffe, *Challenge of Carl Schmitt*; Agamben, *Homo Sacer*.

22. See Marcuse's writing from the time, "The Struggle Against Liberalism in the Totalitarian View of the State," in *Negations: Essays in Critical Theory*, 3–42 (Boston: Beacon Press, 1968), as well as the opening chapter from Scheuermann's *Between the Norm and the Exception: The Frankfurt School and the Rule of Law* (Cambridge, Mass.: MIT Press, 1997).

23. Lenin, *"Left-Wing" Communism*.

24. Lukács, *Marxism and Human Liberation*; Luxemburg, *Reform or Revolution and Other Writings*.

25. Schmitt, *Concept of the Political*, 26–27.

26. To clarify, Schmitt tells us that the practices involved in warfare—decisions about troop deployments, whether to attack by air or sea, and so on—are not indicative of political action, but constitutive of a different sphere with its own dynamics.

Warfare is one mode of conduct, among others, made possible by the political. Schmitt, *Concept of the Political*, 33.
27. Snow, Rochford, Worden, and Benford, "Frame Alignment Processes."
28. Reger, Myers, and Einwohner, *Identity Work in Social Movements*; Polletta and Jasper, "Collective Identity and Social Movements"; Benford and Snow, "Framing Processes and Social Movements."
29. Snow, "Framing Processes, Ideology, and Discursive Fields."
30. Schmitt, *Theory of the Partisan*, 10.
31. Ibid., 13.
32. Tilly, *Contention and Democracy in Europe*.
33. McAdam, "Tactical Innovation"; Berstein, "Celebration and Suppression"; Taylor and Van Dyke, "'Get Up, Stand Up."
34. Piven and Cloward, *Poor People's Movements*.
35. Tarrow, *Power in Movement*; Kriesi et al., *New Social Movements*.
36. Gamson, *Strategy of Social Protest*.
37. Hellman, "Study of New Social Movements in Latin America."
38. Alvarez, "Latin American Feminisms"; Alvarez, "Beyond NGO-ization?"
39. Ondetti, *Land, Protest, and Politics*, 196.
40. Tarlau, "Coproducing Rural Schools."
41. Webber, *From Rebellion to Reform in Bolivia*.
42. Ramirez, "Territorio y estructuras de acción colectiva," 276.
43. Schmitt, *Political Theology*.
44. Hirst, "Carl Schmitt's Decisionism."
45. Mouffe, *Return of the Political*. Also Mouffe, "Carl Schmitt and the Paradox of Liberal Democracy." The same argument is characteristic of the conception of hegemony in Laclau and Mouffe, *Hegemony and Socialist Strategy*.
46. Laclau, *On Populist Reason*.
47. Lenin, *Dual Power*.
48. Rabinowitch, "Evolution of Local Soviets."
49. Jameson, *American Utopia*, 4. Scholars of governance note the centrality of decision-making to the concept. James Rosenau defines the term as control and steering mechanisms. Schmitter discusses governance in his study of the European Union as rule-setting and decision implementation, while others include service provision. Rosenau, "Governance in the Twenty-First Century"; Ronit and Schneider, "Global Governance Through Private Organizations"; Schmitter, "Participation in Governance Arrangements"; Bevir, *Encyclopedia of Governance*. As will become clearer in the next chapter, the MST's style of governing affairs in certain spaces is different from the institutions of participatory governance that have developed in Brazil. See Baiocchi, *Militants and Citizens*; Wampler, *Participatory Budgeting in Brazil*.
50. Negri, *Insurgencies*; Dussel, *Twenty Theses on Politics*.
51. Dussel, *Twenty Theses*, 12.
52. Alvarez, *Engendering Democracy in Brazil*.
53. Abers and Keck, "Mobilizing the State"; Wolford, "Participatory Democracy by Default," 109.

54. Skocpol, *States and Social Revolutions*, 4–5.
55. Arendt, *On Revolution*, 28–35.
56. Tilly, *From Mobilization to Revolution*, 190–93.
57. Selbin, *Modern Latin American Social Revolutions*.
58. Gramsci, *Further Selections from the Prison Notebooks*. For applications, see Tarlau, "Occupying Land"; Meek, "Learning as Territoriality."
59. Jameson, *American Utopia*, 14.
60. Zibechi, *Territories in Resistence*; Holloway, *Change the World*.
61. Wright and Wolford, *To Inherit the Earth*, 115.
62. In 2012, the decision was overturned and movement education in certain schools was allowed to continue.
63. Tarrow, *Power in Movement*.
64. Diani, "Organizational Fields"; Johnston, *Social Movements and Culture*; Castells, *Networks of Outrage and Hope*; McAdam and Boudet, "Putting Movements in Their Place."
65. Despite Ondetti's attempts to resurrect the theory in his analysis of the MST, the conceptual problems remain. I deal more with political opportunity structures in chapters 3 and 5.
66. For more on structures and conditions as relationships, see Tilly, *Big Structures, Large Processes*; Giddens, *Constitution of Society*; Sayer, *Method in Social Science*.
67. Weber, "Profession and Vocation of Politics."
68. Delgado, "Agrarian Question."
69. Scott, *Seeing Like a State*.
70. Serra, "Considerações acerca da evolução da propriedade."
71. Miranda, "Breve histórico."
72. Mota, "Sesmarias e propriedade titulada da terra."
73. Miranda, "Breve histórico."
74. At this time, space was measured in leagues (*leguas*) and fathoms. At various times during the colonial period, alterations were made to how these units of measurement were applied. See Gabaglia, "Evolução histórica."
75. Motta, "Sesmarias e o mito da primeira ocupação."
76. Holston, "Misrule of Law."
77. *Terra devoluta* is best translated in English as "public domain."
78. Ianni, *Origens agrárias do Estado brasileiro*, 14–15.
79. Hoefle, "Beyond Cold War Pipedreams."
80. Pereira, *End of the Peasantry*, 39.
81. Moreira Alves, *State and Opposition*, 46.
82. Wagner, *A saga do João sem terra*.
83. Medeiros, *História dos movimentos*.
84. Besides Tarlau's work on education ("Coproducing Rural Public Schools"), I know of no other studies that foreground the comparative challenges/successes of the movement practices at the subnational level.
85. Amaral and Fusco, "Shaping Brazil."
86. Welch, *Seed Was Planted*, 30.

87. Love, "Political Participation in Brazil."
88. Caires, "O colonato na Usina Tamoio."
89. Da Silva, *A modernização dolorosa*, 44–45.
90. Barros, "Brazil."
91. Maybury-Lewis, *Politics of the Possible*, 5–6.
92. Nakagawara, "Café, do colonato ao bóia-fria."
93. Neves and Silva, *Processos de constituição*, 146–47.
94. Rogers, *Deepest Wounds*, 137; Caires, "O colonato na Usina Tamoio."
95. Skocpol, *States and Social Revolutions*; Migdal, *Peasants, Politics, and Revolution*; Lenin, *"Left Wing" Communism*.
96. Collier and Handlin, "Logics of Collective Action."
97. Yashar, *Contesting Citizenship*.
98. incra.gov.br/assentamento, accessed on December 3, 2015.
99. CNASI, *INCRA–Instrumento básico de realização da reforma agrária*.
100. Fernandes, *A formação do MST no Brasil*, 41.
101. Ondetti, "Repression, Opportunity, and Protest."
102. Leite, *Impactos dos assentamentos*.
103. Ondetti, *Land, Protest, and Politics*, 230.
104. "A educação do MST," last edited October 8, 2009, mst.org.br/2009/10/08/a-educacao-do-mst.html.
105. Of the 2,250 schools, only a fraction of the elementary schools in settlements (three in the state of Paraná, zero in São Paulo, and three in Rio Grande do Sul) operate according to the movement's dictates, with even fewer in the area of secondary education (field notes, ITERRA conference, May 25, 2011).
106. The itinerant schools were closed in Rio Grande do Sul in 2009 and later reopened in 2012. The schools currently exist in Alagoas, Santa Catarina, and Goiás.
107. MST, *Escola itinerante em acampamentos do MST* (1998); MST, *Escola itinerante: Uma pratica pedagogica em acampamentos* (2000); MST, *Escola itinerante do MST: História, projeto e experiencias* (2008).
108. These figures are reached when comparing technical school attendance from the Instituto Nacional de Estudos e Pesquisas Educacionais (INEP) *Censo Escolar* (2010) and INCRA's report on PRONERA, *Relação Geral de Cursos em Execução* (2010).
109. Plummer, "Leadership Development and Formação."
110. MST organizer in the Sector of Production, in discussion with the author, July 11, 2011.

CHAPTER TWO

1. Branford and Rocha, *Cutting the Wire*; Wright and Wolford, *To Inherit the Earth*. Some subsequent research takes a more ethnographic approach to studying the movement: Tarlau, "Occupying Land, Occupying Schools"; Meek, "Learning as Territoriality."
2. The direct translation of *mística* into English is "mystic." Because of the particular meaning given to its practice, as well as the awkward translation, I leave *mística* in

the original Portuguese throughout the text. The first section of this chapter ought to clear up any confusion.

3. Navarro, "Brazilian Landless Movement (MST)." Branford and Rocha also answer this critique in *Cutting the Wire*, 120–25.
4. Monica Weinberg, "Madraçais do MST," *Veja*, September 8, 2004.
5. Former state secretary of education, RS, in discussion with the author, March 11, 2011.
6. Whittier, "Collective Identity in Social Movement Communities"; Kilgore, "Understanding Learning in Social Movements"; Reger, Myers, and Einwohner, *Identity Work in Social Movements*.
7. Thayer, "Translations and Refusals."
8. Stédile and Fernandes, *Brava gente*, 129–39.
9. *JST* (*Jornal dos Trabalhadores Rurais Sem Terra*) has been the MST's newsletter since 1981. Its readership is primarily movement members and allies. *JST* is available at www1.cedem.unesp.br/acervos/acervo_mst.htm.
10. *JST*, July 1989.
11. *JST*, May 1991.
12. *JST*, May 1993.
13. Field notes, encampment near Londrina, PR, June 20, 2011.
14. Fanelli and Sarzynski, "Concept of Sem Terra."
15. Caldart, *Pedagogia do Movimento Sem Terra*, 120.
16. Field notes, Encampment near Londrina, PR, June 28, 2011.
17. Field notes, MST school near Caruaru, PE, September 1, 2009.
18. Field notes, MST school near Rio Bonita, PR, July 23, 2011.
19. Wolford, *This Land Is Ours Now*, 11.
20. Stédile and Fernandes, *Brava gente*; Carter, "Landless Rural Workers Movement"; Carter and de Carvalho, "A luta na terra."
21. Various early reports in the *Jornal Sem Terra* (*JST*) were on nucleo design and management. For example, the April 1982 edition contains an article titled "Os colonos organizam a Nova Ronda Alta" (Settlers Organize Nova Ronda Alta), and in May 1982, there is a piece titled "Nova Ronda Alta: Núcleos." Later, in July 1984 and July 1985, we find articles titled "Reforma agraria e nosso objeto" (Agrarian Reform Is Our Objective) and "Porque apoiamos o plan do governo" (Why We Support the Government's Plan), which also discuss nucleo actions. Furthermore, throughout the 1980s, *JST* publications end with a note describing the MST as "um movimento que tem por objetivo lutar pela terra e reforma agraria. Está organizado em núcleos, commissoes municipais e estaduais, e possui uma coordinaçao nacional composto de lavradores" (a movement with the objective to struggle for land access and agrarian reform. It is organized in nucleos, municipal and state commissions, and has a national coordination that is made up of farmers). I trace the development of and changes in the MST's tactics and mode of organization throughout chapters 3, 4, 5, and 6.
22. Wright and Wolford, *To Inherit the Earth*, 12.

23. Why there are two communist parties and the story of how they developed is analyzed in the next chapter.
24. In the *JST*, the president of the PCB's executive commission is cited as saying that the party was "opposed to the occupations because they are illegal." *JST*, March 1986.
25. Smith, *Rainforest Corridors*; Dos Santos, *Matuchos*; Wright and Wolford, *To Inherit the Earth*.
26. Vergara-Camus, *Land and Freedom*, 260.
27. The IEJC is housed within the other of the MST's flagship educational institutions, the Instituto Técnico de Capacitação e Pesquisa da Reforma Agrária (ITERRA; Technical Institute for Capacity-Building and Research for Agrarian Reform).
28. ITERRA, "Instituto de Educação Josué de Castro," 37–39.
29. Field notes, Instituto Educar, Pontão, RS, March 30, 2011.
30. For her account, see Tarlau, "Occupying Land, Occupying Schools," 83–87.
31. Field notes, Instituto Educar, Pontão, RS, April 5, 2011.
32. Medeiros, Barbosa, Valeria, Esterci, and Leite, "Assentamentos rurais"; Leite, *Impactos dos assentamentos*; Wolford, "Producing Community."
33. Abers and Neck, "Mobilizing the State"; Abers, Serafim, and Tatagiba, "Changing Repertoires," 36.
34. Generative themes, as developed by Paulo Freire and applied by the MST, oppose instruction that is not grounded in students' lives and immediate political, social, and cultural surroundings. Materials—ideational and physical—are primarily located in local, immediate vicinities. For further elaboration of the concept, see Freire, *Pedagogy of the Oppressed*, 87–125.
35. Teacher, in discussion with author, encampment near Londrina, PR, June 21, 2011.
36. Field notes, MST school outside Caruaru, PE, September 5, 2009.
37. Student at the Milton Santos School, in discussion with author, outside of Londrina, PR, July 6, 2011.
38. Salete Campigotto, "Monografia," unpublished text, 2010.
39. Nucleo 1, in discussion with author, outside of Pontão, RS, April 15, 2011; Nucleo 2, in discussion with author, outside of Pontão, RS, April 17, 2011.
40. Article 26 states that curriculum for elementary and secondary education must have a common national base that will be completed in each system and place of instruction. This national common base may allow for diversity, given regional and local social qualities, particularly dealing with culture, economy, and client. For more discussion on the history of rural schools, see Araújo Soares, "Relatório das diretrizes operacionais."
41. Araújo Soares, "Relatório das diretrizes operacionais."
42. Law 9394/1996 ensures that federal authorities have the prerogative to monitor, establish norms, provide financial resources, establish and approve curriculum. The instituting body is composed of various civil society actors, often former or acting teachers, professors, and former educational secretaries, who are nominated by the president.

43. Caldeira, "Failed Marriage."
44. Tarlau, "Coproducing Rural Public Schools."
45. MST organizer in the Sector of Education, in discussion with author, SP, November 8, 2011.
46. Regional secretary of education, instruction supervisor, in discussion with author, SP, November 21, 2011.
47. Another MST cooperative is the CPS (Cooperativas de Prestação de Servicos; Service Cooperatives), which does not collectivize production, but provides technical assistance to members.
48. MST, *Cartilha de Cooperação* (2008), 74.
49. Carvalho, *Another Production Is Possible*, 191.
50. Besides COOPAN, the other CPAs I visited were Cooperativa Agropecuária Vista Alegre (COOPAVA; Agricultural Cooperative Vista Alegre) in São Paulo; Cooperativa de Produção Agropecuária Cascata (COOPTAR; Agricultural Production Cooperative Cascata) in Rio Grande do Sul; and Cooperativa de Produção Agropecuária Vitória (COPAVI; Agricultural Production Cooperative Victory) in Paraná. Each cooperative tends to have the same number of families involved.
51. Bionatur technical assistance team, in discussion with the author, March 30, 2011.
52. Anderson and Valdés, *Distortions to Agricultural Incentives*.
53. Chaddad and Jank, "Evolution of Agricultural Policies"; Martha, Alves, and Contini, "Land Saving Approaches."
54. Bionatur technical assistance team, in discussion with author, outside of Bagé, RS, March 30, 2011.
55. Bionatur grower, in discussion with author, outside of Candiota, RS, April 4, 2011.
56. Field notes, settlement in the Porto Alegre area, RS, March 3, 2011.
57. Former MST state and national director, in discussion with author, outside of Miguel do Iguaçu, PR, July 12, 2011.
58. MST state director, in discussion with author, RS, April 3, 2011.
59. I am neither advocating nor denouncing the view that subsistence is central to understanding the peasantry. There is an extensive literature on defining the peasantry, especially its role in revolutionary contention. While I address difficulties that the MST has encountered due to debates concerning the peasantry in chapter 6, I do not see the analytical value in arguing whether that the movement is essentially peasant or not. Instead, I propose that the movement is revolutionary. For more on the general nature of the peasantry, see Barrington Moore, *Social Origins of Dictatorship and Democracy: Lord and Peasant in the Making of the Modern World* (Boston: Beacon Press, 1968); Eric R. Wolf, *Peasant Wars of the Twentieth Century* (Norman: University of Oklahoma Press, 1969); Teodor Shanin, "The Nature and Logic of the Peasant Economy 1: A Generalisation 1," *Journal of Peasant Studies* 1, no. 1 (1973): 63–80. For work on the MST as a peasant movement, in addition to Vergara-Camus, see Cliff Welch, "Camponeses Brazil's Peasant Movement in Historical Perspective (1946–2004)," *Latin American Perspectives* 36, no. 4 (2009): 126–155; Bernardo Mançano Fernandes, "Re-peasantization, Resistance,

and Subordination: The Struggle for Land and Agrarian Reform in Brazil," *Agrarian South: Journal of Political Economy* 2, no. 3 (2013): 269–89.
60. Vergara-Camus, *Land and Freedom*, 160–70.
61. MST, *Caderno de Cooperação Agricola n8*, 1999.
62. Grzybowski et al., "Relatório Pronaf"; Kozelinski, "Inadimplência de financiamentos."
63. For the story covering the pardon, see Evandro Eboli, "Governo perdoa 80% da dívida de 203 mil famílias de assentados e agricultores familiars," *O Globo*, December 31, 2013, oglobo.globo.com/brasil/governo-perdoa-80-da-divida-de-203-mil-familias-de-assentados-agricultores-familiares-11181395.
64. For the full text, see "Crédito PRONAF," June 27, 2013, accessed April 14, 2015, mstemdados.org/realidade/3-cr%C3%A9dito-pronaf.
65. CPT, *Conflitos no Campo*, 2000–2014. The movement has mobilized more people, but 2000 is the first year when numbers were collected that differentiated between the various rural movements.
66. Areas where the MST is active and the year these areas became formalized within the movement include *formação* (training 1988), *educação* (education 1988), *frente de massa* (mobilization 1989), *finanças* (finance 1989), *projetos* (projects 1989), *produção, cooperação, meio ambiente* (production, cooperation, environment 1992), *relações internacionais* (international relations 1993), *direitos humanos* (human rights 1995), *communicação* (communications 1997), *saúde* (health 1998), *cultura* (culture 2000), *gênero* (gender 2000), *jovens* (youth 2006). Carter and Martins, "A luta na terra."
67. Field notes, Encampment 2 outside Londrina, PR, July 3, 2011.
68. Field notes, Encampment 1 outside of São Paulo, SP, August 5, 2009.
69. Field notes, Encampment 1 outside Londrina, PR, June 20, 2011; field notes, encampment outside Arcoverde, PE, September 10, 2009.
70. Turatti, *Os filhos da lona preta*.
71. Field notes, MST school outside of Caruaru, PE, September 1, 2009.
72. Field notes, Encampment 2 outside of São Paulo, SP, August 5, 2009.
73. Field notes, Encampment 2 outside Londrina, PR, June 21, 2011.
74. Stédile, "Balanço de uma reforma agrária que não existiu."
75. Field notes, Encampment 1 outside of São Paulo, SP, August 10, 2009.
76. Field notes, encampment in INCRA office, Belém, PA, July 1, 2009.
77. Ibid.
78. For a visual account of a land occupation, see Adam Raney and Chad Heeter, *Brazil: Cutting the Wire*, a *Frontline* Rough Cut video, 15:10, December 13, 2005, pbs.org/frontlineworld/rough/2005/12/brazil_cutting.html#.
79. Field notes, Instituto Educar, Pontão, RS, April 5, 2011.
80. The main law that regulates productivity is 8629/1993, which stipulates that 80 percent of a certain parcel must be in operation in order to be classified as productive. More so than the other requirements, the productivity clause is one of the most contentious as well as the one most invoked by the MST.
81. Field notes, outside of Pontão, RS, May 5, 2011.

82. Field notes, roadside encampment near Arcoverde, PE, September 10, 2009.
83. Ondetti, *Land, Protest, and Politics*, 164.
84. Wolford, "Participatory Democracy by Default," 91–109.
85. Carter and Martins, "A luta na terra."
86. COPTEC technician, in discussion with author, RS, March 9, 2011.
87. Ariovaldo Umbelino de Oliveira, "A Reforma Agraria de Lula," *Estadão*, March 6, 2011, accessed April 14, 2015, opiniao.estadao.com.br/noticias/geral,a-reforma-agraria-de-lula-imp-,688397.
88. *Relatório de Demanda Externas*, 2012.
89. Flavio Paes, "Abandonados pelo INCRA, sem acesso a crédito, assentados do Barra Nova abandonam lote," *Regiao News*, February 11, 2013, accessed April 14, 2015, http://www.regiaonews.com.br/noticias/147580--B-Abandonados-pelo-INCRA--sem-acesso-a-credito--assentados-do-Barra-Nova-abandonam-lote--b-.html.
90. MST, *Caderno de Cooperação Agricola n6*, 1998.
91. INCRA official, in discussion with the author, Brasilia, January 31, 2011.
92. Wolford, "Participatory Democracy by Default."
93. Vergara-Camus, "MST and the EZLN Struggle for Land."
94. Fernandes, *A formação do MST no Brasil*.

CHAPTER THREE

1. Movement ally and former CRE official, in discussion with author, Bagé, RS, May 17, 2011.
2. INCRA officials for Rio Grande do Sul, in discussion with author, Porto Alegre, RS, February 28, 2011.
3. CNASI, *INCRA–Instrumento básico de realização da reforma agrária*.
4. Wolford, "Families, Fields, and Fighting for Land."
5. Ondetti, *Land, Protests, and Politics*, 95–96.
6. Carter, "Origins of Brazil's Landless Rural Workers' Movement."
7. *O Boletim* later changed its name to *Sem Terra*, and then in 1984 became *O Jornal dos Trabalhadores Sem Terra* (*JST*; Journal of the Landless Workers), which continues publication today.
8. Darci Maschio, interview, 97.
9. Stédile and Fernandes, *Brava gente*, 22.
10. Carter, *Origins of the Brazil's Landless Movement*.
11. Wright and Wolford, *To Inherit the Earth*, 33.
12. Branford and Rocha, *Cutting the Wire*.
13. *JST*, May 1981.
14. Welch, *Seed Was Planted*.
15. Wagner, *A saga do João Sem Terra*.
16. Ibid., 23.
17. Morais, *História das Ligas Camponesas*, 30–32; Medeiros, *Historia dos movimentos*, 70.

18. Medeiros, *História dos movimentos*, 68.
19. For a detailed account of the Brazilian military government's use of torture, see the *Brasil: Nunca mais* (Never Again) report issued by the Catholic Church in 1985. Others have extensively documented the military government use of repression and censorship. See Maria Helena Moreira Alves, *State and Opposition in Military Brazil* (Austin: University of Texas Press, 1985); Alfred C. Stepan, *Rethinking Military Politics: Brazil and the Southern Cone* (Princeton, N.J.: Princeton University Press, 1988); and Thomas E. Skidmore, *The Politics of Military Rule in Brazil, 1964–1985* (New York: Oxford University Press, 1990).
20. Wagner, *A saga do João Sem Terra*, 58.
21. It is hard to provide a precise number of families who were involved in the early occupations and encampments. The constant attempts by the military government to move families to other areas of Rio Grande do Sul or onto the settlements in the Amazon, as well as the ever-present danger of people succumbing to fatigue and quitting, makes a count for any period variable. Despite these challenges, Wagner mentions 200 active in the region. Marcon notes that 110 families occupied Macali and 170 occupied Brilhante. The lowest number of families involved in occupations at the end of the 1970s is 30. Wagner, *A saga do João Sem Terra*, 57; Marcon, *Acampamento Natalino*, 59; Fernandes, *A formação do MST no Brasil*, 41.
22. Bonavigo and Bavarescro, "Fazenda Annoni," 33.
23. INCRA officials for Rio Grande do Sul, in discussion with author, Porto Alegre, RS, February 28, 2011.
24. De Melo, "Ocupação da Fazenda Burro Branco."
25. Serra, "Conflitos rurais no Paraná."
26. Rogers, *Deepest Wounds*, 169.
27. Pereira, *End of the Peasantry*, 158.
28. Welch, *Seed Was Planted*.
29. Houtzager, "State and Unions."
30. Maybury-Lewis, *Politics of the Possible*, 24–25.
31. Medeiros, *História dos movimentos*, 98–100.
32. Skidmore, *Politics of Military Rule*, 230.
33. Alves, *State and Opposition*, 212.
34. The Brazilian military permitted two political parties to exist in controlled elections: ARENA, which was decidedly pro-military, and PMB (Movimento Democrático Brasileiro; Brazilian Democratic Movement), which was intended to control and channel dissent.
35. Marcon, *Acampamento Natalino*, 54.
36. He claimed, as if part of a dare, that if they wanted to occupy the land, he would join them.
37. Stédile and Fernandes, *Brava Gente*, 17–18.
38. Stédile, interview, 183–85.
39. Dos Santos, *Matuchos*.
40. Ibid., 29.

41. In the 1940s, seven "colonias agricolas nacionais" were established on public lands in the states of Goiás, Amazonas, Para, Maranhao, Paraná, Mato Grosso do Sul, and Piauí. Dos Santos, *Matuchos*, 28.
42. Kay, "Latin America's Agrarian Reform"; Rosset, "Moving Forward."
43. Decree 59.456/1966.
44. Araujo et al., "Politica de credito para a agricultura brasileira," 31–32.
45. Rezende, "Políticas trabalhista e fundiária."
46. Martins, *Militarização da questão agrária no Brasil*.
47. Smith, *Rainforest Corridors*, 22.
48. Ramirez, "Lembrando Casos do INCRA."
49. INCRA official for Brazil, in discussion with author, February 2, 2011.
50. INCRA officials for Rio Grande do Sul, in discussion with author, RS, February 28, 2011; INCRA official for Paraná, in discussion with author, PR, August 1, 2011.
51. Wolford, "State-Society Dynamics."
52. For more discussion of this hierarchy, as well as a map of the agrovila, agropolis, and ruropolis plans, see Smith, *Rainforest Corridors*, 19–20.
53. INCRA official for Rondônia, in discussion with author, Brasília, February 10, 2011.
54. INCRA official for Brazil, in discussion with author, Brasília, February 9, 2011.
55. Former MST state director, in discussion with author, outside of Pontal do Paranapanema, São Paulo, November 7, 2011.
56. Dos Santos, *Matuchos*, 169.
57. Ibid., 177–178.
58. Marcon, *Acampamento Natalino*.
59. Azevedo, *Basic Ecclesiastical Communities*, 26.
60. Levine and Mainwaring, *Religion and Popular Protest in Latin America*.
61. Bruneau, "Brazil."
62. Poletto, "A terra e a vida em tempos neoliberais."
63. Boff, "Eclesiogênese," 13–14.
64. The *Pioneros do MST* features narrative accounts of the first national leadership collective, which was composed of twenty individuals (Scolese, *Pioneiros do MST*). Every actor, regardless of whether or not they remained in the MST, began with involvement in the Catholic Church.
65. Tedesco and Carini, *Conflitos agrários no norte gaúcho*.
66. MST, *Balanço Político da Cooperação no MST*, 2006.
67. Reis, "O Movimento dos Atingidos por Barragens," 269.
68. In Paraná, there was the Movimento de Justica e Terra (Movement for Justice and Land), which was followed by the regional groups MASTRO (Movimento dos Agricultores Sem-Terra do Oeste do Paraná; Movement of Farmers in Western Parana), created in 1981; MASTEL (Movimento dos Agricultores Sem Terra do Litoral do Paraná; Movement of Farmers on the Paranese Coast), in 1982; MASTRECO (Movimento dos Agricultores Sem Terra do Centro-Oeste do Paraná; Movement of Farmers in Center-Western Parana), in 1982; MASTES (Movimento dos Agricultores Sem Terra do Sudoeste do Paraná; Movement of Farmers

in Southeastern Parana), in 1983, MASTEN (Movimento dos Agricultores Sem Terra do Norte do Paraná; Movement of Farmers in Northeast Parana), in 1985. Bonim, *Movimentos sociais no campo*.

69. *JST*, September 1984, March 1986, August 1986.
70. In a seminal 1961 conference of rural worker organizations, a substantial rift arose between those who proposed more radical, direct-action tactics concerning agrarian reform—represented by movements such as the Peasant Leagues and MASTER—and the rural organization ULTRAB, which sought a gradual, negotiated approach. The PCB's focus on negotiation came from its theoretical position, which stated that liberal democracy had to be established before initiating a socialist revolution. This stagist approach included neither land occupations nor armed insurrection, but rather nonviolent cooperation with government elites and demands for public programs. As a result, Brazilian communists tended to favor nonviolent cooperation as the primary orientation with government elites. Morais, "História das Ligas Camponesas do Brasil," 66. Medeiros, *História dos movimentos*, 53–56.
71. Marcon, *Acampamento Natalino*, 67.
72. In the late 1960s, PC do B leaders began mobilizing in the Amazon. Continuing what the Peasant Leagues had inspired, party members became installed in the Araguaia region in the state of Tocantins. Organizing Cuban Revolution-style "focos," or small groups in remote rural areas, around sixty guerrillas gradually gained the trust of local residents by providing security and health services. This effort lasted longer than its urban-guerrilla counterparts also led by the PC do B in the urban southeast, owing partly to the military government's efforts to conceal the very existence of the guerrilla movement. By 1972, the uprising had been crushed by the military government. Central the military's success was Major Curió. Portela, *Guerra de guerrilhas no Brasil*.
73. DOPS was officially dismantled in Rio Grande do Sul in 1982 and in every state by 1983.
74. Marcon, *Acampamento Natalino*, 82.
75. Tedesco and Carini, *Conflitos agrários no norte gaúcho*, 139.
76. Carter, *Ideal Interest*. Antonio Chechin, interview, available at www.ihu.unisinos.br/entrevistas/15724-encruzilhada-natalino-30-anos-o-nascimento-de-um-acampamento-entrevista-especial-com-antonio-cechin.
77. Wagner, *Saga do João Sem Terra*, 115.
78. *JST*, April 1982.
79. *JST*, April 1982.
80. *JST*, May 1982.
81. MST, *Nossa luta é nossa escola*, 1990.
82. Caldart, *Pedagogia*, 224.
83. *JST*, November 1983.
84. *JST*, February 1984.
85. *JST*, Abril 1984.
86. *JST*, June 1981.

87. Scolese, *Pioneiros*.
88. Fernandes, *Formação do MST no Brasil*, 52.
89. Bonavigo and Bavarescro, "Fazenda Annoni," 35.
90. MST, *Caderno de Formação n1*, 1986, 7.
91. Ibid., 13.
92. Prior to Neves, military officials held executive power. Neves was elected by the electoral college that the military had created, but was the first nonmilitary official chosen.
93. Silva, *Buraco negro*.
94. Wagner, *Saga do João Sem Terra*, 127.
95. Medeiros, *Historia dos movimentos*, 182.
96. Selbin, *Modern Latin American Revolutions*.
97. Tedesco and Carini, *Conflitos agrários no norte gaúcho*, 40.
98. *JST*, December 1984, January 1987.
99. Ondetti, *Land, Protest, and Politics*, 80.

CHAPTER FOUR

1. Caldeira and Holston, "Democracy and Violence in Brazil."
2. Eckstein, *Power and Popular Protest*.
3. Alvarez, "Latin American Feminisms."
4. Thayer, "Translations and Refusals"; Alvarez, "Beyond NGO-ization?"
5. Hochstetler and Keck, *Greening Brazil*.
6. Poletto, "Churches."
7. Wolford, *This Land Is Ours Now*.
8. Vergara-Camus, *Land and Freedom*.
9. Ondetti, *Land, Protest, and Politics*.
10. Sluyter-Beltrão, *Rise and Decline*.
11. Brito, *A tomada da Ford*, 92–94.
12. Keck, *Workers' Party*, 110.
13. Brito, *A tomada da Ford*, 47–53.
14. Alves, *State and Opposition*, 195.
15. Keck, *Workers' Party*, 93.
16. Lowy, "New Type of Party."
17. Alves, *State and Opposition*, 199.
18. Scherer-Warren, "O caráter dos novos movimentos sociais"; Dagnino, "Citizenship."
19. Cardoso, Elias, and Pero, "Urban Regeneration and Spatial Discrimination."
20. Skidmore, *Politics of Military Rule*, 180, 246.
21. Huntington, *Third Wave*, vol. 4.
22. Williamson, "What Washington Means by Policy Reform."
23. Weber, "Imposition of a Global Development Architecture"; Stiglitz, "Is There a Post-Washington Consensus?"; Birdsall and Fukuyama, "Post-Washington Consensus-Development."

24. Peck and Tickell, "Neoliberalizing Space."
25. For a discussion of the UDR and its actions at this time, see *Veja*'s article, "O trator da direita," June 18, 1986.
26. In the 1980s, many of the CPT documents do not define "conflict." However, in the 2000 version of their annual *Conflitos no Campo*, the CPT defines conflict as "struggles that involve the means of production, which include acts that take place when claiming possession, ownership, and/or use over a certain piece of land, water, or resource by landless people or squatters." Particular cases of violence include killing, harassment, and death threats. Land occupations by the MST and other actors are included in these figures, as well as documented apart. The CPT collects its data from direct contact with victims, newspapers, and dispatches from movements.
27. The court case is TJ/SP, Apelação cível n. 212.726–1/8, Rel. Des. José Osório, j. December 16, 1994.
28. Metzer, "Inflation and Money in Brazil."
29. Noronha, "Ciclo de greves."
30. Sluyter-Beltrão, *Rise and Decline*, 181.
31. Flores-Macias, *After Neoliberalism?*
32. Prior to the neoliberal turn, the Brazilian system was characterized by price controls for specific crops, subsidized credit for technological investments (e.g., tractors), and particular government agencies being in charge of specific crops (e.g., coffee and sugar). These programs developed in the early twentieth century, based on goals to secure rural to urban population shifts and provide food cheaply to the newly amassing urban populations. Barros, "Brazil."
33. Musacchio and Lazzarini, *Reinventing State Capitalism*.
34. Araujo et al., "Politica de credito para a agricultura brasileira."
35. Sluyter-Beltrão, *Rise and Decline*, 284.
36. Fumes and Oliveira, "MST na era Collor."
37. Kingstone, "Long (and Uncertain) March."
38. Geortzel, *Fernando Henrique Cardoso*.
39. Antunes and Hallewell, "World of Work."
40. Cardoso, *A década neoliberal*.
41. Amann and Baer, "Illusion of Stability."
42. For more on the increased use of fertilizers, see ANDA 2011, "Investimentos no Brasil," anda.org.br/multimidia/investimentos.pdf.
43. For a discussion of *Veja*'s coverage of the MST, as well as the language used by FHC to refer to the movement, see cartamaior.com.br/?/Editoria/Midia/Os-30-anos-de-odio-ao-MST-nas-paginas-de-Veja/12/30253.
44. Fernandes, *Formação do MST no Brasil*, 188.
45. Ondetti, *Land, Protest, and Politics*, 173–77.
46. MDA-SAF official for Brazil, in discussion with author, Brasília, February 11, 2011.
47. INCRA official for Brazil, in discussion with author, Brasília, February 2, 2011.
48. Jungmann, "Agricultura Familiar."

49. FAQ–PRONAF, accessed December 8, 2015, www.bcb.gov.br/pre/bc_atende/port/PRONAF.asp#21.
50. Agronegocio–PRONAF, accessed December 8, 2015, www.bb.com.br/portalbb/page44,8623,10818,0,0,1,1.bb.
51. Correa and Silva, "Perfil das liberações."
52. Van der Ploeg, *New Peasantries*.
53. Lahiff, Borras, and Kay, "Market-Led Agrarian Reform."
54. Dagnino, "Citizenship."
55. Correa and Silva, "Perfil das liberações," 21.
56. Samuels, "From Socialism to Social Democracy."
57. Hunter, "Normalization of an Anomaly."
58. Keck, *Workers' Party*, 106.
59. Sandoval, "Alternative Forms."
60. Tumolo, *Da contestação à conformação*.
61. For more on the MPA, see mpabrasil.org.br/.
62. For more on women's rural movements, see mmcbrasil.com.br/site/node/44.
63. Branford, "Working with Governments."
64. Former state director, in discussion with author, Pontal do Paranapanema, SP, November 7, 2011.
65. Field notes, Encampment 2 outside of São Paulo, SP, August 15, 2009.
66. Scherer-Warren, "Redes para a (re) territorialização"; Benoit, "Assentamento Anita Garibaldi."
67. INCRA official for Paraná, in discussion with author, Curitiba, PR, August 1, 2011.
68. INCRA official for São Paulo State, in discussion with author, São Paulo, SP, November 1, 2011.
69. MST, *Caderno de Cooperação Agrícola n1*, 1995.
70. MST, *Caderno de Educação n9*, 1999.
71. MST, *Caderno de Educação n10*, 2000.
72. MST, *Caderno de Saude n1*, 1999.
73. MST, *Caderno de Formação n31*, 1999.
74. MST, *Caderno de Formação n26*, 1998.
75. For a comparison of the surveys and their results, see "Diminui apoio popular ao MST, diz pesquisa CNI/Ibope," *Folhaonline*, May 31, 2000, www1.folha.uol.com.br/fol/pol/ult31052000264.htm.

CHAPTER FIVE

1. Lula, interview, 56.
2. Lula, interview by Roda Viva, January 10, 1999, accessed July 20, 2017, rodaviva.fapesp.br/materia/67/entrevistados/luiz_inacio_lula_da_silva_1999.htm.
3. Piero Locatelli, "O governo Dilma não fez nada em termos de reforma agrária," *Carta Capital*, February 10, 2014, cartacapital.com.br/sociedade/201co-governo-dilma-nao-fez-nada-em-termos-de-reforma-agraria201d-6758.html; Luciano

Nascimento, "CPT considera reforma agrária do governo Dilma a pior dos ultimos 20 anos," *Agencia Brasil*, agenciabrasil.ebc.com.br/geral/noticia/2015-01/cpt-considera-reforma-agraria-do-governo-dilma-pior-dos-ultimos-20-anos.

4. In 2004, shortly after Lula was elected, the movement organized 286 land occupations. In 2015, the CPT documented 86 MST-led occupations. CPT, *Conflitos no Campo*, 2005, 2014.
5. Pedro Marcondes de Moura, "Ocaso do MST," *IstoÉ*, September 21, 2011.
6. For the statement from the members who left the movement, see "Carta da Saida de Nossas Organizações" (Letter of Resignation from Our Organizations), passapalavra.info/2011/11/48866, April 23, 2016.
7. Roldão Arruda, "Esvaziado por Ações do Governo, MST Chega aos 30 Anos," *O Estado de S. Paulo*, January 20, 2014.
8. For earlier literature, see Fernandes, *Formação do MST no Brasil*; Branford and Rocha, *Cutting the Wire*; Wright and Wolford, *To Inherit the Earth*. Newer accounts include Wolford, *This Land Is Ours Now*; Vergara-Camus, *Land and Freedom*; Pahnke, Tarlau, and Wolford, "Understanding Rural Resistance"; and Carter, *Challenging Social Inequality*.
9. MST organizer in the Sector of Production, in discussion with author, outside of Rio Bonito, PR, August 11, 2011.
10. Field notes, outside of Bagé, RS, May 13, 2011.
11. MST organizer in the Sector of Production, in discussion with author, outside of Rio Bonito, PR, August 11, 2011.
12. MST, *Caderno de Cooperação Agricola n8*, 1999.
13. Souza and Gebara, *PROCERA*.
14. MST, *Caderno de Cooperação Agricola n5*, 1995.
15. Field notes from COOPTAR, outside of Pontão, RS, April 5, 2011.
16. MST, *Balanço Político*, 2006.
17. A similar recognition of problems in the movement's collectivization plans is found in Diniz and Gilbert, "Socialist Values," and also in Wolford, *This Land Is Ours Now*, 188–92.
18. Todorov and Schmidt, "Primeiro Censo."
19. COPERLAT director, in discussion with author, outside of Pontão, RS, April 1, 2011.
20. MST state director, in discussion with author, Porto Alegre, RS, April 3, 2011.
21. MST regional director, in discussion with author, Porto Alegre, RS, March 23, 2011.
22. Corresponding with the embrace of this mode of agricultural production, we find many other movements internationally turning against industrial forms of cultivation. Most of the LVC-affiliated movements adhere to, or at least promote, a form of agroecology. An in-depth account of the international movement for agroecology, as well as its part in the demand for food sovereignty, is beyond the scope of this book. For a succinct discussion of the meaning and practice of agroecology, see Miguel Altieri, *Agroecology: The Scientific Basis of Alternative Agriculture* (Boulder, Colo.: Westview Press, 1987).

23. There have been various high-profile occupations of areas owned by corporations. Details of the occupation of land owned by Petrobras can be found here: g1.globo.com/espirito-santo/noticia/2015/05/familias-do-mst-ocupam-terreno-no-es-reservado-para-polo-da-petrobras.html. One ongoing site of dispute has been territory owned by the Brazilian multinational Cutrale, especially in the state of São Paulo. For more on the years of conflict involving Cutrale, see politica.estadao.com.br/noticias/geral,mst-acusa-cutrale-de-usar-terra-griladas,446913 and g1.globo.com/sp/bauru-marilia/noticia/2015/08/integrantes-do-mst-deixam-fazenda-em-borebi-apos-tres-dias-de-ocupacao.html.
24. Many stories connect the abuse of the environment, through the use of chemicals and promotion of industrial agriculture, to the violation of social function. For a complete transcript of the radio program, see www2.camara.leg.br/camaranoticias/radio/materias/REPORTAGEM-ESPECIAL/335615-ESPECIAL-LUTA-PELA-TERRA:-MOVIMENTO-SEM-TERRA-(06'-44%22).html. Also, www.mst.org.br/2015/08/02/sem-terra-ocupam-fazenda-grilada-pela-cutrale-em-sao-paulo.html and biodiversidadla.org/Principal/Secciones/Noticias/Aliada_ao_agronegocio_brasileiro_a_Syngenta_resiste_ao_decreto_estadual_de_desapropriacao_da_sua_terra.
25. MST, *Caderno de Cooperação Agricola n10*, 2001.
26. *JST*, May 2003.
27. *JST*, September 2005.
28. Both notebooks can be found here: issuu.com/comunicacaompa/docs/caderno_de_estudo_congresso_i.
29. Welch, "Estratégias de resistência."
30. *JST*, March 1995.
31. *JST*, November 2009, June/July 2012.
32. *JST*, July/August 2014.
33. Director of COOPTAT, in discussion with author, Porto Alegre, RS, June 12, 2011.
34. MST, *Cartilha de Cooperação n1*, 2008.
35. Field notes from outside of Rio Bonito, July 23, 2011; director of Mundokide, in discussion with author, outside of Rio Bonito, PR, July 25, 2011.
36. MST, *Caderno de Cooperação Agricola n11*, 2004.
37. MST state director, in discussion with author, RS, April 3, 2011; *colono* literally means settler. The term is still used primarily in the south of Brazil to refer to small farmers, who are usually descendants of immigrants, or rather, settlers from early and mid-twentieth-century immigration.
38. Wolf, *Peasant Wars*; Scott, *Moral Economy*; Moore, *Social Origins*.
39. Field notes from Jornada de Agroecologia, Curitiba, Paraná, July 1, 2011.
40. Field notes from Escola Milton Santos, Londrina, PR, July 6, 2011.
41. See "Carta da Saida de Nossas Organizações" (Letter of Resignation from Our Organizations), accessed April 23, 2017, www.passapalavra.info/2011/11/48866.
42. *Folha de São Paulo*, March 6, 2006, www1.folha.uol.com.br/fsp/brasil/fc060320 0602.htm.

43. Oliveira, "Critérios de avaliação."
44. INCRA official for Brazil, in discussion with author, Brasília, January 31, 2011.
45. Tribunal das Contas da União (TCU), Acórdão no. 557/2004; TCU, *Relatório e Parecer Prévio sobre as Contas do Governo da República Exercício de 2009*; Comissão Parlamentar Parlamentares de Inquerito (CPI) da Terra, 2005.
46. "Dados estatísticos," FNDE, 2014, accessed October 7, 2014, www.fnde.gov.br/programas/alimentacao-escolar/alimentacao-escolar-consultas/alimentacao-escolar-dados-estatisticos.
47. Branford, *Working with Governments*.
48. CONCRAB president, in discussion with author, Brasília, September 1, 2011.
49. COPERLAT director, in discussion with author, outside of Pontão, RS, April 1, 2011.
50. The common phrase used to denote fraud and misuse in each of the congressional inquiries is *"desvio."* Each investigation began with alleged misuse of funds by MST-created nongovernmental organizations, such as ANCA (Associação Nacional de Cooperação Agrícola; National Association for Agricultural Cooperation), which held *convenios* (contracts) with various government entities with specific objectives. Each allegation of fraud led to the temporary suspension of resources. There have not been any indictments or formal criminal investigations resulting from the CPIs.
51. Ariovaldo Umbelino de Oliveira, "A reforma agrária de Lula," *Estadão*, March 6, 2011, accessed April 14, 2015, opiniao.estadao.com.br/noticias/geral,a-reforma-agraria-de-lula-imp-,688397.
52. Field notes, Instituto Educar, outside of Pontão, RS, March 20, 2011.
53. For example, see MST 2001 on PRONAF, and *JST*, April 2008, on the importance of PAA for producers on settlements. More general expressions for more public policies (*politicas publicas*) for rural infrastructure, housing, and production support can be found in *JST*, October 2007, September 2008.
54. Former MST state and national director, in discussion with author, outside of Miguel do Iguaçu, PR, July 12, 2011.
55. MST, *Cadernos de Debates n1*, 2009.
56. Ibid.
57. *Trilhas do campo*, 2011.
58. CNA represents agribusiness in Brazil's corporatist system. CONTAG represents labor.
59. See www.senar.org.br/noticia/rede-e-tec-brasil-no-senar-entra-em-acao-democratizando-o-acesso-ao-ensino-tecnico-no-brasil, accessed July 2, 2016.
60. PRONATEC's course listing can be found at senar.org.br/sites/default/files/portfolio_guia_fic_pronatec_2015.pdf, accessed July 1, 2016.
61. MST, *Caderno de Debates n2*, 2009.
62. MST, *Cartilha de Apoio n2*, 2008.
63. MST, *A constituição e gestão de iniciativas agroindustrias cooperativas*, 2010.
64. Veltmeyer and Petras, "Social Dynamics."

65. ITERRA, "Instituto de Educação Josué de Castro," 5.
66. ITERRA, "IEJC e a Educação Profissional," 17.
67. Student, in discussion with author, Milton Santos School, Londrina, PR, July 6, 2011.
68. MST, *Nossa luta é nossa escola*, 1990.
69. MST, *Por uma educação básica do campo*, 1998; see also Tarlau, "Education of the Countryside."
70. Ondetti, Wambergue, and Gonçalves Fonso, "From Posseiro to Sem Terra."
71. To my knowledge, there is no study that compares developments in Paraná with those in Rio Grande do Sul. Rebecca Tarlau's work on education showcases Rio Grande do Sul and Pernambuco, while David Meek devotes his attention to the Amazon (Pará). There are many theses in Portuguese that analyze specific settlements and experiences in education in each state separately, but I have found none that compare events across the states. See Tarlau, "Reproducing Rural Public Schools" and "Occupying Land, Occupying Schools," and Meek, "Learning as Territoriality."
72. MST, *Escola itinerante em campamentos do MST*, 1998; MST, *Escola Itinerante*, 2000.
73. MST 2003, found in Cesar de David and Ane Carine Meurer, *Espaços-tempos de itinerância: Interlocução entre universidade e escola itinerante do MST* (Santa Maria, RS: Editora UFSM, 2006).
74. These figures are from comparing INEP numbers of students in technical education by state with INCRA/PRONERA figures from 2010.
75. While the majority of students who attend courses at ITERRA are from the south and southeast, many come from all over Brazil. The TAC is also funded with PRONERA resources.
76. ITERRA, "Instituto de Educação Josué de Castro."
77. INCRA-PRONERA, *Relação Geral de Cursos em Execução*.
78. Every CEE in each Brazilian state has norm making, deliberative, and consultative powers for their respective state's educational policies, within the limits set by the Lei de Diretrizes de Base (Basic Legal Directives in Education) of 1996.
79. While not a law, a *parecer* is a legally binding document that regulates specific details of public policy.
80. Every itinerant school has an *escola base* (base school) in a movement settlement, which acts as the pedagogical and administrative center for the itinerant schools in the encampments. The itinerant and base schools differ in that the itinerant schools do not have a permanent structure, which the base schools have because they are located on settlements. Both, however, follow similar pedagogies and fit within the overall movement's educational vision in the same way.
81. Director of the Instituto Federal, Sertão, in discussion with author, Pontão, RS, June 3, 2011.
82. INCRA official, in discussion with author, Porto Alegre, RS, March 23, 2011.
83. MST organizer in the Sector of Education for Rio Grande do Sul, in discussion with author, Porto Alegre, RS, March 9, 2011.

84. MST leader in Sector of Education, Paraná, in discussion with author, Curitiba, PR, July 31, 2011.
85. A *resolução* is not a law but a legally binding order from a nonexecutive body/administration concerning some public policy or matter. An *instrução* is meant to clarify the operation and meaning of practices within policies.
86. Interview with former CRE official, Bagé, RS, May 17, 2011.
87. Constituente Escolar, Department of Education, RS, 2000.
88. Former state secretary of education, RS, March 11, 2011.
89. The schools reopened in 2012. They also exist in Alagoas, Santa Catarina, and Goiás.
90. Marco Aurélio Weissheimer, "Yeda Crusius manda Brigada Militar reprimir protestos contra governo," *Carta Maior*, March 13, 2008.
91. MP official for state of Rio Grande do Sul, March 15, 2011.
92. Public Prosecutor's Office, Act 1.116, 2007.
93. Scalabrin, "Estado de exceção no Rio Grande do Sul."
94. MST state director, in discussion with author, RS, April 3, 2011.
95. Department of Diversity, Department of Education, PR, in discussion with author, August 3, 2011.
96. For more on repression during the Lerner years, see Branford and Rocha, *Cutting the Wire*, 148–70.
97. MST organizer in the Sector of Education, PR, July 31, 2011.
98. MST, *Escola itinerante do MST*, 2008, 6–7.
99. Former Departmento de Diversidade, in discussion with author, Curitiba, PR, August 20, 2011.
100. Former administrator, Department of Diversity, in discussion with author, PR, August 12, 2011.
101. MST organizer in the Sector of Education, in discussion with author, SP, October 29, 2010.
102. Education of the Countryside programs exist in Amapá, Amazonas, Pará, Maranhão, Ceará, Piauí, Rio Grande do Norte, Paraiba, Alagoas, Sergipe, Bahia, Tocantins, Goías, Minas Gerais, Mato Grosso, Mato Grosso do Sul, Paraná, Santa Catarina, and Rio Grande do Sul. In 2012 Rio Grande do Sul formed a working group to discuss the program. Acre, Pernambuco, Espirito Santo, São Paulo, and Rondônia do not have a program.
103. MST organizer in the Sector of Education, in discussion with author, Brasília, February 2010.
104. INCRA official, in discussion with author, PR, August 1, 2011.
105. INCRA official, in discussion with author, SP, November 1, 2011.
106. MST, "MST impõe pauta da Reforma Agrária no governo Dilma," 2014, accessed December 10, 2016, biodiversidadla.org/Portada_Principal/Recomendamos/MST_impoe_pauta_da_Reforma_Agraria_no_governo_Dilma.
107. MST organizer in the Sector of Education, in discussion with author, Pontal do Paranapanema, SP, November 8, 2011.

108. Instruction supervisor, in Secretary of Education, in discussion with author, Pontal do Paranapanema, SP, November 21, 2011.
109. Tarlau, "Coproducing Rural Public Schools."
110. Tarrow, *Power in Movement*.
111. Loman, "Brazil's Social Challenges."
112. ANDA, *Anuário Estatistico*, 2011.
113. For more on the program's nature and results, see "Territórios da Cidadania," Portal de Cidadania, *Governo Federal*, accessed November 23, 2015, http://www.territorios dacidadania.gov.br/dotlrn/clubs/territriosrurais/one-community.
114. Scott, *Seeing Like a State*.
115. Froufe, "Ibope/CAN 92% condenam," accessed April 23, 2017.

CONCLUSION

1. Ohde, "Operação Castra"; Catia Seabra and Angela Bondrini, "Operação policial em escola do MST tem confronto e dois sem-terra detidos," *Folha de Sao Paulo*, November 4, 2016.
2. At the time of concluding this writing (March 2018), Dilma has not been directly connected to any illegal activity uncovered in the Operation Car Wash investigation. The same cannot be said about former President Lula, who was sentenced to ten years in prison for illegally taking $1 million dollars in kickbacks to refurbish a property. He appealed the decision and later lost.
3. The decree is available at planalto.gov.br/ccivil_03/_Ato2015-2018/2016/Mpv/mpv727.htm.
4. Reuters, "Petrobras inicia processo para venda de terminais de GNL e térmicas," republished in *O Globo*, June 7, 2016, br.reuters.com/article/businessNews/idBRKCN0YT2RC.
5. Geralda Doca, "Governo Temer quer abrir capital de Correios e Casa da Moeda," *Globo*. June 15, 2016.
6. Maria Christina Frias and Valdo Cruz, "Temer planeja privatizar Congonhas e Santos Dumont; veja entrevista," *Folha de São Paulo*, July 10, 2016.
7. Rodrigo Polito, "Temer edita MP que facilita privatização do setor electric," *O Valor Econômico*, June 23, 2016.
8. Lais Lis, "Governo marca leilão de quatro aeroportos para março de 2017," *Globo*, November 30, 2016.
9. Darian Alvarenga, "Pacote de privatizações do governo Temer prevê 75 projetos para 2018," *Globo*, January 30, 2018.
10. "Em 1ª privatização do governo Temer, italiana Enel adquire controle da Celg," *UOL Economia*, November 30, 2016.
11. "Governo poderá demitir até 18 mil servidores do Banco do Brasil," *Diario do Brasil*, October 12, 2016; "Governo Temer vai fechar 8 agências do Banco do Brasil em Campinas," *Carta Campinas*, November 23, 2016.

12. Sociedade Nacional de Agricultura, "Michel Temer assume presidência, reduz ministérios e extingue MDA," May 13, 2016.
13. "Porteira aberta: Estrangeiros poderão comprar terras à vontade no Brasil," *Equipe Gazeta do Povo*, May 12, 2017.
14. Renan Truffi, "Entenda a reforma da Previdência (que vai fazer você trabalhar mais)," *Carta Capital*, December 6, 2016.
15. Oganes, "Finance"; Chamon, Garcia, and Souza, "FX Interventions in Brazil."
16. Eduardo Barretto, "Geddel entrega carta de demissão a Temer," *Globo*, November 25, 2016, oglobo.globo.com/brasil/geddel-entrega-carta-de-demissao-temer -20539636.
17. "Governo Temer tem aprovação de 6% e reprovação de 70%, diz Datafolha," *Globo*, January 31, 2018.
18. Castañeda, "Latin America's Left Turn."
19. Cameron, "Latin America's Left Turns"; Sader, *New Mole*; George Ciccariello-Maher, "Constituent Moments"; Ellner, "Latin America's Radical Left."
20. Ciccariello-Maher, "Constituent Moments."
21. García Linera, *Las tensiones creativas*.
22. Ellner, *Latin America's Radical Left*.
23. Burbach, Fox, and Fuentes, *Latin America's Turbulent Transitions*; Sader, *New Mole*.
24. Levitsky and Roberts, *Latin America's Left Turn*.
25. Sader, *New Mole*, 76.
26. Goodwin and Skocpol, *Explaining Revolutions*.
27. Santamarta Luengos, *La campaña de alfabetización*.
28. Abendroth, *Rebel Literacy*.
29. Ibid., 52.
30. Eckstein, "Impact of the Cuban Revolution."
31. Rosset, "Moving Forward."
32. Greeno, interview.
33. "Honoring Nelson Mandela," Jessie Noyes Smith Foundation, noyes.org/news /other-news/honoring-nelson-mandela.
34. St. Peter and Patel, "This Land Is Our Land?"
35. Hoefle, *Beyond Coldwar Pipdreams*.
36. Opie, *The Law of the Land*.
37. Vogeler, *Myth of the Family Farm*, 49.
38. Dunbar-Ortiz, "Land Reform and Indian Survival," 155.
39. Cronon, *Nature's Metropolis*, 27; De Angelis, "Separating the Doing and the Deed"; Harvey, *New Imperialism*.
40. See Chandler, *Land Title Origins*, for a discussion of the multiple conflicting understandings of land title, as well as Wilkins and Lomawaima, *Uneven Ground*.
41. Green, *The Politics of Indian Removal*, 46.
42. Du Bois, *Black Reconstruction in America*, 55.
43. Fierce, "Black Struggle for Land."

44. Foner, *Reconstruction*.
45. Fierce, "Black Struggle for Land."
46. U.S. Department of Agriculture, "Black Farmers in America."
47. Cleaver and Katsiaficas, *Liberation, Imagination, and the Black Panther Party*.
48. Berger and Dunbar-Ortiz, "Struggle Is for Land," 66; Van Deburg, *Modern Black Nationalism*, 197.
49. For figures, see www.gwu.edu/~erpapers/teachinger/glossary/southern-tenant-farmers-union.cfm.
50. Gaither, *Blacks and the Populist Movement*.
51. Geisler and Popper, *Land Reform*, 20.
52. Olsson, "Sharecroppers and Campesinos," 631.
53. Maddox, "Bankhead-Jones Farm Tenant Act."
54. Geisler, "History of Land Reform," 23.
55. McFarland, "Administration of the New Deal Greenbelt Towns."
56. Otis, *Dawes Act*.
57. Strange and Loo, "Holding the Rock."
58. Johnson, "Occupation of Alcatraz Island."
59. Article 16 of U.S. Code.
60. Dunbar-Ortiz, "Land Reform and Indian Survival," 158.
61. White, *Free to Be Kanien'kehaka*.
62. Estes, "Wounded Knee."
63. Jackson, "What Is Property?," 63.

BIBLIOGRAPHY

SECONDARY SOURCES

Abendroth, Mark. *Rebel Literacy: Cuba's National Literacy Campaign and Critical Global Citizenship.* Duluth, Minn.: Litwin Books, 2009.

Abers, Rebecca Neaera, and Margaret E. Keck. "Mobilizing the State: The Erratic Partner in Brazil's Participatory Water Policy." *Politics and Society* 37, no. 2 (2009): 289–314.

Abers, Rebecca, Lizandra Serafim, and Luciana Tatagiba. "Changing Repertoires of State-Society Interaction Under Lula." In *Brazil Under the Workers' Party: Continuity and Change from Lula to Dilma,* edited by Fábio De Castro, Kees Koonings, and Marianne Wiesebron, 36–61. Basingstoke: Palgrave Macmillan, 2014.

Agamben, Giorgio. *Homo Sacer: Sovereign Power and Bare Life.* Stanford, Calif.: Stanford University Press, 1998.

Agarwal, Bina. "Food Sovereignty, Food Security, and Democratic Choice: Critical Contradictions, Difficult Conciliations." *Journal of Peasant Studies* 41, no. 6 (2014): 1247–68.

Alinsky, Saul. *Rules for Radicals: A Pragmatic Primer for Realistic Radicals.* New York: Vintage, 2010.

Alvarez, Sonia. "Beyond NGO-ization? Reflections from Latin America." *Development* 52, no. 2 (2009): 175–84.

———. *Engendering Democracy in Brazil: Women's Movements in Transition Politics.* Princeton, N.J.: Princeton University Press, 1990.

———. "Latin American Feminisms 'Go Global': Trends of the 1990s and Challenges for the New Millennium." In *Cultures of Politics, Politics of Cultures: Revisioning Latin American Social Movements,* edited by Sonia Alvarez, Evelina Dagnino, and Arturo Escobar, 293–325. Boulder, Colo.: Westview Press, 1998.

Alves, Maria Helena Moreira. *State and Opposition in Military Brazil.* Austin: University of Texas Press, 1988.

Amann, Edmund, and Werner Baer. "The Illusion of Stability: The Brazilian Economy Under Cardoso." *World Development* 28, no. 10 (2000): 1805–19.

Amaral, Ernesto Friedrich, and Wilson Fusco. "Shaping Brazil: The Role of International Migration." Migration Policy Institute, June 1, 2005. migrationpolicy.org /article/shaping-brazil-role-international-migration.

Amsden, Alice Hoffenberg. *Asia's Next Giant: South Korea and Late Industrialization*. New York: Oxford University Press, 1992.

ANDA (Associação Nacional para Difusão de Adubos e Corretivos Agrícolas). *Anuário Estatistico do Setor de Fertilizantes, 1987–2006*. São Paulo: 1987–2006.

Anderson, Kym, and Alberto Valdés. *Distortions to Agricultural Incentives in Latin America*. Washington, D.C.: World Bank Publications, 2009.

Ankersen, Thomas T., and Thomas Ruppert. "Tierra y Libertad: The Social Function Doctrine and Land Reform in Latin America." *Tulane Environmental Law Journal* 19 (2006): 69–120.

Antunes, Ricardo, and Laurence Hallewell. "The World of Work, the Restructuring of Production, and Challenges to Trade Unionism and Social Struggles in Brazil." *Latin American Perspectives* 27, no. 6 (November 2000): 9–26.

Araujo, Paulo, Alexandre Barros, José Barros, and Ricardo Shirota. "Politica de credito para a agricultura brasileira." *Revista de Politica Agricola* 16, no. 4 (2007): 31–32.

Araújo Soares, Edla. "Relatório das diretrizes operacionais para a Educação Básica nas escolas do campo." *Resolução CNE/CEB* 1 (2001): 3–38.

Arendt, Hannah. *On Revolution*. 1963. Reprint, New York: Penguin, 1990.

Arroyo, Miguel. "A educação do campo e a pesquisa do campo: Metas." In *Educação do campo e pesquisa: Questões para reflexão*, by Monica Castagna Molina, Antonio Munarim, Beatriz Heredia, Bernardo Mancano Fernandes, Eliana Felipe, Ilse Scherer-Warren, Leonilde Medeiros, Maria do Socorro Silva, Miguel Gonzalez Arroyo, Moacir Palmeira, Pedro Ivan Christoffoli, Rosangela Cintrao, Sergio Pereira Leite, Sonia Meire Santos, and Azevdeo de Jesus, 103–17. Brasília, DF: Ministério do Desenvolvimento Agrario, 2006.

Assies, William. "David versus Goliath in Cochabamba: Water Rights, Neoliberalism, and the Revival of Social Protest in Bolivia." *Latin American Perspectives* 30, no. 3 (2003): 14–36.

Azevedo, Thales. *A religião civil brasileira: Um instrumento político*. Petrópolis: Vozes, 1981.

Badiou, Alain. *The Communist Hypothesis*. London: Verso Books, 2015.

Baiocchi, Gianpaolo. *Militants and Citizens: The Politics of Participatory Democracy in Porto Alegre*. Stanford, Calif.: Stanford University Press, 2005.

Balakrishnan, Gopal. *The Enemy: An Intellectual Portrait of Carl Schmitt*. London: Verso, 2000.

Barros, G. S. A. C. "Brazil: The Challenges in Becoming an Agricultural Superpower." In *Brazil as an Economic Superpower*, edited by Lael Brainard and Leonardo Martinez-Diaz, 81–109. Washington, D.C.: Brookings Institution Press, 2009.

Benford, Robert D., and David A. Snow. "Framing Processes and Social Movements: An Overview and Assessment." *Annual Review of Sociology* 26, no. 1 (2000): 611–39.

Benoit, Hector. "O assentamento Anita Garibaldi: Entrevista com lideranças do Movimento dos Trabalhadores Sem-Teto (MTST)." *Crítica Marxista* 14 (2002): 134–50.
Berger, Dan, with Roxanne Dunbar-Ortiz. "'The Struggle Is for Land!' Race, Territory and National Liberation." In *The Hidden 1970s: Histories of Radicalism*, edited by Dan Berger, 57–76. New Brunswick, N.J.: Rutgers University Press, 2010.
Bernstein, Henry. "'The Peasantry' in Global Capitalism: Who, Where and Why?" *Socialist Register* 37 (2001): 1–51.
Berstein, Mary. "Celebration and Suppression: The Strategic Uses of Identity by the Lesbian and Gay Movement." *American Journal of Sociology* 103 (1997): 531–65.
Bevington, Douglas, and Chris Dixon. "Movement-Relevant Theory: Rethinking Social Movement Scholarship and Activism." *Social Movement Studies* 4, no. 3 (2005): 185–208.
Bevir, Mark. *Encyclopedia of Governance*. Thousand Oaks, Calif.: Sage, 2007.
Birdsall, Nancy, and Francis Fukuyama. "The Post-Washington Consensus: Development After the Crisis." *Foreign Affairs* 90, no. 2 (2011): 45–53.
Boff, Leonardo. *Eclesiogênese: As comunidades eclesiais de base reinventam a Igreja*. Petrópolis: Editora Vozes, 1977.
Bonavigo, Elizabete, and Pedro Bavaresco. "Fazenda Annoni: Da Ocupação ao assentamento definitive." In *Conflitos agrários no norte gaúcho*, edited by João Carlos Tedesco and Joel João Carini, 31–50. Porto Alegre: EST Edições, 2008.
Bonim, Anamaria Aimoré. *Movimentos sociais no campo*. Curitiba: Edições Criar, 1989.
Branford, Sue "Working with Governments: The MST's Experience with the Cardoso and Lula Administrations." In *Challenging Social Inequality: The Landless Rural Worker's Movement and Agrarian Reform in Brazil*, edited by Miguel Carter, 331–51. Durham, N.C.: Duke University Press, 2015.
Branford, Sue, and Jan Rocha. *Cutting the Wire: The Story of the Landless Movement in Brazil*. London: Latin American Bureau, 2002.
Brass, Tom. *Peasants, Populism, and Postmodernism: The Return of the Agrarian Myth*. London: Frank Cass Press, 2000.
Brito, José Carlos Aguiar. *A tomada da Ford: O nascimento de um sindicato livre*. Petrópolis: Editora Vozes, 1983.
Bruneau, Thomas C. "Brazil: The Catholic Church and Basic Christian Communities." In *Religion and Political Conflict in Latin America*, edited by Daniel H. Levine, 106–23. Chapel Hill: University of North Carolina Press, 1986.
Budgen, Sebastian, and Slavoj Žižek. *Lenin Reloaded: Toward a Politics of Truth*. Durham, N.C.: Duke University Press, 2007.
Buechler, Steven M. *Understanding Social Movements: Theories from the Classical Era to the Present*. London: Routledge, 2016.
Burbach, Roger, Michael Fox, and Federico Fuente. *Latin America's Turbulent Transitions*. London: Zed Books, 2013.
Burchardt, Hans-Jürgen, and Kristina Dietz. "(Neo-)extractivism—A New Challenge for Development Theory from Latin America." *Third World Quarterly* 35, no. 3 (2014): 468–86.

Butler, Judith, Ernesto Laclau, and Slavoj Žižek. *Contingency, Hegemony, Universality: Contemporary Dialogues on the Left.* London: Verso, 2000.
Caires, Ângela Cristina Ribeiro. "O colonato na Usina Tamoio." In *Formas tuteladas de condição camponesa,* edited by Delma Pessanha Neves and Maria Aparecida de Moraes Silva, 163–84. São Paulo, Brasília: Edunesp/NEAD, 2008.
Caldart, Roseli Salete. *Pedagogia do Movimento Sem Terra: Escola é mais do que escola.* Petrópolis: Editora Vozes, 2000.
Caldeira, Rute. "The Failed Marriage Between Women and the Landless People's Movement (MST) in Brazil." *Journal of International Women's Studies* 10, no. 4 (2013): 237–58.
Caldeira, Teresa, and James Holston. "Democracy and Violence in Brazil." *Comparative Studies in Society and History* 41, no. 4 (1999): 691–729.
Cameron, Maxwell. "Latin America's Left Turns: Beyond Good and Bad." *Third World Quarterly* 30 (2009): 331–48.
Cardoso, Adalberto Moreira. *A década neoliberal e a crise dos sindicatos no Brasil: E a crise dos sindicatos no Brasil.* São Paulo: Boitempo Editorial, 2003.
Cardoso, Adalberto, Peter Elias, and Valéria Pero. "Urban Regeneration and Spatial Discrimination: The Case of Rio's Favelas." In *Proceedings of the 31st Meeting of the Brazilian Association of Graduate Programs in Economics,* Belo Horizonte, Minas Gerais, 2003. anpec.org.br/encontro2003/artigos/F41.pdf.
Carter, Miguel, ed. *Challenging Social Inequality: The Landless Rural Worker's Movement and Agrarian Reform in Brazil.* Durham, N.C.: Duke University Press, 2015.
———. "Ideal Interest Mobilization: Explaining the Formation of Brazil's Landless Social Movement." PhD diss., Columbia University, 2002.
———. "The Landless Rural Workers Movement and Democracy in Brazil." *Latin American Research Review* 45, no. 4 (2010): 186–217.
———. "Origins and Consolidation of the MST in Rio Grande do Sul." In *Challenging Social Inequality: The Landless Rural Workers Movement and Agrarian Reform in Brazil,* edited by Miguel Carter, 149–82. Durham, N.C.: Duke University Press, 2015.
———. "The Origins of Brazil's Landless Rural Workers' Movement (MST): The Natalino Episode in Rio Grande Do Sul (1981–84): A Case of Ideal Interest Mobilization." PhD diss., University of Oxford Centre for Brazilian Studies, 2003.
Carter, Miguel, and Horacio Matins de Carvalho. "A luta na terra: Fonte de crescimento, inovação, e desafio constante ao MST." In *Combatendo a desigualdade social: O MST e a reforma agraria no Brasil,* edited by Miguel Carter and Cristina Yamagani, 287–331. Sao Paulo: UNESP, 2009.
Carvalho, Horacio Martins. *Another Production Is Possible: Beyond the Capitalist Canon.* London: Verso Books, 2006.
Castañeda, Jorge. "Latin America's Left Turn." *Foreign Affairs New York* 85 (2006): 28–43.
Castells, Manuel. *Networks of Outrage and Hope: Social Movements in the Internet Age.* Cambridge, U.K.: Polity, 2012.
Caume, David José. *O MST e os assentamentos de reforma agrária: A construção de espaços sociais modelares.* Goiânia, Brasil: UPF Editora, 2006.

Chaddad, Fabio R., and Marcos S. Jank. "The Evolution of Agricultural Policies and Agribusiness Development in Brazil." *Choices* 21, no. 2 (2006): 85–90.

Chamon, Marcos, Márcia Garcia, and Laura Souza. "FX Interventions in Brazil: A Synthetic Control Approach." *Journal of International Economics* 108 (September 2017): 157–68.

Chandler, Alfred N. *Land Title Origins: A Tale of Force and Fraud.* Philadelphia: Beard Books, 2000.

Chilcote, Ronald H. *The Brazilian Communist Party: Conflict and Integration 1922–1972.* New York: Oxford University Press, 1974.

Chomsky, Aviva. *A History of the Cuban Revolution.* Hoboken, N.J.: John Wiley & Sons, 2015.

Ciccariello-Maher, George. "Constituent Moments, Constitutional Processes: Social Movements and the New Latin American Left." *Latin American Perspectives* 40 (2013): 126–45.

Cleaver, Kathleen, and George Katsiaficas. *Liberation, Imagination and the Black Panther Party: A New Look at the Black Panthers and Their Legacy.* London: Routledge, 2014.

Collier, Ruth Berins, and Samuel Handlin. "Logics of Collective Action, State Linkages, and Aggregate Traits: The UP-Hub Versus the A-Net." In *Reorganizing Popular Politics: Participation and the New Interest Regime in Latin America,* by Collier and Handlin, 61–94. Pittsburgh: Pennsylvania State University Press, 2009.

Correa, Vanessa, and Fernanda Silva. "Perfil das liberações dos recursos do PRONAF entre 1999–2006: Ocorreu alguma modificação a partir da incorporação dos grupos A e B." *Congresso Brasileiro de Economia, Administração e Sociologia Rural* 47 (2009): 56–86.

Cristofoli, Pedro Ivan. "O desenvolvimento de cooperativas coletivas de trabalhadores rurais no capitalismo: Limites e posibilidades." Master's thesis, Curitiba, Federal University of Paraná, 2000.

Cronon, William. *Nature's Metropolis: Chicago and the Great West.* New York: W. W. Norton, 2009.

Dagnino, Evelina. "Citizenship: A Perverse Confluence." *Development in Practice* 17, no. 4–5 (2007): 549–56.

Danielson. Ross. *Cuban Medicine* New Brunswick, N.J.: Transaction Books, 1979.

Da Silva, José, Francisco Graziano. *A modernização dolorosa: Estrutura agrária, fronteira agrícola e trabalhadores rurais no Brasil.* Rio de Janeiro: Zahar Editores, 1982.

Da Silva, Luiz Inácio Lula. Interview by Felix Guattari. In *The Party Without Bosses: Lessons on Anti-capitalism from Faelix Guattari and Luis Inaacio 'Lula' da Silva,* by Gary Genosko. Winnipeg: Arbeiter Ring, 2003.

De Angelis, Massimo. "Separating the Doing and the Deed: Capital and the Continuous Character of Enclosures." *Historical Materialism* 12, no. 2 (2004): 57–87.

Delgado, Guilherme Costa. "The Agrarian Question and Agribusiness in Brazil." In *Challenging Social Inequality: The Landless Rural Workers Movement and Agrarian Reform in Brazil,* edited by Miguel Carter, 43–68. Durham, N.C.: Duke University Press, 2015.

De Melo, Cristiane Dias. "A ocupação da Fazenda Burro Branco: História, memória e posições–1980." *Revista Cadernos do Ceom* 21, no. 29 (2008): 207–30.

De Oliveira, Ariovaldo Umbelino. "A Reforma Agraria de Lula." *Estadao*, March 6, 2011.

De Souza, José Gilberto, and José Jorge Gebara. *PROCERA: Os resultados de assentamentos rurais frente à inepta política de crédito para a reforma agrária no Brasil.* São Paulo: FUNEP, 2010.

Diani, Mario. "Organizational Fields and Social Movement Dynamics." *The Future of Social Movement Research: Dynamics, Mechanisms, and Processes*, edited by Jacquelien van Stekelenburg, Conny Roggeband, and Bert Klandermans, 145–68. Minneapolis: University of Minnesota Press, 2013.

Diniz, Aldiva Sales, and Bruce Gilbert. "Socialist Values and Cooperation in Brazil's Landless Rural Workers' Movement." *Latin American Perspectives* 40, no. 4 (2013): 19–34.

De Souza, Maria Antônia. *Educação do campo: Propostas e práticas pedagógicas do MST.* Petrópolis: Editora Vozes, 2006.

Domínguez-Alonso, Emma, and Eduardo Zacea. "The Health System in Cuba." *Salud Publica de Mexico* 53 (2011): 168–76.

Dos Santos, José Vicente Tavares. *Matuchos: Exclusão e luta: Do sul para a Amazônia.* Petrópolis: Editora Vozes, 1993.

Du Bois, W. E. B. *Black Reconstruction in America: Toward a History of the Part Which Black Folk Played in the Attempt to Reconstruct Democracy in America, 1860–1880.* New York: Free Press, 2013.

Dunbar-Ortiz, Roxanne. "Land Reform and Indian Survival in the United States." In *Land Reform, American Style*, edited by Charles C. Geisler and Frank J. Popper, 151–71. Totowa, N.J.: Rowman & Allanheld, 1984.

Dussel, Enrique. *Twenty Theses on Politics.* Durham, N.C.: Duke University Press, 2008.

Eckstein, Susan Eva. "The Impact of the Cuban Revolution: A Comparative Perspective." *Comparative Studies in Society and History* 28, no. 3 (1986): 502–34.

———. *Power and Popular Protest: Latin American Social Movements.* Berkeley: University of California Press, 2001.

Ellner, Steve, ed. *Latin America's Radical Left: Challenges and Complexities of Political Power in the Twenty-First Century.* Lanham, Md.: Rowman & Littlefield, 2014.

———. "Latin America's Radical Left in Power: Complexities and Challenges in the Twenty-First Century." *Latin American Perspectives* 40 (2013): 5–25.

Estes, Nick. "Wounded Knee: Settler Colonial Property Regimes and Indigenous Liberation." *Capitalism Nature Socialism* 24, no. 3 (2013): 190–202.

Evans, Peter B. *Embedded Autonomy: States and Industrial Transformation.* Princeton, N.J.: Princeton University Press, 1995.

Fabricant, Nicole. *Mobilizing Bolivia's Displaced: Indigenous Politics and the Struggle Over Land.* Chapel Hill: University of North Carolina Press, 2012.

Fanelli, Lua, and Sarah Sarzynski. "The Concept of Sem Terra and the Peasantry in Brazil." *Journal of Developing Societies* 19, no. 2–3. (2003): 334–64.

Fernandes, Bernardo Mançano. *A formação do MST no Brasil*. Petrópolis: Editora Vozes, 2000.

——. "Questão agrária: Conflitualidade e desenvolvimento territorial." 2004. bibspi.planejamento.gov.br/bitstream/handle/iditem/564/Quest%E30%20agr%E1ria_conflitualidade%20e%20desenvolvimento%20territorial.pdf?sequence=1.

Fierce, Milfred C. "Black Struggle for Land During Reconstruction." *Black Scholar* 5, no. 5 (1974): 13–18.

Flores-Macias, Gustavo *After Neoliberalism? The Left and Economic Reforms in Latin America*. Oxford: Oxford University Press, 2012.

Foner, Eric. *Reconstruction: America's Unfinished Revolution, 1863–1877*. 1988. Reprint, New York: Harper Collins, 2011.

Freire, Paulo. *Pedagogy of the Oppressed*. New York: Continuum, 1996.

Froufe. Celia. "Ibope/CNA 92% condenam ocupações do MST." politica.estadao.com.br/noticias/geral,ibopecna-92-condenam-ocupacoes-do-mst,485449.

Fuentes, Federico. "'Bad Left Government' versus 'Good Left Social Movements'?" In *Latin America's Radical Left: Challenges and Complexities of Political Power in the Twenty-first Century*, 103–27. Lanham, Md.: Rowman & Littlefield, 2014.

Fumes, Rodrigo César Paes, and Leandro Rodrigues de Oliveira. "O MST na era Collor." Paper presented at the XIX Encontro Nacional de Geografia Agrária, São Paulo, 2009.

Gabaglia, F. R. "Evolução histórica e cultural dos povos Americanos." *Revista Geográfica* 5, no. 13 (1949): 77–86.

Gaither, Gerald H. *Blacks and the Populist Movement: Ballots and Bigotry in the New South*. Tuscaloosa: University of Alabama Press, 2005.

Gamson, William. *The Strategy of Social Protest*. Homewood, Ill.: Dorsey Press, 1975.

Ganz, Marshall. *Why David Sometimes Wins: Leadership, Organization, and Strategy in the California Farm Worker Movement*. Oxford: Oxford University Press, 2009.

García Linera, Álvaro. *Las tensiones creativas de la revolución*. La Paz: Vicepresidencia del Estado Plurinacional Presidencia de la Asamblea Legislativa Plurinacional, 2011.

Geisler, Charles. "A History of Land Reform in the United States: Old Wine, New Battles." In *Land Reform, American Style*, edited by Charles C. Geisler and Frank J. Popper, 7–34. Totowa, N.J.: Rowman & Allanheld, 1984.

Geortzel, Ted George. *Fernando Henrique Cardoso: Reinventing Democracy in Brazil*. Boulder, Colo.: Lynne Rienner, 1999.

Giddens, Anthony. *The Constitution of Society: Outline of the Theory of Structuration*. Berkeley: University of California Press, 1984.

Giron, Loraine Slomp, and Heloisa Eberle Bergamaschi. *Terra e homens: Colônias e colonos no Brasil*. Caixas do Sul, RS: EDUCS, 2004.

Goodwin, Jeff, and Theda Skocpol. "Explaining Revolutions in the Contemporary Third World." *Politics and Society* 17, no. 4 (1989): 489–509.

Gramsci, Antonio. *Further Selections from the Prison Notebooks*. Minneapolis: University of Minnesota Press, 1995.

Green, Michael D. *The Politics of Indian Removal: Creek Government and Society in Crisis.* Lincoln: University of Nebraska Press, 1985.

Greeno, Joel. Interview by Daniel Tucker and Anne Hamersky. In *Farm Together Now*, edited by Amy Franceschini, Daniel Tucker, and Anne Hamersky, 26–37. San Francisco: Chronicle Books, 2010.

Grisaffi, Thomas. "We Are Originarios . . . 'We Just Aren't from Here': Coca Leaf and Identity Politics in the Chapare, Bolivia." *Bulletin of Latin American Research* 29, no. 4 (2010): 425–39.

Grzybowski, Cândido, et al. *Relatório PRONAF: Resultados da Etapa Paraná.* Brasília: IBASE, 2006.

Guhur, Dominique Michèle Perioto. "Contribuições do diálogo de saberes à educação profissional em agroecologia no MST: Desafios da educação do campo na construção do Projeto Popular." Master's thesis, Universidade Estadual de Maringá, Brazil, 2010.

Hammond, John L. "Law and Disorder: The Brazilian Landless Farmworkers' Movement." *Bulletin of Latin American Research* 18, no. 4 (1999): 469–89.

Harvey, David. *The New Imperialism.* Oxford: Oxford University Press, 2003.

Hellman, Janice. "The Study of New Social Movements in Latin America and the Question of Autonomy." In *The Making of Social Movements in Latin America: Identity, Strategy, and Democracy*, edited by Arturo Escobar and Sonia E. Alvarez, 52–61. Boulder, Colo.: Westview Press, 1992.

Hirst, Paul. "Carl Schmitt's Decisionism." In *The Challenge of Carl Schmitt*, edited by Chantal Mouffe, 7–18. London: Verso, 2010.

Hochstetler, Kathryn, and Margaret E. Keck. *Greening Brazil: Environmental Activism in State and Society.* Durham, N.C.: Duke University Press, 2007.

Hoefle, Scott William. "Beyond Cold War Pipedreams: What the West Was Not." *Journal of Peasant Studies* 30, no. 2 (2003): 95–123.

Holloway, John. *Change the World Without Taking Power.* London: Pluto Press, 2002.

Holston, James. "The Misrule of Law: Land and Usurpation in Brazil." *Comparative Studies in Society and History* 33, no. 4 (1991): 695–725.

Holt-Giménez, Eric, and Miguel A. Altieri. "Agroecology, Food Sovereignty, and the New Green Revolution." *Agroecology and Sustainable Food Systems* 37, no. 1 (2013): 90–102.

Houtzager, Peter. "State and Unions in the Transformation of the Brazilian Countryside, 1964–1979." *Latin American Research Review* 33, no. 2 (1998): 103–42.

Hunter, Wendy. "The Normalization of an Anomaly: The Workers' Party in Brazil." *World Politics* 59, no. 3 (2007): 440–75.

———. *The Transformation of the Workers' Party in Brazil, 1989–2009.* New York: Cambridge University Press, 2010.

Huntington, Samuel P. *The Third Wave: Democratization in the Late Twentieth Century.* Vol. 4. Norman: University of Oklahoma Press, 1993.

Ianni, Octávio. *Origens agrárias do Estado brasileiro.* São Paulo: Brasiliense, 1984.

Jackson, Janet Thompson. "What Is Property? Property Is Theft: The Lack of Social Justice in US Eminent Domain Law." *St. John's Law Review* 84, no. 1 (2010): 63–116.

Jameson, Fredric. "An American Utopia." In *An American Utopia: Dual Power and the Universal Army*, edited by Slavoj Žižek, 1–104. London: Verso Books, 2016.

Jasper, James M. "Social Movement Theory Today: Toward a Theory of Action?" *Sociology Compass* 4, no. 11 (2010): 965–76.

Johnson, Chalmers. *MITI and the Japanese Miracle: The Growth of Industrial Policy: 1925–1975*. Stanford, Calif.: Stanford University Press, 1982.

Johnson, Troy. "The Occupation of Alcatraz Island: Roots of American Indian Activism." *Wicazo Sa Review* 10, no. 2 (1994): 63–79.

Johnston, Hank. *Social Movements and Culture*. London: Routledge, 2013.

Judson, Fred. *Cuba and the Revolutionary Myth: The Political Education of the Cuban Rebel Army, 1953–1963*. Boulder, Colo.: Westview Press, 1984.

Jungmann, Raul. "Agricultura Familiar, Reforma Agraria, e Desenvolvimento Local para um Novo Mundo Rural." Policy paper. Brasília, 1999.

Kay, Cristóbal. "Latin America's Agrarian Reform: Lights and Shadows." *Land Reform, Land Settlement and Cooperatives* 2 (1998): 9–31.

Keck, Margaret E. *The Workers' Party and Democratization in Brazil*. New Haven, Conn.: Yale University Press, 1995.

Kilgore, David. "Understanding Learning in Social Movements: A Theory of Collective Learning." *International Journal of Lifelong Education* 18, no. 3 (1999): 191–202.

Kingstone, Peter. "The Long (and Uncertain) March to Energy Privatization in Brazil." In *Critical Issues in Brazil's Energy Sector*, edited by James A. Baker III Institute for Public Policy, 1–61. Houston, Tex.: James A. Baker III Institute for Public Policy of Rice University, 2004.

Kozelinski, Benigno. "Inadimplência de financiamentos da agricultura familiar no Pronaf C: Um estudo no município de Marmeleiro, Paraná." Master's thesis, Universidade Federal do Rio Grande do Sul, 2009.

Kriesi, Hanspeter, Ruud Koopmans, Jan Willem Duyvendak, and Marco G. Giugni, eds. *New Social Movements in Western Europe: A Comparative Analysis*. Minneapolis: University of Minnesota Press, 1995.

Laclau, Ernesto. *On Populist Reason*. London: Verso, 2005.

———. "Os novos movimentos sociais e a pluralidade do social." *Revista Brasileira de Ciências Sociais* 1, no. 2 (1986): 41–47.

Laclau, Ernesto, and Chantal Mouffe. *Hegemony and Socialist Strategy: Towards a Radical Democratic Politics*. 2nd ed. London: Verso, 2001.

Lahiff, Edward, Saturnino M. Borras Jr, and Cristóbal Kay. "Market-Led Agrarian Reform: Policies, Performance, and Prospects." *Third World Quarterly* 28, no. 8 (2007): 1417–36.

Lefebvre, Stephan, and Jeanette Bonifaz. "Lessons from Bolivia: Re-nationalising the Hydrocarbon Industry." OpenDemocracyUK, November 24, 2014. opendemocracy.net/ourkingdom/stephan-lefebvre-jeanette-bonifaz/lessons-from-bolivia-renationalising-hydrocarbon-indust.

Leite, Sergio. *Impactos dos assentamentos: Um estudo sobre o meio rural brasileiro*. São Paulo: UNESP, 2004.

Lenin, Vladimir. *The Dual Power*. Pamphlet, 1918. marxists.org/archive/lenin/works/1917/apr/09.htm.
———. *"Left-Wing" Communism: An Infantile Disorder*. Pamphlet, 1920. marxists.org/archive/lenin/works/1920/lwc/index.htm.
Levine, Daniel H., and Scott Mainwaring. *Religion and Popular Protest in Latin America*. Notre Dame, Ind.: Kellogg Institute, 1986.
Levitsky, Steven, and Kenneth Roberts. *Latin America's Left Turn*. Baltimore: Johns Hopkins University Press, 2011.
Loman, Herman, et al. "Brazil's Social Challenges." *Economic Report*, January 9, 2014. economics.rabobank.com/publications/2014/january/brazils-social-challenges/.
Love, Joseph L. "Political Participation in Brazil, 1881–1969." *Luso-Brazilian Review* 7, no. 2 (1970): 3–24.
Lowy, Michael. "A New Type of Party: The Brazilian PT." *Latin American Perspectives* 14, no. 4 (1987): 453–64.
Lukács, Georg. *Marxism and Human Liberation: Essays on History, Culture and Revolution*. New York: Dell, 1973.
Luxemburg, Rosa. *Reform or Revolution and Other Writings*. Mineola, N.Y.: Dover, 2006.
Maddox, James G. "The Bankhead-Jones Farm Tenant Act." *Law and Contemporary Problems* 4, no. 4 (1937): 434–55.
Marcon, Telmo. *Acampamento Natalino: História da luta pela reforma agrária*. Passo Fundo, RS: Ed. da UPF, 1997.
Martha, Geraldo B., Jr., Eliseu Alves, and Elisio Contini. "Land Saving Approaches and Beef Production Growth in Brazil." *Agricultural Systems* 110 (2012): 173–77.
Martínez-Torres, Maria Elena, and Peter M. Rosset. "La Vía Campesina: The Birth and Evolution of a Transnational Social Movement." *Journal of Peasant Studies* 37, no. 1 (2010): 149–75.
Martins, José de Souza. *A militarização da questão agrária no Brasil: Terra e poder, o problema da terra na crise política*. Petrópolis: Vozes, 1985.
Maschio, Darci. Interview. In *Uma foice longe da terra: A repressão aos sem-terra nas ruas de Porto Alegre*, edited by Sérgio Antônio Görgen. Petrópolis: Vozes, 1991.
Maybury-Lewis, Biorn. *The Politics of the Possible: The Brazilian Rural Workers' Trade Union Movement, 1964–1985*. Philadelphia: Temple University Press, 1994.
McAdam, Doug. *Political Process and the Development of Black Insurgency, 1930–1970*. Chicago: University of Chicago Press, 2010.
———. "Tactical Innovation and the Pace of Insurgency." *American Sociological Review* 48, no. 6 (1983): 735–54.
McAdam, Doug, and Hilary Boudet. *Putting Social Movements in Their Place: Explaining Opposition to Energy Projects in the United States, 2000–2005*. Cambridge: Cambridge University Press, 2012.
McCarthy, John D., and Mayer N. Zald. "Resource Mobilization and Social Movements: A Partial Theory." *American Journal of Sociology* 82, no. 6 (1977): 1212–41.
McFarland, John R. "The Administration of the New Deal Greenbelt Towns." *Journal of the American Institute of Planners* 32, no. 4 (1966): 217–25.

Medeiros, Leonilde Sérvolo de. *História dos movimentos sociais no campo*. Rio de Janiero: FASE, 1988.
Medeiros, Leonilde, Franco Pantoja Mariana Barbosa, Maria Valeria, Neide Esterci, and Sergio Leite. *Assentamentos rurais: Uma visão multidisciplinar*. São Paulo: UNESP, 1994.
Meek, David. "Learning as Territoriality: The Political Ecology of Education in the Brazilian Landless Workers' Movement." *Journal of Peasant Studies* 42, no. 6 (2015): 1179–1200.
Mészáros, George. "The MST and the Rule of Law in Brazil." In *Challenging Social Inequality: The Landless Rural Workers Movement and Agrarian Reform in Brazil*, edited by Miguel Carter, 351–71. Durham, N.C.: Duke University Press, 2015.
Metzer, Allan. "Inflation and Money in Brazil." In *Proceedings of a Conference on Currency Substitution and Currency Boards*, edited by Nissan Liviatan. Washington, D.C.: World Bank, 1993. repository.cmu.edu/cgi/viewcontent.cgi?article=1897&context=tepper.
Meurer, Ane Carine. "O projeto político-pedagógico da Escola Itinerante: Contribuições que me ajudaram a repensar o projeto político-pedagógico da Universidade." In *Espaços-tempos de itinerância: Interlocução entre universidade e escola itinerante do MST*, edited by Cesar de David and Ane Carine Meurer. Santa Maria, RS: Editora UFSM, 2006.
Migdal, Joel. *Peasants, Politics, and Revolution: Pressures Toward Political and Social Change in the Third World*. Princeton, N.J.: Princeton University Press, 1975.
Miranda, Newton Rodrigues. "Breve histórico da questão das terras devolutas no Brasil e dos instrumentos legais de posse sobre esses bens." *Revista do Centro Acadêmico Afonso Pena* 17, no. 2 (2011): 153–76.
Moore, Barrington. *Social Origins of Dictatorship and Democracy: Lord and Peasant in the Making of the Modern World*. Boston: Beacon Press, 1968.
Morais, Clodimir. "História das Ligas Camponesas do Brasil." In *História e natureza das Ligas Camponesas, 1954–1964*, edited by João Pedro Stédile and Douglas Estevam, 33–66. São Paulo: Editora Espressão Popular, 2006.
Mota, Maria Sarita. "Sesmarias e propriedade titulada da terra: O individualismo agrário na América Portuguesa." *Sæculum–Revista de História* 26 (2012): 29–46.
Motta, Márcia Maria Menendes. "Sesmarias e o mito da primeira ocupação." *Revista Justiça and História* 4, no. 1 (2004): 61–83.
Mouffe, Chantal. "Carl Schmitt and the Paradox of Liberal Democracy." In *The Challenge of Carl Schmitt*, edited by Chantal Mouffe, 38–54. London: Verso, 1999.
———, ed. *The Challenge of Carl Schmitt*. London: Verso, 1999.
———. *The Return of the Political*. London: Verso, 2005.
Mujal-León, Eusebio. "Tensions in the Regime." *Journal of Democracy* 20, no. 1 (2009): 20–35.
Müller, Jan-Werner. *A Dangerous Mind: Carl Schmitt in Post-war European Thought*. New Haven, Conn.: Yale University Press, 2003.
Musacchio, Aldo, and Sergio G. Lazzarini. *Reinventing State Capitalism*. Cambridge: Harvard University Press, 2014.

Nakagawara, Yoshiya. "Café, do colonato ao bóia-fria." *Semina: Ciências Sociais e Humanas* 15, no. 3 (2004): 270–79.

Navarro, Zander. "The Brazilian Landless Movement (MST): Critical Times." *Redes* 15, no. 1 (2010): 196–223.

Negri, Antonio. *Insurgencies: Constituent Power and the Modern State.* Minneapolis: University of Minnesota Press, 1999.

Neves, Delma Pessanha, and Maria Aparecida de Moraes Silva, eds. *Processos de constituição e reprodução do campesinato no Brasil: Formas dirigidas de constituição do campesinato.* São Paulo: Editora UNESP, 2008.

Nimtz, August. *Lenin's Electoral Strategy from Marx and Engels Through the Revolution of 1905: The Ballot, the Streets—or Both.* New York: Palgrave Macmillan, 2016.

———. *Marx and Engels: Their Contribution to the Democratic Breakthrough.* Albany: State University of New York Press, 2000.

Noronha, Eduardo Garuti. "Ciclo de greves, transição política e estabilização no Brasil, 1978–2007." *Lua Nova*, no. 76 (2009): 119–68.

Oganes, Luis. "Finance: The Importance of Foreign Exchange Reserves." *Americas Quarterly*, Winter 2012. americasquarterly.org/node/3286.

Ohde, Mariana. "Operação Castra não tem como objetivo reprimir o MST, diz delegado." ParanáPortal, November 5, 2016.

Oliveira, Augusto de Andrade. "Critérios de avaliação de qualidade e a consolidação de assentamentos de reforma agrária no Brasil: A experiência do Programa de Consolidação e Emancipação (auto-suficiência) de assentamentos resultantes de reforma agrária–PAC." PhD diss., Universidade Federal de Rio de Janeiro, 2010.

Olsson, Tore C. "Sharecroppers and Campesinos: The American South, Mexico, and the Transnational Politics of Land Reform in the Radical 1930s." *Journal of Southern History* 81, no. 3 (2015): 607–46.

Ondetti, Gabriel. *Land, Protest, and Politics: The Landless Movement and the Struggle for Agrarian Reform in Brazil.* University Park: Penn State Press, 2008.

———. "Repression, Opportunity, and Protest: Explaining the Takeoff of Brazil's Landless Movement." *Latin American Politics and Society* 48, no. 2 (2006): 61–94.

Ondetti, Gabriel, Emmanuel Wambergue, and José Batista Gonçalves Fonso. "From Posseiro to Sem Terra: The Impact of MST Land Struggles in the State of Pará." In *Challenging Social Inequality: The Landless Rural Worker's Movement and Agrarian Reform in Brazil*, edited by Miguel Carter, 202–27. Durham, N.C.: Duke University Press, 2015.

Opie, John. *The Law of the Land: Two Hundred Years of American Farmland Policy.* Lincoln: University of Nebraska Press, 1987.

Otis, Delos Sacket. *The Dawes Act and the Allotment of Indian Lands*, edited by Francis Paul Prucha. Norman: University of Oklahoma Press, 2014.

Page, Joseph A. *The Revolution That Never Was: Northeast Brazil, 1955–1964.* New York: Grossman, 1972.

Pahnke, Anthony, Rebecca Tarlau, and Wendy Wolford. "Understanding Rural Resistance: Contemporary Mobilization in the Brazilian Countryside." *Journal of Peasant Studies* 42, no. 6 (2015): 1069–85.

Patel, Raj. "Food Sovereignty." *Journal of Peasant Studies* 36, no. 3 (2009): 663–706.
Peck, Jamie, and Adam Tickell. "Neoliberalizing Space." *Antipode* 34, no. 3 (2002): 380–404.
Pereira, Anthony. *End of the Peasantry: The Rural Labor Movement in Northeast Brazil, 1961–1988*. Pittsburgh: University of Pittsburgh Press, 1997.
Pérez-Stable, Marifeli. *The Cuban Revolution: Origins, Course, and Legacy*. Oxford: Oxford University Press, 1999.
Pessoa, Luisa. "Propriedades de mais de mil hectares ocupam 45% da área rural do Brasil." *Folha de S. Paulo*, June 1, 2015. www1.folha.uol.com.br/poder/2015/01/1571133-propriedades-de-mais-de-mil-hectares-ocupam-45-da-area-rural-do-brasil.shtml.
Petras, James, and Henry Veltmeyer. "Are Latin American Peasant Movements Still a Force for Change? Some New Paradigms Revisited." *Journal of Peasant Studies* 28, no. 2 (2001): 83–118.
———. *Social Movements and State Power: Argentina, Brazil, Bolivia, Ecuador*. London: Pluto Press, 2005.
Piven, Frances, and Richard Cloward. *Poor People's Movements: Why They Succeed, How They Fail*. New York: Vintage, 1979.
Plummer, Dawn. "Leadership Development and Formação in Brazil's Landless Workers Movement (MST)." PhD diss., City University of New York, 2008.
Poletto, Ivo. "Churches, the Pastoral Land Commission, and the Mobilization for Agrarian Reform." In *Challenging Social Inequality: The Landless Rural Worker's Movement and Agrarian Reform in Brazil*, edited by Miguel Carter, 90–115. Durham, N.C.: Duke University Press, 2015.
———. "A terra e a vida em tempos neoliberais: Uma releitura da história da CPT." In *A Luta pela Terra: A Comissão Pastoral da Terra 20 Anos Depois*, 21–69, 1997.
Polletta, Francesca, and James M. Jasper. "Collective Identity and Social Movements." *Annual Review of Sociology* 27, no. 1 (2001): 283–305.
Portela, Fernando. *Guerra de guerrilhas no Brasil: A saga do Araguaia*. São Paulo: Terceiro Nome, 2002.
Price, Richard. *Maroon Societies: Rebel Slave Communities in the Americas*. Baltimore: Johns Hopkins University Press, 1996.
Rabinowitch, Alexander. "The Evolution of Local Soviets in Petrograd, November 1917–June 1918: The Case of the First City District Soviet." *Slavic Review* 46 (1987): 20–37.
Ramirez, Júlio Lizarraga. "Lembrando Casos do INCRA." In *Memoria INCRA, 35 Anos*, 62–79. Núcleo de Estudos Agrários e Desenvolvimento Rural (NEAD). Brasília: MDA-INCRA, 2006.
Ramirez, Pablo Mamani. "Territorio y estructuras de acción colectiva: Microgobiernos barriales." *Ephemera* 6, no. 3 (2006): 276–86.
Reger, Jo, Daniel Myers, and Racehl Einwohner, eds. *Identity Work in Social Movements*. Minneapolis: University of Minnesota Press, 2008.
Reis, Maria José. "O Movimento dos Atingidos por Barragens: Atores, estratégias de luta e conquistas." In *Lutas camponesas contemporâneas: Condições, dilemas e conquistas*, edited by Cliff Welch, 265–87. São Paulo: UNESP, 2009.

Rezende, Gervásio Castro de. "Políticas trabalhista e fundiária e seus efeitos adversos sobre o emprego agrícola, a estrutura agrária e o desenvolvimento territorial rural no Brasil." No. 1108, Discussion Papers from Instituto de Pesquisa Econômica Aplicada (IPEA), 2005.

Robles, Wilder, and Henry Veltmeyer. "The Politics of Agrarian Reform in Brazil: A Historical Background." In *The Politics of Agrarian Reform in Brazil: The Landless Rural Workers Movement*, 65–84. New York: Palgrave Macmillan, 2015.

Rogers, Thomas D. "Agricultural Transformations in Sugarcane and Labor in Brazil." In *Oxford Research Encyclopedia of Latin American History*, 1–15. Oxford: Oxford University Press, 2015.

———. *The Deepest Wounds: A Labor and Environmental History of Sugar in Northeast Brazil*. Chapel Hill: University of North Carolina Press, 2010.

Ronit, Karsten, and Volker Schneider. "Global Governance Through Private Organizations." *Governance* 12, no. 3 (1999): 243–66.

Rosenau, James N. "Governance in the Twenty-First Century." *Global Governance* 1, no. 1 (1995): 13–43.

Rosset, Peter. "Food Sovereignty and Alternative Paradigms to Confront Land Grabbing and the Food and Climate Crises." *Development* 54, no. 1 (2011): 21–30.

———. "Food Sovereignty and the Contemporary Food Crisis." *Development* 51, no. 4 (2008): 460–63.

———. "Moving Forward: Agrarian Reform as a Part of Food Sovereignty." In *Promised Land: Competing Visions of Agrarian Reform*, 301–21. New York: Food First Books, 2006.

Rosset, Peter Michael, and María Elena Martínez Torres. "Rural Social Movements and Diálogo de Saberes: Territories, Food Sovereignty, and Agroecology." Food Sovereignty: A Critical Dialogue conference, Yale University, 2013.

Sader, Emir. *The New Mole: Paths of the Latin American Left*. London: Verso, 2001.

Samuels, David "From Socialism to Social Democracy Party Organization and the Transformation of the Workers' Party in Brazil." *Comparative Political Studies* 37, no. 9 (2004): 999–1024.

Sándor, John. *Bolivia's Radical Tradition: Permanent Revolution in the Andes*. Tucson: University of Arizona Press, 2009.

Sandoval, Salvador. "Alternative Forms of Working-Class Organization and the Mobilization of Informal-Sector Workers in Brazil in the Era of Neoliberalism." *International Labor and Working-Class History* 72, no. 1 (2007): 63–89.

Santamarta Luengos, Juan Ignacio. "La campaña de alfabetización en Cuba (1ª parte)." *Revista Pedagógica*, no. 5 (1989): 201–16.

Sayer, Andrew. *Method in Social Science: A Realist Approach*. Hove, U.K.: Psychology Press, 1992.

Scalabrin, Leandro Gaspar. "Estado de exceção no Rio Grande do Sul e a criminalização do MST." *Filosofazer* 33, no. 2 (2016): 161–82.

Scherer-Warren, Ilse. "O caráter dos novos movimentos sociais." In *Uma revolução no cotidiano? Os novos movimentos sociais na América Latina*, edited by Ilse Scherer-Warren and Paulo José Krischke, 35–54. São Paulo: Editora Brasiliense, 1987.

———. "Redes para a (re) territorialização: Os casos de MST e MTST no Brasil." *Interface* 1, no. 1: 105–24.
Scherer-Warren, Ilse, and Paulo José Krischke, eds. *Uma revolução no cotidiano? Os novos movimentos sociais na América Latina*. São Paulo: Editora Brasiliense, 1987.
Scheuerman, William E. *Carl Schmitt: The End of Law*. Lanham, Md.: Rowman & Littlefield, 1999.
Schmitt, Carl. *The Concept of the Political*. Chicago: University of Chicago Press, 1995.
———. *Political Theology: Four Chapters on the Concept of Sovereignty*. Chicago: University of Chicago Press, 1985.
———. *Theory of the Partisan: Intermediate Commentary on the Concept of the Political*. Candor, N.Y.: Telos Press, 2004.
Schmitter, Phillip. "Participation in Governance Arrangements: Is There Any Reason to Expect It Will Achieve Sustainable and Innovative Policies in a Multi-level Context?" In *Participatory Governance: Political and Societal Implications*, edited by Jürgen R. Grote and Bernard Gbikpi, 51–69. Wiesbaden: Springer Fachmedien, 2002.
Schultz, James "A New Day for Bolivia." *NACLA Report on the Americas* 37, no. 3 (2003): 8–10.
Scolese, Eduardo. *Pioneiros do MST: Caminhos e descaminhos de homes e mulheres que criaram o movimento*. Rio de Janeiro: Editora Record, 2008.
Scott, James C. *The Moral Economy of the Peasant: Rebellion and Subsistence in Southeast Asia*. New Haven, Conn.: Yale University Press, 1977.
———. *Seeing Like a State: How Certain Schemes to Improve the Human Condition Have Failed*. New Haven, Conn.: Yale University Press, 1999.
Selbin, Eric. *Modern Latin American Revolutions*. New York City: Guilford Press, 1998.
Serra, Carlos Alberto Teixeira. "Considerações acerca da evolução da propriedade da terra rural no Brasil." *Revista de Comunicação, Cultura e Política* 4, no. 7 (2003): 231–38.
Serra, Elpidio. "Conflitos rurais no Paraná: Como foi que tudo começou." *Boletim de Geografia* 28, no. 1 (2010): 75–89.
Skidmore, Thomas. *The Politics of Military Rule in Brazil, 1964–1985*. Oxford: Oxford University Press, 1988.
Skocpol, Theda. *States and Social Revolutions: A Comparative Analysis of France, Russia, and China*. Cambridge: Cambridge University Press, 1979.
Silva, José Gomes da. *Buraco negro: A reforma agrária na constituinte de 1987–88*. Rio de Janeiro: Paz e Terra, 1989.
Slater, David. *New Social Movements and the State in Latin America*. Amsterdam: CEDLA, 1985.
Sluyter-Beltrão, Jeffrey. *Rise and Decline of Brazil's New Unionism: The Politics of the Central Única dos Trabalhadores*. Bern: Peter Lang AG, 2010.
Smith, Nigel. *Rainforest Corridors: The Transamazon Colonization Scheme*. Berkeley: University of California Press, 1982.
Snow, David A. "Framing Processes, Ideology, and Discursive Fields." In *The Blackwell Companion to Social Movements*, edited by David A. Snow, 380–412. Malden, Mass.: Blackwell, 2004.

Snow, David A., E. Burke Rochford Jr., Steven K. Worden, and Robert D. Benford. "Frame Alignment Processes, Micromobilization, and Movement Participation." *American Sociological Review* 51, no. 4 (1986): 464–81.
Stédile, João Pedro. "Balanço de uma reforma agrária que não existiu." *MST Informa*, ano 1, n. 7 (January 2002).
———. Interview by Vandeck Santiago. In *Historia e natureza das Ligas Camponesas, 1954–1964*, edited by João Pedro Stedile, 183–85. São Paulo: Editora Expressão Popular, 2006.
Stedile, João Pedro, and Bernardo Mançano Fernandes. *Brava gente: A trajetória do MST e a luta pela terra no Brasil*. São Paulo: Editora Fundação Perseu Abramo, 1999.
Stiglitz, Joseph E. "Is There a Post-Washington Consensus?" In *The Washington Consensus Reconsidered: Towards a New Global Governance*, edited by Narcis Serra and Joseph E. Stiglitz, 41–56. Oxford: Oxford University Press, 2008.
St. Peter, Bob, and Raj Patel. "This Land Is Our Land?" Raj Patel website, November 21, 2013. rajpatel.org/2013/11/21/this-land-is-our-land/.
Strange, Carolyn, and Tina Loo. "Holding the Rock: The 'Indianization' of Alcatraz Island, 1969–1999." *Public Historian* 23, no. 1 (2001): 55–74.
Tarlau, Rebecca. "Coproducing Rural Public Schools in Brazil Contestation, Clientelism, and the Landless Workers' Movement." *Politics and Society* 41, no. 3 (2013): 395–424.
———. "Education of the Countryside at a Crossroads: Rural Social Movements and National Policy Reform in Brazil." *Journal of Peasant Studies* 42, no. 6 (2015): 1157–77.
———. "Occupying Land, Occupying Schools: Transforming Education in the Brazilian Countryside." PhD diss., University of California–Berkeley, 2014.
Tarrow, Sidney. *Power in Movement: Social Movements and Contentious Politics*. Cambridge: Cambridge University Press, 2011.
Taylor, Verta, and Nella Van Dyke. "'Get Up, Stand Up': Tactical Repertoires of Social Movements." *The Blackwell Companion to Social Movements*, edited by David A. Snow, Sarah A. Soule, and Hanspeter Kriesi, 262–93. Malden, Mass.: Blackwell, 2004.
Tedesco, João Carlos, and Joel João Carini. *Conflitos agrários no norte gaúcho, 1960–1980: O Master, indígenas e camponeses*. Porto Alegre: EST Edições, 2007.
Thayer, Maggie. "Translations and Refusals: Resignifying Meanings as Feminist Political Practice." *Feminist Studies* 36, no. 1 (2010): 200–30.
Tilly, Charles. *Big Structures, Large Processes, Huge Comparisons*. New York: Russell Sage Foundation, 1984.
———. *Contention and Democracy in Europe, 1650–2000*. Cambridge: Cambridge University Press, 2004.
———. *From Mobilization to Revolution*. Reading, Mass.: Addison-Wesley, 1977.
Todorov, Joao Claudio, and Benicio Viero Schmidt. *Primeiro Censo da reforma agraria do Brasil*. Brasilia: Universidade de Brasilia/INCRA, 1997.
Tumolo, Paulo Sergio. *Da contestação à conformação: A formação sindical da CUT e a reestruturação capitalista*. Campinas, SP: Editora da Unicamp, 2002.
Turatti, Maria Cecilia Manzoli. *Os filhos da lona preta: Identidade e cotidiano em acampamentos do MST*. São Paulo: Alameda, 2005.

U.S. Department of Agriculture. "Black Farmers in America: 1865–2000: The Pursuit of Independent Farming and the Role of Cooperatives." RBS Research Report 194. Washington, D.C.: USDA, 2003.

Van Deburg, William L. *Modern Black Nationalism: From Marcus Garvey to Louis Farrakhan.* New York: New York University Press, 1997.

Van der Ploeg, Jan. *The New Peasantries: Struggles for Autonomy and Sustainability in an Era of Empire and Globalization.* London: Routledge, 2009.

Veltmeyer, Henry, and James Petras. "The Social Dynamics of Brazil's Rural Landless Workers' Movement: Ten Hypotheses on Successful Leadership." *Canadian Review of Sociology* 39, no. 1 (2002): 79–96.

Vergara-Camus, Leandro. *Land and Freedom: The MST, the Zapatistas, and Peasant Alternatives to Neoliberalism.* London: Zed Books, 2014.

———. "The MST and the EZLN Struggle for Land: New Forms of Peasant Rebellions." *Journal of Agrarian Change* 9, no. 3 (2009): 365–91.

Viana, Natalia. "Cablegate: How the US Sees the Landless Movement in Brazil." Last modified December 22, 2010. wikileaks.org/Brazil-Cablegate-how-the-US-sees.html.

Vogeler, Ingolf. *The Myth of the Family Farm: Agribusiness Dominance of U.S. Agriculture.* Boulder, Colo.: Westview Press, 1981.

Wagner, Carlos. *A saga do João Sem Terra.* Petrópolis: Vozes, 1989.

Wampler, Brian. *Participatory Budgeting in Brazil: Contestation, Cooperation, and Accountability.* University Park: Pennsylvania State University Press, 2007.

Webber, Jeffrey. *From Rebellion to Reform in Bolivia: Class Struggle, Indigenous Liberation, and the Politics of Evo Morales.* Chicago: Haymarket Books, 2011.

Weber, Heloise. "The Imposition of a Global Development Architecture: The Example of Microcredit." *Review of International Studies* 28, no. 3 (2002): 537–55.

Weber, Max. "The Profession and Vocation of Politics." In *Weber: Political Writings,* edited by Peter Lassman and Ronald Speirs, 309–69. Cambridge: Cambridge University Press, 1994.

Welch, Clifford. "Estratégias de resistência do movimento camponês brasileiro em frente das novas táticas de controle do agronegócio transnacional." *Revista NERA* 8, no. 6 (January/June 2005): 35–45.

———. *The Seed Was Planted: The São Paulo Roots of Brazil's Rural Labor.* University Park: Pennsylvania State University Press, 1999.

———. "Wikileaks, o globo, historia y EU." Last modified July 2011. snh2011.anpuh.org/resources/anais/14/1296843706_ARQUIVO_WELCHWikileaksImprensaMstMim2010_ANPUH2011.pdf.

Wetzel, Deborah. "Bolsa Família: Brazil's Quiet Revolution." World Bank, November 4, 2013. worldbank.org/en/news/opinion/2013/11/04/bolsa-familia-Brazil-quiet-revolution.

White, Louellyn. "Free to Be Kanien'kehaka: A Case Study of Educational Self-Determination at the Akwesasne Freedom School." PhD diss., University of Arizona, 2009.

Whittier, Nancy. "Collective Identity in Social Movement Communities: Lesbian Feminist Mobilization." In *Social Perspectives in Lesbian and Gay Studies*, edited by Peter M. Nardi and Beth E. Schneider, 349–65. New York: Routledge, 1998.

Wickham-Crowley, Timothy P. *Guerrillas and Revolution in Latin America: A Comparative Study of Insurgents and Regimes Since 1956.* Princeton, N.J.: Princeton University Press, 1992.

———. "Terror and Guerilla Warfare in Latin America, 1956–1970." *Comparative Studies in Society and History* 32, no. 2 (1990): 201–37.

Wilkins, David Eugene, and K. Tsianina Lomawaima. *Uneven Ground: American Indian Sovereignty and Federal Law.* Norman: University of Oklahoma Press, 2001.

Williamson, John. "What Washington Means by Policy Reform." In *Latin American Adjustment: How Much Has Happened?* Washington, D.C.: Institute for International Economics, 1990. piie.com/commentary/speeches-papers/what-washington-means-policy-reform.

Windfuhr, Michael, and Jennie Jonsén. *Food Sovereignty: Towards Democracy in Localized Food Systems.* UK: ITDG, 2005.

Wittman, Hannah. "Reworking the Metabolic Rift: La Vía Campesina, Agrarian Citizenship, and Food Sovereignty." *Journal of Peasant Studies* 36, no. 4 (2009): 805–26.

Wittman, Hannah, Annette Aurélie Desmarais, and Nettie Wiebe. "The Origins and Potential of Food Sovereignty." In *Food Sovereignty: Reconnecting Food, Nature, and Community*, edited by Wittman, Desmarais, and Wiebe, 1–14. Oakland, Calif.: Food First Books, 2010.

Wolf, Eric R. *Peasant Wars of the Twentieth Century.* Norman: University of Oklahoma Press, 1969.

Wolford, Wendy. "Agrarian Moral Economies and Neoliberalism in Brazil: Competing Worldviews and the State in the Struggle for Land." *Environment and Planning A* 37, no. 2 (2005): 241–61.

———. "Families, Fields, and Fighting for Land: The Spatial Dynamics of Contention in Rural Brazil." *Mobilization* 8, no. 2 (June 2003): 157–72.

———. "Participatory Democracy by Default: Land Reform, Social Movements and the State in Brazil." *Journal of Peasant Studies* 37, no. 1 (2010): 91–109.

———. "Producing Community: The MST and Land Reform Settlements in Brazil." *Journal of Agrarian Change* 3, no. 4 (2003): 500–520.

———. "State-Society Dynamics in Contemporary Brazilian Land Reform." *Latin American Perspectives* 43, no. 2 (2016): 77–95.

———. *This Land Is Ours Now: Social Mobilization and the Meanings of Land in Brazil.* Durham, N.C.: Duke University Press, 2010.

Woo-Cumings, Meredith. *The Developmental State.* Ithaca, N.Y.: Cornell University Press, 1999.

Wright, Angus, and Wendy Wolford. *To Inherit the Earth: The Landless Movement and the Struggle for a New Brazil.* Oakland: Food First Books, 2003.

Wright, Thomas C. *Latin America in the Era of the Cuban Revolution*. Westport, Conn.: Greenwood, 2001.
Yashar, Deborah. *Contesting Citizenship in Latin America: The Rise of Indigenous Movements and the Postliberal Challenge*. Cambridge, U.K.: Cambridge University Press, 2005.
Zibechi, Raul. *Territories in Resistence*. Oakland, Calif.: AK Press, 2012.
Žižek, Slavoj. *Revolution at the Gates: A Selection of Writings from February to October 1917*. London: Verso, 2002.

PRIMARY SOURCES

"A educação do MST." mst.org.br/2009/10/08/a-educacao-do-mst.html.
Act 1.116. Public Prosecutor's Office, Rio Grande do Sul, 2007.
ANVISA (Agência Nacional de Vigilância Sanitária). *Programa de Análise de Resíduos de Agrotóxicos em Alimentos (PARA)*. Available at portal.anvisa.gov.br/documents /111215/446359/Programa+de+An%C3%A1lise+de+Res%C3%ADduos+de+Agrot%C3 %B3xicos+-+Relat%C3%B3rio+2012+%282%C2%BA+etapa%29/3bc220f9-8475-44ad -9d96-cbbc988e28fa.
CNASI (Confederação Nacional das Associações dos Servidores do INCRA). *INCRA– Instrumento básico de realização da reforma agrária e do ordenamento da estrutura fundiária a ser mantido e fortalecido*. Unpublished document, 2011.
CPT, *Conflitos no Campo*, 1985–2014. Available at cptnacional.org.br/.
Field notes, encampment in INCRA office, Belém, PA, July 1, 2009.
Field notes, Encampment 1 outside of São Paulo, SP, August 10, 2009.
Field notes, Encampment 2 outside of São Paulo, SP, August 15, 2009.
Field notes, MST school near Caruaru, PE, September 1, 2009.
Field notes, MST school outside Caruaru, PE, September 5, 2009.
Field notes, encampment outside Arcoverde, PE, September 10, 2009.
Field notes, settlement in the Porto Alegre area, RS, March 3, 2011.
Field notes, Instituto Educar, outside of Pontão, RS, March 20, 2011.
Field notes, Instituto Educar, Pontão, RS, March 30, 2011.
Field notes, Instituto Educar, Pontão, RS, April 5, 2011.
Field notes, from COOPTAR, outside of Pontão, RS, April 5, 2011.
Field notes, outside of Pontão, RS, May 5, 2011.
Field notes, outside of Bagé, RS, May 13, 2011.
Field notes, ITERRA conference, May 25, 2011.
Field notes, encampment near Londrina, PR, June 20, 2011.
Field notes, encampment near Londrina, PR, June 28, 2011.
Field notes, from Jornada de Agroecologia Curitiba, PR, July 1, 2011.
Field notes, Encampment 2 outside Londrina, PR, July 3, 2011.
Field notes, MST school near Rio Bonita, PR, July 23, 2011.
Incra.gov.br/assentamento. Accessed December 3, 2015.

IBGE (Instituto Brasileiro de Geografia e Estatística). *Censo Agricola*, Rio de Janeiro, RJ. 1950, 1960.
IBGE (Instituto Brasileiro de Geografia e Estatística). *Censo Agropecuario*, Rio de Janeiro, RJ. 1970, 1980, 1985, 1995–96, 2006. (1995–1996 and 2006 *Censo* are available at ww2.ibge.gov.br/home/estatistica/economia/agropecuaria/censoagro/default.shtm.)
INCRA-PRONERA. *Relação Geral de Cursos em Execução*, 2010.
Inep (Instituto Nacional de Estudos e Pesquisas Educacionais). *Censo Escolar*, 2010. Available at censobasico.inep.gov.br/censobasico/.
ITERRA. "Instituto de Educação Josué de Castro: Método Pedagogico." *Cadernos do ITERRA* 4, no. 9 (December 2004).
ITERRA. "O IEJC e a Educação Profissional." *Cadernos do ITERRA* 8. Veranópolis, RS, ITERRA, 2008.
Interview with MST organizer in the Sector of Education, SP, October 29, 2010.
Interview with INCRA official for Brazil (federal government), Brasília, January 31, 2011.
Interview with INCRA official for Brasília, February 2, 2011.
Interview with INCRA official for Brasília, February 9, 2011.
Interview with INCRA official for Rondônia (in Brasília), February 10, 2011.
Interview with MDA-SAF official, Brasília, February 11, 2011.
Interview with INCRA officials for Rio Grande do Sul, Porto Alegre, RS, February 28, 2011.
Interview with COPTEC technician, RS, March 9, 2011.
Interview with MST organizer in the Sector of Education, RS, March 9, 2011.
Interview with former state secretary of education, RS, March 11, 2011.
Interview with MP official for state of Rio Grande do Sul, RS, March 15, 2011.
Interview with MST regional director March 23, 2011.
Interview with INCRA official, Porto Alegre, RS, March 23, 2011.
Interview with Bionatur technical assistance team, RS, March 30, 2011.
Interview with COPERLAT director, former MST state director, outside of Pontão, RS, April 1, 2011.
Interview with MST state director, RS, April 3, 2011.
Interview with Bionatur grower, RS, April 4, 2011.
Interview with Nucleo 1, outside of Pontão, RS, April 15, 2011.
Interview with Nucleo 2, outside of Pontão, RS, April 17, 2011.
Interview with movement ally and former CRE official, Bagé, RS, May 17, 2011.
Interview with director of the Instituto Federal, Sertão, RS, June 3, 2011.
Interview with director of COOPTAT, RS, June 12, 2011.
Interview with teacher, encampment near Londrina, PR, June 21, 2011.
Interview with student at the Milton Santos School, PR, July 6, 2011.
Interview with former MST state director, SP, July 7, 2011.
Interview with MST organizer in the Sector of Production, PR, July 11, 2011.
Interview with former MST state and national director, outside of Miguel do Iguaçu, PR, July 12, 2011.
Interview with director of Mundokide, PR, July 25, 2011.

Interview with MST organizer in the Sector of Education, PR, July 31, 2011.
Interview with INCRA official, Curitiba, PR, August 1, 2011.
Interview with Department of Diversity, Department of Education, PR, August 3, 2011.
Interview with MST organizer in the Sector of Education, Curitiba, PR, August 5, 2011.
Interview with MST organizer in the Sector of Production, outside of Rio Bonito, PR, August 11, 2011.
Interview with former Departmento de Diversidade, Curitiba, PR, August 20, 2011.
Interview with CONCRAB president, Brasília, September 1, 2011.
Interview with INCRA official for São Paulo State, SP, November 1, 2011.
Interview with former MST state director, outside of Pontal de do Paranapanema, SP, November 7, 2011.
Interview with MST organizer in the Sector of Education, Pontal de do Paranapanema, SP, November 8, 2011.
Interview with instruction supervisor in the Secretary of Education, Pontal do Paranapanema, SP, November 21, 2011.
JST, June 1981, May 1981, April 1982, November 1983, February 1984, April 1984, March 1986, July 1989, May 1991, May 1993, May 2003, September 2005, July/August 2012, March 2014, July/August 2015.
MEC (Ministério de Educacao e Cultura). *Censos Escolar*, 2010.
MST, *Caderno de Formação n1: Organização do movimento—Quem é quem na luta pela terra*, 1986.
MST, *Nossa luta é nossa escola: A educação das crianças nos acampamentos e assentamentos*, 1990.
MST, *Caderno de Cooperação Agrícola n1: Uma concepção de desenvolvimento rural*, 1995.
MST, *Caderno de Cooperação Agricola n5: O sistema cooperativista dos assentados*, 1995.
MST, *Caderno de Formação n26: A vez dos valores*, 1998.
MST, *Escola itinerante em acampamentos do MST*, 1998.
MST, *Caderno de Cooperação Agricola n6: A emancipação dos assentamentos: Os direitos e cuidados que os assentados devem ter*, 1998.
MST, *Caderno de textos do 1º Encontro Estadual Minas Gerais—Por uma educação básica do campo*, 1998.
MST, *Caderno de Cooperação Agricola n8: A evolução da concepção da cooperação Agricola do MST 1989–1999*, 1999.
MST, *Caderno de Educação n9: Como fazemos a escola de educação fundamental*, 1999.
MST, *Caderno de Formação n31: O movimento campones no Brasil e a luta pela reforma agrária*, 1999.
MST, *Caderno de Saude n1: Lutar por saúde e lutar pela vida*, 1999.
MST, *Caderno de Educação n10: Ocupamos a biblia*, 2000.
MST, *Escola itinerante: Uma pratica pedagogica em acampamentos*, 2000.
MST, *Caderno de Cooperação Agricola n10: O que levar em conta no acampamento*, 2001.
MST, *Caderno de Cooperação Agricola n11: A constituição e o desenvolvimento de formas coletivas de organização e gestão do trabalho em assentamentos de reforma agrária*, 2004.
MST, *Balanço Político da Cooperação no MST*, 2006.

MST, *Cartilha de Cooperação n1*, 2008.
MST, *Cartilha de Apoio n2: Programa de formação para a cooperação e organização dos assentamentos*, 2008.
MST, *Escola itinerante do MST: História, projeto, e experiencias*, 2008.
MST, *Cadernos de Debates n1: Os desafios daluta pela reforma agrária popular e do MST*, 2009.
MST, *Caderno de Debates n2: Para debater os desafios internos do MST*, 2009.
MST, *A constituição e gestão de iniciativas agroindustrias cooperativas em areas de reforma agrária*, 2010.
MST, *História, projeto e experiencias*, 2010.

INDEX

Agência Nacional de Vigilância Sanitária (ANVISA), 175, 176
agrarian reform, 6, 12, 19, 35, 51, 56, 59, 62, 66, 87, 99, 102, 103, 105–6, 119–20, 121, 138, 148; beneficiaries of, 144–45, 171; demand for, 134, 167, 178, 190, 205; development of, 112, 135, 151, 195, 203–4; efforts at, 50, 96, 121, 156, 157, 169; figures for, 49t, 50; governance, 78–84, 85; Landless Movement and, 54, 55, 78, 117, 167, 194; neoliberalization of, 144, 150–51; political action and, 116, 204–13; settlements, 88, 107, 162, 177, 187
Agrarian Reform Census (1996), 163
agribusiness, 15, 17, 39, 60, 73, 74, 81, 166, 173, 175, 176–77, 186, 191, 192
agriculture, 7, 46, 138, 145, 153; export, 15, 188; multinational companies and, 165–66; production, 18, 51, 65, 98t, 121, 141, 141t, 164, 165, 168, 169, 188,189t
agroecology, 50, 51, 57, 59, 64, 70–77, 160, 177, 179, 204; incorporation of, 167–68; politicization of, 77, 164–69; promotion of, 74, 74f, 75, 168, 178
Alcatraz, 211, 212, 213, 214

Aliança Renovadora Nacional (ARENA), 43, 100, 229n34
Alinsky, Saul, 24
Alvarez, Sonia, 10, 33, 125, 220n12
Alves, Darcy, 135
Alves, Maria, 42
Amazon, 46, 111, 112, 113, 118; settlements/colonization and, 101–7
American Indian Movement (AIM), 212–13, 215
Amorim, Jaime, 121
Annoni, Ernesto, 88, 96, 110–16, 116–20, 137
Araújo Neto, Brazílio de, 150
Arendt, Hannah, 34
Arraes, Miguel, 42, 122
Arroyo, Miguel, 21
Articulação Nacional de Mulheres Trabalhadoras Rurais, 150
Assambleia Nacional Constituente (ANC), 117
Associação de Cooperação Agrícola e Reforma Agrária do Paraná, 182
Associação Nacional de Defesa Vegetal (ANDEF), 175, 176
Azevedo, Sebastião, 150

Banco do Brasil (Bank of Brazil), 145, 194
Batista, Fulgencio, 14, 202, 204
Bernstein, Henry, 10
Bevington, Douglas, 24
Bezerra, Gregorio, 42
Bionatur, 71, 72, 73, 162, 173, 226n51, 226n54, 226n55
Boff, Leonardo, 58
Bogo, Ademar, 58, 109
Bolsa Familia (Family Fund), 125, 177, 188, 197
Branford, Sue, 8, 55, 91, 151, 171
Brass, Tom, 10
Brazilian Constitution (1988), 4, 15, 81, 115, 134, 139, 146, 148, 186; legal changes with, 135–36; revolutionary political action and, 116–20
Brazilian Democratic Movement Party (PMDB), 117, 122, 131, 183, 184, 194
Brilhante ranch, 48, 90, 96, 100, 101, 111, 116, 229n21
Brizola, Leonel, 42, 93
Buechler, Steven, 9
Burbach, Roger, 197

Caiado, Ronaldo, 135
Caldart, Roseli, 59
Calixto, Jair, 93
Campigotto, Salette, 113
Cardoso, Fernando Henrique (FHC), 83, 124, 126, 142, 144, 145, 155, 158, 163, 170, 173, 179, 191; agrarian reform and, 151; economic stabilization and, 139; labor movement and, 140; Medida Provisória by, 169; neoliberalism and, 138–39, 153, 156; Plano Real and, 125, 139
Carta de Saida de Nossas Organizações, 169
Carter, Miguel, 4, 8, 88
Castañeda, Jorge, 197
Castro, Fidel, 14
Catholic Church, 89, 90, 114, 115, 120, 128; economics/unity and, 107–10, 119

Central Única dos Trabalhadores (CUT), 12, 47, 124, 126, 127, 138, 139, 146, 149, 151, 155, 199; decline of, 147; deradicalization of, 125; growth of, 128, 131; labor code and, 148; social relations and, 129, 132; unions and, 140
Chávez, Hugo, 196, 198
Ciccariello-Maher, George, 197
civil rights, 24, 43, 99, 133, 209, 214
civil society, 35, 100, 117, 198, 201, 203, 225n42
Cloward, Richard, 22, 29
collective action, 5, 7, 13, 22, 24, 28–29, 30, 46, 52, 63, 122–23, 199; conditions for, 125, 126–27
Collier, Ruth, 47
Collor de Mello, Fernando, 124, 125, 137–38
Comisión Nacional de Alfabetización, 202
Comissão dos Atingidos pela Hidreléctrica de Tucuruí (CAHTU), 109
Comissão do Vale do São Francisco (CVSF), 102
Comissão Pastoral da Terra (CPT), 14, 48, 78, 80, 89, 108, 109, 110, 115, 128, 158, 219n25
Comissão Regional dos Atingidos do Rio Iguaçu (CRABI), 109
Comissão Regional dos Atingidos por Barragens (CRAB), 109
Comissões de Atingidos, 109
Comissões Parlamentares de Inquerito (CPIs), 171, 172, 175, 237n50
Comuna da Terra, 151
Comunidades Eclesiales de Base (CEBs), 62, 63, 89, 108, 109, 128
Confederação da Agricultura e Pecuária do Brasil (CNA), 176, 177, 194, 237n58
Confederação das Cooperativas de Reforma Agrária do Brasil (CONCRAB), 117
Confederação Nacional da Indústria (CNI), 154
Confederação Nacional dos Trabalhadores na Agricultura (CONTAG), 43, 48, 89, 98, 99, 124, 149, 179, 237n58

Conferência Nacional do Bispos do Brasil (CNBB), 48, 112–13, 124, 149, 179
Conselho Estadual de Educação (CEE), 181, 238n78
Conselho Nacional de Educação (CNE), 68
Consolidação das Leis do Trabalho (CLT), 4, 45, 99, 148, 150
Constitutional Convention, 132–37, 149
Cooperativa Agrícola Novo Sarandi (COANAL), 162, 168
cooperativa de produção agrícola (CPA), 71, 72, 75, 226n50; photo of, 162
Cooperativa de Produção Agropecuária Cascata (COOPTAR), 75, 119, 164, 226n50
Cooperativa de Produção Agropecuária dos Assentados de Tapes (COOPTAT), 167–68
Cooperativa de Produção Agropecuária Nova Santa Rita (COOPAN), 71, 72, 164, 168, 226n50
Cooperativa de Produção Agropecuária Vitória (COPAVI), 162, 168, 226
Cooperativa de Produção de Trabalho Integração (COPTIL), 162; photo of, 162
Cooperativa de Serviços Técnicos (COPTEC), 73, 74, 172, 228n86
Cooperativa Nacional de Terra e Vida (CONATERRA), 71, 162
Cooperativa Regional dos Agricultores Assentados (COOPERAL), 161; photo of, 161
Cooperativas de Prestação de Serviços (CPS), 226n47
Costa Muniz, Francisco Orlando, 150
Council for Mutual Economic Assistance (COMECON), 203
critical theory, 9, 22, 24, 26, 200
Crusius, Yeda, 70, 183, 184, 187, 193
cultural relations, 12, 22, 52, 55, 77, 82, 84, 85, 113, 119, 126, 180, 198, 200, 204
culture, 11, 12, 15, 84, 114, 153, 173, 187; Indigenous, 213; revolutionary, 57–62; transformation of, 148, 204

Curió, Sebastião, 111, 112, 195, 231n72
Cutrale corporation, 191, 236n23

Da Silva, José, 45
Dagnino, Evelina, 146
Davis, Jefferson, 208
Delgado, Guilherme Costa, 39
democracy, 25, 26, 69, 85, 88, 132–37, 146, 147; ascending, 64, 64f, 65; descending, 64, 64f, 65; liberal, 33, 38, 42, 43, 125, 126–27, 132, 133, 134, 135
De Oliveira, Ariovaldo Umbelino, 83, 172
Departamento de Ordem Política e Social (DOPS), 111
De Souza, José Augusto Amaral, 100
Dilma Rousseff, 14, 38, 47, 70, 72, 77, 159, 166, 170, 186, 190, 195, 196, 197; impeachment/removal of, 147, 193–94; Landless Movement and, 157, 158, 174
Dixon, Chris, 24
Dos Santos, João Machado (João Sem Terra), 93
Du Bois, W. E. B., 207
Dunbar-Ortiz, Roxanne, 206
Dussel, Enrique, 23, 26, 33, 34, 36, 37, 55–56, 65, 76, 82, 85, 90, 153, 200, 201

Eckstein, Susan, 125, 220n12
economic conditions, 39, 98, 104, 137–40, 140–41, 147, 156, 188, 201
economic development, 6, 50, 51, 56, 82, 84, 85, 86, 98, 112, 137, 154, 159; alternative, 70–77; figures for, 49t; Landless Movement and, 55, 122, 159; economic instability, extralegal action and, 90–91, 93–98
economic production, 15, 54, 70, 146, 159, 161, 165, 166, 171, 172, 174, 177, 202; collective form of, 51, 108, 110
economic reform, 19, 62, 124, 126, 204, 214
economic relations, 12, 44, 52, 55, 82, 84, 113, 129, 132, 156, 163, 180, 198, 204; destabilization of, 200; transforming, 22, 77, 85, 119, 126, 148, 204

Educação do Campo, 37, 70, 175, 179, 183, 185, 187, 188, 239n102
education, 6, 7, 11, 12, 33, 54, 56, 62, 72, 73, 78, 82, 84, 85, 120, 144, 154, 159, 160; access to, 67, 182, 183; figures for, 49t, 50; Landless Movement and, 55, 64, 69, 175, 179, 180, 183, 185, 187; reform, 19, 21, 70, 76; revolutionary, 64–70, 86; secondary, 50, 70, 178, 181, 182
El Ejército Zapatista de Liberación Nacional (EZLN), 63, 198
elites, 70, 99, 104, 159; economic/political, 33, 94, 95, 116, 188, 191
Ellner, Steve, 197
Empresa Brasileria de Pesquisa Agropecuária (EMBRAPA), 72, 103–4
encampments, 3, 22, 51, 78, 79–80, 82, 94, 95, 110, 114, 120, 174f, 188; establishment of, 54; itinerant schools in, 50; photo of, 91, 92
Encontro Nacional de Educadores da Reforma Agrária, 179
Encruzilhada Natalino, 90, 91, 107, 109, 110–16, 120, 195
Engenho do Complexo de Suape, 121
environment, 19, 32, 129, 166, 191, 195, 210; contamination of, 81; economic production and, 174
environmental law, 4, 136
Escobar, Arturo, 10, 220n12
Escola Latino-Americana de Agroecologia, 166
Escola Milton Santos, 178; wall painting at, 178f
escolas itinerantes (itinerant schools), 50, 66, 184, 185
Estação Experimental da Secretaria da Agricultura do Estado de Rio Grande do Sul, 115, 116
Estatuo do Trabalhador Rural (ETR) (1963), 45–46, 98, 149
extralegal actions, 13, 30, 32, 90–91, 93–98, 101, 148

extralegal tactics, 27–37, 39, 46, 52, 78, 86, 107, 110–11, 130, 153, 159, 166, 171–72, 214

Farm Security Administration (FSA), 209, 210
Fazenda Annoni, 89, 115, 116, 117, 118–19, 120, 137
Fazenda Brilhante, 100
Fazenda Burro Branco, 96; map of, 97
Fazenda Sarandi, 93, 94, 96; map of, 97
Federação dos Trabalhadores e Trabalhadoras na Agricultura (FETAGRI), 180
Federation of Southern Cooperatives, 205, 208
Fernandes, Bernardo Mançano, 8, 9, 10, 85, 217n2
Figueiredo, João, 133
food sovereignty, 12, 13, 23, 25, 26, 34, 55, 71, 73, 84, 119, 167, 201
Força Sindical, 138
Fort Laramie Treaty (1868), 211, 212, 214
Franco, Itamar, 125, 138
Freedman's Bureau, 208
Freire, Paulo, 79, 225n34
Frente Brasil Popular (FBP), 194, 196
Friedman, Milton, 11, 132
friend/enemy distinction, 27, 28, 29, 31, 32, 60, 153, 203
Fritzen, Arnildo, 100, 101, 109
Fundo de Apoio ao Trabalhador Rural (FUNRURAL), 99

Galeano, Eduardo, 198
Gamson, William, 22, 30
Ganz, Marshall, 24
García Linera, Álvaro, 197, 198
Geisler, Charles, 210
Goodwin, Jeff, 7, 9, 199, 218n16
Görgen, Sergio, 149
Goulart, João, 42
Graciano, Xico, 150
Gramsci, Antonio, 24
Greeno, Joel, 205

Grupo Executivo da Reforma Agrária
    (GERA), 102
Grupo Executivo de Terras do Araguaia-
    Tocantins (GETAT), 112
Guazzelli, Sinval, 100
Guevara, Che, 6, 14, 59

Hackbart, Rolf, 150
Hammond, Jack, 5
Handlin, Samuel, 47
Harvey, David, 206
Hellman, Janice, 30
Holston, James, 40
Hunter, Wendy, 147
Huntington, Samuel, 132

identity, 18, 61, 67, 120; changes in, 152–55, 164–69; construction of, 28, 57, 58, 59, 60; work, 37, 59, 62, 114, 194
IMF, 140, 157, 189
Indigenous people, 47, 185, 206, 207, 211
individualism, 5, 29, 70, 77, 79, 82, 83, 84, 153
industrialization, 15, 104, 130, 132
inequality, 56, 146, 177, 188; economic/political, 13, 14, 39, 214
Instituo Preservar, 182
Institutional Act 5 (1968) (AI-5), 43, 99, 108, 133
Instituto Brasileiro de Opinião Pública e Estatística (IBOPE), 154, 191
Instituto Brasileiro de Reforma Agrária (IBRA), 102, 103
Instituto de Educação Josué de Castro (IEJC), 64, 65, 178, 225n27
Instituto Educar, 59, 65, 69, 182
Instituto Nacional de Imigração e Colonização (INIC), 102
Instituto Nacional de Reforma Agrária (INCRA), 4, 17, 53, 54, 63, 78, 79, 80, 81, 82, 83, 87, 88, 96, 112, 116, 144, 145, 154, 158; agrarian reform and, 107, 169; budget of, 170f; emancipation and, 152; executive and, 150–51; land purchases and, 170; settlements/ colonization and, 101–7, 108, 120, 122, 123
Instituto Nacional do Desenvolvimento Agrário (INDA), 102, 103
Instituto Técnico de Capacitação e Pesquia da Reforma Agrária (ITERRA), 68, 180, 181, 223n10, 225n27, 238n75

Jameson, Frederic, 26, 33, 35
Jara, Victor, 60
Jasper, James, 9, 218n16
Jobim, Nelson, 142
Jornada de Agroecologia, 61, 167; photo of, 60
Julião, Francisco, 42, 100, 122
Jungmann, Raul, 150

labor code, 128–29, 131, 148
labor law, 4, 45, 124, 134, 136
labor movement, 12, 129, 130, 138, 140, 142, 147, 148, 152
labor relations, 46, 98, 112, 141, 201, 210
Laclau, Ernesto, 9–10, 31, 220n22
La Confederación de Nacionalidades Indígenas de Ecuador (CONAIE), 198
land: expropriations, 95, 214; ownership, 54, 106, 119, 152; redistribution of, 40, 57, 78–84, 91, 100, 102, 103, 106, 107, 110, 116, 126, 149, 172, 191–92; tenure, 40, 206, 214
land conflicts, 110, 135f, 142f, 190, 190f; people involved in, 136f, 143f, 190f
Land Law (1850), 40–41, 44, 205, 206
Landless Movement: actions of, 19, 51, 52; analysis of, 7, 16, 18, 22; challenges for, 69, 159–60, 163, 177; changes for, 56, 126, 174; growth of, 6, 10, 47–48, 52, 195; internal divisions within, 164–69; leadership of, 17, 54, 185; organization of, 5, 42, 110; resistance by, 7, 19, 34, 37, 80, 122, 192, 199; as revolutionary project, 35, 126, 127, 148–49, 202; studies of, 10–11, 14, 36, 127, 159
land titles, 40, 152–55, 241n40
latifundio, 44, 45, 46, 114–15, 135–36, 166

La Via Campesina (LVC), 12, 13, 17, 25, 119, 167, 201, 205
legal tactics, 6, 31, 32, 46, 52, 107, 159; embrace of, 98–101; extralegal tactics and, 110–11
Lei de Diretrizes de Bases da Educação (LDB), 68, 238n78
Lei de Sesmarias, 39
Lei de Terras, 40
Leite, Sergio, 49
Lenin, Vladimir, 22, 24, 26, 27, 30, 32, 33, 35, 37, 46, 82, 90, 200, 201; dual power and, 23, 34, 85
Lerner, Jaime, 184
Levitsky, Steven, 179
Lincoln, Abraham, 207
literacy, 14, 67, 112, 179, 202, 203
Locke, John, 15
Lorscheiter, Ivo, 113
Lukács, Georg, 27
Lula da Silva, Luiz Inácio, 14, 15, 38, 47, 70, 72, 83, 159, 163, 166, 188, 189, 190, 195, 197; Diretas Já and, 125; election of, 8, 157, 169, 174, 219n25; Landless Movement and, 157, 158, 169–70, 172, 174
Lumiar, 143, 154, 156
Luxemburg, Rosa, 23, 27

Macali ranch, 48, 90, 96, 100, 101, 111, 116
Macri, Mauricio, 196
Maduro, Nicolaus, 196
Makarenko, Anton, 59
Mandela, Nelson, 205
Mao Zedong, 23, 219n4
Marcos, Subcommandante, 63
Marighella, Carlos, 6–7, 59
Martins, José de Souza, 104
Marx, Karl, 18, 23, 24, 37, 184, 219n4
Marxism, 9–10, 22, 23–27, 200
Maschio, Darci, 90, 109, 115
Mato Grosso, 83, 95, 101, 106, 230n41, 239n102
Maybury-Lewis, Biorn, 46
McAdam, Doug, 22, 24
McCarthy, John, 24
Medici, General, 103

Medida Provisória, 154, 169
Mendes, Chico, 135
Meneghetti, Ildo, 95
Mészáros, George, 5
Migdal, Joel, 46, 200
migration, 103, 131, 141, 180, 212
military government, 45, 88, 99, 103–4, 110, 130, 134, 138, 147, 156; political conditions and, 98–101
Ministério da Agricultura, Pecuaria e Abastecimento (MAPA), 6
Ministério da Educação e Cultura (MEC), 68, 69, 176
Ministério de Desenvolvimento Agrário (MDA), 6, 54, 144, 145, 194
Ministério Extraordinário para o Desenvolvimento e a Reforma Agrária, 150
Ministério Público (MP), 37, 69, 175, 183, 184, 187
Ministry of Education, 202–3
mística, 56, 57–62, 149–50, 223n2; photo of, 60
mobilization, 22, 24, 44, 51, 107, 111, 112, 129–30, 178, 180, 184, 195, 214; mass, 202; political, 101; rural worker, 18, 137; transnational, 168
monoculture, 13, 15, 54, 72, 204, 218n24
Morales, Evo, 30
Mouffe, Chantal, 10, 26, 31, 220n12
Movimento Democrático Brasileiro (MDB), 43, 229n34
Movimento de Pescadores e Pescadores Artesanais (MPP), 167
Movimento dos Agricultores Sem Terra (MASTER), 42, 93, 94, 96, 100, 101, 103, 115, 118; occupations of, 95, 122, 123
Movimento dos Atingidos por Barragens (MAB), 48, 80, 89, 150, 166, 167, 169, 179
Movimento dos Pequenos Agricultores (MPA), 48, 149–50, 152, 166–67, 179, 185
Movimento dos Trabalhadores Desempregados (MTD), 9, 80, 169
Movimento dos Trabalhadores Rurais Sem Terra (MST): agrarian reform and, 34, 35, 48, 66, 82, 86, 119–20, 167, 191, 204, 212;

agroecology and, 74, 167, 169; cooperatives and, 153, 161, 163, 164; economic development and, 55, 70–77; education and, 21, 50, 55, 56, 68, 69, 73, 79, 159, 178, 179, 180, 181, 182, 183, 188; emergence of, 63, 88, 120; Landless Movement and, 13, 55, 78, 88, 89, 90, 127, 149, 150, 154, 166, 187; occupations by, 110, 121, 128, 134, 189, 191, 214, 233n26; revolutionary actions by, 57, 62, 83, 116, 121, 128, 132, 155, 171; settlements of, 19, 75f, 82, 151, 152–53, 177; studies of, 8, 55, 90
Movimento dos Trabalhadores Sem-Teto (MTST), 152
Movimiento al Socialismo (MAS), 30

National Agricultural Workers Union, 209
National Family Farm Coalition (NFFC), 13
National Farmers Organization (NFO), 19
Native Americans, 207, 211, 212, 213
Navarro, Zander, 56
Negri, Antonio, 26, 34, 36, 55–56, 65, 76, 82, 90, 153, 200, 201; work of, 23, 33, 37, 85, 219n5
neoliberalism, 11, 39, 72, 75, 77, 83, 125, 127, 132–37, 139, 198, 199, 215; challenging, 47, 73, 146–52, 153, 196; institutionalization of, 126; privatization and, 156; repression and, 140–43, 143–46; rollback vs. rollout, 133, 138, 144
neoliberal restructuring, 15, 30, 47, 125, 126, 127, 132, 146, 155, 156, 199; economic conditions/ repression during, 137–40
Neves, Tancredo, 117, 133, 232n92
Nimtz, August, 26
Nonoai, 42, 90, 93, 95, 100, 101, 107, 121, 122
Nova Ronda Alta, 89, 90, 112, 113, 119, 120; nucleo governance at, 114f, 115
Novo Lei Organica de Partidos, 100
nucleos, 4, 17, 55, 56, 62–63, 64, 65, 67–71, 73, 77, 78, 79, 81, 113, 115, 129; nature of, 84–86

Obama, Barack, 198–99
occupations, 22, 31, 37, 51, 78, 80, 82, 95, 107, 110, 114, 121, 122, 126, 128, 134, 149, 152, 155–56, 155, 155f, 163, 173, 174f, 188, 190, 214; extralegal, 101, 120; military, 206
Ondetti, Gabriel, 8, 30, 48, 81, 88, 121, 127, 180, 222n65

Page, Joseph, 200
Pará, 17, 53, 101, 142, 143, 180
Paraná, 17–18, 44, 46, 67, 72, 78, 79, 96, 97, 105, 121, 162, 164, 165, 166, 168; agroecology in, 74, 169; CEE and, 181; education in, 50, 65, 160, 181, 183; encampment in, 92f; land conflicts in, 110; learning at, 180–88; legislation in, 180–88
Partido Comunista Brasileiro (PCB), 63, 93, 110, 111, 112, 131, 225n24, 231n70, 231n72
Partido Democratico Social (PSD), 133
Partido dos Trabalhadores (PT), 47, 70, 124, 126, 127, 134, 146, 148, 149, 151, 155, 191, 194, 197, 199; agrarian reform and, 195; cultural changes by, 131; deradicalization of, 125; Landless Movement and, 158, 160, 169–74, 193; organization by, 129, 157; political/economic/social relations and, 132; power for, 157–60, 169–74, 188, 196; revolutionary political action and, 128, 147, 160
Partido Liberal (PL), 157
Partido Socialista Popular (PSP), 202
Partido Trabalhista Brasileiro (PTB), 93
Passo Real Dam project, 87, 96, 97, 105
Pastoral da Juventude (PJR), 167
Patel, Raj, 25, 205
Peasant Leagues, 42, 94, 100, 103, 118, 121, 122, 231n70, 231n72
Peck, Jamie, 133
Pereira, Anthony, 42
Pernambuco, 3, 17, 78, 81, 94, 103, 121, 122, 142, 180
Petra, James, 10
Petrobras, 125, 138, 139, 140, 193, 236n23
Pine Ridge Reservation, 211, 212, 213
Piven, Frances, 22, 29
Plano Collor, 137–38
Plano de Integração Nacional (PIN), 103

Plano Nacional de Reforma Agrária (PNRA), 117–18, 120, 134, 137, 150, 172
Plano Real, 139
Plano Verão, 137
Poletto, Ivo, 126
political action, 11, 12, 27, 28, 52, 85, 90, 95, 192, 197, 200; agrarian reform and, 116, 204–13; contradictions of, 6–9; extralegal, 29, 32; revolutionary, 19, 22, 23, 25, 26, 32, 35, 37, 38, 48, 62–63, 116–20, 122, 127, 132, 152, 155, 160, 196, 201, 204–13
political conditions, 51, 52, 144, 188, 199; changing, 98–101, 126, 204, 214
political relations, 12, 52, 55, 82, 84, 113, 132, 156, 180, 198, 200, 204, 218n24; transforming, 22, 77, 85, 119, 126
politics, 11, 15, 36, 124, 187, 189, 215; alternative practices in, 153; as-anti-politics, 12; revolutionary, 7, 13, 19, 28; transformation of, 148, 204
Pontal do Paranapanema, 70, 186, 187
poverty, 32, 77, 83, 93, 103, 108, 188, 197, 203
power, 32, 85, 146, 177, 197; dual, 7, 14, 23, 27–37, 201; public/private, 33, 52, 120; state, 7, 35, 40, 201, 204
private property, 15, 43, 44, 71, 95, 119, 153, 206, 215; development of, 152, 156
privatization, 77, 125, 138, 139, 156, 194, 198, 199
production, 15, 71, 80; agroecological, 179; collectivization of, 76, 82, 162–63, 199, 226n47; commercializing, 104; cooptation of, 215; economic, 78, 97, 109, 119; technologies, 169
Programa de Aquisão de Alimentos (PAA), 51, 72, 75, 157, 170, 172, 173
Programa de Crédito Especial para a Reforma Agrária (PROCERA), 76, 144, 145, 161, 163, 168, 173
Programa de Desenvolvimento de Áreas Integradas do Nordeste (POLONORDESTE), 103
Programa de Pólos Agropecuários e Agrominerais da Amazônia (POLAMAZONIA), 103

Programa de Redistribuição de Terras e de Estímulo a Agro-indústria do Norte e do Nordeste (PROTERRA), 103
Programa Especial para o Vale do São Francisco (PROVALE), 103
Programa Nacional Alimentar Escolar (PNAE), 72, 75, 157, 170–71, 172
Programa Nacional de Acesso ao Ensino Técnico e Emprego (PRONATEC), 176, 237n60
Programa Nacional de Melhoramento de Cana-de-Açúcar (PLANALSUCAR), 104
Programa Nacional de Fortalecimento da Agricultura Familiar (PRONAF), 77, 144, 145, 156, 163, 172
Programa Nacional para Educação na Reforma Agrária (PRONERA), 144, 179, 181, 182, 186, 223n108, 238n74, 238n75
property, 15, 83, 96, 106; ownership of, 96, 117, 205, 206; rights, 44, 47, 131, 152
public policy, 6, 22, 31, 125, 153, 160, 171, 180, 183, 187, 200, 204; acceptance of, 3, 32
public/private divide, 33, 34, 51, 56, 63, 82
public programs, 8, 70, 170, 172, 181, 199, 231n70

Ramirez, Pablo, 30
Reagan, Ronald, 11, 211
recognition, 4, 9, 10, 23, 37, 131, 149, 206, 212; de jure, 78, 84; legal, 54, 128
redistribution, 93, 94–95, 100, 113, 143, 208, 210, 212, 213
Republic of New Africa, 209
Requião, Roberto, 184
resistance, 5, 8, 10, 14, 15, 17, 35, 47, 51, 55, 191, 196, 200; diagram of, 36f; expansion of, 37, 121; mobilizing contradictions of, 21–23
revolution, 23, 26, 27, 34, 42, 56, 85, 128, 148; landless, 47–51, 52, 196–99; researching, 9–16; social movements and, 199–204
revolutionary contention, 22, 34, 156, 199; consolidating, 174–80

revolutionary movements, 7, 9, 22–23, 35, 38, 43, 200
Rezende, Gervásio, 104
Rigotto, Germano, 183
Rio Grande do Sul, 17, 18, 37, 42, 44, 48, 72, 87, 88, 93, 95, 97, 100, 101, 105, 107, 111–12, 115–16, 118, 121, 122, 137; agroecology in, 74; dam projects and, 109; education in, 50, 65, 160, 182, 183, 184; land redistribution in, 94, 106, 110; learning in, 180–88; legislation in, 180–88; MST and, 70, 162, 184, 187–88; poverty in, 103; territorial claims in, 96
Roberts, Kenneth, 197
Robles, Wilder, 25
Rocha, Jan, 8, 55, 91
Rodrigues, Milton Serres, 93
Rodrigues de Freitas, Osvaldino, 95
Roosevelt, Eleanor, 210
Rosenau, James, 221n49
Rosset, Peter, 25
Rural Land Statute (1964), 102, 104, 114, 118, 120, 134, 136
Russo, Osvaldo, 150

Sader, Emir, 197
Saldanha, Ari, 93
Salto Santiago Hydroelectric Power Plant and Dam, 96; map of, 97
Santa Catarina, 88, 96, 97, 107, 109, 121, 223n106, 239n89, 239n102
São Bernardo do Campo Metalworkers' Union, 130
São Paulo, 44, 45, 70, 80, 101, 105, 129, 130, 131, 136, 151; MST in, 17; schools in, 65; settlements in, 152–53
Sarandi, 93, 94, 96
Sarney, José, 117, 133, 134, 137, 150
Schmitt, Carl, 23, 26, 27, 30, 60, 85, 90, 116, 200, 201, 220n19, 220n26; illegality/extralegality and, 29, 35; partisan and, 34, 81; political action and, 28, 31; sovereignty and, 31–32
Scott, James, 39, 190, 200

security, 12, 33, 54, 65, 78, 79–80, 120, 167, 212, 231n72; national, 102, 105, 106, 112, 119, 134, 151; technology and, 104
Selbin, Eric, 34, 35, 118, 156
Sem Terra, 59, 114, 116, 120; identity construction and, 58, 60, 70
Service Employees International Union (SEIU), 12
Serviço Nacional de Aprendizagem Rural (SENAR), 176
settlements, 44, 63, 82, 101–7, 122, 159, 161, 164, 175, 210; agrarian reform, 88, 107, 162, 187; legal recognition of, 54; photo of, 75; privatization of, 152–53
Sherer-Warren, Ilse, 10
Sherman, William Tecumseh, 208
Silva, José Alencar Gomes da, 157
Sioux Treaty (1868), 211, 212
Skocpol, Theda, 22, 34, 46, 126, 199, 200
Slater, Daniel, 10
Smith, Nigel, 104
Snow, David, 28
social actors, 71, 76, 79, 85, 128, 134
social movements, 7, 10, 12, 19, 28, 29, 37, 38, 42, 46, 49, 57, 66, 95, 99, 100, 102, 108, 118, 128; connections, 129; education and, 185; government and, 197; Landless Movement and, 85, 187, 205; political action of, 84; researching, 18, 24, 30, 201; resistance/neoliberalism and, 47; revolution and, 199–204; studies, 22, 23–27; theory, 22, 24, 30–31, 199, 200
social programs, 27, 49, 83, 140, 146, 195; resources for, 203
social relations, 11, 44, 62, 120, 132, 156, 192, 204; transforming, 10, 33, 77, 127
social services, 11, 83, 99, 134, 146, 198
Southern Tenant Farmers' Union (STFU), 209, 210, 214
sovereignty, 23, 25, 26, 31, 38, 41, 55, 119, 132, 200; colonial, 207; fractured, 45; Native American, 212; social movement action and, 201; understanding of, 27
squatters, 13, 40, 41, 54, 95, 96, 106, 117, 206, 211

Standing Rock Reservation, 214
Stédile, João Pedro, 57, 63, 90, 100, 101, 109
St. Peter, Bob, 205
strikes, 4, 124, 130, 138–39, 140, 147, 148, 207
Superintendência do Desenvolvimento Econômico do Nordeste (SUDENE), 102
Superintendência do Plano de Valorização Econômica da Amazônia (SPVEA), 102
Superintendência do Plano de Valorização Econômica da Região da Fronteira Sudoeste do Pais (SUDOESTE), 102
Supreme Electoral Tribunal, 147
Supremo Tribunal Federal, 4
Syngenta, 15, 165, 174, 175

Tannenbaum, Frank, 209–10, 215
Tarlau, Rebecca, 10, 30, 37, 65, 187, 238n71
Tarrow, Sidney, 24, 187, 199
technology, 97, 104, 123, 141; labor-intensive, 165; labor-saving, 46, 140
Técnico em Administração de Cooperativas (TAC), 68
Técnico em Cooperativismo (TAC), 181
Temer, Michel, 194, 195, 196
Territórios da Cidadania, 46–47, 189
Thatcher, Margaret, 11
Thayer, Maggie, 57
Thomas, Norman, 209
Tickell, Adam, 133
Tilly, Charles, 9, 24, 29, 34
Trabalho de Conclusão de Curso (TCC), 68
transformation, 26, 54, 156, 164, 203, 213; peasant-worker, 169; revolutionary, 126, 204; social, 22, 34, 35, 159, 204; technological, 46

Tribunal das Contas da União (TCU), 69–70, 170, 175, 186, 187
Trotsky, Leon, 24
Trump, Donald, 11
26th of July Movement, 14, 202, 21n24

União Democrática Ruralista (UDR), 134–35, 137, 233n25
unicidade (union tax), 128, 129, 134, 148
unions, 18, 43, 93, 115, 134, 180; agrarian reform and, 149; formation of, 45–46, 130, 148; membership of, 140; mobilization by, 129–30; revolutionary, 128–32; social-movement, 128; worker-managed, 129
United Farmworkers Movement, 24

Van der Ploeg, Jan, 145
Vargas, Getúlio, 45, 101, 128, 138, 148
Veltmeyer, Henry, 10, 25
Vergara-Camus, Leandro, 8, 10, 85, 218n20

Wagner, Carlos, 112, 229n21
Washington Consensus, 133, 140
Webber, Jeffrey, 30
Webber, Lucia, 113
Weber, Max, 38
Welch, Cliff, 93
Wolford, Wendy, 4, 8, 9, 10, 36, 37, 55, 63, 77, 85, 90, 105, 127
Wright, Angus, 4–5, 8, 36, 55, 63, 90

Yashar, Deborah, 47

Zald, Mayer, 24
Žižek, Slavoj, 26

ABOUT THE AUTHOR

Anthony Pahnke received his PhD in political science from the University of Minnesota–Twin Cities. His work on social movements, Latin American politics, and political economy has appeared in *Monthly Review*, *New Politics*, *The Journal of Peasant Studies*, *Latin American Politics and Society*, *Social Movement Studies*, and *Third World Quarterly*. His current projects include analyzing the dynamics of transnational rural mobilization in the Americas and the development of sovereignty in the United States.